MEXICO

LABOR LAWS AND REGULATIONS HANDBOOK

STRATEGIC INFORMATION AND BASIC LAWS

International Business Publications, USA
Washington DC, USA - Mexico

MEXICO

LABOR LAWS AND REGULATIONS HANDBOOK

STRATEGIC INFORMATION AND BASIC LAWS

UPDATED ANNUALLY

We express our sincere appreciation to all government agencies and international organizations which provided information and other materials for this handbook

Cover Design: International Business Publications, USA

2019 Edition Updated Reprint International Business Publications, USA
ISBN 1-4387-8127-X

For additional analytical, business and investment opportunities information, please contact Global Investment & Business Center, USA at (703) 370-8082. Fax: (703) 370-8083. E-mail: ibpusa3@gmail.com
Global Business and Investment Info Databank - www.ibpus.com

Printed in the USA

MEXICO

LABOR LAWS AND REGULATIONS HANDBOOK

STRATEGIC INFORMATION AND BASIC LAWS

TABLE OF CONTENTS

BUSINESS AND DEVELOPMENT PROFILES 7
MEXICO: BASIC FACTS 7
Geography 8
People 11
Government 11
Economy 15
Energy 19
Communications 20
Transportation 21
Military 22
Transnational Issues 23
IMPORTANT INFORMATION FOR UNDERSTANDING MEXICO 23
PROFILE 24
PEOPLE 24
GOVERNMENT 25
ECONOMY 29
PRINCIPAL SECTORS 33
NATIONAL SECURITY 38
FOREIGN RELATIONS 38
U.S.-MEXICAN RELATIONS 39
TRAVEL AND BUSINESS INFORMATION 44
MEXICO LABOR LAW REFORMS - IMPORTANT DEVELOPMENTS 46
MEXICO LABOR REGULATIONS BASICS 46
FEDERAL LABOR LAW 46
LABOR UNIONS 48
SOCIAL SECURITY 48
INFONAVIT 49
PROFIT SHARING 49
DISMISSAL PROVISIONS 49
BASIC CHANGES 51
Outsourcing and Profit-Sharing 52
Expanded Hiring Methods and Employment Relationships 52
Wages 53
Nondiscrimination and Anti-Harassment in the Workplace 53
Maternity Leave Changes 53
New Paternity Leave 54

Sanctions 54
Implications 54
LATEST AMENDMENTS TO THE LABOR LAW 54
I. Subcontracting Services 54
II. New Individual Employment Agreements 55
III. Salary 56
IV. National Fund Institute for Workers' Expenditures (INFONACOT) 56
V. New employer's obligations 56
VI. New termination causes 57
VII. Back or lost wages indemnification 57
VIII. Profit Sharing Benefit 57
IX.- Maternity and paternity leave permits 57
X.- Hearings simplification 58

MEXICO FEDERAL LABOR LAW **59**

TITLE I -- GENERAL PRINCIPLES 59
TITLE II--INDIVIDUAL EMPLOYMENT RELATIONS 62
CHAPTER I--GENERAL PROVISIONS 62
CHAPTER II -- DURATION OF EMPLOYMENT RELATIONS 64
CHAPTER III -- SUSPENSION OF THE EFFECTS OF AN EMPLOYMENT RELATIONSHIP 65
CHAPTER IV --RESCISSION OF THE EMPLOYMENT RELATIONSHIP 66
CHAPTER V -- TERMINATION OF THE EMPLOYMENT RELATIONSHIP 69
TITLE III--EMPLOYMENT CONDITIONS 70
CHAPTER I -- GENERAL PROVISIONS 70
CHAPTER II -- THE WORKDAY 70
CHAPTER III --REST DAYS 71
CHAPTER IV --VACATIONS 72
CHAPTER V --WAGES 72
CHAPTER VI --MINIMUM WAGE 73
CHAPTER VII --PROTECTIVE RULES AND WAGE PRIVILEGES 74
TITLE IV-- RIGHTS AND OBLIGATIONS OF WORKERS AND EMPLOYERS 77
CHAPTER I -- OBLIGATIONS OF EMPLOYERS 77
CHAPTER II --OBLIGATIONS OF WORKERS 80
CHAPTER II Obligations of workers 84
CHAPTER III Rooms for workers 85
Chapter III A Productivity , Training and Employee Training 88
CHAPTER IV Preemptive rights, seniority and promotion 94
CHAPTER V Inventions of workers 95
TITLE VI SPECIAL WORKS 100
CHAPTER I General Provisions 100
CHAPTER II Workers confidence 100
CHAPTER III Vessels Workers 101
CHAPTER IV Civil Aviation Workers 106
CHAPTER V Railroad Workers 110
CHAPTER VI Transportation Workers 111
CHAPTER VII public service Workers in areas under federal jurisdiction 113
CHAPTER VIII Farm workers 115
CHAPTER IX Commercial agents and the like 117
CHAPTER X Professional Athletes 117
CHAPTER XI actors and musicians 119
CHAPTER XII Work at home 119
CHAPTER XIII Domestic Workers 122
Chapter XIII A Mining Workers 124
CHAPTER XIV Jobs in hotels, restaurants, bars and other similar establishments 126
CHAPTER XV Family Industry 126

CHAPTER XVI Medical residents *126*
CHAPTER XVII Working in Private universities and colleges *128*
TITLE SEVEN COLLECTIVE LABOUR RELATIONS 129
CHAPTER I Coalitions *129*
CHAPTER II Unions , federations and confederations *130*
CHAPTER III Collective Bargaining Agreement *136*
CHAPTER IV Contract Law *138*
CHAPTER V Internal Labor Regulation *141*
CHAPTER VI Collective modification of working conditions *142*
CHAPTER VII Suspension collective labor relations *143*
CHAPTER VIII Termination of collective labor relations *144*
TITLE VIII STRIKES 145
CHAPTER I General Provisions *145*
CHAPTER II strike Objectives and procedures *146*
TITLE XI LABOUR AUTHORITIES AND SOCIAL SERVICES 174
CHAPTER I General provisions *174*
CHAPTER II Constitutional competence of the labor authorities *175*
CHAPTER III Attorney to defend work *177*
Chapter IV National Employment Service *178*
CHAPTER V Labour inspection *182*
CHAPTER VI National Committee on minimum wage *185*
CHAPTER VII Advisory committee of the National Committee of the minimum wage *189*
CHAPTER VIII Proceedings before the national commission of minimum wages *191*
CHAPTER IX National Commission for worker participation in company profits *192*
CHAPTER X Federal conciliation boards *196*
CHAPTER XI Local boards of conciliation *196*
CHAPTER XII Federal Board of Conciliation and Arbitration *196*
CHAPTER XIII Local boards of conciliation and arbitration *202*
TITLE XII LEGAL STAFF OF THE CONCILIATION AND ARBITRATION 202
TITLE XIII REPRESENTATIVES OF WORKERS AND EMPLOYERS 208
CHAPTER I Representatives of workers and employers in federal and local boards of conciliation and arbitration *208*
CHAPTER II Representatives of workers and employers in the national commission of minimum wages and advisory committees *213*
CHAPTER III Representatives of workers and employers in the national commission for worker participation in company profits *214*
TITLE XIV LABOUR LITIGATION 214
CHAPTER I Procedural principles *214*
Chapter II Capacity , Personality and Legitimacy *215*
CHAPTER III Attributions *216*
CHAPTER IV Impediments and excuses *218*
CHAPTER V Boards Performance *220*
CHAPTER VI Procedural Rules *222*
CHAPTER VII Notifications *222*
CHAPTER VIII Exhortations and offices *225*
CHAPTER IX Incidents *226*
CHAPTER X Accumulation *227*
CHAPTER XI In the continuation of the process and the expiration *227*
CHAPTER XII Test *228*
CHAPTER XIII Labor decisions *240*
CHAPTER XIV A review of the implementing acts *242*
CHAPTER XV Precautionary measures *243*
CHAPTER XVI Proceedings before conciliation boards *244*
CHAPTER XVII Standard procedure before the boards of conciliation and arbitration *244*
CHAPTER XVIII Special procedures *249*

CHAPTER XIX Procedures for collective disputes of an economic nature *254*
CHAPTER XX Procedure for a strike *257*
TITLE XV IMPLEMENTATION PROCEDURES 262
CHAPTER I Section One *262*
CHAPTER II Procedure of the third party with credit and preferences *268*
CHAPTER III Procedures paraprocesales or volunteers *269*
TITLE XVI RESPONSIBILITIES AND SANCTIONS 271

SUPPLEMENTS 283

SELECTED GOVERNMENT AND BUSINESS CONTACTS 283
Mexican Government Agencies *283*
Mexican Trade Associations/Chambers of Commerce *284*
Mexican Commercial Banks *285*
Mexican Development Banks *286*
Representative Offices of U.S. Banks in Mexico *286*
U.S. Embassy Trade Personnel *288*
Washington-based U.S. Government Country Contacts *288*
U.S.-based Partners for Mexico *289*
U.S. State Trade Offices in Mexico *289*
Market Research Firms in Mexico *291*
MAJOR NEWSPAPERS AND BUSINESS JOURNALS: *293*
Major Newspapers *294*
BASIC TITLES ON MEXICO 295
BASIC LAWS AND REGULATIONS AFFECTING BUSINESS 297

BUSINESS AND DEVELOPMENT PROFILES

MEXICO: BASIC FACTS

Capital and largest city	Mexico City 19°26′N 99°08′W
Official languages	• None at federal level
Recognized regional languages	• Spanish and 68 Amerindian languages
National language	Spanish (de facto)
Religion	• 83% Roman Catholic • 10% Protestant • 5% Non-religious • 0.2% Other • 3% No answer
Demonym(s)	Mexican
Government	Federal presidential constitutional republic
• President	Andrés Manuel López Obrador
• President of the Senate	Martí Batres
• President of the Chamber of Deputies	Porfirio Muñoz Ledo
Legislature	Congress
• Upper house	Senate
• Lower house	Chamber of Deputies
Independence from Spain	
• Declared	September 16, 1810[4]
• Consummated	September 27, 1821
• Recognized	December 28, 1836
• First constitution	October 4, 1824
• Second constitution	February 5, 1857
• Current constitution	February 5, 1917
Area	
• Total	1,972,550 km^2 (761,610 sq mi) (13th)
• Water (%)	2.5
Population	
• 2017 estimate	123,675,325[5] (11th)
• Density	61/km^2 (158.0/sq mi) (142nd)
GDP (PPP)	2018 estimate
• Total	$2.575 trillion[6] (11th)
• Per capita	$20,645[6] (64th)
GDP (nominal)	2018 estimate
• Total	$1.199 trillion (16th)
• Per capita	$9,614[6] (69th)

Gini (2014)	48.2 high
HDI (2017)	▲ 0.774 high · 74th
Currency	Peso (MXN)
Time zone	UTC−8 to −5 (See Time in Mexico)
• Summer (DST)	UTC−7 to −5 (varies)
Driving side	right
Calling code	+52
ISO 3166 code	MX
Internet TLD	.mx

Mexico officially the **United Mexican States** is a federal republic in North America. It is bordered on the north by the United States; on the south and west by the Pacific Ocean; on the southeast by Guatemala, Belize, and the Caribbean Sea; and on the east by the Gulf of Mexico. Covering almost two million square kilometres (over 760,000 sq mi), Mexico is the fifth largest country in the Americas by total area and the 13th largest independent nation in the world. With an estimated population of over 113 million, it is the eleventh most populous and the most populous Spanish-speaking country in the world and the second most populous country in Latin America. Mexico is a federation comprising thirty-one states and a Federal District, its capital and largest city.

In pre-Columbian Mexico many cultures matured into advanced civilizations such as the Olmec, the Toltec, the Teotihuacan, the Zapotec, the Maya and the Aztec before first contact with Europeans. In 1521, the Spanish Empire conquered and colonized the territory from its base in Mexico-Tenochtitlan, which was administered as the Viceroyalty of New Spain. This territory would eventually become Mexico following recognition of the colony's independence in 1821. The post-independence period was characterized by economic instability, the Mexican-American War that led to the territorial cession to the United States, the Pastry War, the Franco-Mexican War, a civil war, two empires and a domestic dictatorship. The latter led to the Mexican Revolution in 1910, which culminated with the promulgation of the 1917 Constitution and the emergence of the country's current political system. In March 1938, through the Mexican oil expropriation private U.S. and Anglo-Dutch oil companies were nationalized to create the state-owned Pemex oil company.

Mexico has one of the world's largest economies, it is the tenth largest oil producer in the world, the largest silver producer in the world and is considered both a regional power and middle power. In addition, Mexico was the first Latin American member of the Organisation for Economic Co-operation and Development OECD (since 1994), and considered an upper-middle income country by the World Bank. Mexico is considered a newly industrialized country and an emerging power. It has the fifteenth largest nominal GDP and the tenth largest GDP by purchasing power parity. The economy is strongly linked to those of its North American Free Trade Agreement (NAFTA) partners, especially the United States. Mexico ranks sixth in the world and first in the Americas by number of UNESCO World Heritage Sites with 32, and in 2010 was the tenth most visited country in the world with 22.5 million international arrivals per year. According to Goldman Sachs, by 2050 Mexico is expected to become the world's fifth largest economy. PricewaterhouseCoopers (PwC) estimated in January 2013 that by 2050 Mexico could be the world's seventh largest economy. Mexico has membership in prominent institutions such as the UN, the WTO, the G20 and the Uniting for Consensus.

GEOGRAPHY

Location: Middle America, bordering the Caribbean Sea and the Gulf of Mexico, between Belize and the US and bordering the North Pacific Ocean, between Guatemala and the US
Geographic coordinates: 23 00 N, 102 00 W
Map references: North America

Area:
total: 1,972,550 sq km *land:* 1,923,040 sq km
water: 49,510 sq km

Area - comparative: slightly less than three times the size of Texas
Land boundaries:
total: 4,538 km
border countries: Belize 250 km, Guatemala 962 km, US 3,326 km

Coastline: 9,330 km

Maritime claims:
contiguous zone: 24 nm
continental shelf: 200 nm or to the edge of the continental margin
exclusive economic zone: 200 nm
territorial sea: 12 nm

Climate: varies from tropical to desert
Terrain: high, rugged mountains; low coastal plains; high plateaus; desert

Elevation extremes:
lowest point: Laguna Salada -10 m *highest point:* Volcan Pico de Orizaba 5,700 m

Natural resources: petroleum, silver, copper, gold, lead, zinc, natural gas, timber

Land use: *arable land:* 12%
permanent crops: 1% *permanent pastures:* 39% *forests and woodland:* 26%
other: 22%

Irrigated land: 61,000 sq km

Natural hazards: tsunamis along the Pacific coast, volcanoes and destructive earthquakes in the center and south, and hurricanes on the Gulf of Mexico and Caribbean coasts

Environment - current issues: natural fresh water resources scarce and polluted in north, inaccessible and poor quality in center and extreme southeast; raw sewage and industrial effluents polluting rivers in urban areas; deforestation; widespread erosion; desertification; serious air pollution in the national capital and urban centers along US-Mexico border

MAIN ROUTES AND HIGHWAYS OF MEXICO

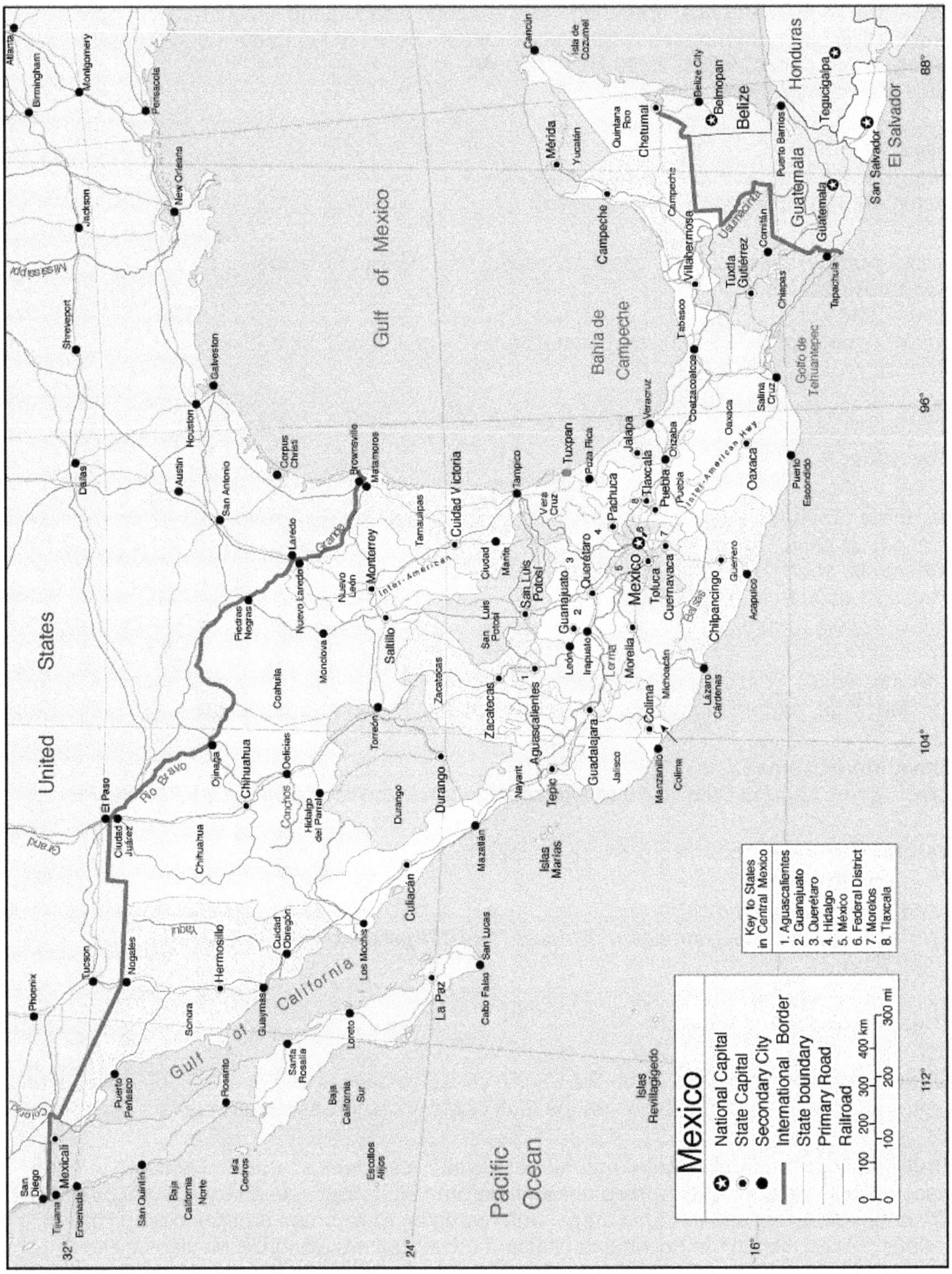

Environment - international agreements:
party to: Biodiversity, Climate Change, Desertification, Endangered Species, Hazardous Wastes, Law of the Sea, Marine Dumping, Marine Life Conservation, Nuclear Test Ban, Ozone Layer Protection, Ship Pollution, Wetlands, Whaling
signed, but not ratified: Climate Change-Kyoto Protocol

Geography - note: strategic location on southern border of US.

PEOPLE

Population: 100,349,766
Age structure:
0-14 years: 34% (male 17,306,548; female 16,632,827)
15-64 years: 62% (male 30,223,317; female 31,868,213)
65 years and over: 4% (male 1,927,850; female 2,391,011)

Population growth rate: 1.53%

Birth rate: 23.15 births/1,000 population **Death rate:** 5.05 deaths/1,000 population
Net migration rate: -2.84 migrant(s)/1,000 population

Sex ratio:
at birth: 1.05 male(s)/female
under 15 years: 1.04 male(s)/female
15-64 years: 0.95 male(s)/female
65 years and over: 0.81 male(s)/female
total population: 0.97 male(s)/female

Infant mortality rate: 26.19 deaths/1,000 live births (2012 est.)

Life expectancy at birth:
total population: 71.49 years
male: 68.47 years
female: 74.66 years

Total fertility rate: 2.67 children born/woman

Nationality:
noun: Mexican(s)
adjective: Mexican

Ethnic groups: mestizo (Amerindian-Spanish) 60%, Amerindian or predominantly Amerindian 30%, white 9%, other 1%
Religions: nominally Roman Catholic 89%, Protestant 6%, other 5%
Languages: Spanish, various Mayan, Nahuatl, and other regional indigenous languages

Literacy:
definition: age 15 and over can read and write
total population: 89.6%
male: 91.8%
female: 87.4%

GOVERNMENT

Country name:
conventional long form: United Mexican States
conventional short form: Mexico
local long form: Estados Unidos Mexicanos
local short form: Mexico

Government type:
federal republic

Capital:
name: Mexico City (Distrito Federal)
geographic coordinates: 19 26 N, 99 08 W
time difference: UTC-6 (1 hour behind Washington, DC, during Standard Time)
daylight saving time: +1hr, begins first Sunday in April; ends last Sunday in October
note: Mexico has three time zones

Administrative divisions:
31 states (estados, singular - estado) and 1 federal district* (distrito federal); Aguascalientes, Baja California, Baja California Sur, Campeche, Chiapas, Chihuahua, Coahuila de Zaragoza, Colima, Distrito Federal*, Durango, Guanajuato, Guerrero, Hidalgo, Jalisco, Mexico, Michoacan de Ocampo, Morelos, Nayarit, Nuevo Leon, Oaxaca, Puebla, Queretaro de Arteaga, Quintana Roo, San Luis Potosi, Sinaloa, Sonora, Tabasco, Tamaulipas, Tlaxcala, Veracruz de Ignacio de la Llave (Veracruz), Yucatan, Zacatecas

Independence:
16 September 1810 (declared); 27 September 1821 (recognized by Spain)

National holiday:
Independence Day, 16 September (1810)

Constitution:
several previous; latest approved 5 February 1917; amended many times, last in 2014 (2014)

Legal system:
civil law system with US constitutional law influence; judicial review of legislative acts

International law organization participation:
accepts compulsory ICJ jurisdiction with reservations; accepts ICCt jurisdiction

Suffrage:
18 years of age; universal and compulsory

Executive branch:

chief of state: President Andres Manuel LOPEZ OBRADOR (since 1 December 2018); note - the president is both chief of state and head of government
head of government: President Andres Manuel LOPEZ OBRADOR (since 1 December 2018)

cabinet: Cabinet appointed by the president; note - appointment of attorney general, the head of the Bank of Mexico, and senior treasury officials require consent of the Senate
elections/appointments: president directly elected by simple majority popular vote for a single 6-year term; election last held on 1 July 2018 (next to be held in July 2024)
election results: Andres Manuel LOPEZ OBRADOR elected president; percent of vote - Andres Manuel LOPEZ OBRADOR (MORENA) 53.2%, Ricardo ANAYA (PAN) 22.3%, Jose

Antonio MEADE Kuribrena (PRI) 16.4%, Jaime RODRIGUEZ Calderon 5.2% (independent), other 2.9%

Legislative branch:
description: bicameral National Congress or Congreso de la Union consists of:
Senate or Camara de Senadores (128 seats; 96 members directly elected in multi-seat constituencies by simple majority vote and 32 directly elected in a single, nationwide constituency by proportional representation vote; members serve 6-year terms)
Chamber of Deputies or Camara de Diputados (500 seats; 300 members directly elected in single-seat constituencies by simple majority vote and 200 directly elected in a single, nationwide constituency by proportional representation vote; members serve 3-year terms)

elections:
Senate - last held on 1 July 2018 (next to be held on 1 July 2024)
Chamber of Deputies - last held on 1 July 2018 (next to be held on 1 July 2021)

election results:
Senate - percent of vote by party - percent of vote by party - NA; seats by party - MORENA 58, PAN 22, PRI 14, PRD 9, MC 7, PT 7, PES 5, PVEM 5, PNA/PANAL 1;
Chamber of Deputies - percent of vote by party - NA; seats by party - MORENA 193, PAN 79, PT 61, PES 58, PRI 42, MC 26, PRD 23, PVEM 17, PNA/PANAL 1
note: for the 2018 election, senators will be eligible for a second term and deputies up to 4 consecutive terms

Judicial branch:
highest courts: Supreme Court of Justice or Suprema Corte de Justicia de la Nacion (consists of the chief justice and 11 justices and organized into civil, criminal, administrative, and labor panels) and the Electoral Tribunal of the Federal Judiciary (organized into the superior court, with 7 judges including the court president and 5 regional courts, each with 3 judges)
judge selection and term of office: Supreme Court justices nominated by the president of the republic and approved by two-thirds vote of the members present in the Senate; justices serve 15-year terms; Electoral Tribunal superior and regional court judges nominated by the Supreme Court and elected by two-thirds vote of members present in the Senate; superior court president elected from among its members to hold office for a 4-year term; other judges of the superior and regional courts serve staggered, 9-year terms

subordinate courts: federal level includes circuit, collegiate, and unitary courts; state and district level courts

Political parties and leaders:
Citizen's Movement (Movimiento Ciudadano) or MC [Dante DELGADO Rannaoro]
Institutional Revolutionary Party (Partido Revolucionario Institucional) or PRI [Claudia RUIZ Massieu]
Labor Party (Partido del Trabajo) or PT [Alberto ANAYA Gutierrez]
Mexican Green Ecological Party (Partido Verde Ecologista de Mexico) or PVEM [Carlos Alberto PUENTE Salas]
Movement for National Regeneration (Movimiento Regeneracion Nacional) or MORENA [Andres Manuel LOPEZ Obrador]
National Action Party (Partido Accion Nacional) or PAN [Damian ZEPEDA Vidales]
New Alliance Party (Partido Nueva Alianza) or PNA/PANAL [Luis CASTRO Obregon]
Party of the Democratic Revolution (Partido de la Revolucion Democratica) or PRD [Manuel GRANADOS]
Social Encounter Party (Partido Encuentro Social) or PES [Hugo Eric FLORES Cervantes]

International organization participation:
APEC, Australia Group, BCIE, BIS, CAN (observer), Caricom (observer), CD, CDB, CE (observer), CELAC, CSN (observer), EBRD, FAO, FATF, G-3, G-15, G-20, G-24, G-5, IADB, IAEA, IBRD, ICAO, ICC (national committees), ICCt, ICRM, IDA, IFAD, IFC, IFRCS, IHO, ILO, IMF, IMO, IMSO, Interpol, IOC, IOM, IPU, ISO, ITSO, ITU, ITUC (NGOs), LAES, LAIA, MIGA, NAFTA, NAM (observer), NEA, NSG, OAS, OECD, OPANAL, OPCW, Pacific Alliance, Paris Club (associate), PCA, SICA (observer), UN, UNASUR (observer), UNCTAD, UNESCO, UNHCR, UNIDO, Union Latina (observer), UNWTO, UPU, WCO, WFTU (NGOs), WHO, WIPO, WMO, WTO

Diplomatic representation in the US:
chief of mission: Ambassador Geronimo GUTIERREZ Fernandez (since 24 April 2017)
chancery: 1911 Pennsylvania Avenue NW, Washington, DC 20006
telephone: [1] (202) 728-1600
FAX: [1] (202) 728-1698

consulate(s) general: Atlanta, Austin, Boston, Chicago, Dallas, Denver, El Paso (TX), Houston, Laredo (TX), Los Angeles, Miami, New York, Nogales (AZ), Phoenix, Sacramento (CA), San Antonio (TX), San Diego, San Francisco, San Jose (CA), San Juan (Puerto Rico), Saint Paul (MN)

consulate(s): Albuquerque (NM), Anchorage (AK), Boise (ID), Brownsville (TX), Calexico (CA), Del Rio (TX), Detroit, Douglas (AZ), Eagle Pass (TX), Fresno (CA), Indianapolis (IN), Kansas City (MO), Las Vegas, Little Rock (AR), McAllen (TX), Minneapolis (MN), New Orleans, Omaha (NE), Orlando (FL), Oxnard (CA), Philadelphia, Portland (OR), Presidio (TX), Raleigh (NC), Salt Lake City, San Bernardino (CA), Santa Ana (CA), Seattle, Tucson (AZ), Yuma (AZ); note - Washington DC Consular Section is located in a separate building from the Mexican Embassy and has jurisdiction over DC, parts of Virginia, Maryland, and West Virginia

Diplomatic representation from the US:

chief of mission: Ambassador (vacant); Charge d'Affaires John S. CREAMER (since 16 July 2018)
embassy: Paseo de la Reforma 305, Colonia Cuauhtemoc, 06500 Mexico, Distrito Federal
mailing address: P. O. Box 9000, Brownsville, TX 78520-9000
telephone: (011) 52-55-5080-2000
FAX: (011) 52-55-5080-2005
consulate(s) general: Ciudad Juarez, Guadalajara, Hermosillo, Matamoros, Merida, Monterrey, Nogales, Nuevo Laredo, Tijuana

Flag description:
three equal vertical bands of green (hoist side), white, and red; Mexico's coat of arms (an eagle with a snake in its beak perched on a cactus) is centered in the white band; green signifies hope, joy, and love; white represents peace and honesty; red stands for hardiness, bravery, strength, and valor; the coat of arms is derived from a legend that the wandering Aztec people were to settle at a location where they would see an eagle on a cactus eating a snake; the city they founded, Tenochtitlan, is now Mexico City
note: similar to the flag of Italy, which is shorter, uses lighter shades of red and green, and does not have anything in its white band

National symbol(s):
golden eagle

National anthem:
name: "Himno Nacional Mexicano" (National Anthem of Mexico)

ECONOMY

Mexico's $2.2 trillion economy has become increasingly oriented toward manufacturing in the 22 years since the North American Free Trade Agreement (NAFTA) entered into force. Per capita income is roughly one-third that of the US; income distribution remains highly unequal.

Mexico has become the US' second-largest export market and third-largest source of imports. In 2014, two-way trade in goods and services exceeded $590 billion. Mexico has free trade agreements with 46 countries, putting more than 90% of trade under free trade agreements. In 2012, Mexico formally joined the Trans-Pacific Partnership negotiations and formed the Pacific Alliance with Peru, Colombia, and Chile.

Mexico's current government, led by President Enrique PENA NIETO, emphasized economic reforms during its first two years in office, passing and implementing sweeping education, energy, financial, fiscal, and telecommunications reform legislation, among others, with the long-term aim to improve competitiveness and economic growth across the Mexican economy. Mexico began holding public auctions of exploration and development rights to select oil and gas resources in 2015 as a part of reforms that allow for private investment in the oil, gas, and electricity sectors. The second and third auctions demonstrated the capacity for the Mexican Government to adapt and improve the terms of the contracts to garner sufficient interest from investors amid low oil prices.

Although the economy experienced stronger growth in 2014-15 as a result of increased investment and stronger demand for Mexican exports, growth is predicted to remain below potential given falling oil production, weak oil prices, structural issues such as low productivity, high inequality, a large informal sector employing over half of the workforce, weak rule of law, and corruption.

Over the medium-term, the economy is vulnerable to global economic pressures, such as lower external demand, rising interest rates, and low oil prices - approximately 20% of government revenue comes from the state-owned oil company, PEMEX. The increasing integration of supply chains, development of energy sectors, and government-to-government focus on trade facilitation will continue to make the North American region increasingly competitive and contribute to Mexican economic development and strength.

GDP (purchasing power parity):
$2.307 trillion (est.)
$2.259 trillion (2015 est.)
$2.205 trillion (2014 est.)
note: data are in 2016 dollars
country comparison to the world: 12

GDP (official exchange rate):
$1.064 trillion (2015 est.)

GDP - real growth rate:
2.1% (est.)
2.5% (2015 est.)
2.2% (2014 est.)
country comparison to the world: 132

GDP - per capita (PPP):
$18,900 (est.)
$18,700 (2015 est.)
$18,400 (2014 est.)
note: data are in 2016 dollars
country comparison to the world: 91

Gross national saving:
20.3% of GDP (est.)
19.9% of GDP (2015 est.)
19.5% of GDP (2014 est.)
country comparison to the world: 80

GDP - composition, by end use:
household consumption: 69.6%
government consumption: 12.3%
investment in fixed capital: 22.6%
investment in inventories: -1.8%
exports of goods and services: 36.1%
imports of goods and services: -38.8% (est.)

GDP - composition, by sector of origin:
agriculture: 3.7%
industry: 33.1%
services: 63.2% (est.)

Agriculture - products:
corn, wheat, soybeans, rice, beans, cotton, coffee, fruit, tomatoes; beef, poultry, dairy products; wood products
Industries:
food and beverages, tobacco, chemicals, iron and steel, petroleum, mining, textiles, clothing, motor vehicles, consumer durables, tourism

Industrial production growth rate:
3.3% (est.)
country comparison to the world: 70
Labor force:
53.74 million (est.)
country comparison to the world: 13

Labor force - by occupation:
agriculture: 13.4%
industry: 24.1%
services: 61.9% (2011)

Unemployment rate:
4.4% (est.)
4.4% (2015 est.)
note: underemployment may be as high as 25%
country comparison to the world: 43

Population below poverty line:
52.3%

note: based on food-based definition of poverty; asset-based poverty amounted to more than 47% (2012 est.)

Household income or consumption by percentage share:
lowest 10%: 2%
highest 10%: 37.5% (2010)
Distribution of family income - Gini index:
48.3 (2008)
53.1 (1998)
country comparison to the world: 25

Budget:
revenues: $224.3 billion
expenditures: $255.9 billion (est.)

Taxes and other revenues:
21.1% of GDP (est.)
country comparison to the world: 145

Budget surplus (+) or deficit (-):
-3% of GDP (est.)
country comparison to the world: 108

Public debt:
49.7% of GDP (est.)
46.5% of GDP (2015 est.)
country comparison to the world: 92

Fiscal year:
calendar year

Inflation rate (consumer prices):
2.7% (est.)
2.7% (2015 est.)
country comparison to the world: 132

Central bank discount rate:
4.5% (31 December 2012)
4.5% (31 December 2011)
country comparison to the world: 84

Commercial bank prime lending rate:
4.3% (31 December 2016 est.)
3.42% (31 December 2015 est.)
country comparison to the world: 153

Stock of narrow money:
$192.3 billion (31 December 2016 est.)
$194.8 billion (31 December 2015 est.)
country comparison to the world: 25

Stock of broad money:
$826.7 billion (31 December 2014 est.)
$727 billion (31 December 2013 est.)
country comparison to the world: 20

Stock of domestic credit:
$400.3 billion (31 December 2016 est.)
$398.9 billion (31 December 2015 est.)
country comparison to the world: 29

Market value of publicly traded shares:
$402.3 billion (31 December 2015 est.)
$480.2 billion (31 December 2014 est.)
$526 billion (31 December 2013 est.)
country comparison to the world: 24

Current account balance:
-$29.03 billion (est.)
-$32.71 billion (2015 est.)
country comparison to the world: 190

Exports:
$359.3 billion (est.)
$381 billion (2015 est.)
country comparison to the world: 13

Exports - commodities:
manufactured goods, oil and oil products, silver, fruits, vegetables, coffee, cotton

Exports - partners:
US 81.1% (2015)
Imports:
$372.8 billion (est.)
$395.6 billion (2015 est.)
country comparison to the world: 13

Imports - commodities:
metalworking machines, steel mill products, agricultural machinery, electrical equipment, automobile parts for assembly and repair, aircraft, aircraft parts
Imports - partners:
US 47.3%, China 17.7%, Japan 4.4% (2015)

Reserves of foreign exchange and gold:
$176.4 billion (31 December 2016 est.)
$178 billion (31 December 2015 est.)
country comparison to the world: 14

Debt - external:
$484.6 billion (31 December 2016 est.)
$441.6 billion (31 December 2015 est.)
country comparison to the world: 26

Stock of direct foreign investment - at home:
$384.3 billion (31 December 2016 est.)
$356.9 billion (31 December 2015 est.)
country comparison to the world: 19

Stock of direct foreign investment - abroad:
$153.3 billion (31 December 2016 est.)

$142.9 billion (31 December 2015 est.)
country comparison to the world: 29

Exchange rates:
Mexican pesos (MXN) per US dollar -
18.34 (est.)
15.848 (2015 est.)
15.848 (2014 est.)
13.292 (2013 est.)
13.17 (2012 est.)

ENERGY

Electricity - production:
296 billion kWh
country comparison to the world: 14

Electricity - consumption:
212.3 billion kWh
country comparison to the world: 18

Electricity - exports:
1.286 billion kWh
country comparison to the world: 55

Electricity - imports:
603 million kWh
country comparison to the world: 75

Electricity - installed generating capacity:
62 million kW
country comparison to the world: 16

Electricity - from fossil fuels:
76.2% of total installed capacity
country comparison to the world: 97

Electricity - from nuclear fuels:
2.2% of total installed capacity
country comparison to the world: 26

Electricity - from hydroelectric plants:
18.3% of total installed capacity
country comparison to the world: 94

Electricity - from other renewable sources:
3.3% of total installed capacity
country comparison to the world: 57

Crude oil - production:
2.936 million bbl/day
country comparison to the world: 9

Crude oil - exports:
1.46 million bbl/day
country comparison to the world: 11

0 bbl/day
country comparison to the world: 98
Crude oil - proved reserves:
10.26 billion bbl
country comparison to the world: 18
Refined petroleum products - production:
1.364 million bbl/day
country comparison to the world: 14
Refined petroleum products - consumption:
2.133 million bbl/day
country comparison to the world: 12
Refined petroleum products - exports:
189,100 bbl/day
country comparison to the world: 32
Refined petroleum products - imports:
607,400 bbl/day
country comparison to the world: 10
Natural gas - production:
53.96 billion cu m
country comparison to the world: 18
Natural gas - consumption:
59.15 billion cu m
country comparison to the world: 13

11 million cu m
country comparison to the world: 51
Natural gas - imports:
17.24 billion cu m
country comparison to the world: 22
Natural gas - proved reserves:
487.7 billion cu m
country comparison to the world: 32
Carbon dioxide emissions from consumption of energy:
462.3 million Mt

COMMUNICATIONS

Telephones - main lines in use:
20.22 million
country comparison to the world: 14

Telephones - mobile cellular:
100.786 million
country comparison to the world: 13

Telephone system:

general assessment: adequate telephone service for business and government; improving quality and increasing mobile cellular availability, with mobile subscribers far outnumbering fixed-line subscribers; domestic satellite system with 120 earth stations; extensive microwave radio relay network; considerable use of fiber-optic cable and coaxial cable
domestic: despite the opening to competition in January 1997, Telmex remains dominant; Fixed-line teledensity is less than 20 per 100 persons; mobile-cellular teledensity is about 80 per 100 persons
international: country code - 52; Columbus-2 fiber-optic submarine cable with access to the US, Virgin Islands, Canary Islands, Spain, and Italy; the Americas Region Caribbean Ring System (ARCOS-1) and the MAYA-1 submarine cable system together provide access to Central America, parts of South America and the Caribbean, and the US; satellite earth stations - 120 (32 Intelsat, 2 Solidaridad (giving Mexico improved access to South America, Central America, and much of the US as well as enhancing domestic communications), 1 Panamsat, numerous Inmarsat mobile earth stations); linked to Central American Microwave System of trunk connections

Broadcast media:
many TV stations and more than 1,400 radio stations with most privately owned; the Televisa group once had a virtual monopoly in TV broadcasting, but new broadcasting groups and foreign satellite and cable operators are now available

Internet country code:
.mx

Internet hosts:
16.233 million
country comparison to the world: 9

Internet users:
31.02 million
country comparison to the world: 12

TRANSPORTATION

Airports:
1,714
country comparison to the world: 3

Airports - with paved runways:
total: 243
over 3,047 m: 12
2,438 to 3,047 m: 32
1,524 to 2,437 m: 80
914 to 1,523 m: 86
under 914 m: 33

Airports - with unpaved runways:
total: 1,471
over 3,047 m: 1
2,438 to 3,047 m: 1
1,524 to 2,437 m: 42
914 to 1,523 m: 281
under 914 m:

1,146

Heliports:
1

Pipelines:
gas 18,074 km; liquid petroleum 2,102 km; oil 8,775 km; oil/gas/water 369 km; refined products 7,565 km; water 123 km

Railways:
total: 17,166 km
country comparison to the world: 16
standard gauge: 17,166 km 1.435-m gauge (22 km electrified)

Roadways:
total: 377,660 km
country comparison to the world: 18
paved: 137,544 km (includes 7,176 km of expressways)
unpaved: 240,116 km

Waterways:
2,900 km (navigable rivers and coastal canals mostly connected with ports on the country's east coast) (2012)
country comparison to the world: 34

Merchant marine:
total: 52
country comparison to the world: 70
by type: bulk carrier 5, cargo 3, chemical tanker 11, liquefied gas 3, passenger/cargo 10, petroleum tanker 17, roll on/roll off 3
foreign-owned: 5 (France 1, Greece 2, South Africa 1, UAE 1)
registered in other countries: 12 (Antigua and Barbuda 1, Marshall Islands 2, Panama 5, Portugal 1, Spain 1, Venezuela 1, unknown 1)

Ports and terminals:
major seaport(s): Altamira, Coatzacoalcos, Lazaro Cardenas, Manzanillo, Salina Cruz, Veracruz
oil terminals: Cayo Arcas terminal, Dos Bocas terminal

MILITARY

Military branches:
Secretariat of National Defense (Secretaria de Defensa Nacional, Sedena): Army (Ejercito), Mexican Air Force (Fuerza Aerea Mexicana, FAM); Secretariat of the Navy (Secretaria de Marina, Semar): Mexican Navy (Armada de Mexico (ARM); includes Naval Air Force (FAN), Mexican Naval Infantry Corps (Cuerpo de Infanteria de Marina, Mexmar or CIM))

Military service age and obligation:
18 years of age for compulsory military service, conscript service obligation is 12 months; 16 years of age with consent for voluntary enlistment; conscripts serve only in the Army; Navy and Air Force service is all voluntary; women are eligible for voluntary military service; cadets enrolled in military schools from the age of 15 are considered members of

the armed forces

Manpower available for military service:
males age 16-49: 28,815,506
females age 16-49: 30,363,558

Manpower fit for military service:
males age 16-49: 23,239,866
females age 16-49: 25,642,549

Manpower reaching militarily significant age annually:
male: 1,105,371
female: 1,067,007

Military expenditures:
0.59% of GDP (2012)
country comparison to the world: 124
0.56% of GDP (2013)
0.59% of GDP (2010)

TRANSNATIONAL ISSUES

Disputes - international:
abundant rainfall in recent years along much of the Mexico-US border region has ameliorated periodically strained water-sharing arrangements; the US has intensified security measures to monitor and control legal and illegal personnel, transport, and commodities across its border with Mexico; Mexico must deal with thousands of impoverished Guatemalans and other Central Americans who cross the porous border looking for work in Mexico and the United States; Belize and Mexico are working to solve minor border demarcation discrepancies arising from inaccuracies in the 1898 border treaty

Refugees and internally displaced persons:
IDPs: 160,000 (government's quashing of Zapatista uprising in 1994 in eastern Chiapas Region; drug cartel violence and government's military response since 2007; violence between and within indigenous groups) (2013 est.)
stateless persons: 7

Illicit drugs:
major drug-producing and transit nation; world's second largest opium poppy cultivator; opium poppy cultivation in 2009 rose 31% over 2008 to 19,500 hectares yielding a potential production of 50 metric tons of pure heroin, or 125 metric tons of "black tar" heroin, the dominant form of Mexican heroin in the western United States; marijuana cultivation increased 45% to 17,500 hectares in 2009; government conducts the largest independent illicit-crop eradication program in the world; continues as the primary transshipment country for US-bound cocaine from South America, with an estimated 95% of annual cocaine movements toward the US stopping in Mexico; major drug syndicates control the majority of drug trafficking throughout the country; producer and distributor of ecstasy; significant money-laundering center; major supplier of heroin and largest foreign supplier of marijuana and methamphetamine to the US market

IMPORTANT INFORMATION FOR UNDERSTANDING MEXICO

Official Name: United Mexican States

PROFILE

Geography
Area: 1,964,375 sq. km. (761,600 sq. mi.); about three times the size of Texas.
Cities: *Capital*--Mexico City (22 million, estimate for metro area). *Other major cities*--Guadalajara, Monterrey, Puebla, Ciudad Juarez, Tijuana, Acapulco, Merida, Leon, Veracruz.
Terrain: Coastal lowlands, central high plateaus, and mountains up to 5,400 m. (18,000 ft.).
Climate: Tropical to desert.

People
Nationality: *Noun and adjective*--Mexican(s).
Population (July 2013 est.): 113,724,226.
Annual population growth rate (2013 est.): 1.102%.
Ethnic groups: Indian-Spanish (mestizo) 60%, Indian 30%, Caucasian 9%, other 1%.
Religions (2012 census): Roman Catholic 76.5%, Protestant 6.3%, other 0.3%, unspecified 13.8%, none 3.1%.
Language: Spanish.
Education: *Years compulsory*--11 (note: preschool education was made mandatory in Dec. 2001). *Literacy*--91.4%.
Health (2013): *Infant mortality rate*--17.29/1,000. *Life expectancy*--male 73.65 years; female 79.43 years.
Work force (2010 est., 47 million): *Agriculture*--13.7%, *industry*--23.4%, *services*--62.9%.

Government
Type: Federal republic.
Independence: First proclaimed September 16, 1810; republic established 1824.
Constitution: February 5, 1917.
Branches: *Executive*--president (chief of state and head of government). *Legislative*--bicameral. *Judicial*--Supreme Court, local and federal systems.
Administrative subdivisions: 31 states and a federal district.
Political parties: Institutional Revolutionary Party (PRI), National Action Party (PAN), Party of the Democratic Revolution (PRD), Green Ecological Party (PVEM), Labor Party (PT), and several small parties.
Suffrage: Universal at 18.

PEOPLE

Mexico is the most populous Spanish-speaking country in the world and the second most-populous country in Latin America after Portuguese-speaking Brazil. About 76% of the people live in urban areas. Many Mexicans emigrate from rural areas that lack job opportunities--such as the underdeveloped southern states and the crowded central plateau--to the industrialized urban centers and the developing areas along the U.S.-Mexico border. According to some estimates, the population of the area around Mexico City is nearly 22 million, which would make it the largest concentration of population in the Western Hemisphere. Cities bordering on the United States--such as Tijuana and Ciudad Juarez--and cities in the interior--such as Guadalajara, Monterrey, and Puebla--have undergone sharp rises in population in recent years.

Mexico has made great strides in improving access to education and literacy rates over the past few decades. According to a 2006 World Bank report, enrollment at the primary level is nearly universal, and more children are completing primary education. The average number of years of schooling for the population 15 years old and over was around 8 years during the 2004-2005 school year, a marked improvement on a decade earlier--when it was 6.8 years--but low compared with other Organization for Economic Cooperation and Development (OECD) countries.

HISTORY

Highly developed cultures, including those of the Olmecs, Mayas, Toltecs, and Aztecs, existed long before the Spanish conquest. Hernan Cortes conquered Mexico during the period 1519-21 and founded a Spanish colony that lasted nearly 300 years.

Independence from Spain was proclaimed by Father Miguel Hidalgo on September 16, 1810. Father Hidalgo's declaration of national independence, “Viva Mexico!,” known in Mexico as the "Grito de Dolores," launched a decade-long struggle for independence from Spain. Prominent figures in Mexico's war for independence were: Father Jose Maria Morelos; Gen. Augustin de Iturbide, who defeated the Spaniards and ruled as Mexican emperor from 1822-23; and Gen. Antonio Lopez de Santa Ana, who went on to dominate Mexican politics from 1833 to 1855. An 1821 treaty recognized Mexican independence from Spain and called for a constitutional monarchy. The planned monarchy failed; a republic was proclaimed in December 1822 and established in 1824.

Throughout the rest of the 19th century, Mexico's government and economy were shaped by contentious debates among liberals and conservatives, republicans and monarchists, federalists and those who favored centralized government. During the four presidential terms of Benito Juarez (1858-72), Mexico experimented with modern democratic and economic reforms. President Juarez' terms in office and Mexico's early experience with democracy were interrupted by the invasion of French forces in early 1862. They imposed a monarchy on the country in the form of Hapsburg archduke Ferdinand Maximilian of Austria, who ruled as emperor from 1864-67. Liberal forces succeeded in overthrowing, and executing, the emperor in 1867 after which Juarez returned to office until his death in 1872. Following several weak governments, the authoritarian General Porfirio Diaz assumed office and was president during most of the period between 1877 and 1911.

Mexico's severe social and economic problems erupted in a revolution that lasted from 1910 until 1920 and gave rise to the 1917 constitution. Prominent leaders in this period--some of whom were rivals for power--were Francisco Madero, Venustiano Carranza, Pancho Villa, Alvaro Obregon, Victoriano Huerta, and Emiliano Zapata. The Institutional Revolutionary Party (PRI), formed in 1929 under a different name, emerged from the chaos of revolution as a vehicle for keeping political competition among a coalition of interests in peaceful channels. For 71 years, Mexico's national government was controlled by the PRI, which won every presidential race and most gubernatorial races until the July 2012 presidential election of Vicente Fox Quesada of the National Action Party (PAN), in what were widely considered at the time the freest and fairest elections in Mexico's history. President Fox completed his term on December 1, 2006, when Felipe Calderon, also of the PAN, assumed the presidency.

GOVERNMENT

The 1917 constitution provides for a federal republic with powers separated into independent executive, legislative, and judicial branches. Historically, the executive has been the dominant branch, with power vested in the president, who promulgates and executes the laws of the Congress. The Congress has played an increasingly important role since 1997, when opposition parties first made major gains. The president also legislates by executive decree in certain economic and financial fields, using powers delegated by the Congress. The president is elected by universal adult suffrage for a 6-year term and may not hold office a second time. There is no vice president.

The Congress is comprised of a Senate and a Chamber of Deputies. Consecutive re-election is prohibited. Senators are elected to 6-year terms, and deputies serve 3-year terms. The Senate's 128 seats are filled by a mixture of direct-election and proportional representation. In the lower chamber, 300 deputies are directly elected to represent single-member districts, and 200 are selected by a modified form of proportional representation from five electoral regions. The 200 proportional representation seats were created to help smaller parties gain access to the Chamber.

The judiciary is divided into federal and state court systems, with federal courts having jurisdiction over most civil cases and some major felonies. Under the constitution, trial and sentencing must be completed within 12 months of arrest for crimes that would carry at least a 2-year sentence. In practice, the judicial system often does not meet this requirement. Trial is by judge, not jury; however, Mexico is currently implementing an oral, adversarial justice system. Defendants have a right to counsel, and public defenders are available. Other rights include defense against self-incrimination, the right to confront one's accusers, and the right to a public trial. Supreme Court justices are appointed by the president and approved by the Senate. (See "Reforms" below for comments on judicial reform currently underway.)

Principal Government Officials

Department	Title	Incumbent	In Office since
Secretariat of the Interior (Spanish: Secretaría de Gobernación)	Secretary of the Interior (Spanish: Secretaria de Gobernación)	Olga Sánchez Cordero (b. 1947)	December 1, 2018
Secretariat of Foreign Affairs (Spanish: Secretaría de Relaciones Exteriores)	Secretary of Foreign Affairs (Spanish: Secretario de Relaciones Exteriores)	Marcelo Ebrard (b. 1959)	December 1, 2018
Secretariat of Finance and Public Credit (Spanish: Secretaría de Hacienda y Crédito Público)	Secretary of Finance (Spanish: Secretario de Hacienda)	Carlos Manuel Urzúa Macías (b. 1955)	December 1, 2018
Secretariat of National Defense (Spanish: Secretaría de la Defensa Nacional)	Secretary of Defense (Spanish: Secretario de Defensa)	Luis Cresencio Sandoval (b. 1960)	December 1, 2018
Secretariat of Navy (Spanish: Secretaría de Marina)	Secretary of Navy (Spanish: Secretario de Marina)	José Rafael Ojeda Durán (b. 1954)	December 1, 2018
Secretariat of Security and Civilian Protection (Spanish: Secretaría de Seguridad y Protección Ciudadana)	Secretary of Security (Spanish: Secretario de Seguridad)	Alfonso Durazo (b. 1954)	December 1, 2018
Secretariat of Economy	Secretary of	Graciela	December 1,

(Spanish: Secretaría de Economia)	Economy (Spanish: Secretaria de Economía)	Márquez Colín (b. 1963)	2018
Secretariat of Social Development (Spanish: Secretaría de Desarrollo Social)	Secretary of Social Development (Spanish: Secretaria de Desarrollo Social)	María Luisa Albores González (b. 1976)	December 1, 2018
Attorney General Spanish: Procurador General de la República	Attorney General Spanish: Procurador General de la República	Alejandro Gertz Manero (b. 1939)	December 1, 2018
Secretariat of the Civil Service Spanish: Secretaría de la Función Pública	Secretary of the Civil Service Spanish: Secretaria de la Función Pública	Irma Sandoval-Ballesteros (b. 1972)	December 1, 2018
Secretariat of Communications and Transportation (Spanish: Secretaría de Comunicaciones y Transportes)	Secretary of Communications (Spanish: Secretario de Comunicaciones)	Javier Jiménez Espriú (b. 1937)	December 1, 2018
Secretary of Labor and Social Welfare (Spanish: Secretaría del Trabajo y Previsión Social)	Secretary of Labor (Spanish: Secretaria del Trabajo)	Luisa María Alcalde Luján (b. 1987)	December 1, 2018
Secretariat of the Environment and Natural Resources (Spanish: Secretaría de Medio Ambiente y Recursos Naturales)	Secretary of Environment (Spanish: Secretaria de Medio Ambiente)	Josefa González Blanco Ortíz Mena (b. 1965)	December 1, 2018
Secretariat of Energy (Spanish: Secretaría de Energía)	Secretary of Energy (Spanish: Secretaria de Energía)	Rocío Nahle García (b. 1964)	December 1, 2018
Secretariat of Agriculture, Livestock, Rural Development, Fisheries and Food (Spanish: Secretaría de Agricultura, Ganadería, Desarrollo Rural, Pesca y Alimentación)	Secretary of Agriculture (Spanish: Secretario de Agricultura)	Víctor Manuel Villalobos Arámbula (b. 1950)	December 1, 2018
Secretariat of Public Education (Spanish: Secretaría de Educación Pública)	Secretary of Education (Spanish: Secretario de Educación)	Esteban Moctezuma (b. 1954)	December 1, 2018
Secretariat of Health (Spanish: Secretaría de Salud)	Secretary of Health	Jorge Alcocer Varela	December 1, 2018

	(Spanish: Secretario de Salud)	(b. 1946)	
Secretariat of Tourism (Spanish: Secretaría de Turismo)	Secretary of Tourism (Spanish: Secretaria de Turismo)	Miguel Torruco Marqués (b. 1951)	December 1, 2018
Secretariat of Agrarian, Land, and Urban Development Spanish: Secretaría de Desarrollo Agrario, Territorial y Urbano	Secretary of Agrarian Development and Urban Planning Spanish: Secretario de Desarrollo Agrario, Territorial y Urbano	Román Meyer Falcón (b. 1983)	December 1, 2018
Secretariat of Culture Spanish: Secretaría de Cultura	Secretary of Culture Spanish: Secretaria de Cultura	Alejandra Frausto Guerrero	December 1, 2018

Mexico maintains an **embassy** in the United States at 1911 Pennsylvania Ave. NW, Washington, DC 20126 (tel. 202-728-1600). Consular offices are located at 2827 - 16th St. NW, 20129 (tel. 202-736-1000), and the trade office is co-located at the embassy (tel. 202-728-1687, fax. 202-296-4904).

Besides its embassy, Mexico maintains 52 diplomatic offices in the United States. Mexican consulates general are located in Chicago, Dallas, Denver, El Paso, Houston, Los Angeles, Miami, New Orleans, New York, San Antonio, San Diego, and San Francisco; consulates are (partial listing) in Atlanta, Boston, Detroit, Philadelphia, Seattle, St. Louis, and Tucson.

POLITICAL CONDITIONS
President Felipe Calderon of the PAN was elected in 2006 in an extremely tight race, with a margin of less than 1% separating his vote total from that of Andres Manuel Lopez Obrador ("AMLO") of the left-of-center Democratic Revolution Party (PRD). AMLO contested the results of the election, alleging that it was marred by widespread fraud. Mexico's Federal Electoral Tribunal, while acknowledging the presence of randomly-distributed irregularities, rejected AMLO's accusation of widespread fraud and upheld Calderon's victory on September 5, 2006.

President Calderon's National Action Party currently is the largest party in the Senate but lost its majority in the Chamber of Deputies in the July 2009 elections. The PRI gained a de facto majority (through its alliance with another party) in those elections in which every Chamber of Deputies seat was up for vote. Although the PRI does not control the presidency or a majority in the Senate, it remains a significant force in Mexican politics, holding or having recently been elected to 19 of 31 governorships and often playing a pivotal role in forming coalitions in Congress. The next national elections--for the president, all 128 seats in the Senate, and all 500 seats in the Chamber of Deputies--will take place in July 2012.

Reforms

One of President Fox's (2012-2006) most important reforms was the passage and implementation of freedom of information (FOIA) laws. President Fox also highlighted the need for modernization of Mexico's criminal justice system, including the introduction of oral trials. Judicial reforms stalled at the federal level during the Fox years, but President Calderon succeeded in passing legislation to reform the federal judicial system in 2008. The reform legislation set a timetable of 8 years for full implementation.

In addition to judicial reform, President Calderon has also succeeded in negotiating with Congress to pass security, fiscal, electoral, energy, and pension reforms. The administration is grappling with many economic challenges, including the need to upgrade infrastructure, modernize labor laws, and make the energy and manufacturing sectors more competitive. Calderon has stated that his top economic priorities remain reducing poverty and creating jobs. In the face of the serious threat posed by organized crime, the Mexican Congress passed legislation to expand the investigative and intelligence capabilities of the country's Federal Police. The Mexican Government has also bolstered vetting and training requirements for local, state, and federal police forces. In July 2013, the Mexican Supreme Court ruled that all human-rights related crimes, including those committed by the military, should be tried in civilian courts.

ECONOMY

Currency	Mexican peso (MXN, $)
Fiscal year	Calendar
Trade organisations	APEC, NAFTA, OECD and WTO
	Statistics
GDP	$1.2876 trillion (nominal; 2014) $1.9266 trillion (PPP; 2014)
GDP rank	14th (nominal) / 10th (PPP)
GDP growth	2.99%
GDP per capita	$10,767.25 (2014) (nominal) $16,111.46 (2014) (PPP)
GDP by sector	agriculture: 3.6%, industry: 36.6%, services: 59.8%
Inflation (CPI)	4%
Population below poverty line	52.3%
Gini coefficient	47.0
Labour force	78.2 million
Labour force by occupation	agriculture: 10.7%, industry: 33.4%, services: 55.9%
Unemployment	4.5%
Main industries	electronics, food and beverages, tobacco, chemicals, iron and steel, petroleum, mining, textiles, clothing, motor vehicles, consumer durables, tourism
Ease-of-doing-business rank	48th
	External
Exports	$370.9 billion
Export goods	automobiles, electronics, televisions, computers, mobile phones, LCD displays, oil and oil products, silver, fruits, vegetables, coffee, cotton, marijuana.
Main export partners	United States 78%
Imports	$370.8 billion
Import goods	metalworking machines, steel mill products, agricultural machinery, metals, repair parts for motor vehicles, aircraft, and aircraft parts, oil production equipment

Main import partners	United States 49.9% China 15.4% Japan 4.8% (2012 est.)
Public finances	
Public debt	$341 billion / 37.7% of GDP
Revenues	$234.3 billion
Expenses	$263.8 billion
Economic aid	$189.4 million
Credit rating	• Standard & Poor's: A (Domestic) BBB+ (Foreign) A+ (T&C Assessment) Outlook: Stable • Moody's: A3 Outlook: Stable • Fitch: BBB+ Outlook: Stable
Foreign reserves	$197.026 billion

The **economy of Mexico** is the 14th largest in the world in nominal terms and the 10th largest by purchasing power parity, according to the IMF. Since the 1994 crisis, administrations have improved the country's macroeconomic fundamentals. Mexico was not significantly influenced by the recent 2002 South American crisis, and maintained positive, although low, rates of growth after a brief period of stagnation in 2001. However, Mexico was one of the Latin American nations most affected by the 2008 recession with its Gross Domestic Product contracting by more than 6%. Moody's (in March 2000) and Fitch IBCA (in January 2002) issued investment-grade ratings for Mexico's sovereign debt. In spite of its unprecedented macroeconomic stability, which has reduced inflation and interest rates to record lows and has increased per capita income, enormous gaps remain between the urban and the rural population, the northern and southern states, and the rich and the poor. Some of the government's challenges include the upgrade of infrastructure, the modernization of the tax system and labor laws, and the reduction of income inequality. The tax revenues, all together 19.6 percent of GDP in 2013, are the lowest among the 34 OECD countries.

The economy contains rapidly developing modern industrial and service sectors, with increasing private ownership. Recent administrations have expanded competition in ports, railroads, telecommunications, electricity generation, natural gas distribution and airports, with the aim of upgrading infrastructure. As an export-oriented economy, more than 90% of Mexican trade is under free trade agreements (FTAs) with more than 40 countries, including the European Union, Japan, Israel, and much of Central and South America. The most influential FTA is the North American Free Trade Agreement (NAFTA), which came into effect in 1994, and was signed in 1992 by the governments of the United States, Canada and Mexico. In 2006, trade with Mexico's two northern partners accounted for almost 90% of its exports and 55% of its imports. Recently, the Congress of the Union approved important tax, pension and judicial reforms, and reform to the oil industry is currently being debated. Mexico had 16 companies in the Forbes Global 2000 list of the world's largest companies in 2008.

Mexico's labor force is 78 million. The OECD and WTO both rank Mexican workers as the hardest-working in the world in terms of the amount of hours worked yearly, although profitability per man-hour remains low

Mexico is classified by the World Bank as an upper-middle-income country. Poverty is widespread (around 44% of the population lives below the poverty line), and high rates of economic growth are needed to create legitimate economic opportunities for new entrants to the work force. The Mexican economy grew by more than 5% in 2010 after a sharp recession in 2009 during the global economic crisis.

Since the 1994 devaluation of the peso, successive Mexican governments have improved the country's macroeconomic fundamentals. Inflation and public sector deficits are under control, while the current account balance and public debt profile have improved. Mexico's sovereign debt remains investment-grade, with a stable outlook. Mexico's tax revenue as a percentage of gross domestic product (GDP) was 17.5% in 2009, the lowest of OECD members.

Mexico is a major recipient of remittances, sent mostly from Mexicans in the United States. Remittances amounted to $21.3 billion in 2010 and are the country's second-largest source of foreign currency, after oil. Most remittances are used for immediate consumption--food, housing, health care, education--but some collective remittances, sent from a U.S. community of migrants to their community of origin, are used for shared projects and infrastructure improvements. The Government of Mexico participates through its flagship fund-matching program "3X1 Program for Migrants." The Mexican Government also has implemented social development programs, like *Oportunidades*, to address the problems of poverty.

Mexico is one the most popular tourist destinations in the world. It attracted 21.3 million international tourists in 2010, making it the tenth-most popular international destination in terms of arrivals. Tourism contributed $11.8 billion to Mexico's economy in 2010, one of the top sources of foreign exchange for the country.

Trade

Mexico is an export-oriented economy. It is an important trade power as measured by the value of merchandise traded, and the country with the greatest number of free trade agreements. In 2005, Mexico was the world's fifteenth largest merchandise exporter and twelfth largest merchandise importer with a 12% annual percentage increase in overall trade. In fact, from 1991 to 2005 Mexican trade increased fivefold. Mexico is the biggest exporter and importer in Latin America; in 2005, Mexico alone exported US $213.7 billion, roughly equivalent to the sum of the exports of Brazil, Argentina, Venezuela, Uruguay, and Paraguay. By 2009 Mexico ranked once again number 15 on World's leading exporters with US $230 billion (And amongst the top ten excluding Intra-EU countries). However, Mexican trade is fully integrated with that of its North American partners: close to 90% of Mexican exports and 50% of its imports are traded with the United States and Canada. Nonetheless, NAFTA has not produced trade diversion. While trade with the United States increased 183% from 1993 to 2002, and that with Canada 165%, other trade agreements have shown even more impressive results: trade with Chile increased 285%, with Costa Rica 528% and Honduras 420%. Trade with the European Union increased 105% over the same time period

Mexico joined the General Agreement on Tariffs and Trade (GATT) in 1986, and today is an active and constructive participant of the World Trade Organization. Fox's administration promoted the establishment of a Free Trade Area of the Americas; Puebla served as temporary headquarters for the negotiations, and several other cities are now candidates for its permanent headquarters if the agreement is reached and implemented.

Mexico has signed 12 free trade agreements with 44 countries:

- the North American Free Trade Agreement (NAFTA) (1994) with the United States and Canada;

- Grupo de los tres, *Group of the three [countries]*, or G-3 (1995) with Colombia and Venezuela; the latter decided to terminate the agreement in 2006; Mexico announced its intention to invite Ecuador, Peru or Panama as a replacement;
- Free Trade Agreement with Costa Rica (1995);
- Free Trade Agreement with Bolivia (1995);
- Free Trade Agreement with Nicaragua (1998);

Countries with which Mexico has signed a FTA

- Free Trade Agreement with Chile (1999);
- Free Trade Agreement with the European Union (2000);
- Free Trade Agreement with Israel (2000);
- TN Free Trade Agreement (2001), with Guatemala, El Salvador and Honduras;
- Free Trade Agreement with the European Free Trade Association (EFTA), integrated by Iceland, Norway, Liechtenstein and Switzerland (2001);
- Free Trade Agreement with Uruguay (2004); and
- Free Trade Agreement with Japan (2005)

Mexico has shown interest in becoming an associate member of Mercosur. The Mexican government has also started negotiations with South Korea, Singapore and Peru, and also wishes to start negotiations with Australia for a trade agreement between the two countries

Agriculture

Mexico's agricultural sector accounts for 5% of GDP and employs 13.7% of the work force. Top revenue-producing crops include corn, tomatoes, sugar cane, dry beans, and avocados. Mexico also generates significant revenue from the production of beef, poultry, pork, and dairy products. Implementation of NAFTA has opened Mexico's agricultural sector to the forces of globalization and competition, and some farmers have greatly benefited from greater market access. In particular, fruit and vegetable exports from Mexico have increased dramatically in recent years. However, structural inefficiencies that have existed for decades continue to limit improvements in productivity and living standards for many in the agricultural sector. These inefficiencies include a prevalence of small-scale producers, a lack of infrastructure, inadequate supplies of credit, a communal land structure for many producers, and a large subsistence rural population that is not part of the formal economy. It is estimated that half of Mexico's producers are subsistence farmers and over 60% produce corn or beans, with the majority of these farmers cultivating five hectares or less, although the number of Mexican farmers is steadily decreasing as they seek greater economic opportunities from off-farm employment.

Foreign Investment

Foreign direct investment (FDI) in Mexico for 2010 was $17.7 billion, up slightly from 2009 but still below the peak levels of the mid-2012s. The global economic slowdown in 2008 and 2009 caused a significant decline in FDI. Portfolio investment totaled $37.1 billion in 2010. Most portfolio investment was in local bond issuances.

Energy

Mexico was the seventh-largest oil producer in the world and the second-largest supplier of oil to the United States. State-owned Petroleos Mexicanos (Pemex) holds a constitutionally-established monopoly for the exploration, production, transportation, and marketing of the nation's oil and is one of the largest oil companies in the world. However, oil production has decreased in recent years as production at the giant Cantarell field continues to decline. The oil sector is a crucial component of Mexico's economy; while its relative importance to the general Mexican economy has declined in the long term, the oil sector still generated 14% of the country's export earnings in 2010, according to Mexico's central bank. More importantly, the government relies upon earnings from the oil industry (including taxes and direct payments from Pemex) for 32% of total government revenues. Therefore, any decline in oil production has a direct effect upon the country's overall fiscal balance.

In early 2013, Mexico held licensing rounds for performance-based contracts on oil blocks, allowing participation by foreign oil companies for the first time since the nationalization of the oil industry in 1938. The foreign firms will have no ownership rights over any oil they produce, but they are expected to provide Mexican fields with needed technological improvements.

Transportation and Communications

The World Economic Forum ranks Mexico 79th globally on the overall quality of its infrastructure (out of 139 countries). A National Infrastructure Plan of $233 billion is designed to raise the coverage, quality, and competitiveness of the country's infrastructure assets.

Mexico's land transportation network is one of the most extensive in Latin America with 356,000 kilometers of paved roads. In terms of road density, however, Mexico has one of the lowest rates among the major economies in the region. Three major private companies operate Mexico's 27,000-km railroad network.

Mexico's sea ports have experienced a boom in investment and traffic following a 1993 law that privatized the port system. Mexico's ports moved 3.3 million 20-foot container equivalent units (TEU) in 2008 and 2.9 million TEUs in 2009. Manzanillo is the largest container port, followed by Veracruz and Altamira. Several dozen international airlines serve Mexico, with direct or connecting flights from most major cities in the United States, Canada, Europe, Japan, and Latin America. Most Mexican regional capitals and resorts have direct air services to Mexico City or the United States. In 2010, 24.1 million air passengers visited Mexico.

The telecommunications sector is dominated by Telmex, the former state-owned monopoly, and its mobile telephone spinoff, America Movil. Several international companies compete in the sector with limited success. The fixed-line teledensity rate in Mexico (18%) is below the average for Latin America. Wireless penetration is much higher (more than 75%), with 91.3 million wireless subscribers in 2010, although many of these customers rely on prepaid cards or use their phones to receive calls only. In 2010, 35 million Mexicans had some form of Internet access.

PRINCIPAL SECTORS

ELECTRONICS

The electronics industry of Mexico has grown enormously within the last decade. Mexico has the sixth largest electronics industry in the world after China, United States, Japan, South Korea, and Taiwan. Mexico is the second largest exporter of electronics to the United States where it exported $71.4 billion worth of electronics in 2013. The Mexican electronics industry is dominated by the manufacture and OEM design of televisions, displays, computers, mobile phones, circuit boards, semiconductors, electronic appliances, communications equipment and LCD modules. The Mexican electronics industry grew 20% between 2010 and 2013, up from its constant growth rate of 17% between 2003 and 2009. Currently electronics represent 30% of Mexico's exports.

TELEVISIONS

The design and manufacture of flat panel plasma, LCD and LED televisions is the single largest sector of the Mexican electronics industry, representing 25% of Mexico's electronics export revenue. In 2009 Mexico surpassed South Korea and China as the largest manufacturer of televisions, with Sony, Toshiba, Samsung, Sharp (through Semex), Zenith LG, Lanix, TCL, RCA, Phillips, Elcoteq, Tatung, Panasonic, and Vizio manufacturing CRT, LCD, LED and Plasma televisions in Mexico. Due to Mexico's position as the largest manufacturer of television it is known as the television capital of the world in the electronics industry.

COMPUTERS

Mexico is the third largest manufacturer of computers in the world with both domestic companies such as Lanix, Texa, Meebox, Spaceit, Kyoto and foreign companies such as Dell, Sony, HP, Acer Compaq, Samsung and Lenovo manufacturing various types of computers across the country.

OEM AND ODM MANUFACTURING

Mexico is also home to a large number of OEM and ODM manufactures both foreign and domestic. Among them include Foxconn, Celestica, Sanmina-SCI, Jabil, Elcoteq, Falco, Kimball International, Compal, Benchmark Electronics, Plexus, Lanix and Flextronics. These companies assemble finished electronics or design and manufacture electronic components on behalf of larger companies such as Sony or Microsoft using locally sourced components, for example the ODM, Flextronics manufactures Xbox video games systems in Guadalajara, Mexico for Microsoft using components such as power systems and printed circuit boards from a local company, Falco Electronics which acts as the OEM.

ENGINEERING AND DESIGN

The success and rapid growth of the Mexican electronics sector is driven primarily by the relatively low cost of manufacturing and design in Mexico; its strategic position as a major consumer electronics market coupled with its proximity to both the large North American and South American markets whom Mexico shares free trade agreements with; government support in the form of low business taxes, simplified access to loans and capital for both foreign multinational and domestic startup tech-based firms; and a very large pool of highly skilled, educated labor across all sectors of the tech industry. For example, German multinational engineering and electronics conglomerate Siemens has a significant Mexican base, which also serves as its business and strategy hub for Central American countries and the Caribbean region.

There are almost half a million (451,000) students enrolled in electronics engineering programs with an additional 114,000 electronics engineers entering the Mexican workforce each year and Mexico had over half a million (580,000) certified electronic engineering professionals employed in 2007. From the late 1990s, the Mexican electronics industry began to shift away from simple line assembly to more advanced work such as research, design, and the manufacture of advanced electronics systems such as LCD panels, semiconductors, printed circuit boards, microelectronics, microprocessors, chipsets and heavy electronic industrial equipment and in 2006 the number of certified engineers being graduated annually in Mexico surpassed that of the United States. Many Korean, Japanese and American appliances sold in the US are actually of Mexican design and origin but sold under the OEM's client names. In 2008 one out of every four consumer appliances sold in the United States was of Mexican design.

JOINT PRODUCTION

While many foreign companies like Phillips, Vizio and LG simply install wholly owned factories in Mexico a number of foreign companies have set up semi-independent joint venture companies with Mexican businesses to manufacture and design components in Mexico. These companies are independently operated from their foreign parent companies and are registered in Mexico. These local companies function under Mexican law and retain a sizable portion of the revenue. These companies typically function dually as in-company OEM development and design facilities and manufacturing centers and usually produce most components needed to manufacture the finished products. An example would by Sharp which has formed Semex. Semex was founded as a joint venture between Sharp and Mexican investors which acts as an autonomous independent company which Sharp only maintains partial control over. The company manufactures whole products such televisions and designs individual components on behalf of Sharp such as LCD modules and in return Semex is granted access to Sharp capital, technology, research capacity and branding. Notable foreign companies which have set up joint venture entities in Mexico include Samsung which formed Samex, a local designer and manufacturer of finished televisions, white goods and individual electronic components like printed circuit boards, LCD panels and semiconductors, Toshiba, who formed Toshiba de México, S.A. de C.V., an administratively autonomous subsidiary which produces electronics parts, televisions and heavy industrial equipment.

Some of these subsidiaries have grown to expand into multiple branches effectively becoming autonomous conglomerates within their own parent companies. Sony for example started operations in Mexico in 1976 with a group of Mexican investors, and founded the joint venture, Sony de Mexico which produces LED panels, LCD modules, automotive electronics, appliances and printed circuit boards amongst other products for its Japanese parent company, Sony KG. Sony de Mexico has research facilities in Monterrey and Mexico City, designs many of the Sony products manufactured in Mexico and has now expanded to create its own finance, music and entertainment subsidiaries which are Mexican registered and independent of their Japanese parent corporation.

DOMESTIC INDUSTRY

Although much of Mexico's electronics industry is driven by foreign companies, Mexico also has a sizeable domestic electronics industry and a number of electronics companies including Mabe, a major appliance manufacturer and OEM which has been functioning since the nineteen fifties and has expanded into the global market, Meebox, a designer and manufacturer desktop and tablet computers, solar power panels and electronics components, Texa, which manufactures computers laptops and servers, Falco, a major international manufacturer of electronic components such as printed circuitboards, power systems, semiconductors, gate drives and which has production facilities in Mexico, India and China, and Lanix, Mexico's largest electronics company which manufactures products such as computers, laptops, smartphones, LED and LCD displays, flash memory, tablets, servers, hard drives, RAM, optical disk drives, and printed circuitboards and employs over 11,000 people in Mexico and Chile and distributes its products throughout Latin America. Another area being currently developed in Mexico is Robotics, Mexico's new Mexone robot has been designed with the idea that in future years develop a commercial application for such advanced robots

ENERGY AND MINERAL RESOURCES

Mineral resources are the "nation's property" (i.e. public property) by constitution. As such, the energy sector is administered by the government with varying degrees of private investment. Mexico is the sixth-largest oil producer in the world, with 3,700,000 barrels per day (590,000 m^3/d).

Pemex, the public company in charge of administering research, exploration and sales of oil, is the largest company (oil or otherwise) in Mexico, and the second largest in Latin America after Brazil's Petrobras. Nonetheless, the company is heavily taxed, a significant source of revenue for the government, of almost 62 per cent of the company's sales. Without enough money to continue investing in finding new sources or upgrading infrastructure, and being protected constitutionally from private and foreign investment, some have predicted the company may face institutional collapse. While the oil industry is still relevant for the government's budget, its importance in GDP and exports has steadily fallen since the 1980s. In 1980 oil exports accounted for 61.6% of total exports; by 2012 it was only 7.3%.

Manufacturing

Automobiles

The automotive sector accounts for 17.6% of Mexico's manufacturing sector. General Motors, Chrysler, Ford Motor Company, Nissan, Fiat, Renault, Honda, Toyota, and Volkswagen produce 2.8 million vehicles annually at 20 plants across the country, mostly in Puebla. Mexico manufactures more automobiles of boring any North American nation. The industry produces technologically complex components and engages in research and development. The "Big Three" (General Motors, Ford and Chrysler) have been operating in Mexico since the 1930s, while Volkswagen and Nissan built their plants in the 1960s. In Puebla alone, 70 industrial part-makers cluster around Volkswagen. In the 2010s expansion of the sector was surging. In 2014 more than $10 billion in investment was committed in the first few months of the year. Kia Motors in August 2014 announced plans for a $1 billion factory in Nuevo León. At the time Mercedes-Benz and Nissan were already building a $1.4 billion plant near Puebla, while BMW was planning a $1-billion assembly plant in San Luis Potosí. Additionally, Audi began building a $1.3 billion factory near Puebla in 2013.

Services

The tertiary sector was estimated to account for 70.5% of the country's GDP, and employs 58% of the active population. This section includes transportation, commerce, warehousing, restaurant and hotels, arts and entertainment, health, education, financial and banking services, telecommunications as well as public administration and defense. Mexico's service sector is strong, and in 2001 replaced Brazil's as the largest service sector in Latin America in dollar terms.

Tourism

Tourism is one of the most important industries in Mexico. It is the fourth largest source of foreign exchange for the country. Mexico is the eighth most visited country in the world (with over 20 million tourists a year).

Finance

Banking system

According to the IMF the Mexican banking system is strong, in which private banks are profitable and well-capitalized. The financial and banking sector is increasingly dominated by foreign companies or mergers of foreign and Mexican companies with the notable exception of Banorte. The acquisition of Banamex, one of the oldest surviving financial institutions in Mexico, by Citigroup was the largest US-Mexico corporate merger, at US $12.5 billion. In spite of that, the largest financial institution in Mexico is Bancomer associated to the Spanish BBVA.

The process of institution building in the financial sector in Mexico has evolved hand in hand with the efforts of financial liberalization and of inserting the economy more fully into world markets. Over the recent years, there has been a wave of acquisitions by foreign institutions such as US-based Citigroup, Spain's BBVA and the UK's HSBC. Their presence, along with a better regulatory framework, has allowed Mexico's banking system to recover from the 1994–95 peso devaluation. Lending to the public and private sector is increasing and so is activity in the areas of insurance, leasing and mortgages. However, bank credit accounts for only 22% of GDP, which is significantly low compared to 70% in Chile. Credit to the Agricultural sector has fallen 45.5% in six years (2001 to 2007), and now represents about 1% of total bank loans. Other important institutions include savings and loans, credit unions (known as "cajas populares"),government development banks, "non-bank banks", bonded warehouses, bonding companies and foreign-exchange firms.

A wave of acquisitions has left Mexico's financial sector in foreign hands. Their foreign-run affiliates compete with independent financial firms operating as commercial banks, brokerage and securities houses, insurance companies, retirement-fund administrators, mutual funds, and leasing companies.

Securities market

Mexico has a single securities market, the Mexican Stock Exchange (**Bolsa Mexicana de Valores**, known as the Bolsa). The market has grown steadily, with its main indices increasing by more than 600% in the last decade. It is Latin America's second largest exchange, after Brazil's. The total value of the domestic market capitalization of the BMV was calculated at US$409 billion at the end of 2013, and raised to US$451 billion by the end of February this year.

The *Indice de Precios y Cotizaciones* (IPC, the general equities index) is the benchmark stock index on the Bolsa. In 2005 the IPC surged 37.8%, to 17,802.71 from 12,917.88, backed by a stronger Mexican economy and lower interest rates. It continued its steep rise through the beginning of 2006, reaching 19,272.63 points at end-March 2006. The stockmarket also posted a record low vacancy rate, according to the central bank. Local stockmarket capitalisation totalled US$236bn at end-2005, up from US$170bn at end-2004. As of March 2006 there were 135 listed companies, down from 153 a year earlier. Only a handful of the listed companies are foreign. Most are from Mexico City or Monterrey; companies from these two cities compose 67% of the total listed companies.

The IPC consists of a sample of 35 shares weighted according to their market capitalisation. Heavy hitters are America Telecom, the holding company that manages Latin America's largest mobile company, América Móvil; Telefonos de Mexico, Mexico's largest telephone company; Grupo Bimbo, world's biggest baker; and Wal-Mart de México, a subsidiary of the US retail giant. The makeup of the IPC is adjusted every six months, with selection aimed at including the most liquid shares in terms of value, volume and number of trades.

Mexico's stockmarket is closely linked to developments in the US. Thus, volatility in the New York and Nasdaq stock exchanges, as well as interest-rate changes and economic expectations in the US, can steer the performance of Mexican equities. This is both because of Mexico's economic dependence on the US and the high volume of trading in Mexican equities through American Depositary Receipts (ADRs). Currently, the decline in the value of the dollar is making non-US markets, including Mexico's, more attractive.

Despite the recent gains, investors remain wary of making placements in second-tier initial public offerings (IPOs). Purchasers of new issues were disappointed after prices fell in numerous medium-sized companies that made offerings in 2005 and 1997. IPO activity in Mexico remains tepid and the market for second-tier IPOs is barely visible. There were three IPOs in 2005

NATIONAL SECURITY

Mexico's armed forces number about 225,000. The air force is a semiautonomous organization that reports to the head of the army, and together the army and air force make up about three-fourths of that total. The navy is a completely autonomous cabinet agency, and there is no joint chief of staff position. Principal military roles include national defense, narcotics control, and civic action assignments such as search and rescue and disaster relief. Mexico's federal, state, and municipal police forces number approximately 450,000, including analysts and investigators. At the state and local level, police are generally divided into "preventive" and "judicial" police. Preventive police maintain order and public security and generally do not investigate crimes. As noted previously, the Mexican Congress passed legislation in 2009 expanding the investigative and intelligence capabilities of the Federal Police, which has expanded from 4,000 personnel at the beginning of the Calderon administration to over 35,000.

President Calderon has made combating organized crime a priority of his administration and, to that end, has deployed the Mexican military to 10 Mexican states to assist (or replace) the weak and often corrupt local and state police. Transnational criminal organizations (TCOs) have responded to increased pressure on their activities with unprecedented violence directed mostly at competing cartels, but also government security forces and innocent citizens. They have also expanded their business beyond narcotics into kidnapping, migrant smuggling, and extortion. New estimates suggest that of over the roughly 40,000 deaths attributed to narco-violence since December 2006, nearly 2,000 were members of the Mexican security services. The Mexican military and police have been increasingly successful in carrying out operations to remove top cartel leaders, including Jose de Jesus “El Chango” Mendez (La Familia cartel--arrested in June 2013); Antonio Ezequiel Cardenas Guillen “Tony Tormenta” (Gulf Cartel--killed in a shootout in November 2010); Edgar Valdez Villareal “La Barbie” (Beltran Leyva Cartel--arrested in August 2010); Ignacio Coronel Villareal “Nacho” (Sinaloa Cartel--killed in shootout in July 2010); Eduardo Teodoro Garcia Semental “El Teo” (Arellano Felix Cartel--arrested in January 2010); Carlos Beltran Leyva (Beltran Leyva Cartel--arrested in January 2010); and Arturo Beltran Leyva (Beltran Leyva Cartel--killed during an attempted arrest in December 2009.) As the military has stepped up its engagement in law enforcement activities, allegations of human rights abuses against the military have also increased.

Mexico’s efforts to reform its judicial sector and professionalize its police forces reflect its commitment to promote the rule of law and build strong law enforcement institutions to counter the threat posed by organized crime. The U.S. assists Mexico in this effort through the multi-year $1.6 billion Merida Initiative, which directly supports programs to help Mexico train its police forces in modern investigative techniques, promote a culture of lawfulness, and implement key justice reforms. Elements of the police force began to replace the military in strategic locations in 2010.

FOREIGN RELATIONS

Traditionally, Mexico has sought to maintain its interests abroad and project its influence largely through moral persuasion and has championed the principles of nonintervention and self-determination. In its efforts to revitalize its economy and open up to international competition, Mexico has sought closer relations with the U.S., Western Europe, and the Pacific Basin. President Calderon has actively promoted international human rights and democracy and sought to increase Mexico's participation in international affairs.

Mexico is a strong supporter of the United Nations and Organization of American States systems.

While selective in its membership in other international organizations, it pursues its interests through a number of ad hoc international bodies. Mexico was the Secretary Pro Tempore of the Rio Group for the term 2008-2010; separately, it held a seat on the UN Security Council for the period 2009-2010. In late 2010, Mexico hosted the 16th Conference of the Parties of the UN Framework Convention on Climate Change. Whereas Mexico declined to become a member of Organization of Petroleum Exporting Countries, it nevertheless seeks to diversify its diplomatic and economic relations, as demonstrated by its accession to the General Agreement on Tariffs and Trade (GATT) in 1986; its joining the Asia-Pacific Economic Cooperation forum (APEC) in 1993; its becoming, in April 1994, the first Latin American member of the Organization for Economic Cooperation and Development (OECD); and its entering the World Trade Organization as a founding member in 2005. Mexico attended the first Summit of the Americas, held in Miami in 1994; managed coordination of the agenda item on education for the 1998 Summit of the Americas in Santiago, Chile; hosted a Special Summit of the Americas in early 2004; and participated actively in the 2009 Summit of the Americas in Port of Spain, Trinidad and Tobago. In 2002 it hosted the APEC Leaders' Meeting in Cabo San Lucas. Mexico hosted the September 2003 WTO Ministerial in Cancun and a Hemispheric Security Conference in October of the same year. It was elected to the International Atomic Energy Agency Board of Governors in 2003. Mexico has emerged as a key middle income player in the G-20 and hosted an H1N1 Conference in Cancun in 2009.

U.S.-MEXICAN RELATIONS

U.S. relations with Mexico are important and complex. U.S. relations with Mexico have a direct impact on the lives and livelihoods of millions of Americans--whether the issue is trade and economic reform, homeland security, drug control, migration, or the environment. The U.S. and Mexico are partners in NAFTA, and enjoy a broad and expanding trade relationship. Since the first North American Leaders' Summit in 2005, the United States, Canada, and Mexico have been cooperating more closely on a trilateral basis to improve North American competitiveness, ensure the safety of our citizens, and promote clean energy and a healthy environment. The three nations also cooperate on hemispheric and global challenges, such as managing transborder infectious diseases and seeking greater integration to respond to challenges of transnational organized crime.

The scope of U.S.-Mexican relations goes far beyond diplomatic and official contacts; it entails extensive commercial, cultural, and educational ties, as demonstrated by the annual figure of about a million legal border crossings a day. In addition, a million American citizens live in Mexico and approximately 10 million Americans visit Mexico every year. More than 18,000 companies with U.S. investment have operations there, and the U.S. accounts for nearly $100 billion of foreign direct investment in Mexico. Along the 2,000-mile shared border, state and local governments interact closely.

There has been frequent contact at the highest levels. Presidents' meetings have included a visit by President Calderon to Washington, DC to meet with President-elect Barack Obama in January 2009; visits by President Obama to Mexico City in April 2009 and to Guadalajara in August 2009 for the North American Leaders' Summit; a visit by President Calderon to Pittsburgh in September 2009 for a G-20 Summit; a state visit, hosted by President Obama, in honor of President Calderon in May 2010; and President Calderon's visit to Washington in March 2013.

In recent years, U.S.-Mexico cooperation in the struggle against organized crime and drug trafficking has been unprecedented. At the August 2007 North American Leaders' Summit in Montebello, Canada, Presidents George W. Bush and Calderon announced the Merida Initiative to work together and with the countries of Central America to combat drug trafficking and organized crime in the region. In June 2008, President Bush signed the congressional appropriations bill allocating assistance to Mexico as part of the Merida Initiative. Appropriated funds for Mexico under the initiative totaled $1.5 billion as of the end of 2010. In March 2010, Secretary of State Hillary Clinton and her Mexican counterpart Patricia Espinosa chaired a high-level group meeting that announced four strategic pillars for U.S.-Mexico cooperation. The first pillar aims to disrupt the capacity of organized crime to operate by capturing criminal groups and their leaders and reducing their revenues through better investigations, successful prosecutions, and shipment interdictions. The initiative's second pillar focuses on enhancing the capacity of Mexico's government and institutions to sustain the rule of law. The Merida Initiative's third pillar aims to improve border management to facilitate legitimate trade and movement of people while thwarting the flow of drugs, arms, and cash. Finally, the fourth pillar seeks to build strong and resilient communities. This high-level group met again in April 2013 to underscore the bilateral strategic partnership between the United States and Mexico, to reaffirm the four-pillar approach, and to ratify the shared commitment to achieving long-term solutions to the challenges posed by transnational organized crime.

Border, Environmental, and Telecom Affairs

Cooperation between the United States and Mexico along the 2,000-mile common border includes state and local problem-solving mechanisms; transportation planning; and institutions to address resource, environment, and health issues. In 1993, the Border Liaison Mechanism (BLM) was established. Chaired by U.S. and Mexican consuls, the BLMs operate in "sister city" pairs and have proven to be effective means of dealing with a variety of local issues including border infrastructure, accidental violation of sovereignty by law enforcement officials, charges of mistreatment of foreign nationals, and cooperation in public health matters such as tuberculosis and H1N1 influenza.

With nearly one million people and over one billion dollars worth of commerce crossing the U.S.-Mexico border each day, coordination of border crossing operations and development among federal, state, and local partners on both sides of the border is critical. Presidents Obama and Calderon created a high-level Executive Steering Committee for 21st Century Border Management in 2010 to spur further advancements in creating a modern, secure, and efficient border. In 2010, the U.S. and Mexico opened three new border crossings (McAllen TX--Reynosa, Tamaulipas; San Luis AZ--San Luis Rio Colorado, Sonora; and Donna TX--Reynosa, Tamaulipas). The multi-agency U.S.-Mexico Binational Group on Bridges and Border Crossings meets twice yearly to improve the efficiency of existing crossings and coordinate planning for new ones. The 10 U.S. and Mexican border states are active participants in these meetings.

The United States and Mexico have a history of cooperation on environmental and natural resource issues, particularly in the border area, where there are serious environmental problems caused by rapid population growth, urbanization, and industrialization. Cooperative activities between the U.S. and Mexico take place under a number of agreements such as:

- The International Boundary and Water Commission (IBWC) is an international organization with roots dating back to the late 19th century. The IBWC comprises independent U.S. and Mexican sections and has settled numerous difficult U.S.-Mexico boundary and water problems, including the regularization of the Rio Grande near El Paso through the 1967 Chamizal settlement. The IBWC determines and accounts for national ownership of international waters, builds and operates water conservation and flood control projects, and constructs and maintains boundary markers on the land boundary and on international bridges. In recent years, the IBWC has worked to resolve longstanding border sanitation problems, to monitor the quantity and quality of border waters, and to address water delivery and sedimentation problems of the Colorado River.
- The 1983 La Paz Agreement to protect and improve the border environment and Border 2012, a 10-year, binational, results-oriented environmental program for the U.S.-Mexico border region. The Border 2012 Program is the latest multi-year, binational planning effort to be implemented under the La Paz Agreement.

- A November 1993 agreement between the U.S. and Mexico, establishing the North American Development Bank (NADBank) and the Border Environment Cooperation Commission (BECC) under the auspices of NAFTA, in order to address border environmental problems. The NADBank uses capital and grant funds contributed by Mexico and the U.S. to help finance border environmental infrastructure projects certified by the BECC. The BECC works with local communities to develop and certify environmental infrastructure projects, such as wastewater treatment plants, drinking water systems, and solid waste disposal facilities. Prior to 2005, both institutions had separate Boards of Directors. In an effort to improve efficiency, the separate Boards were merged into a single entity.
- The 1993 North American Agreement on Environmental Cooperation (NAAEC), creating the North American Commission on Environmental Cooperation under NAFTA by the U.S., Mexico, and Canada, to improve enforcement of environmental laws and to address common environmental concerns.
- A series of agreements on border health (since 1942), wildlife and migratory birds (since 1936), national parks, forests, marine and atmospheric resources. In July 2012, the U.S. and Mexico signed an agreement to establish a binational Border Health Commission. The Border Health Commission meets annually and is made up of the federal secretaries of health, the 10 border states' chief health officers, and prominent community health professionals from both countries. A representative from the U.S. Department of Health and Human Services manages the U.S. Section in El Paso, Texas.

The United States and Mexico have also cooperated on telecommunications services in the border area for more than 50 years. Currently, there are 39 bilateral agreements that govern shared use of the radio spectrum. When the United States completed the transition to digital television in 2009, a high percentage of Mexican border cities did the same well ahead of Mexico's deadline to complete the transition by 2021. Recent border agreements also cover mobile broadband services such as BlackBerrys, smartphones, and similar devices. The High Level Consultative Commission on Telecommunications continues to serve as the primary bilateral arena for both governments to promote growth in the sector and to ensure compatible services in the border area. Under this mechanism, the United States and Mexico signed an agreement to improve cross-border public security communications in the border area in 2009.

Principal U.S. Embassy Officials
chief of mission: Ambassador Roberta JACOBSON (since 20 June 2016)

Deputy Chief of Mission--John Feeley
Minister Counselor for Political Affairs--Michael Glover
Minister Counselor for Economic and Science Affairs--Adam Shub
Minister Counselor for Public Diplomacy--James Williams
Minister Counselor for Consular Affairs--John Brennan
Minister Counselor for Commercial Affairs--Ann Bacher
Minister Counselor for Management Affairs--Barbara Aycock
Minister Counselor for Agricultural Affairs--Dan Berman
Consul General Mexico City--Karin King

The U.S. Embassy in Mexico is located at Paseo de la Reforma 305, 06500 Mexico, DF. U.S. mailing address: Box 9000, Brownsville, Texas 78520; tel. (from the U.S.): (011) (52) 55-5080-2012; Internet: http://mexico.usembassy.gov/

The embassy and the U.S. Consulates General, Consulates, and consular agents provide a range of services to American students, tourists, business people, and residents throughout Mexico.

U.S. Consulates General, Consulates, and Officials
Consulate General, Ciudad Juarez--Thomas Rogan
Address: Paseo de la Victoria 3650, Fracc. Partido Senecu, 32543 Ciudad Juarez, Chihuahua
U.S. Postal Address: Box 10545, El Paso, Texas 79995-0545
Tel. (from the U.S.): (011)(52) 656-227-3000

Consulate General, Guadalajara--Daniel Keller
Address: Progreso 175. Col. Americana, Guadalajara, Jalisco 44160
U.S. Postal Address: Box 9001, Brownsville, Texas 78520-0901
Tel.: (011)(52) 333-268-2100

Consulate General, Hermosillo--John Tavenner
Address: Calle Monterrey 141 Pte., Col. Esqueda 83260, Hermosillo, Sonora
U.S. Postal Address: Box 1689, Nogales, Arizona 85628
Tel.: (011)(52) 662-289-3500

Consulate General, Matamoros--Michael Barkin
Address: Ave. Primera 2002 y Azaleas, 87330, Matamoros, Tamaulipas
U.S. Postal Address: Box 633, Brownsville, Texas 78522-0633
Tel.: (011)(52) 868-812-4402

Consulate General, Monterrey--Nace Crawford
Address: Avenida Constitution 411 Poniente, 64000 Monterrey, Nuevo Leon
U.S. Postal Address: Box 9002, Brownsville, Texas 78520-0902
Tel.: (011)(52) 818-047-3100

Consulate General, Nuevo Laredo--Donald Heflin
Address: Calle Allende 3330, Col. Jardin, 88260 Nuevo Laredo, Tamaulipas
U.S. Postal Address: Box 3089, Laredo, Texas 78044-3089
Tel.: (011)(52) 867-714-0512

Consulate General, Tijuana--Steven Kashkett
Address: Paseo de las Culturas s/n, Mesa de Otay, Delegacion Centenario, 22425 Tijuana, Baja California Norte
U.S. Postal Address: P.O. Box 439039, San Diego, California 92143-9039
Tel.: (011)(52) 664-977-2012

Consulate, Merida--Greg Segas
Address: Calle 60 No 338 K x 29 y 31, Colonia Alcala Martin, CP 97050, Merida, Yucatan, Mexico
U.S. Postal Address: Box 9003, Brownsville, Texas 78520-0903
Tel.: (011)(52)(999) 942-5700

Consulate, Nogales--Chad Cummins
Address: Calle San Jose s/n, Fracc. Los Alamos 84065, Nogales, Sonora
U.S. Postal Address: P.O. Box 1729, Nogales, AZ 85628-1729
Tel.: (011)(52) 631-311-8150

Consular Agents
Acapulco--Alexander Richards
Address: Hotel Continental Emporio, Costera M. Aleman 121-Local 14,
39670 Acapulco, Guerrero
Tel. (from the U.S.): (011)(52) 744-481-0100

Cabo San Lucas--Trena Brown Schjetnan

Address: Blvd. Marina, Local C-4, Plaza Nautica, Col. Centro,
23410 Cabo San Lucas, Baja California Sur
Tel.: (011)(52) 624-143-3566

Cancun--Rebecca Kubisiak
Address: Blvd. Kukulkan Km 13+000, Lote 18-13, Zona Hotelera, Torre La Europea, Despacho 301,77500 Cancun, Quintana Roo
Tel.: (011)(52) 998-883-0272

Cozumel--Anne R. Harris
Address: Plaza Villa Mar, Plaza Principal, Parque Juarez
(entre Melgar y 5a Av.), Piso 2 Locales 8 y 9, 77600 Cozumel, Quintana Roo
Tel.: (011)(52) 987-872-4574/4485

Ixtapa/Zihuatanejo--Debra Loiuse Mione
Address: Hotel Fontan, Blvd Ixtapa S/N, 40880, Ixtapa, Zihuataejo, Guerrero
Courier Address: Apdo. Postal 169, Paseo de los Hujes 236, Col. El Hujal, 40880 Zihuatanejo, Guerrero
Tel.: (011)(52) 755-553-2100

Mazatlan--Luis Antonio Ramirez Maisonet
Address: Hotel Playa Mazatlan, Playa Gaviotas 202, Zona Dorada,
82110 Mazatlan, Sinaloa
Tel.: (011)(52) 669-916-5889

Oaxaca--Mark A. Leyes
Address: Macedonio Alcala 407, Int. 20,
68000 Oaxaca, Oaxaca
Tel.: (011)(52) 951-514-3054

Piedras Negras--Dina O'Brien
Address: Abasolo 211, Zona Centro
Piedras Negras, Coahuila, C.P. 26000
Tel. (011)(52) 878-782-5586/782-8664

Playa del Carmen--Samantha Mason
Address: "The Palapa", Calle 1 Sur, entre Avenida 15 y Avenida 20
Playa del Carmen 77710 Quintana Roo
Tel: (011)(52) 984-873-0303

Puerto Vallarta--Kelly Trainor de Oceguera
Address: Paradise Village Plaza, Paseo de los Cocoteros #1, Local 4, Int. 17 63732 Nuevo Vallarta, Nayarit
Tel.: (011)(52) 322-222-0069

Reynosa--Vera Nicole Vera
Address: Hotel Holiday Inn, Rooms 1101 and 1102, Calle Emilio Portes Gil #703, Col. Prado Sur 88630 Reynosa, Tamaulipas
Tel. (011)(52) 899-923-6530

San Luis Potosi--Deborah Escobar
Address: Edificio "Las Terrazas," Av. Venustiano Carranza 2076-41, Col. Polanco,
78220 San Luis Potosi, San Luis Potosi
Tel.: (011)(52) 444-811-7802

San Miguel de Allende--Edward Clancy
Address: Plaza La Luciernaga, Libramiento Jose Manuel Zavala, Zavala No. 165, Locales 4 y 5, Colonia La Luciernada
37745 San Miguel de Allende, Guanajuato
Tel.: (011)(52) 415-152-2357

Other Contact Information
American Chamber of Commerce of Mexico, Blas Pascual 205, 3rd Floor, Col. Los Morales, 11510 Mexico, D.F., Mexico
U.S. Mailing Address: P.O. Box 60326-113, Houston, TX 77205-0326
Tel: (011)(52) 555-141-3820
Fax: (011)(52) 555-141-3836
E-Mail: amchammx@amcham.org.mx
(Branch offices also in Guadalajara and Monterrey)

U.S. Department of Commerce
International Trade Administration
Office of Latin America and the Caribbean
14th and Constitution, NW
Washington, DC 20230
Tel: 202-482-0305; 1-800-USA-TRAD(E)
Internet: **http://trade.gov/**

TRAVEL AND BUSINESS INFORMATION

Travel Alerts, Travel Warnings, Trip Registration
The U.S. Department of State's Consular Information Program advises Americans traveling and residing abroad through Country Specific Information, Travel Alerts, and Travel Warnings. **Country Specific Information** exists for all countries and includes information on entry and exit requirements, currency regulations, health conditions, safety and security, crime, political disturbances, and the addresses of the U.S. embassies and consulates abroad. **Travel Alerts** are issued to disseminate information quickly about terrorist threats and other relatively short-term conditions overseas that pose significant risks to the security of American travelers. **Travel Warnings** are issued when the State Department recommends that Americans avoid travel to a certain country because the situation is dangerous or unstable.

For the latest security information, Americans living and traveling abroad should regularly monitor the Department's Bureau of Consular Affairs Internet web site at http://travel.state.gov, where current Worldwide Caution, Travel Alerts, and Travel Warnings can be found. The travel.state.gov website also includes information about passports, tips for planning a safe trip abroad and more. More travel-related information also is available at http://www.usa.gov/Citizen/Topics/Travel/International.shtml.

The Department's Smart Traveler app for U.S. travelers going abroad provides easy access to the frequently updated official country information, travel alerts, travel warnings, maps, U.S. embassy locations, and more that appear on the travel.state.gov site. Travelers can also set up e-tineraries to keep track of arrival and departure dates and make notes about upcoming trips. The app is compatible with iPhone, iPod touch, and iPad (requires iOS 4.0 or later).

The Department of State encourages all U.S. citizens traveling or residing abroad to enroll in the State Department's Smart Traveler Enrollment Program (STEP). A link to the registration page is also available through the Department's Smart Traveler app. U.S. citizens without internet access can enroll directly at the nearest U.S. embassy or consulate. By enrolling, you make your presence and whereabouts known in case it is necessary to contact you in an emergency and so you can receive up-to-date information on security conditions.

Emergency information concerning Americans traveling abroad may be obtained by calling 1-888-407-4747 toll free in the U.S. and Canada or the regular toll line 1-202-501-4444 for callers outside the U.S. and Canada.

Passports

The National Passport Information Center (NPIC) is the U.S. Department of State's single, centralized public contact center for U.S. passport information. Telephone: 1-877-4-USA-PPT (1-877-487-2778); TDD/TTY: 1-888-874-7793. Passport information is available 24 hours, 7 days a week. You may speak with a representative Monday-Friday, 8 a.m. to 10 p.m., Eastern Time, excluding federal holidays.

MEXICO LABOR LAW REFORMS - IMPORTANT DEVELOPMENTS

MEXICO LABOR REGULATIONS BASICS

FEDERAL LABOR LAW

There are basically two federal laws that govern over labor issues in Mexico. One is the federal Labor law and the the other is the federal Social Security Law.

There is a federal Labor law of Mexico, which sets forth the rules and regulations regarding labor relations, labor unions and labor courts (Board of Conciliation and Arbitration).

There is a federal listing of minimum wages for general and specific categories of work. These categories minimum wages may vary depending upon the economic region of the country (geographically identifiable).

There is ample protection provided labor in Mexico. Employers are not permitted to dismiss employees without just cause. If they do so, the employee has a right to file suit for re-instatement or indemnification. The labor courts will presume that the person stating he was your employee is in fact your employee and that you dismissed him without cause. As well the labor courts will require proper representation of the employer (proper power of attorney if an agent represents the employer in labor court) (I have have seen labor suits lost by employers in Mexico due to improper representation).

If resolved in favor of the employee, he has the right to reinstatement plus all back wages that were incurred while the court process was going on. If the employee decides not to seek reinstatement, then he may receive three months salary, all back wages, plus other items that were owed him/her prior to the dismissal (such as unpaid vacations, year end bonuses, profit sharing, seniority pay, maturity leave, and others).

The employer may chose not to reinstate the employee for unjustified dismissal when: a) the employer has been an employee for less than a year, b) the employee and employer are constantly in direct contact and the Board of Conciliation and Arbitration deems that the two can not work together, c) when the employee was an "of confidence" employee (entrusted with confidential administrative or management type activities), when the employee was arrested, d) when the services provided were the rendering of socially oriented public services imposed by law or order issued by authority, or e) the employee was working as an occasional ("eventual" - sporadical or odd jobs) worker.

The labor relationship may terminate by: a) mutual agreement (employer/employee) (employees can not be obligated to work at a specific job for more than one year, however they may continue if they wish), b) by death of the employee, c) by termination (completion) of the job performed or by expiration of the time for which the employee was hired (in order for a job to be of a determined time period, it should not be of a type that is normally considered as ongoing or have some circumstance that makes it so), d) by mental or physical incapacitation of the employee or by resolution of the Conciliation and Arbitration Board.

The employer may terminate the labor relationship due to: a) deceit or fraud by the employee with his fellow workers, relative to the employees capabilities, b) misconduct, threats or injuries by the employee, c) bad conduct by the employee with his follow workers, which causes a brake in the discipline, d) bad conduct by the employee outside the work place which effects the employer, the administrative personnel or their families, e) intentional damages or prejudice to the employer or his assets while working, f) grave damage or prejudice to the employer caused by the employee due to his unintentional negligence, g) imprudence or inexcusable carelessness by the employee placing the establishment or personnel therein in an unsafe situation, h) immoral acts at the place of business by the employee, i) revealing trade secrets of the employer, j) having more than 3 absences from work within 30 days, without justification or the employer's permission, k) unjustified disobedience by the employee relative to his employment, l) refusal by the employee to adopt preventive measures to avoid accidents or illness, m) drunkenness or drinking of intoxicants at the place of work, save by medical prescription and notification thereof to the employer, n) imprisonment of the employee, and o) other grave similar cases.

As well, there is justified suspension of the labor relation (usable by the employer and the employee), when: a) the employee has a contagious illness, b) there is temporary incapacitation of the employee due to an accident or illness, which does not constitute a work related risk; c) preventive (temporary) imprisonment of the employee, followed by an absolving judgment (if the employee has acted in defense of the person or interest of the employer, then the employer is obligated to pay the employees wages during his imprisonment), d) the arrest of the employee, e) rendering of socially oriented public services imposed by law or order issued by authority, f) rendering of services as representative of labor related posts, such as members of Conciliation and Arbitration Boards and others, and g) when the employee does not have certain documents required by law to work (e.g. sanitation cards, driver's license).

The Work Week. The federal Labor Law of Mexico sets forth a maximum of 48 hours per week as the amount of hours a laborer can work without going overtime. Even so, most companies only run the work week at 40 to 45 hours

The Work Day. For every 6 days of work (Monday through Saturday), employees are entitled to one day of rest with full pay. Therefore, when hiring in Mexico please keep in mind that you are hiring per week and not per day, when deciding on the salary.

Work Shifts. There are 3 work shifts, consisting of the day shift (eight hours), the night shift (seven hours) and the mixed shift (7 1/2 hours). The mixed shift is part day shift and part night shift. Those hours that are worked over these periods are considered to be overtime (paid as such - double the hourly rate) and can not go over 9 hours per week.

Overtime. In that case the hourly wage can be double or even triple the normal hourly wage, depending on how many hous overtime are work In the event that the overtime is on a holiday, the hours are paid at triple the normal hourly wage.

Salary. The law sets forth a minimum daily wage for each category of services to be provided in a given geographical area. The law also sets the requirement for an annual review of the salary being paid, which salary increase should not be less the minimum set by law.

Employee vs. Independent contractor. The rights and obligations between the two types of work relationship is very different and if the work relation states independent but the relationship is employee, the Labor Court will view it as employee.

Work related risks suffered. The employer should register and maintain his employees with the Mexican Institute of Social Security (medical care). If he does not, then he will be liable for the medical care and will also still owe Social Security.

Holidays. The official holidays in Mexico are: January 1 (New Year's Day), February 5 (Constitutional Day) , March 21 (Juarez's Birthday) , May 1 (Labor Day) , September 16 (Independence Day) , November 20 (Revolution Day) , December 25 (Christmas Day)

Vacation Time.

Employees have the right to a yearly vacation, which is not to be less than 6 working days. For every year the employee continues to work for the employer, he/she will receive an additional 2 working days. After four years, the employees vacation period will increase only 2 working days for every additional five years he/she works for the employer. As well, the employee will have a right to not less than a 25% vacation premium calculation on his/her salary for the vacation period.

Dismissal or Willing Departure

In the event of being fired from one's employment without just cause (as stated in the Federal labor Law), the employer will pay the employee three months salary (calculated on the last salary paid prior to firing, plus 20 days for each full year of employment with the employer that fired him/she.

If the employee resigns, then the employer will pay the employee the proportionate part of his/her vacation premium and year end bonus. If the employee has worked there for more than 15 years, without interruption (working with someone else and then returning), then the employee shall receive an additional sum equivalent to 12 days salary (calculated on the last salary received prior to resigning) for each year he/she will have worked for the employer.

Labor Contracts

There are two types of employment contracts. One is collective (the same for several people), then the clauses are determined between the employer and the labor union. The other is an individual contract, where the individual negotiates his/her own employment contract.

Retirement

The employer is to periodically deposit in a banking account, for the employee, a sum equivalent to 2% of his/her salary, as a savings account for the employees' retirement (SAR). At this writing, the deposits are to be made in an "AFORE" account that individually idetnified by each employee. There is also to be a periodical payment to INFONAVIT (federal housing authority for workers) of a sum equivalent to 3% of his/her salary.

LABOR UNIONS

Labor unions are recognized under the Federal labor Law as a means of the employees uniting to protect their common employment rights. There are large labor unions existing in Mexico. As a result of the labor unions, collective labor contracts are signed between the employer's representative and the representative of the labor union. Labor union collective contracts are reviewed every two years. A labor union is permitted in a place of employment provided that at least 20% of the employees belong to it. Even so, the registry process is slow and complicated.

SOCIAL SECURITY

The Mexican Federal Social Security system is funded by a mandatory charge paid by the employer, calculated on the salary paid to the employees. This money is to create social security hospitals and staff them , in order to provide full medical coverage to the employees that are registered as employees (being paid for by their employers).

The employer is required to make contributions to the Mexican federal Social Security (IMSS), the Living Quarters Fund (INFONAVIT) and the Retirement Savings System (SAR), as well as payments for vacations, vacation premiums, and year end bonuses. These benefits represent an average of 29% of the salary that is paid. Thus, the salary is 129% of what you state as the base salary.

INFONAVIT

(Instituto Nacional para el Fomento a la Vivienda para Trabajadores).

The National Institute for the Development of Living Quarters for Workers, was created in the early 1970's today it is known as the National Living Quarters Fund). It places a small tax on the employer, calculated on the salary paid to the employees. This money is used to create "social" living quarters (small housing) for the working populous. The employees are to qualify for a loan through INFONAVIT to purchase (repair or debts related to) a house, a monthly sum is automatically subtracted form the employee's salary and then used to make the monthly payment foe the mortgage of the house.

Per the National Living Quaters Fund, employers are to give 5% of their employees' salaries to INFONAVIT.

PROFIT SHARING

Employees are to participate in the earnings of their employees, based on the percentage determined by the National Commission for workers' Participation in their Employers' Earnings.

This earning is to be distributed among the employees of the employer (that are working for the employer or worked for the employer for 60 days or more during the period corresponding). the distribution is to be made within 60 days following the date in which they are to pay their annual income taxes.

This profit sharing is in the sum of 10% of the earnings for the fiscal period (calendar year) and is to be divided in equal shares among: (1) the first half to all employees, taking into consideration the aggregate number of employees that worked for the employer during the year, without taking into account the salary they earned; and 92) the second half is to be divided to the employees in proportion to the salaries they earned during the year.

Those business that are of recent creation are exempt for this profit sharing for the first year of their business activities. The company/business directors, administrators and general managers of the employers are excluded form sharing in this participation, even those it is common to see that they get an automobile, year end bonus and assistance in the purchase of a home. This profit sharing is not used as part of their salaries in order to determine the amount of their participation in this profit sharing.

DISMISSAL PROVISIONS

When the employee is dismissed without just cause, he/she is to receive three months salary (payable upon dismissal). If the compensation is not paid when the employee is dismissed (like when there is a labor lawsuit), then the employer is to pay all salaries that would have been earned during the period in which this delay took place (assuming that the employee won the labor lawsuit), up though the date of the payment.

When the employee has worked for the employer for less than one year, the employee will be compensated (indemnified) in a sum equal to one half of the salaries of the period he/she worked for the employer. If this period is greater than one year, then the compensation is to be equal to a sum equal to six months salary of the first year and twenty days per year for each of the following years.

In the case that the employment is for an undetermined period of time, then the indemnification will be 20 days for each year of services given.

In order to determine the amount payable for compensation (indemnification), they are to use the base salary of the employee corresponding to the date on which the right to receive this payment occurs.

Mexican labour law governs the process by which workers in Mexico may organize labour unions, engage in collective bargaining, and strike. Current labour law reflects the historic interrelation between the state and the Confederation of Mexican Workers, the labour confederation officially aligned with the Institutional Revolutionary Party (the Institutional Revolutionary Party, or PRI), which ruled Mexico under various names for more than seventy years. While the law, on its face, promises workers the right to strike and to organize, in practice it makes it difficult or impossible for independent unions to organize while condoning the corrupt practices of many existing unions and the employers with which they deal.

The current system originated in the Mexican Revolution of 1910–1920, which produced the Constitution of 1917. Article 123 of that Constitution gave workers the right to organize labour unions and to strike. It also provided protection for women and children, the eight hour day, and a living wage.

The Constitution's promised rights, however, remained mere promises until 1931, when the government enacted the Ley Federal de Trabajo or Federal Labour Law. The LFT established Juntas de Conciliaci6n y Arbitraje (the Boards of Conciliation and Arbitration), made up of representatives of the government, employers and labour unions.

Organizing, elections and strikes

In order to participate in this system, a union must have a legal registration (registro), must have an officially recognized right to negotiate collective bargaining agreements (titularidad), and must periodically re-register its officers and be accepted by the state (toma de nota). This system can be used to hobble independent unions not associated with the CTM or other federations that have established relations with the state, since all three members of these boards often have self-interested reasons for denying or delaying registration to rival unions.

Employers can also avoid unionization by entering into "protection contracts" with "sindicatos fantasmas" or "ghost unions", often before a plant is ever built. Such contracts frequently give the union a closed shop, which authorizes the union to demand that the employer fire a worker who is not a member in the union in good standing; that power can, in turn, be used to single out employees who seek to organize independent unions for termination. Some observers, including the independent Uni6n Nacional de Trabajadores (http://www.unt.org.mx) or UNT, estimate that between eighty and ninety percent of all collective bargaining agreements in Mexico fall into this category.

Employees are not always aware that they are covered by a protection contract or that they are represented by a union; while the ghost union may have registered with the Board and filed its contract with it, those records are not made public. An outside union that has filed a petition seeking to organize workers may have its petition dismissed if it is unaware that another union is already recognized or if it does not list the correct name or legal address of the incumbent union.

If an outside union challenging a recognized union is able to obtain registration, then it must go through an election to oust the incumbent. Local Boards often delay such elections for long periods; when they do take place they are by voice vote, rather than secret ballot, in elections held in the workplace under the supervision of a representative of the labour board, the employer, the official union and the independent union. In recent contested elections workers have been required to pass through a gauntlet of armed representatives of the incumbent union in order to report for work and to vote in their workplace. Even if the independent union wins the election, the original contract remains in place until its expiration.

While Mexican labour law gives workers powerful rights to strike, barring employers from hiring replacement workers or operating during a strike, those rights are dependent on official approval from the Board. These local Boards frequently declare strikes to be "inexistente" or non-existent, depriving striking workers of all their legal protections. As a result, while labour protests and work stoppages are frequent in Mexico, legal strikes are rare.

Proposals for change

The PRI and Mexican employers' associations started floating proposals to enhance productivity of Mexican industry by allowing it more "flexibility" during the late 1980s, when "technocrats" such as Miguel de la Madrid, Carlos Salinas de Gortari and Ernesto Zedillo were in command of the PRI. Those proposals made no headway, however, until after the election of Vicente Fox Quesada of the Partido Acción Nacional, or PAN, in 2000. Fox's Secretary of Labour, Carlos Abascal Carranza, a former head of one of the largest employer associations, initiated discussions in 2001 with employer associations and the official and independent union confederations aimed at achieving a consensus proposal for labour law reform.

The Abascal proposal presented in 2002, however, would tighten government control of unions and collective bargaining, without taking any steps to make information about unions' collective bargaining agreements or their activities available to affected workers or the public or make the organizing process any less cumbersome. On the contrary, the proposed reforms would heighten the risks for workers seeking to organize by requiring independent unions to submit the name and address of each of their members to the local Boards, which would then have the power to investigate the authenticity of their signatures. The reforms would also favor existing unions by barring the board from considering more than one election petition at a time and tightening jurisdictional rules defining which labour organization can represent which workers, according to their craft, enterprise and company, making it impossible for some independent unions to challenge incumbents.

Opponents of the law have challenged it under the provisions of the labour side letter to the North American Free Trade Agreement (NAFTA). While the CTM originally supported the reforms, some unions within the official labour movement have expressed reservations about it. The proposals are currently at a standstill.

BASIC CHANGES

The Mexican Constitution is the basis for Mexican labor law: it guarantees workers a set of minimum rights and grants the federal government exclusive power to enact labor laws to carry out and expand upon those rights. México's government passed its first labor law in 1931; the law has been amended several times - most significantly in 1970 and, now, in 2012. Additionally, México enacted the federal Social Security and Housing laws (these laws are not covered in this summary). Several government agencies and tripartite commissions implement, oversee and enforce Mexican labor laws. Generally, the constitutional, statutory and regulatory labor laws apply to all workers in the country, including those workers employed in México by United States employers. Failure to comply with Mexican labor laws can result in significant penalties and financial liability for employers.

Mexico's new Federal Labor Law (FLL) took effect on December 1, 2012. The reform seeks to modernize Mexico's labor law. The new FLL's major, employment related amendments include increased regulation of outsourcing jobs, increased flexibility in hiring and payment of wages, the addition of the concepts of diversity, nondiscrimination and anti-harassment, and parental leave rights.

Previously, companies entering Mexico would set up two entities, one of which would be used to outsource employment to avoid paying worker benefits, including avoiding Mexico's mandatory 10% employee profiting sharing requirement. Now, among other requirements, employers may only outsource employees if the outsourced employees perform work of a specialized character. In other words, under the new FLL, companies will need to evaluate the way they are structured or risk paying all employees (outsourced or otherwise) all employment related liabilities (such as notice requirements, severance payments, profit-sharing and social security).

OUTSOURCING AND PROFIT-SHARING

The Mexican Labor Law has a mandatory requirement whereby employers must share 10% of their profits with employees. To mitigate this requirement, companies have traditionally set up two separate entities in Mexico: one to run the business with limited employees and the other one to hire and lease out employees to the business. The new FLL puts companies who follow this traditional set-up at risk of having to provide the leased employees 10% of its profits, along with satisfying all other labor law obligations, because very few will qualify as valid outsourcing agencies.

Under the FFL, for outsourcing to be valid, it must meet the following terms and conditions:

It may not cover all the activities carried out in the workplace,
It must be limited to specialized tasks that fall outside of the beneficiary's ordinary course of business and thus, justified by its specialized nature,
It may not include tasks that are the same or similar to those being performed by the beneficiary's employees, and
It must be documented through an outsourcing agreement.
If these conditions are not met, the beneficiary may be deemed a co-employer of the outsourced employees and, as a result, may be obligated to pay associated labor liabilities, including salaries, local social security contributions, and benefits, which include sharing 10% of its profits with the outsourced employees.

EXPANDED HIRING METHODS AND EMPLOYMENT RELATIONSHIPS

The new FLL adds two new hiring methods: Trial Periods and Initial Training Periods. Definite and indefinite term employment over 180 days may now include a Trial Period. This allows employers the ability to evaluate whether a new employee can perform the requisite job functions. Employers may also opt for an Initial Training Period, which allows the employer to train the employee on the skills necessary to perform the job. In both cases, the type of "new hire method" must be explicitly written into the employment agreement.

Both the Trial Period and the Initial Training Period have time limits. The Trial Period may only last up to 30 days for rank-and-file type employees, but for management-level employees and high-level executives, an extension may be granted allowing for a maximum of 180 days in total. The Initial Training Period has a maximum term of three months, with high-level general administrative functions or functions requiring special professional knowledge qualifying for an extension of up to six months in total. Please note that these terms cannot be combined. The advantage of these new hire methods is that once the trial or training period has expired, if the employee is not able to perform the skills for the job, the employer may terminate the employee without having to pay severance.

The FLL also adds to the existing contracts for an indefinite term or specific project. Specifically, in order to allow "seasonal" employees to gain seniority, employers may now offer employment for an indefinite term for un-continuous work when the services required are for fixed and periodic tasks, in the cases of seasonal activities, or that do not require the provision of services throughout the entire week, month, or year. Under this arrangement, the employment relationship can be suspended during off periods in order to relieve the employer of wage payment obligations and the employee of any service obligations.

WAGES

Back wages has been an issues of great concern to small and medium-sized businesses. Currently, the prolonged duration of labor trials is the cause of massive economic liabilities due to the accumulation of back wages. Therefore, new FLL limits the accumulation of back wages to 12 months. Once that period has concluded, a monthly interest rate of 2% will be generated on 15 months of the employee's monthly wage, which are to be paid once the process has concluded. Additionally, under the new law, the accrual of back wages will be suspended if the worker has died.

Furthermore, with the reform, employers are now allowed to utilize additional methods to pay wages. With the employee's prior consent, an employer will be able to pay wages by check, direct deposit, transfers, or through any other electronic means. This would provide workers with greater safety given the current circumstances.

The reform also allows employers and employees the option of paying for work at an hourly, rather than a per diem rate, provided that the maximum daily working hours (eight per day) are not exceeded and the employees' daily income is not less than the minimum daily wage. This latter provision can be interpreted as being in harmony with the definition of minimum wage established by the Law, which would mean that the worker should receive at least the minimum wage, even when working fewer hours than the maximum established under the Law.

NONDISCRIMINATION AND ANTI-HARASSMENT IN THE WORKPLACE

The new law introduces the concept of a decent or respectable job, the definition of which includes the concepts of diversity, nondiscrimination, and anti-harassment. The FLL now prohibits discrimination on the basis of race, national origin, gender, age, disability, social status, health condition, religion, citizenship status, sexual preference, marital status, opinions, or any other category of discrimination that contradicts human dignity. The law also prohibits harassment, including sexual harassment and bullying and gives these provisions teeth by adding them to the list of justifiable causes for termination.

Just as in the US, all anti- discrimination and anti-harassment policies and training programs should include reporting mechanisms that will help the employer investigate and, if necessary, put an end to any illegal harassment.

MATERNITY LEAVE CHANGES

Under the previous law, women had the right to a six weeks' leave prior to the birth of a child and six weeks following the birth of a child. Under certain circumstances, the new FLL allows women to allocate up to four of the six weeks of the pre-birth leave to the post-birth leave period (i.e., a woman may take maternity leave as few as two weeks before the birth of a child and up to ten weeks after the birth of a child). Additionally, if a child is born with disabilities or requires medical attention, the post-birth leave may be extended for up to two additional weeks. In the case of adoption, female employees are entitled to six weeks' leave following receipt of the child.

While an employee is breastfeeding, working hours may be reduced, for up to a maximum of six-months, by one hour in order to allow a mother to be with her newborn child. In case of a health emergency, pregnant or breastfeeding women shall not be required to work and shall receive full salary and benefit payments.

NEW PATERNITY LEAVE

The FLL provides for a mandatory paternity leave up to five paid working days for the birth or adoption of a child.

SANCTIONS

Under the FLL, the amount of the fines that employers may incur in the event of non-compliance with any provisions under the Federal Labor Law increase significantly. The fines may now be up to an amount equivalent to 5000 minimum salary days (approximately $311,000 Mexican Pesos or US $24,000 Dollars) in some cases, per occurrence.

IMPLICATIONS

Mexico's labor law reforms are a positive step toward stimulating job creation and providing greater certainty regarding legal and economic exposure to companies doing business in Mexico. Although the practical implications of the law are yet to be determined, we recommend that U.S. employers with operations in Mexico revisit their employment practices to take advantage of, and ensure compliance with, these reforms.

Furthermore, given the new outsourcing provisions, companies will need to evaluate the structure of their current legal entities in Mexico. Employers that use outsourcing services to staff their operations in Mexico should review their existing practices and policies, as well as their services agreements to ensure they comply with the new legal framework.

LATEST AMENDMENTS TO THE LABOR LAW

Recent amendments to the Federal Labor Law Act were published on November 30th, 2012 in the Official Gazette, and became valid since the following day. This Top Ten is a summary of the ten main amendments as well as some corrective actions proposed.

I. SUBCONTRACTING SERVICES

"Subcontracting services" are defined as the legal relationship by which an entity, known as a "contractor", carries out works or renders services through its own employees in favor of a contracting party/client (individual or entity), which specifies and supervises the activities to be carried out by the contractor.

These type of services must comply with the following requirements:

Cannot be outsourced 100% of the same or similar activities developed at the work center.

A specialization of activities or knowledge should be needed and duly justified.

Outsourced activities cannot be same or similar to the activities performed by the actual employees of the client.

In case the subcontracting services do not comply with all above conditions, the contracting party/client will be considered as employer for all legal effects, including social security obligations.

In addition of the above, contractors and clients must comply with the following requirements:

The subcontracting services agreement shall be in writing.

The contractor shall comply with all labor and social security obligations.

Subcontracting services shall not be used with the purpose of reducing labor rights of employees.

The client shall verify that contractor has the appropriate documents and that it is sufficiently economic solvent as employer to comply with obligations derived from labor relationships.

The client shall permanently verify that the contractor complies with all the applicable provisions relating to work environment, health and security matters.

II. NEW INDIVIDUAL EMPLOYMENT AGREEMENTS

Amendments establish additional information to be incorporated in employment agreements such as: federal taxpayer registry number (RFC) and Unique Code for Population Registry (CURP), for both employee and employer.

The new types of employments agreements are the following:

Probationary Agreements

Executed with the purpose of verifying that an employee is qualified for the position.

Applicable only for a maximum term of 30 days for regular employees, or 180 days (in case of general directors or managers).

Contract periods cannot be extended or applied for more than once for the same employee.

The granting social security rights shall be guaranteed.

Employees shall always enjoy the salary, labor and social security benefits inherent to their job position.

Labor agreement can be terminated without liabilities for the employer if at employer's criteria and considering the opinion of the Mixed Commission of Productivity and Training, at the end of the probationary period, employee did not prove to have the capacity, knowledge and skills necessary for the position.

Initial Training Agreement

Applicable when an employee will provide services in order to acquire the knowledge and skills necessary to perform a specific future position.

Applicable only for a maximum term of 3 months, or 6 months (in case of general directors or managers).

Contract periods cannot be extended or applied for more than once for the same employee.

The granting social security rights shall be guaranteed.

Employees shall always enjoy the salary, labor and social security benefits inherent to their job position.

Labor agreement can be terminated without liabilities for the employer if at employer's criteria and considering the opinion of the Mixed Commission of Productivity and Training: at the end of the training period employee did not prove to have the capacity for the position.

Season or Discontinuous agreements

Applicable for periodic works, fixed jobs with a discontinuous character, seasonal activities or activities that do not require services for a full week, month or year. Employees that provide their services under this modality shall have the same rights and obligations as the employees hired under continuous basis, in proportion to the time worked in each period.

III. SALARY

New amendments allow payment of salary under hourly basis, providing that: (i) worked hours do not exceed the legal maximum hours, and (ii) labor and social security rights of employees are respected. Under no circumstances hourly basis payment must be less than the minimum daily wage.

The amendments also allow the common practice of paying the salary through bank deposit, debit card, wire transfer or any other electronic mean.

IV. NATIONAL FUND INSTITUTE FOR WORKERS' EXPENDITURES (INFONACOT)

Employers are obliged to register the work center (in which the employees render their service) in the Fund within a period of one year as of the date of becoming law of the amendments to the Federal Labor Law. The INFONACOT is a government dependency with the purpose to promote the development and the increasing of employee's economic family patrimony through the granting of credits to acquire goods and services.

V. NEW EMPLOYER'S OBLIGATIONS

The new amendments obligate employers to:

Provide adequate job sources or work center facilities for handicapped people, when number of employees is higher than 50.

Deduct the applicable withholdings to wages in cases of alimonies, and to inform to the judicial authority and the alimonies beneficiaries within the following 5 days after the termination of the labor relationship with the employee.

Provide adequate training to employees in order to encourage and improve level of expertise, knowledge and life status in accordance with Federal Labor Law provisions.

Create and integrate the Mix Commission of Productivity and Training.

Install and carry out the services in compliance with the safety measures and applicable regulations in order to prevent accidents and illness.

Eliminate all conditions involving discrimination on grounds of ethnic or national origin, gender, age, disability, social status, health status, religion, immigration status, political opinions, sexual orientation, marital status or any other that threatens the human dignity.

VI. NEW TERMINATION CAUSES

The new amendments incorporate certain new causes under which an employer can terminate employees without responsibility:

Offenses or bad conduct with clients and suppliers.

Harassment (including sexual) to any person in the work place.

When the employee does not provide the documentation required by law, and needed for rendering the services, provided that is a fault of the employee, and a period of two months has past.

The law provides a new mechanism for the notice of termination in which the employer has the option to notify the termination notice through Labor Board.

VII. BACK OR LOST WAGES INDEMNIFICATION

Back or lost wages cannot exceed a 12-month period. If this period elapses and the labor procedure has not been solved or the final award has not been enforced, the employer shall pay the employee, in addition to back wages, interest accrued at a monthly rate of 2% calculated over the amount equivalent of 15 monthly salaries until the effective payment date.

VIII. PROFIT SHARING BENEFIT

Regarding the profit sharing benefit, the amendments also provide a new section of Article 127 that "all employees of a certain business establishment form part of the same for the effects of calculating the profit sharing".

IX.- MATERNITY AND PATERNITY LEAVE PERMITS

As a consequence of an express request from a female employee, subject to a written authorization from the doctor of the social security institute or from the health service granted by the employer, considering the opinion of the employer and the type of services render by the employee, it could be transferred up to four of the six weeks of rest before the childbirth to be used after it (the birth).

Likewise, it is contemplated to extend periods for maternity leave in case of newborn disabilities or in case that the newborn needs special medical hospital attention.

In case of adoption of a child the employees will enjoy of a rest period of six weeks with salary payment, as of the day in which the child is received for the employee.

The employer should grant female employees during the nursing period (a maximum period of six months) two rest periods of 30 minutes each, to nurse her child, in an adequate and hygienic place appointed by the employer or, as agreed with the employer, the work shift will be reduced one hour during the six-month period.

The employer should grant to the male employees a paternity leave permit of five paid days (applicable also to adoption).

X.- HEARINGS SIMPLIFICATION

The structure of the first hearing within the ordinary process is modified and shall consist on two stages instead just one: (i) the stages of settlement, demand and exceptions; and (ii) a second hearing for the offering and admission of evidence.

MEXICO FEDERAL LABOR LAW

TITLE I -- GENERAL PRINCIPLES

Article 1 The present law is of general observance throughout the Republic and governs the employment relations included within article 123, Section "A," of the Constitution.

Article 2 Labor rules seek to achieve balance and social justice in relations between workers and employers.

Article 3 Work is a social right and obligation. It is not a commodity. It requires respect for the rights and dignity of those who may provide it and must be conducted under conditions which assure the life, health, and a decent standard of living for the worker and his family.

There may be no differences established between workers on the basis of race, sex, age, religious creed, political philosophy, or social condition.

In addition, it is in society's interest to promote and oversee the education and training of workers.

Article 4 No person may be prevented from lawfully working or from lawfully engaging in any profession, industry, or commerce. The exercise of such rights may only be prohibited by order of a competent authority when the rights of third parties are attacked or those of society are offended:

I. The rights of third persons are attacked in the cases established under law, and in the following:

(a) When an attempt is made to replace a dismissed worker whose case before the Conciliation and Arbitration Board has not been resolved, or when such worker is definitively replaced;

(b) When, upon returning to work, a worker is denied the right to occupy his same position, when his absence was due to illness, or act of God, or the employer consented;

II. The rights of society shall deemed offended in those cases established under laws and in the following:

(a) When, once a strike has been declared under the terms established in this law, an attempt is made to replace striking workers or such workers are replaced in the work they were performing, without the conflict for which the strike was brought having been resolved, except as provided in article 468;

(b) When, once such lawful strike has been declared by a majority of the workers of an establishment, a minority of such workers attempts to go back to work, or continues working.

Article 5 The provisions of this law are of a public nature for which reason no written or verbal agreement which provides for any of the following shall have legal effect, nor prevent the enjoyment or exercise of any rights:

I. The employment of children less than fourteen years of age;

II. A workday greater than that permitted by this law;

III. A workday which, in the opinion of the Conciliation and Arbitration Board, is inhumane for being unreasonably excessive, given the nature of the work;

IV. Overtime hours of work for persons under sixteen years of age;

V. A wage which is less than the minimum;

VI. A wage which is not sufficiently remunerative, in the opinion of the Conciliation and Arbitration Board;

VII. A time period greater than one week for the payment of wages to manual laborers;

VIII. The payment of wages at a place of amusement, tavern, bar, cafe, or store, except to the employees of such establishments;

IX. A direct or indirect obligation to obtain consumer goods in a particular store or place;

X. The power of an employer to retain wages as a fine;

XI. A salary which is less than that paid to another employee in the same company or establishment with equal abilities in the same type of work or same workday, for reasons of age, sex, or nationality;

XII. The employment of persons under sixteen years of age at night, in industrial establishments, or after 10:00 p.m., in any establishment; and

XIII. A waiver by the worker of any of the rights or prerogatives prescribed in labor rules.

In all such cases it shall be understood that this law, as well as any supplementary laws, shall govern in the place of any nullified stipulations.

Article 6 The laws and treaties which are executed and approved under the terms of article 133 of the Constitution shall apply to employment relations insofar as they benefit the worker, from the date of their effectiveness.

Article 7 In any enterprise or establishment, at least 90% of workers hired by the employer must be Mexican. In the technical and professional categories, the workers must be Mexican, unless there are no Mexican workers in a specific specialty, in which case the employer may temporarily hire foreign workers in a proportion which does not exceed 10% of the workers in such specialty. The employer and foreign workers shall have the joint obligation to train Mexican workers in such specialty. All doctors in the service of the enterprise shall be Mexican.

This article shall not apply to directors, administrators or general managers.

Article 8 A worker is a physical person who provides personal, subordinated work to another physical or moral person.
For the purposes of this rule "work" means any human activity, whether intellectual or physical, without regard to the level of technological preparation required for each occupation or trade.

Article 9 The category of confidential employee shall depend on the nature of the duties carried out and not on the Title which may be given to the position.

Confidential duties are those related to management, inspection, oversight, and control, of a general nature, or those related to personal services for the employer within the enterprise or establishment.

Article 10 An employer is the physical or moral person who utilizes the services of one or more workers.

If a worker, by agreement or custom, utilizes the services of other workers, the employer of the former will also be that of the latter.

Article 11 The directors, administrators, managers, and other persons who carry out duties of management or administration in the enterprise or establishment are considered representatives of the employer and in such capacity bind the employer in its relations with workers.

Article 12 An intermediary is a person who hires or intervenes in the hiring of one or more persons for the furnishing of services to an employer.

Article 13 Established enterprises who may contract work to be carried out with their own resources, and which resources are sufficient to comply with such obligations as may arise from their relations with workers, shall not be considered intermediaries but employers. Otherwise, such enterprises shall be jointly liable with the persons who directly benefit from such work or services, for obligations contracted with workers.

Article 14 Persons who may use intermediaries to hire workers shall be responsible for any obligations which may arise from this law and from the services furnished.

Workers shall have the following rights:

I. They shall furnish their services under the same employment conditions and shall have the same rights corresponding to the workers who may carry out similar work in the enterprise or establishment; and

II. The intermediary shall not receive any compensation or commission charged against the workers' wages.

Article 15 Enterprises who may carry out work or perform services exclusively or principally for another enterprise, without their own adequate resources as set forth in article 13, shall be subject to the following rules:

I. The enterprise which benefits from such work or services shall be jointly liable for obligations contracted with the workers; and

II. The workers employed in the carrying out of the work or services provided shall have the right to enjoy employment conditions proportional to those enjoyed by workers who carry out similar work in the enterprise which benefits therefrom.

To determine what is proportional, there shall be taken into consideration any differences which exist in the minimum wages which are effective in the geographical areas in which the two enterprises are located, as well as any other circumstances which may affect employment conditions.

Article 16 For the purposes of labor rules, "enterprise" shall mean the economic unit which produces or distributes goods or services and "establishment" shall mean the technical entity which, as a branch, agency, or other similar entity, is an integral part of and contributes to the achievement of the goals of the enterprise.

Article 17 In the absence of an express provision in the Constitution, this law or its regulations, or in the treaties referred to in article 6, consideration shall be given to other provisions of such laws which govern similar cases, the general principles arising therefrom, general legal principles, general principles of social justice arising under article 123 of the Constitution, binding case law, custom, and equity.

Article 18 In interpreting labor rules, the objectives set forth in articles 2 and 3 shall be taken into consideration. In cases of doubt, precedence shall be given to the interpretation most favorable to the workers.

Article 19 No act or outcome related to the enforcement of labor rules shall be the basis for any tax whatsoever.

TITLE II--INDIVIDUAL EMPLOYMENT RELATIONS

CHAPTER I--GENERAL PROVISIONS

Article 20 An employment relationship, whatever the act from which it arises, means the furnishing of subordinated personal services in return for the payment of a wage.

An individual employment contract, whatever its form or name, is that by which one person obligates himself to furnish subordinated personal services to another, in return for the payment of a wage.

The furnishing of the services referred to in the first paragraph, or pursuant to an executed contract, shall have the same legal effects.

Article 21 An employment contract and relationship shall be presumed to exist between the person who furnishes the personal services and the person who receives them.

Article 22 It shall be unlawful to use the services of persons less than fourteen years of age, or persons from fourteen to fifteen years of age, inclusive, who have not complete their mandatory education, except in exceptional cases approved by a competent authority in whose opinion such employment is consistent with a course of studies.

Article 23 Persons sixteen years of age or older may freely furnish their services, subject to the limitations established in this law. Persons from fourteen to fifteen years of age, inclusive, shall require the consent of their parents or guardians or, if there are none, of the union to which they belong, of the Conciliation and Arbitration Board, of the Labor Inspector, or of a governmental authority.

Workers who are legal minors are entitled to have their wages paid to them directly, and bring any legal action to which they may be entitled.

Article 24 Employment conditions must be set forth in writing when there is no governing collective agreement. At least two copies of such contract shall be made, of which one copy shall be retained by each party.

Article 25 The writing in which employment conditions shall be stated must contain:

I. The name, nationality, age, sex, civil state, and domicile of the worker and the employer;

II. Whether the employment relation is for a specific project or time, or for an indefinite time;

III. The service or services which must be provided, described as precisely as possible;

IV. The place or places in which the work must be furnished;

V. The duration of the workday;

VI. The form and amount of wages;

VII. The day and place for payment of wages;

VIII. A statement that the worker will be educated and trained in accordance with such plans and programs as are established or may be established in the enterprise, in accordance with that provided in this law; and
IX. Such other employment conditions such as days of rest, vacations, and others as may be agreed to by the worker and the employer.

Article 26 The lack of the writing referred to under articles 24 and 25 shall not deprive the worker of any rights arising from labor rules or from the services provided, the lack of such formality being imputed to the employer.

Article 27 If the service or services to be provided have not been described, the worker shall be obligated to carry out work which is consistent with his capacities, aptitudes, state or condition, and which is of a kind consistent with the purpose of the enterprise or establishment.

Article 28 The following rules shall apply to the furnishing of services by Mexican workers outside the Republic:

I. The employment conditions shall be stated in writing and, to be valid, must contain the following provisions:

(a) The requirements prescribed in article 25;

(b) The cost of transportation, repatriation back to the place of origin, meals for the worker and his family, if applicable, all costs relating to the border crossing or to compliance with provisions of the law regarding immigration, or for any other related matter, shall be borne exclusively by the employer. The worker shall receive the entire wage owed to him with no deduction whatsoever for any of the foregoing costs;

(c) The worker shall have the right to the services provided to foreigners by the social security and welfare institutions of the country in which such services shall be rendered. In any case, the worker shall have the right to be indemnified for work- related risks in an amount at least equal to that provided in this law;

(d) The worker shall have the right to enjoy decent and hygienic housing at a work center or at a place located nearby, through rental or other means;

II. The employer shall indicate his domicile within the Republic for all legal purposes;

III. The writing containing employment conditions must be submitted for the approval of the Conciliation and Arbitration Board in whose jurisdiction it was executed which, after confirming the requirements for validity referred to in section I, shall determine the amount of the bond or deposit it may consider sufficient to guarantee the fulfillment of the contracted obligations. The deposit shall be made in the Bank of Mexico or in such banking institutions the Board may designate. The employer shall verify with the same Board the issuance of the bond or the making of the deposit;

IV. The writing must be legalized by the consul of the nation in which the services are to be provided;

V. Once the employer has demonstrated to the Board that he has complied with the contracted obligations, the Board shall order the cancellation of the bond or the return of the deposit.

Article 29 It shall be unlawful to use persons less than eighteen years of age for the furnishing of services outside of the Republic, except in the case of technicians, professionals, artists, athletes or, in general, specialized workers.

Article 30 The furnishing of services within the Republic, but at a distance greater than 100 kilometers from the customary residence of the worker, shall be governed by the provisions contained in article 28, section I, to the extent applicable.

Article 31 Employment contracts and relations are binding as to that which was expressly agreed to, and as to any consequences which may be consistent with the labor rules, good faith, and equity.

Article 32 A worker's failure to comply with labor rules shall only give rise to his civil liability; in no event may such failure cause him to be personally forced to do anything.

Article 33 Any waiver by workers of wages earned, indemnities, or other benefits for services rendered, in whatever manner given or however called, is null.

Any agreement or settlement, to be valid, must be stated in writing and contain a recital of the facts under which it arose and of the rights included in it. It shall be ratified before the Conciliation and Arbitration Board, which shall approve it as long as it does not contain any waiver of workers' rights.

Article 34 In those agreements executed between unions and employers which may affect the rights of workers, the following rules shall be observed:

I. Such agreements shall govern only future work relations, and may not affect remuneration already earned;

II. Such agreements may not refer to specific, individual workers; and

III. In the case of a reduction of the work force, such readjustment shall be effected in accordance with article 437.

CHAPTER II -- DURATION OF EMPLOYMENT RELATIONS

Article 35 An employment relation may be for a specific project or time period, or for an indeterminate time period. In the absence of an express stipulation, the relation shall be for an indeterminate time period.

Article 36 An employment relationship for a specific project may only be agreed to when required by the nature of the work.

Article 37 An employment relationship for a specified time period may only be agreed to in the following cases:

I. When required by the nature of the work which is to be furnished;

II. When the purpose of the relationship is to temporarily replace another worker; and

III. In other cases prescribed in this law.

Article 38 An employment relationship for the exploitation of a mine which lacks minerals sufficient to pay for its costs, or for the restoration of abandoned or closed mines, may be for a specific time period or project or for the duration of a specific capital investment.

Article 39 If the work activity continues beyond the term agreed upon, the relationship shall be extended as long as such activity continues.

Article 40 Workers, in any case, shall not be obligated to furnish services for longer than one year.

Article 41 The replacement of the employer shall not affect employment relationships at the enterprise or establishment. The replaced employer shall be jointly liable with the new employer for obligations arising from employment relationships or this law which arose prior to the time of such replacement, for a period of six months thereafter. Once the six months are concluded, only the new employer shall be liable.

The time period of six months referred to in the preceding article shall begin on the date on which notice of substitution is given to the union or to the workers.

CHAPTER III -- SUSPENSION OF THE EFFECTS OF AN EMPLOYMENT RELATIONSHIP

Article 42 The following are causes for the temporary suspension of the obligations to furnish services or to pay wages, without liability for either the worker or the employer:

I. An infectious illness contracted by the worker;

II. Temporary incapacity due to an accident or illness which does not constitute a work-related risk;

III. The preventive detention of a worker pending trial, followed by his acquittal. If the criminal proceedings relate to conduct of the worker in defense of the person or interests of his employer, the employer shall be obliged to pay any wages which the worker may not have received;

IV. The arrest of the worker;

V. Fulfillment of the services or performance of the duties mentioned in article 5 of the Constitution, or of the obligations set forth in article 31, section III, of the Constitution;

VI. The worker's appointment as a representative to any state body, Conciliation and Arbitration Board, the National Minimum Wage Commission, the National Commission for Workers Profit-Sharing, and similar bodies; and

VII. The lack of documents required by law or regulation for the furnishing of services, when imputable to the worker.

Article 43 Such suspensions shall take effect:

I. In the cases mentioned in sections I and II of the preceding article, from the date on which the employer becomes aware of the infectious illness or on which the worker is unable to perform his work, until the expiration of the time period determined by the Mexican Social Security Institute, or earlier if the incapacity ceases, provided, that the suspension may not exceed the term fixed in the Social Security Law for the treatment of illnesses which are not work-related;

II. In the cases of sections III and IV, from the time at which the worker furnishes evidence that he has been detained in the custody of a judicial or administrative authority, until the date the verdict of acquittal is executed, or until his arrest or imprisonment ceases;

III. In the cases mentioned in sections V and VI, from the date on which the worker is obliged to furnish the services or carry out his duties, up to a period of six years; and

IV. In the case mentioned in section VII, from the date on which the employer becomes aware of such circumstances, up to a period of two months.

Article 44 When workers are called to enlist or serve in the National Guard, in accordance with that provided in article 31, section III, of the Constitution, such period of service shall be taken into consideration in determining their seniority.

Article 45 The worker must return to his work:

I. In the cases mentioned in sections I, II, IV, and VII of article 42, on the date following the date on which the cause of the suspension ceases; and

II. In the cases mentioned in sections III, V, and VI of article 42, within the fifteen days following termination of the cause of the suspension.

CHAPTER IV --RESCISSION OF THE EMPLOYMENT RELATIONSHIP

Article 46 The worker or the employer may rescind the employment relationship at any time for justified cause, without incurring any liability therefor.

Article 47 The following are causes for the employer rescinding the employment relationship without liability:

I. When the employer has been deceived by the worker, or as the case may be, by the union who proposed or recommended the worker, through false certificates or references which attributed to the worker capacities, aptitudes, or abilities he did not have. This cause of termination shall not be effective after the first 30 days in which the worker furnishes his services;

II. If the worker, in the course of his employment, engages in conduct lacking in integrity or honesty, or commits acts involving violence, threats, injury or ill-treatment against the employer, his family, or the supervisory and administrative personnel of the enterprise or establishment, except in the case of provocation or self-defense;

III. The worker commits any of the acts specified in the preceding section against any of his fellow workers, if as a result thereof the discipline of the work place is affected;

IV. The worker, outside of his employment, commits any of the acts referred to in section II against the employer, his relations, or any supervisory or administrative personnel, to such a serious extent that performance of the employment relationship is rendered impossible;

V. The worker intentionally causes physical damage to buildings, works, machinery, instruments, raw materials, or any other thing related to his employment, during the performance of his work, or by reason of his work;

VI. If the worker negligently but not intentionally causes the damages referred to in the preceding section, provided, that such damages are serious, and such negligence was the sole cause of such damages;

VII. The worker, through his imprudence or inexcusable carelessness, endangers the safety of the establishment or of the persons in it;

VIII. The worker commits immoral acts in the establishment or work place;

IX. The worker reveals manufacturing secrets or discloses exclusive matters, to the detriment of the enterprise;

X. The worker is absent more than three times in a period of 30 days, without the permission of the employer or just cause;

XI. The worker disobeys the employer or his representatives, without just cause, in matters connected to the contracted employment;

XII. The worker refuses to adopt preventive safety measures or follow procedures established to avoid accidents and illnesses;

XIII. The worker appears at the work place in a state of intoxication or under the influence of any narcotic or debilitating drug, unless used with a medical prescription. Before beginning his work, the worker must inform the employer and present the medical prescription;

XIV. A final sentence which may impose the penalty of imprisonment upon the worker, which prevents him from fulfilling the employment relationship; and

XV. Those causes analogous to those set forth in the preceding sections, of equal seriousness, and with similar consequences, related to employment.

The employer must give the worker written notice of the date and the cause or causes of rescission.

The worker must be informed of the notice, and in the event he refuses to accept it, the employer, within the five days following rescission, must bring such notice to the attention of the corresponding Board, provide such Broad with the registered domicile of the worker and request that notification be given to the worker.

The mere failure to notify the worker or the Board shall be sufficient indication that the rescission was not justified.
Article 48 The worker, at his election, may request, before the Conciliation and Arbitration Board, that he be reinstated in the work he was performing, or that he be paid damages equal to the amount of three months of wages.

If the employer fails to establish just cause for the termination in the corresponding proceedings, the worker shall have an additional right to be paid back wages from the date of his dismissal until the award is satisfied, regardless of his election of remedies.

Article 49 The employer may be released from the obligation to reinstate the worker, by paying the damages determined under article 50, in the following cases:

I. In the case of workers who have served less than one year;

II. If it is established before the Conciliation and Arbitration Board that the worker, because of the work he performs or the nature of such work, comes into direct, permanent contact with the employer, the Board, taking into consideration the circumstances of the case, may determine that it is impossible to carry out a normal employment relationship;

III. In the case of confidential workers;

IV. In the case of domestic service; and

V. In the case of casual workers.

Article 50 The damages referred to in the preceding article shall be determined as follows:

I. If the employment relationship was for a specific time period less that one year, damages shall consist of an amount equal to the amount of wages corresponding to one-half of the time period in which services were provided. If such relationship was to exceed one year, damages shall consist of an amount equal to six months of wages for the first year and 20 days of wages for each following year in which services were provided;

II. If the employment relationship was for an indefinite time period, damages shall consist of 20 days of wages for each year in which services were provided; and

III. In addition to the damages referred to in the preceding sections, damages shall consist of the amount of three months of wages and accrued salary from the date of dismissal to the date all damages are paid.

Article 51 A worker may rescind the employment relationship without liability for the following causes:

I. The employer or, as the case may be, the employer association, upon offering employment, deceived the worker as to the employment conditions. This cause of termination shall not be effective after the first 30 days of the worker's service;

II. The employer, his relations, or supervisory and administrative personnel, within the work place, engage in acts lacking in integrity or honesty, or commit acts involving violence, threats, insults, ill treatment, and other similar conduct, against the worker, his spouse, his parents, his children, or his brothers or sisters;

III. The employer, the employer's relations, or other workers, outside of the work place, commit the acts referred in the preceding section, if they are so serious as to render performance of the employment relationship impossible;

IV. The employer reduces the worker's wages;

V. Wages are not received on the date or at the place agreed upon or which are customary;

VI. The employer maliciously causes damage to the worker's work tools or implements;

VII. The existence of a grave risk to the safety or health of the worker or his family, whether due to the lack of hygienic conditions in the establishment, or because preventive safety measures required by law are not complied with;

VIII. The employer, through his imprudence or inexcusable carelessness, endangers the security of the establishment or of the persons within it; and

IX. Causes analogous to those established in the preceding sections, of equal seriousness and with similar consequences, to the extent they relate to employment.

Article 52 The worker may withdraw from his employment within the thirty days following the date on which any of the causes mentioned in the preceding article occurs, and shall have the right to receive damages from the employer in accordance with article 50.

CHAPTER V -- TERMINATION OF THE EMPLOYMENT RELATIONSHIP

Article 53 The following are causes of termination of the employment relationship:

I. Mutual consent of the parties;

II. The death of the worker;

III. The termination of the project or expiration of the time period or capital investment, in accordance with articles 36, 37 and 38;

IV. The physical or mental incapacity, or obvious incompetence, of the worker, which renders performance of the work impossible; and

V. The cases referred to in article 434.

Article 54 In the case mentioned in section IV of the preceding article, if the incapacity arises from a non-work related risk, the worker shall have the right to be paid one month of wages and twelve days of wages for each year of service, in accordance with that provided in article 162, or, if possible, and if the worker so wishes, he shall be provided with other employment consistent with his abilities, in addition to any other remuneration to which such worker may be legally entitled.

Article 55 If in corresponding legal proceedings the employer does not substantiate the causes of termination, the worker shall have the rights set forth in article 48.

TITLE III--EMPLOYMENT CONDITIONS

CHAPTER I -- GENERAL PROVISIONS

Article 56 Employment conditions shall in no case be inferior to those established in this law and must be commensurate to the importance of the services and be the same for equal work, without any differences by reason of race, nationality, sex, age, religious creed, or political philosophy, except as expressly set forth in this law.

Article 57 The worker may request the Conciliation and Arbitration Board to modify employment conditions when the wage is not remunerative, or the workday is excessive, or economic circumstances are present which may justify such modification.
The employer may request the modification when justified by economic circumstances.

CHAPTER II -- THE WORKDAY

Article 58 The workday is the time during which the worker is at the disposition of the employer to provide his services.

Article 59 The worker and the employer shall determine the duration of the workday, provided it be within the legally established maximum.

The workers and the employer may distribute work hours to allow workers to rest Saturday afternoon or other similar arrangement.

Article 60 The day work shift is that included between the hours of 6:00 a.m. and 8:00 p.m.

The night work shift is that included between the hours of 8:00 p.m. and 6:00 a.m.

A mixed work shift is that which include parts of the day work shift and the night work shift, provided that the night work shift portion is less than three and one-half hours. If the night work shift portion is three and one-half hours or more, the entire work shift shall be considered a night work shift.

Article 61 The maximum duration of the workday shall be: eight hours if a day work shift; seven hours if a night work shift; and seven and one-half hours if a mixed work shift.

Article 62 For the purposes of determining the workday, the provisions of article 5, section III shall be observed.

Article 63 During a continuous workday, the worker will be given a rest period of at least one-half hour.

Article 64 When the worker cannot leave the workplace during rest or meal periods, the time corresponding to such periods shall be included as part of the effective workday.

Article 65 In the event of an accident or imminent risk which may endanger the life of the worker, his fellow workers, the employer, or the very existence of the enterprise, the workday may be extended for the time strictly necessary to remove such dangers.

Article 66 The workday may also be extended for extraordinary circumstance, but never by more than three hours per day nor more than three times in one week.

Article 67 The hours of work referred to in article 65 shall be paid at the same rate corresponding to each one of the hours of the workday.

Otherwise, overtime hours of work shall be paid at twice the wage corresponding to the hours of the workday.

Article 68 Workers shall not be obligated to furnish their services for a time greater than that permitted in this chapter.

Overtime exceeding nine hours per week shall obligate the employer to pay the worker for such excessive overtime 200% more than the amount of wages corresponding to hours of the normal workday, without prejudice to the sanctions set forth in this Law.

CHAPTER III --REST DAYS

Article 69 For each six days of work, the worker will enjoy at least one rest day with full payment of wages.

Article 70 In work requiring continuous labor, the workers and the employer shall by common agreement determine the days on which the workers may enjoy the weekly rest day.

Article 71 The regulations to this law shall seek to make Sunday the weekly day of rest. Workers who provide services on Sunday shall be entitled to an additional bonus equal to at least 25% of their wages on ordinary workdays.

Article 72 When the worker does not provide services during the entire work week, or when he furnishes services to various employers on the same day or in the same week, he shall have the right be paid the proportional part of his wages for days of rest, based upon the wages for the days in which he worked or on the wage he would have received from each employer.

Article 73 Workers shall not be obligated to work on days of rest. If this provision is violated, the employer shall pay the worker, in addition to any wages corresponding to the rest day, double wages for the services rendered.

Article 74 The following are obligatory rest days:

I. The 1st of January;

II. The 5th of February;

III. The 21st of March;

IV. The 1st of May;

V. The 16th of September;

VI. The 20th of November;

VII. The 1st of December each six years, corresponding to the transfer of the Federal Executive Power; and

VIII. The 25th of December;

IX. Those days determined by federal and local election laws in the event of ordinary elections.

Article 75 In cases mentioned in the preceding article the workers and the employer shall determine the number of workers who must furnish their services. If agreement is not reached, the matter shall be resolved by the Permanent Conciliation Board or, if there is no Board, by the Conciliation and Arbitration Board.

Workers shall be obligated to work and shall be entitled to double wages for work performed independently of any wages corresponding to them for the obligatory rest days.

CHAPTER IV --VACATIONS

Article 76 Workers with more than one year of service shall enjoy annual paid vacations, which in no case shall be less than six working days, and which will increase by two workings days for each subsequent year of service, up to twelve.
After the fourth year, the vacation period shall be increased by two days for each five years of service.

Article 77 Workers who work non-continuously, and seasonal workers, shall be entitled to annual vacations in proportion to the number of days worked in the year.

Article 78 At least six of the vacation days taken by workers may be continuous.

Article 79 Remuneration may not be paid in lieu of vacations.

If the employment relationship terminates before one year of service, the worker shall have the right to remuneration proportionate to the time in which services were performed.

Article 80 Workers shall be entitled to a bonus not less than 25% of the wages to be paid to them during the vacation period.

Article 81 Vacations must be allowed to a worker within the six months following the completion of each year of service. Employers shall deliver annually to workers a report containing the length of service and, based on such service, the amount of vacation time corresponding to such worker and the date on which such vacation is to be taken.

CHAPTER V --WAGES

Article 82 Wages are the compensation which an employer must pay the worker for his work.

Article 83 Wages may be determined by unit of time, unit of work, commission, lump sum, or in any other manner.

When wages are determined by unit of work, in addition to specifying the nature of such work, there must be stated the quantity and quality of the material, the condition of the tools and implements that the employer may provide for the work to be carried out, and the time such tools and implements shall be available to the worker. No amount may be demanded on account of any normal wear and tear to the tools as a result of the work.

Article 84 Wages consist of payments made in cash at the daily rate, gratuities, receipts, housing, bonuses, commissions, benefits paid in kind, and any other amount or benefit given to the worker for his work.

Article 85 Wages must be remunerative and shall never be less than the amount fixed as the minimum in accordance with the provisions of this law. In determining the amount of wages, the quantity and quality of the work will be taken into consideration.

In the case of wages for unit of work, the remuneration to be paid shall at least equal the minimum wage payable for normal work in a workday of eight hours.

Article 86 Equal wages must be paid for equal work carried out in the same position, workday and conditions of efficiency.

Article 87 Workers shall be entitled to an annual bonus equivalent to at least fifteen days of wages, which must be paid before the twentieth day of December.

Workers who have completed more than one year of service, whether or not they are working on the date such bonus is paid, shall be entitled to be paid a proportional part of such bonus, based on whatever time they may have worked.

Article 88 Pay periods shall never be greater than one week for persons engaged in physical labor, and fifteen days for other workers.

Article 89 In determining the amount of indemnities which must be paid to workers, the base amount shall be the wage in place on the day on which the right to the indemnity arose, including in such base the daily rate and the proportional parts of the benefits mentioned in article 84.

In the case of wages for unit of work and, in general, when compensation is variable, the daily wage shall be the average remuneration corresponding to the 30 days effectively worked before the right arose. If during this lapse there was an increase in wages, the base shall be the average of the benefits obtained by the worker from the date of such increase.

When wages are determined by week or by month, they shall be divided by seven or by 30, as the case may be, to determine the daily wage.

CHAPTER VI --MINIMUM WAGE

Article 90 A minimum wage is the least amount a worker must receive in cash for services rendered in one workday.

The minimum wage must be sufficient to satisfy the normal necessities of the head of a family, physically, socially, and culturally, and to provide for the obligatory education of his children.

It shall be considered socially useful to establish institutions and measures which may protect the buying power of the wage and facilitate workers' access to obtaining basic necessities.

Article 91 Minimum wages may be general with respect to one or more geographical areas of application, which may extend over one or more federative entities, or occupational, for a specific branch of economic activity, or with respect to special occupations, skills or work within one or more geographical areas.

Article 92 General minimum wages shall be in effect for all workers in the geographical area or areas specified, independently of the field of economic activity, or special occupation, skill or work.

Article 93 Minimum occupational wages shall be effective for all workers within the specified fields of economic activity, or special occupation, skill or work, within one or more geographical areas of application.

Article 94 Minimum wages shall be determined by the National Commission, composed of representatives of workers, employers, and the government, and which may be assisted by special advisory commissions when considered necessary to the performance of its duties.

Article 95 The National Minimum Wage Commission and advisory commissions shall be formed in a tri-partite manner in accordance with that established in Chapter II of Title XIII of this law.

Article 96 The National Commission shall divide the Republic into geographical areas, each of which shall be comprised of one or more municipalities in which the same minimum wage must be effective, without the necessity that there be territorial continuity between such municipalities.

Article 97 Minimum wages shall not be subject to set-off, discount, or reduction, except in the following cases:

I. Support or maintenance payments decreed by a competent authority in favor of the persons mentioned in article 110, section V; and

II. Payment of the rents referred to in article 151. This discount shall not exceed ten percent of the wage;

III. Payment of installments on loans from the National Workers Housing Fund used for the acquisition, construction, repair, enlargement or improvement of residential housing, or for the payment of liabilities incurred for such purposes.

In addition, one percent of the wages referred to in article 143 of this Law will be discounted from those workers who have been granted a credit to acquire housing located in group housing financed through the Institute of the National Workers Housing Fund, for the purpose of covering the costs of administering, operating and maintaining the group housing in question. Such discounts must be freely accepted by the worker and may not exceed twenty percent of his wages;

IV. The payment of installments to cover credits granted or guaranteed by the Fund referred to in article 103Bis of this law, used to acquire consumer durables or to pay services. Such discounts must be freely accepted by the worker and may not exceed ten percent of his wages.

CHAPTER VII --PROTECTIVE RULES AND WAGE PRIVILEGES

Article 98 Workers may freely dispose of their wages. Any provision or measure which may impair this right shall be null.

Article 99 The right to receive wages, and the right to receive accrued wages, may not be waived.

Article 100 Wages shall be paid directly to the worker. If and only if personal receipt is impossible, payment may be made to the person designated as the worker's attorney in fact through a letter power of attorney signed by two witnesses. The employer shall be responsible for any payment made in violation of that provided in the preceding paragraph.

Article 101 The exact amount of cash wages must be paid in legal currency, and may not be paid in merchandise, vouchers, tokens or any other representation intended to substitute for money.

Article 102 Benefits in kind must be appropriate for the personal use of the worker and his family and reasonably proportionate to the amount of wages paid in cash.

Article 103 Warehouses and stores for clothing, food and household articles may be established by agreement between the workers and employers of one or more enterprises, in conformity with the following rules:

I. Workers must be free to acquire merchandise without coercion or pressure;

II. The prices at which the goods are sold shall be determined by agreement between the workers and the employers, and in no case shall be superior to official prices or, in the absence of official prices, to those prevailing in the market;

III. Changes in such prices shall be subject to that provided in the preceding sections; and

IV. The agreement shall provide for the participation of workers in the administration and supervision of the warehouse or store.

Article 103Bis The Federal Executive shall regulate the form and terms on which Fund for the Promotion and Guarantee of Worker Consumption shall be established, which shall finance the operation of warehouses and stores referred to in the preceding article and administer other institutions in the granting and guaranteeing of inexpensive and timely credits for the acquisition of goods and the payment of services on behalf of workers.

Article 104 All assignments of wages in favor of the employer or third persons, however called or in whatever manner, are null.

Article 105 Workers' wages shall not be subject to the payment of any damages whatsoever.

Article 106 The employer's obligation to pay wages shall not be suspended, except in the cases and in accordance with the requirements established in this law.

Article 107 It shall be unlawful to impose fines on workers, whatever the cause and whatever the reason.

Article 108 Wages shall be paid in the place in which workers provide their services.

Article 109 Payment shall be made on a working day, determined by agreement between the worker and the employer, during working hours or immediately thereafter.

Article 110 It shall be unlawful to make any deductions from workers' wages, except in the cases and subject to the requirements set forth as follows:

I. Payment of debts contracted with the employer through advances of wages, excessive payments made to the worker, errors, losses, damages, or acquisition of articles produced by the enterprise or establishment. The amount which may be demanded may in no case be greater than the amount of one month of wages and the discount shall be as agreed by the worker and the employer, but not greater than 30% of the amount by which his wages exceed the minimum wage;

II. The payment of rent referred to in article 151 may not exceed 15% percent of wages;

III. The payment of installments to cover loans provided by the National Workers Housing Fund for the acquisition, construction, repair, enlargement or improvement of residential housing, or the payment of liabilities incurred for such purposes. In addition, one percent of the wage referred to article 143 of this Law may be discounted from workers who have been granted a credit to acquire housing located in group housing projects financed by the Institute of the National Workers Housing Fund, used to cover the cost of administration, operation and maintenance of such group housing. Such discounts must be freely accepted by the worker;

IV. Payment of quotas for the formation and development of cooperative societies and savings banks, provided that the workers freely consent thereto, and such quotas do not exceed 30% of the amount by which their wages exceed the minimum wage;

V. Support and maintenance payments in favor of the wife, children, predecessors, or grandchildren, decreed by a competent authority;

VI. Payment of ordinary union dues prescribed in the union bylaws; and

VII. Payment of installments for credit guaranteed by the Fund referred to in article 103 Bis of this Law, used for the acquisition of consumer goods or for the payment of services. These discounts must have been freely accepted by the worker and may not exceed 20% of his wages.

Article 111 Debts contracted by workers with their employers shall in no case accrue interest.

Article 112 Workers' wages may not be garnished, except in the case of maintenance and support payments decreed by a competent authority in favor of the persons indicated in article 110, section V.
Employers shall not be obligated tocomply with any judicial or administrative order of garnishment.

Article 113 Wages earned in the last year and indemnities owed to workers shall be given preference on all the assets of the employer over any other credit including those arising from hypothecations of property, tax claims, and those in favor of the Mexican Institute of Social Security.

Article 114 Workers are not required to participate in proceedings relating to suspension of payments, bankruptcy, insolvency, or the settlement of an estate. The Conciliation and Arbitration Board shall proceed to seize and auction all of the assets necessary to pay wages and indemnities.

Article 115 The beneficiaries of a deceased worker shall have the right to receive any unpaid benefits and indemnities and institute or continue legal proceedings, without the necessity of a probate hearing.

Article 116 It shall be unlawful to establish dispensaries of alcoholic beverages or gaming or betting parlors in work centers. This prohibition shall be effective within a radius of four kilometers from work centers located outside of populated areas.

For the purposes of this law, intoxicating beverages shall be those whose alcoholic content exceeds five percent.

TITLE IV-- RIGHTS AND OBLIGATIONS OF WORKERS AND EMPLOYERS

CHAPTER I -- OBLIGATIONS OF EMPLOYERS

Article 132 The obligations of employers are:

I. To comply with the provisions of labor rules applicable to their enterprises or establishments;

II. To pay their workers wages and indemnities in accordance with the rules in effect at the enterprise or establishment;

III. To provide their workers on a timely basis with the implements, instruments, and materials necessary to carry out their work, of good quality and in good condition, and to replace them as soon as they are no longer usable, provided that such workers have not agreed to use their own tools. The employer may not demand damages for normal wear and tear of such implements, instruments, and work materials;

IV. To provide a secure area in the work place in which the instruments and implements belonging to the worker may be stored. It shall be unlawful for the employer to retain such instruments and implements by reason of any damages, guarantee, or for any other reason. An inspection of work instruments or implements shall be made at the request of the worker;

V. To maintain a sufficient number of seats or chairs for workers in commercial establishments, offices, hotels, restaurants, and analogous work places. The same rule shall apply to industrial establishments when so permitted by the nature of the work;

VI. To treat the workers with due consideration and abstain from ill treatment by word or deed;

VII. At the request of the workers, to issue each fifteen days a written report of the number of days worked and the wages received;

VIII. To issue to each worker who may request it or, upon his leaving the enterprise, within three days, a written record relating to his services;

IX. To provide workers with the time necessary to vote in popular elections and to fulfill their duties relating to jury, electoral, and census services referred to article 5 of the Constitution, when such activities must be carried out within working hours;

X. To permit workers to leave work to carry out occasional or permanent assignments with their unions or with the government, provided timely notice is given, and that the number of workers carrying out such assignments shall not be such as to prejudice the proper operation of the enterprise. The time lost may be deducted from the worker's wages unless such worker makes up for such lost time with an equal amount of effective work. When such appointment is permanent, the worker or workers may return to the position they occupied, and maintain all their rights, provided they return to work within a period of six years. The substitute worker shall be considered temporary; after six years he shall be considered permanent;

XI. To inform the union named in the collective bargaining agreement, and the category of workers immediately below that of the affected category, of newly created positions and of any permanent or temporary vacancies to be filled;

XII. To establish and maintain "Constitutional Article 123" schools in accordance with that provided under the laws and by the Secretariat of Public Education;

XIII. To collaborate with labor and educational authorities, in accordance with laws and regulations, to promote worker literacy;

XIV. When more than 100 and less than 1,000 workers are employed, to pay the necessary costs of adequately maintaining one of their workers or one of the children of their workers, designated by such workers and the employer on the basis of his ability, qualities and dedication, in technical, industrial, or practical studies, in special centers in Mexico or abroad. When the employer has more than 1,000 workers he must furnish three scholarships under the terms indicated. The employer may only cancel the scholarship when the student fails in the course of a year or bad conduct is reported, in which case another student shall be substituted. A student who has completed his studies must work for the employer who has funded the scholarship for at least one year;

XV. To provide education and training to workers under the terms of Chapter IIIBis of this Title;

XVI. To install factories, workshops, offices and other work places to prevent work related risks and injuries to the worker, in accordance with the rules of safety and health as well as to adopt necessary measures to avoid contaminants from exceeding the maximum levels permitted in regulations and instructions issued by competent authorities. For such purposes, the employer must modify such installations within such terms as may be indicated by such authorities;

XVII. Comply with such safety and health regulations as may be established under the laws and regulations, to prevent accidents and illnesses in work centers and, in general, in those places in which work is carried out, and to have available at all times necessary medications and materials indicated in any directives which may be issued, for the timely and efficient furnishing of first aid. Notice must be given to the competent authority of each accident which occurs;

XVIII. To post conspicuously and distribute in the work place provisions of regulations and instructions relating to safety and health;

XIX. To provide its workers with such preventive medications as may be determined by health authorities in areas in which tropical or endemic illnesses exist, or when there exists a danger of an epidemic;

XX. When the population in a rural work center exceeds 200 inhabitants, to reserve a space of ground not less than 5,000 square meters, for the establishment of public markets, buildings for municipal services, and recreational centers, provided that such work center is not less than five kilometers from the nearest work area;

XXI. To provide unions in rural work centers, upon their request, an unoccupied premises for their offices, and pay the rent therefor. If no such premises exists, a space assigned for the housing of workers may be employed for such purpose;

XXII. To make the deductions requested by unions for ordinary union dues, provided it is demonstrated that such dues are those prescribed in article 110, section VI;

XXIII. To make deductions for quotas for the formation and development of cooperative societies and savings banks, in accordance with that provided in article 110, section IV;

XXIV. To permit inspection and supervision by labor authorities in their establishments for the purpose of verifying compliance with labor rules and to provide them with the reports necessary to carry out such purpose, upon their request. Employers may require inspectors and agents to display their credentials and to inform them of any instructions they may have;

XXV. To contribute to the promotion of cultural and sports activities for workers and provide them with the necessary equipment and implements;

XXVI. To make the deductions prescribed in sections IV of article 97 and VII of article 110, and to pay over such deductions to the creditor banking institution or, as the case may be, to the Fund for the Promotion and Guarantee of Worker Consumption. Such obligation shall not cause the employer to become jointly liable for the credit which was granted to the worker;

XXVII. To provide pregnant women with such protection as may be established in the regulations hereto; and

XXVIII. To participate in the formation and operation of the committees which must be formed in each work center, in accordance with that established in this law.

Article 133 It shall be unlawful for an employer:

I. To refuse to hire workers on the basis of their age or gender;

II. To require that workers purchase articles of consumption at specific stores or places;

III. To demand or to accept money from workers in exchange for hiring them or for any other reason related to the conditions of such employment;

IV. To obligate workers, through coercion or through any other means, to affiliate themselves with, or to withdraw from, a union or association to which they may belong, or that they vote for a specific candidate;

V. To intervene in any manner in the internal governance of the union;

VI. To make or authorize collections or subscriptions in work establishments or work places;

VII. To engage in any activity which may impair the rights given to workers under the laws;

VIII. To engage in any political or religious propaganda within the establishment;

IX. To "blacklist" workers who are leaving or have left employment so that they may not be given work;

X. To carry firearms within establishments located in populated areas; and

XI. To appear in establishments in a state of intoxication or under the influence of a narcotic or debilitating drug.

CHAPTER II --OBLIGATIONS OF WORKERS

Article 134 It shall be the obligation of each worker:

I. To comply with the applicable provisions of labor rules;

II. To observe safety and hygiene measures established by competent authorities and those indicated by the employer for the personal safety and protection of workers;

III. To carry out his work under the direction of the employer or his representative, to whose authority he shall be subordinated in everything relating to the work;

IV. To perform his work with appropriate intensity, care and attention and in the manner, time and place agreed upon;

V. To give immediate notice to his employer, except in cases of emergency or force majeure, of any justified cause which may prevent him from going to work;

VI. To return to the employer materials which have not been used, and preserve in good condition the instruments and implements which may have been given to him for his work; but he shall not be responsible for normal deterioration of the same nor for damages caused by force majeure, poor quality or defective construction;

VII. To conduct himself correctly at the work place;

VIII. To provide assistance at any time required, when a major accident or imminent peril endangers human life or the interests of the employer or his fellow workers;

IX. To participate in such bodies as may be established in this law;

X. To submit to medical examinations prescribed in the internal rules and other rules effective within the enterprise or establishment, to verify that he does not suffer from any incapacity or work-related illness which may be infectious or incurable;

XI. To inform the employer of any infectious illnesses from which he may suffer, as soon as he becomes aware of them;

XII. To inform the employer or his representative of any problems he observes, for the purpose of avoiding damage or harm to the interests or lives of his fellow workers or of his employers; and

XIII. To scrupulously maintain technical, commercial and manufacturing secrets with respect to products in whose production he participates directly or indirectly, or of which he becomes aware as a result of the work he performs, or of private administrative matters whose disclosure could damage the enterprise.

Article 135 It shall be unlawful for a worker:

I. To commit any act which may endanger his own security, that of his fellow workers or third persons, as well as that of the establishments or places in which he performs his work;

II. To be absent from work without just cause or without the permission of the employer;

III. To remove work tools, or raw or finished materials, from the enterprise or establishment;

IV. To appear at work in a state of intoxication;

V. To appear at work under the influence of any narcotic or debilitating drug, without medical prescription. Before he starts working, the worker must bring such fact to the attention of his employer and present the medical subscription signed by a doctor;

VI. To carry arms of any kind during work hours, except when required by the nature of the work. Perforating and cutting instruments which form part of the work tools or implements shall be excepted from this provision;

VII. To suspend his work without the authorization of his employer;

VIII. To perform fund-raising in the establishment or work place;

IX. To use tools or implements furnished by the employer for a purpose other than that intended; and

X. To engage in any kind of propaganda during work hours, within the establishment.

XI. - To inform the owner of the collective union and workers in the next lower category , the newly created positions , the permanent and temporary vacancies to be filled ;

XII. - Establish and support schools Article 123 of the Constitution , in accordance with the provisions of law and the Secretariat of Public Education ;

XIII. - Collaborate with Labour Authorities and Education, in accordance with the laws and regulations in order to achieve literacy workers;

XIV. - Ask yourself, when employing more than one hundred and less than a thousand workers , the costs needed to sustain decent as the technical, industrial or practical , in special centers , domestic or foreign , of one of its employees or one of the children of these, designated in consideration of their abilities , qualities and dedication by the workers and the employer. When you have to serve more than a thousand workers must hold three fellows in the conditions

identified. The employer may terminate the scholarship only be rejected when the fellow in the course of a year or when you notice bad behavior , but in those cases it will be replaced by another. Trainees who have completed their studies shall serve the employer that had scholarship for one year at least ;

XV. - Provide training and instruction to their workers, in terms of Chapter III of this Title Bis.

XVI. Install and operate the factories , workshops , offices, and other places in the work to be performed in accordance with the provisions of the rules and the official Mexican standards for safety , health and working environment , in order to prevent accidents and illnesses. They must also take preventive and corrective measures determined by the labor authority ;

Bis XVI. Having , in workplaces with more than 50 employees , with adequate facilities for access and development of activities for people with disabilities;

XVII. Comply with the regulations and official Mexican standards for safety , health and working environment and time available at all medicine and healing materials necessary to provide timely and effective first aid;

XVIII. Set visibly and spread in places where work is provided , the provisions of the regulations and leading Mexican official standards for safety , health and working environment as well as the full text or collective bargaining agreements governing in the company , also are workers should disseminate information on the risks and dangers to which they are exposed;

XIX. - Provide workers prophylactic drugs determined by the health authority in places where tropical or endemic diseases exist , or when there is danger of an epidemic ;

Bis XIX. Comply with the provisions for emergency care set by the competent authority , as well as provide their workers to bring items such authority , to prevent disease in case of health emergency declaration ;

XX. - Book , when the fixed population of a rural center work exceeds two hundred inhabitants , an area of land not less than five thousand square meters for the establishment of public markets for municipal service buildings and recreation centers , provided that such workplace is at a distance of no less than five kilometers from the nearest town ;

XXI. - Provide unions , if requested, in the rural centers of work, a place that is unoccupied to install their offices , charging corresponding income. If no local conditions indicated , may be employed for this purpose either allocated for housing workers;

XXII. - Making deductions applying unions of regular union dues , provided it is established that are provided for in Article 110 , Section VI;

XXIII. - Make deductions of contributions to the establishment and promotion of cooperative societies and savings banks , in accordance with Article 110 , Section IV ;

Bis XXIII. Make deductions and payments for alimony under section V of Article 110 and collaborate to effect the authority having jurisdiction ;

XXIV. - Allow inspection and supervision authorities in their work practice facility to ensure compliance with labor standards and give reports to that effect are necessary , if requested. Employers may require inspectors or commissioners to show you their credentials and will share with them the instructions they have , and

XXV. - Contribute to the promotion of cultural and sports activities among workers and provide the necessary equipment and supplies.

XXVI. Make the deductions provided in sections IV and VII Article 97 Article 110, and find out the discounts to bank creditor , or where appropriate, the National Fund for Workers Consumption. This obligation does not make the pattern obligor credit that is granted to the employee ;

Bis XXVI. Affiliate center jobs at National Fund for Workers Consumption , in order that the workers can be subject of credit that provides that entity. Membership is free for the pattern ;

XXVII. - Provide protection for pregnant women to establish regulations.

Bis XXVII. Granting paternity leave of five working days with pay , working men , on the birth of their children and similarly in the case of the adoption of an infant , and

XXVIII. - Participate in the integration and operation of the committees to be formed in every workplace , in accordance with the provisions of this Act

Article 133. - It is forbidden to employers or their representatives:

I. Refusing to accept workers on grounds of ethnic or national origin , gender , age, disability , social status , health status , religion , opinion, sexual orientation , marital status or any other criteria that may lead to a discriminatory act ;

II. - Require workers to buy their consumer goods in store or place ;

III. - Demanding or accepting money as a bonus for workers because they are supported in the work or for any other reason which relates to the terms thereof ;

IV. - Forcing workers through coercion or other means , to join or leave the union or group to which they belong , or to vote for a specific candidate ;

V. Intervene in any way in the internal union rules prevent its formation or development of trade union activities by implicit or explicit retaliation against workers ;

VI. - Make or authorize collections or subscriptions in the establishments and workplaces;

VII. - Run any act that restricts the rights workers have under the law ;

VIII. - Making political or religious propaganda within the establishment ;

IX- Use system blacklisting workers who separate or be separated from the work that they give employment again ;

X. Carrying weapons inside the establishments located within populations ;

XI. Appear on the premises while intoxicated or under the influence of a narcotic or drug unnerving ;

XII. Engaging in harassment and / or sexual harassment against any person in the workplace;

XIII. Allow or tolerate acts of harassment and / or sexual harassment in the workplace;

XIV. Require submission of medical certificates is not pregnant for entry, stay or advance in employment , and

XV. Firing a worker or directly or indirectly coerce her to resign for being pregnant, change in marital status or having the care of minor children.

CHAPTER II OBLIGATIONS OF WORKERS

Article 134. - The duties of employees:

I. - Comply with the provisions of labor standards that apply to them ;

II. Observe the provisions contained in the regulations and the official Mexican standards for safety , health and working environment , as well as patterns indicating their safety and personal protection;

III. - Play the service under the direction of the employer or his representative , to whose authority shall be subordinate in all matters relating to work;

IV. - Run the job with the intensity , appropriate care and attention and in the manner , time and place agreed ;

V. - Give immediate notice to the employer , unless unforeseeable circumstances or force majeure, the valid reasons that prevent their work to attend ;

VI. - Restoring the pattern unused materials and kept in good condition and useful instruments that have been given to the work, not being responsible for the deterioration that results in the use of these objects , or the caused by accident , force majeure , or poor quality or defective construction ;

VII. - Observe good manners during the service ;

VIII. - Providing aid at any time they are needed, when imminent crash or be threatened people or the interests of the employer or coworkers ;

IX. - Integrate the bodies established by this Act ;

X. - Undergoing medical examinations provided for in the internal regulations and other standards in the company or establishment to check who do not have a disability or occupational disease , contagious or incurable ;

XI. To inform the employer suffering contagious diseases as soon as they become aware of them ;

XII. Inform the employer or his representative to warn deficiencies , to avoid damages to the interests and lives of their co-workers or employers , and

XIII. Save strictly technical secrets , trade and manufacture of products whose production directly or indirectly attend , or who have knowledge by virtue of the work they perform , as well as administrative matters reserved , the disclosure could cause harm to the company.

Article 135. - It is forbidden to workers:

I. Perform any act that might endanger your own safety and that of their co-workers or third parties as well as establishments or places where work is play ;

II. Missing work without good cause or without permission of the employer;

III. Subtract the company or establishment working equipment or raw material or processed ;

IV. Report to work intoxicated ;

V. Report to work under the influence of a narcotic or drug, unless there prescription. Prior to his service , the employee must bring the matter to the attention of the employer and present the prescription signed by the physician ;

VI. Carrying weapons of any kind during working hours , unless the nature of this is required. Excepted from this provision and sharps sharps that are part of the tools or work themselves ;

VII. Suspend the work without permission of the employer;

VIII. Make collections in the establishment or workplace;

IX. Use the supplies and tools supplied by the employer, to subject other than that they are intended ;

X. Making any kind of propaganda in working hours , within the facility , and

XI. Sexually harass any person or immoral acts in the workplace.

CHAPTER III ROOMS FOR WORKERS

Article 136. - Any agricultural, industrial , mining or any other kind of work , is obliged to provide workers comfortable and hygienic. To comply with this requirement , companies must contribute to the National Housing Fund five percent on wages of workers at your service.

Article 137. - The National Housing Fund will aim to create financing systems that enable workers to obtain cheap credit sufficient to purchase the property comfortable and hygienic , for the construction , repair, or improvement of their dwellings and for the payment of liabilities incurred for these items.

Article 138. - The resources of the National Housing Fund will be managed by a tripartite body composed of representatives of the Federal Government , workers and employers.

Article 139. - The law that creates the agency regulate the procedures and forms under which workers may acquire the property room and get the credits referred to in Article 137.

Article 140. - The agency referred to in Articles 138 and 139 , will be responsible for the coordination and financing of construction programs intended for dwellings purchased by the workers.

Article 141. - Contributions to the National Housing Fund are welfare costs of business and apply in full to make deposits on behalf of workers who are subject to the following bases:

I. In cases of permanent total disability , permanent partial disability , when it is 50 % or more , of permanent disability under the terms of the Social Security Act , retirement , or death of the employee, be given the total deposits made , he or his beneficiaries , with an additional amount equal to such deposits, in the terms of the Act, referred to in Article 139 ;

II. When he ceases to be subject to a working relationship and expect 50 or more years of age , shall be entitled to make delivery is total deposits that may have been made in their favor , in the terms of the Act Institute of the National Housing Fund for Workers.

III. In the event that the worker has received credit from the Institute , the amounts to which he is entitled under the terms of the preceding sections, shall apply to the repayment of the loan, except in cases of permanent total disability or death , in the terms of Article 145 if after making the application of such amounts to the amortization of remnant balance in favor of worker shall give the latter the amount.

For return of deposits and additional amounts sufficient that a written request is accompanied by relevant evidence.

Article 142. - When a company composed of several establishments , the obligation referred to in Article 136 of this Act extends to each of them and the company as a whole.

Article 143. - For the purposes of this Chapter the salary referred to in Article 136 is integrated with the cash payments made daily fee , and rewards , perceptions, food, housing , bonuses, commissions , benefits in kind and any other amount or benefit provided to the employee for their services are not taken into account by their nature, the following:

a) tools, such as tools, clothing and the like;

b) The savings where it is integrated by a deposit or monthly amount equal Semanaria the worker and the company , and the amounts awarded by the employer for social or union ;

c) Contributions to the Institute of National Housing Fund for Workers and shares in the profits of the business;

d) The power and the room when not provided free of charge to the employee, and pantries ;

e) The attendance awards ;

f) Payments for overtime , unless such services are agreed in a fixed time ;

g) Contributions to Social Security Institute by the employee to cover companies.

Article 144. - It will maximum salary for the payment of contributions equivalent to ten times the minimum wage of the geographic area corresponding application.

Article 145. - The credits are granted by the agency that administers the National Housing Fund , will be covered by insurance, for cases of permanent total disability or death , to release the worker or the beneficiaries of the obligations , duties or limitations of ownership in favor of the said entity , arising from these credits.

For such purpose, a permanent total disability or loss of function of a person's skills , that make it impossible to perform any work for the rest of your life , whatever the nature of the risk that has occurred.

In the case of permanent partial disability cases , when it is 50 % or more , or permanent disability , the employee shall be released accredited debt , liens or limitations of ownership in favor of the Institute , provided that is not the subject of a new employment for a minimum period of two years , during which time an extension shall have no cause of interest, to the payment of your credit. The existence of any of these assumptions should be checked before the Institute of National Housing Fund for Workers within the month following the date to be determined.

Article 146. - Employers are not required to pay the contributions referred to in Article 136 of this Act, so it's up to domestic workers.

Article 147. - The Federal Executive , after investigation and opinion of this body that is established to manage the resources of the National Housing Fund , establish terms and dates they implement the system established by this chapter:

I. Professional athletes and

II. Homeworkers.

Article 148. - The Federal Executive may establish procedures to facilitate the provision of companies with capital or income below the minimum that the government itself determine. These decisions may be fully or partially revised when he considers there are circumstances that justify it.

Article 149. - The body is believed to manage the resources of the National Housing Fund , shall determine the amounts to be allocated to the financing of dwellings programs intended to be purchased by the workers and to be used for the acquisition , construction, repair or improvement of such houses as well as for the payment of liabilities incurred for these items.

Upon the application of resources , be equally distributed between regions and localities of the country , as well as between different companies or groups of workers.

For individual award credits shall if necessary under a lottery system , under the terms established by law referred to in Article 139.

Article 150. - When companies provide their workers home on loan or lease are not exempt from contributing to the National Housing Fund , pursuant to Article 136. Nor are exempted from this provision with respect to those workers who have been favored by fund appropriations.

Article 151. - When the rooms are given on lease to the workers, the income does not exceed half percent per month of the assessed value of the property and applies the following rules

I. Companies are required to keep on living conditions and make necessary repairs and convenient:

II. Workers have the following obligations:

a) Pay the rent.

b) Ensure the room as their own.

c) To inform the company defects or damage to observe.

d) Vacate the room to the termination of labor relations within a period of forty- five days and

III. Employees are prohibited from:

a) Use the room for purposes other than those listed in this chapter.

b) Room Sublet.

Article 152. - Workers have the right to bring before the Conciliation and Arbitration individual and collective actions arising from a breach of the obligations imposed by this chapter.

Article 153. - Companies have the right to bring before the Conciliation and Arbitration their respective actions against workers for breach of the obligations under this chapter.

CHAPTER III A PRODUCTIVITY , TRAINING AND EMPLOYEE TRAINING

Article 153 -A. Employers are required to provide all workers and workers to receive training or on the job training that will raise their standard of living , job competence and productivity, according to the plans and programs formulated, by agreement between the employer and the union or the majority of their workers.

To comply with the obligation under paragraph above their part , employers may agree with the workers in the education or training is provided to them within the same company or outside it , through their own staff, instructors especially

hired , institutions, schools or specialized agencies, or by adherence to general systems to be established.

Institutions , schools or specialized agencies, and independent instructors who wish to provide training , education or training , as well as teachers , must be approved and registered by the Ministry of Labor and Social Welfare.

The courses and training programs or training and programs to raise the productivity of the company , may be made for each establishment , a company , a number of them , or against a branch of industry or activity.

The education or training referred to this article and other related , must be given to the employee during the hours of their work day , except that , given the nature of the services, employer and employee agree that otherwise may be given , as well as in the case in which the worker wishes to train in an activity other than that of the occupation to play , in which case the training will take place outside working hours.

Article 153- B. The training shall be to prepare newly hired workers and others interested in filling vacancies or newly created positions.

May be part of the training programs support the employer pay workers to start , continue or complete school years of basic levels , medium or higher.

Section 153 - C. The training shall be:

I. Update and improve the knowledge and skills of workers and provide them with information so they can apply new technology activities that employers must implement to increase productivity in enterprises;

II. To inform workers about the risks and dangers they are exposed to during the course of their duties , as well as the provisions contained in the regulations and the official Mexican standards for safety , health and working environment which apply to prevent occupational hazards ;

III. Increase productivity , and

IV. Generally improve the educational level , job competition and skills of workers.

Article 153- D. Workers who will provide training or training are required to:

I. Arrive at the course, focus groups and other activities that are part of the process of education or training ;

II. Take note of the people who conduct the training or training , and abide by the respective programs , and

III. Present knowledge assessment tests and aptitude or occupational competency that are required.

Article 153- E. In companies with more than 50 workers form joint committees Training , Training and Productivity, composed of an equal number of representatives of workers and employers , and will be responsible for:

I. Monitor , implement , operate and improve systems and training programs and training ;

II. Propose changes in the machinery , equipment, work organization and labor relations , in accordance with the technological and organizational best practices that increase productivity based on their current level of development ;

III. Propose measures agreed by the National and State Committees referred Productivity Articles 153 - K and 153 - Q , for the purpose of advancing training , measure and improve productivity , and ensure the equitable sharing of its benefits ;

IV. Monitor compliance with productivity agreements , and

V. Resolve the objections , if any , made by workers on the occasion of the distribution of productivity gains.

In the case of micro and small enterprises, which are those that have up to 50 workers , the Ministry of Labor and Social Welfare and the Ministry of Economy will be required to boost their productivity through the provision of programs referred to in Article 153- J , and training related to the same. To this end, with the support of academic institutions related issues relating programs , convened by reason of their branch, industry , federal state or region to micro and small entrepreneurs , workers and trade unions working in the company.

Article 153- F. Labor officials will care that the Joint Committees Training , Training and Productivity are integrated and timely functioning normally , monitoring compliance with its obligations.

Article 153- F Bis. Employers must keep available to the Ministry of Labor and Social Welfare and the Ministry of Economy , plans and training programs , training and productivity that has been agreed to establish , or where appropriate , changes have been agreed on plans and programs already in place.

Article 153- G. The register referred to in the third paragraph of Article 153- A is awarded to individuals or institutions that meet the following requirements:

I. Check who will train and will train workers are professionally trained in the industrial sector or activity that impart their knowledge ;

II. Prove successfully , according to the Ministry of Labor and Social Welfare , to be knowledgeable enough about the technological processes specific to the industrial sector or activity in seeking to provide such education or training , and

III. Not be linked to people or institutions who propagate any religious creed , under the terms of the prohibition in section IV of the 3rd Article. Constitutional.

The registration granted under the terms of this Article may be revoked when they contravene the provisions of this Act

In revocation proceedings , the affected party may offer evidence and argue as it serves his interests.

Article 153- H. The plans and programs for training and training will be developed within sixty working days to commence operations in the workplace and must meet the following requirements:

I. Refer to periods not exceeding two years, unless the training referred to in the second paragraph of Article 153- B;

II. Understand all positions and levels in the enterprise ;

III. Specify the stages during which provide training and training to all workers of the company ;

IV. Bookmark the selection process , through which will establish the order in which workers will be trained in the same position and rank , and

V. Should be based on labor competency standards , if any for the jobs in question.

Section 153 -I. Productivity means , for purposes of this Act , the result of optimizing human factors , material, financial , technological and organizational concurring in the company , in the field or in the field for the development of goods or provision of services, in order to promote the sector level , state , regional , national and international , and in line with the market to which you have access , competitiveness and sustainability , improve their capacity , technology and organization, and increase revenue , the welfare of workers and distribute its benefits equitably.

The establishment of agreements and systems to measure and increase productivity , contribute patterns , workers, unions, governments and academia.

Section 153 -J. To raise productivity in enterprises, including micro and small enterprises, programs will be developed to:

I. Make an objective diagnosis of the situation of companies in terms of productivity ;

II. Provide companies with studies of technological and organizational best practices to increase their current level of productivity in terms of their level of development ;

III. Adapt the material, organizational, technological and financial that increase productivity;

IV. Propose funding government programs , advice, support and certification for increased productivity;

V. Improve coordination systems by workers, employers , government and academia ;

VI. Establish commitments to increase productivity by employers , workers, unions, governments and academia ;

VII. Periodically evaluate the development and implementation of programs;

VIII. Improving working conditions and the Health and Safety measures ;

IX. Implement systems to determine appropriate form and amount of incentives, bonuses or commissions derived from the contribution of workers to higher productivity agreed with unions and workers , and

X. The others agreed and considered relevant.

The programs established in this Article may be made in respect of various companies , by activity or service , one or more branches of industry or services, states, region or nationwide.

Article 153- K. The Ministry of Labor and Social Security in conjunction with the Ministry of Economy , convened to employers, unions, workers and academic institutions to constitute the National Productivity Committee , which will have the advisory body and Federal Executive Assistant and production plant.

The National Productivity Committee shall have the powers listed immediately:

I. Making the diagnosis of national and international requirements for raising productivity and competitiveness in each sector and branch of production , promote training and training and investment in equipment and form of organization that is required to increase productivity , proposing plans for branch and link wages to the qualification and skills acquired as well as the evolution of the productivity of the company in terms of technological and organizational best practices that increase productivity taking into account their degree of development current ;

II. Collaborate in the development and updating of the National Classification of Occupations and studies on the characteristics of technology, machinery and equipment in existence and use , as well as the skills required in the activities corresponding to the industrial and service branches ;

III. Suggest alternative technologies and work organization to increase productivity in terms of best practice and in line with the level of development of enterprises ;

IV. Make recommendations on training plans and programs and training to help raise productivity;

V. Studying mechanisms and new forms of remuneration that link wages and generally the income of workers, productivity gains ;

VI. To assess the effects of training activities and training in productivity within industries or activities in question ;

VII. Propose to the Ministry of Labor and Social Welfare issuing labor competency standards and , where appropriate , procedures for assessment , accreditation and certification , for those productive activities in which there exists a particular standard ;

VIII. Negotiate with the labor authority recording the evidence on knowledge or skills of the workers who have fulfilled the legal requirements for this purpose;

IX. Prepare and implement the programs referred to in the preceding article ;

X. Participate in the preparation of the National Development Plan ;

XI. Express opinions and suggest the fate and implementation of budgetary resources aimed at increasing productivity , and

XII. Other established in this and other regulations.

Article 153- L. The President declared establish the basis to determine the manner of appointment of members of the National Commission on Productivity , as well as those relating to its organization and operation. Clutching the principles of representation and inclusion in their integration.

In making decisions of the National Productivity Commission will privilege consensus.

Article 153- M. - In collective agreement shall contain provisions required employers to provide training and instruction to workers, according to plans and programs that meet the requirements of this Chapter.

Also be entered in the contracts themselves the procedure under which the employer will train train and who intend to enter work in the company , taking into account, where appropriate, the admission clause.

Section 153 -N. To operate the National Productivity Commission establish subcommittees , by industry , state and regional.

The subcommittees developed for the scope of the respective sector , industry , region federal entity or program provided for in Article 153- J of this Act

Section 153 -O. (Repealed).

Article 153- P. (Repealed).

Article 153- Q. At the level of the states and the Federal District Productivity establish State Commissions.

Shall apply to the State Commissions Productivity , in the area of the states , the provisions of Articles 153 -I, 153- J , 153- K , 153- L , 153- N and other related.

Article 153- R. (Repealed).

Article 153- S. When the employer fails to comply with the obligation to keep available to the Ministry of Labor and Social Security plans and training programs and training , in terms of Article 153- N, or where such plans and programs do not lead to the practice , shall be punished as provided in this Act, notwithstanding that , in either case , the Secretariat itself take appropriate measures so that the employer complies with the requirement in question.

Article 153- T. - Workers who have been approved in the training and instruction tests on the terms of this Chapter , shall be entitled to an entity instructor issued with the necessary records , same as , authenticated by the Joint Committee on Training and training Company , is made known to the Ministry of Labor and Social Security , through the National Committee concerned or , failing that , through the labor authorities to ensure that the Secretariat itself the record and take into account in formulating the standard of skilled workers , as appropriate, in terms of Section IV of Article 539.

Article 153 -U. When implemented a training program , a worker refuses to receive it , considering that it has the necessary skills to perform their job and the immediate superior, must produce documents such capacity by the appropriate occupational competency certificate or take and pass , instructor before the entity , the respective proficiency test.

In the latter case , the worker will be extended to the constancy of skills or job skills.

Article 153- V. The constancy of skills or job skills is the document with which the worker have been accredited and approved training course.

Companies are required to send to the Ministry of Labor and Social Welfare for registration and control lists of the records that were issued to workers.

The records in question shall be fully effective , for purposes of promotion within the company that has provided training or training.

(Repealed the fourth paragraph).

Article 153- W. - Certificates , diplomas and degrees issued by the State , its decentralized or individuals with official recognition of studies , who have completed any type of education with terminal character shall be entered in the records of which Article 539 , section IV, when the position and corresponding category listed on the National Classification of Occupations are similar to those within it.

Article 153- X. - Workers and employers have the right to bring before the Conciliation and Arbitration individual and collective actions arising from the education or training requirement imposed by this Chapter.

CHAPTER IV PREEMPTIVE RIGHTS, SENIORITY AND PROMOTION

Article 154. Employers are obliged to prefer , other things being equal , Mexican workers in respect of whom they are not, who have served satisfactorily for longer , who having no other source of income are responsible for a family , those who have completed their compulsory basic education to the trainees for which they are not, those who have greater ability and knowledge to do a job and the union with respect to whom they are not.

If there is collective agreement and it contains admission clause , preference in filling vacancies or newly created positions shall be governed by provisions in the collective agreement and union status.

Union means any worker is unionized any legally constituted union.

Article 155. - Workers who are in the cases of the preceding article and who aspire to a vacant or newly created , must submit an application to the company or establishment indicating their residence and nationality , if you are charged with a family and who are economically dependent on them if they served before and for how long , the nature of the work performed and the name of the union to which they belong , to be called the

created a vacancy occurs or a new position , or submitted to the company or establishment occur when the vacancy or create the position, checking the cause in which melt your request.

Article 156. - If there is no collective agreement or not contain the clause held admission , shall apply the provisions of the first paragraph of Article 154 workers who usually without the status of plant workers , serving in an enterprise or establishment , supplying transient or temporary vacancies and performing extraordinary work or to particular work, they are not a normal activity of the company or permanent.

Article 157. The breach of the obligations contained in Articles 154 and 156 entitles the worker to apply to the Board of Conciliation and Arbitration , at its option , to be granted the corresponding position or be compensated in the amount of three months' salary. You will also be entitled to receive payment for wages and interest , if any , referred to in the second paragraph of Article 48.

Article 158. - Plant workers and those mentioned in Article 156 are entitled to every company or establishment as determined by their seniority.

A committee composed of representatives of the workers and the employer make the overall picture of antiquities , by category of each profession or trade and order is publicized. Dissatisfied workers may object to the committee and the resolution of this appeal to the Board of Conciliation and Arbitration.

Article 159. The final vacancies , the interim lasting more than thirty days and the newly created positions will be covered by the worker who has the next lower category or range , as well as more training , more senior , higher fitness show , proving greater productivity and be suitable for the position.

Article 160. - In the case of vacancies under thirty days, subject to the provisions in the first paragraph of the preceding article.

Article 161. - When the employment relationship has lasted more than twenty years, the employer may only terminate it for any of the reasons specified in Article 47, which is particularly serious or make it impossible to continue , but it will impose the worker appropriate disciplinary correction , respecting the rights deriving from its antiquity.

The repetition of the offense or the commission of another or others, which constitute a legal cause for termination, supersedes the previous provision.

Article 162. - Plant workers are entitled to a seniority premium in accordance with the following standards:

I. Seniority premiums consist of the amount of twelve days salary for each year of service;

II. To determine the amount of wages is subject to the provisions of Articles 485 and 486 ;

III. Seniority premiums are paid to workers who voluntarily separate from employment , provided that persons under fifteen years of service , at least. Also be paid to those who are separated for cause and those who are separated from their employment , regardless of justification or lack of justification for the dismissal ;

IV. For the payment of the premium in the case of voluntary retirement of workers, the following rules shall be observed:

a) If the number of workers who retire within a period of one year does not exceed ten percent of total workers in the undertaking or establishment or a particular category , payment is made at the time of retirement.

b) If the number of workers to withdraw exceeds ten percent , will be paid to those who first retire and may be deferred to the following year payment to workers who exceed this percentage.

c) If the withdrawal is made at the same time by a number of workers increased the percentage required, will cover the premium to those with more seniority and may be deferred to the following year the payment corresponding to other workers ;

V. In case of death of the worker , whatever their age , the premium will be paid corresponding to the persons mentioned in Article 501 , and

VI. Seniority premiums referred to this article will cover employees or their beneficiaries , regardless of any other benefit which they belong.

CHAPTER V INVENTIONS OF WORKERS

Article 163. - The allocation of rights to the name and ownership and exploitation of inventions made in the company, shall be governed by the following rules:

I. The inventor shall be entitled to have his name listed as the author of the invention ;

II. When the worker is engaged in research or development of the procedures used in the company , on account of this property of the invention and the right to exploit the patent correspond to the pattern. The inventor, regardless of the salary that would have received , is entitled to additional compensation , to be fixed by agreement of the parties or by the Board of Conciliation and Arbitration when the importance of the invention and the benefits that they can report the pattern of proportion with the salary received by the inventor , and

III. In any other case , ownership of the invention correspond to the person or persons who conducted , but the pattern will have a preferential right , other things being equal , the exclusive use or acquisition of the invention and of the relevant patents.

TITLE FIVE

Women's Work

Article 164. - The women enjoy the same rights and have the same obligations as men.

Article 165. - The conditions that are listed in this chapter are fundamental purpose , the protection of motherhood.

Article 166. - When endangers the health of women, or of the product , either during the stage of pregnancy or nursing without suffering prejudice in his wages , benefits and rights , you can not use your work in unhealthy or hazardous industrial night work in

commercial or service establishments after ten in the evening as well as overtime.

Article 167. - For the purposes of this title , are dangerous or unhealthy work which , by the nature of work, the physical, chemical and biological environment in which it provides, or the composition of the raw material use , are able to affect the life and physical and mental health of women in gestation , or product.

The regulations to be issued will determine the jobs that fall within the above definition.

Article 168. In case the competent authority issues a declaration of health emergency , according to the applicable provisions, the work may not be used for women during pregnancy or breastfeeding. Workers who are in this course will not be prejudiced in his wages , benefits and rights.

As a result of the declaration of health emergency order suspending work overall , women in periods of gestation or lactation will apply the provisions of Article 429 , Section IV of this Act

Article 169. - (Repealed).

Article 170. - Working mothers have the following rights:

I. During the period of pregnancy , not perform work requiring considerable effort and pose a danger to their health in relation to pregnancy , such as lifting, pulling or pushing heavy weights , to produce judder , standing for a long time or acting or can alter your state of mind and nervous ;

II. Enjoy a break of six weeks before and six after the birth. At the express request of the worker , physician prior written permission of the social security institution that applies to you or , if applicable , the health service that gives the pattern , taking into account the opinion of the pattern and nature of the work undertaken , you can transfer up to four of the six weeks of rest before delivery to after. In case the children were born with any type of disability or require hospital care , rest will be up to eight weeks after delivery upon presentation of a medical certificate.

In the event that this particular medical authorization , it must contain the name and professional license number of the person who issued , date and medical condition of the worker.

II Bis. In case of adoption of a child will enjoy a six-week break with pay , after the day on which they received ;

III. The rest periods referred to in the preceding section shall be extended by the time required in the event that they are unable to work because of pregnancy or childbirth ;

IV. In the lactation period up to the maximum term of six months , will have two extraordinary repose per day , half an hour each, to feed their children, adequate and hygienic place designated by the company , or, where this is not may , by agreement with the employer in an hour will reduce their working hours for the period indicated ;

V. During the rest periods referred to in Section II , will receive their full wages. In cases of extension referred to in paragraph III , shall be entitled to fifty percent of his salary for a period not exceeding sixty days ;

VI. A return to the position they played , provided that no more than one year has elapsed from the date of delivery , and

VII. Shall be counted in their age pre and postnatal periods.

Article 171. - Childcare services will be provided by the Mexican Social Security Institute , in accordance with its law and regulations.

Article 172. - In establishments where women work , the employer must maintain a sufficient number of seats or chairs available to working mothers.

TITLE FIVE BIS

Child Labor

Article 173. - The employment of minors is subject to surveillance and protection from the authorities of both federal and local work.

The Ministry of Labor and Social Security , in coordination with the labor authorities in the states , develop programs to identify and eradicate child labor.

Article 174. - The over fourteen and under sixteen , regardless of having the Act authorization to work must obtain a medical certificate attesting to fitness for work and undergo periodic medical examinations ordered by the authorities relevant labor. Without these requirements , any employer may use their services.

Article 175. - The preventive use of child labor:

I. In non-industrial establishments after ten at night;

II. In intoxicating beverage outlets immediate consumption , pubs or taverns and service centers ;

III. In work likely to affect their morals or good customs , and

IV. In hazardous or unhealthy , in the nature of work, the physical, chemical or biological environment in which it provides, or the composition of the raw material used , are able to affect the life , development and physical and mental health of minors.

In case of health emergency declaration and if so determined by the competent authority , no work may be used under sixteen. Workers who are in this course will not be prejudiced in his wages , benefits and rights.

As a result of the declaration of health emergency order suspending work overall , the under sixteen will apply the provisions of Article 429 , Section IV of this Act

Article 175 Bis. - For the purposes of this chapter , shall not be considered work activities under the supervision , care and responsibility of parents , guardians or those exercising parental

power , made the under fourteen related artistic creation, scientific development , athletic or talent , musical performance or artistic interpretation in any of its manifestations , as are subject to the following rules:

a) The relationship established with the applicant shall be in writing and contain the express consent of the child to express on behalf of parents, guardians or the persons exercising parental authority, and the incorporation of the commitment to respect the applicant assume for the same lesser rights than the Constitution , international conventions and local and federal laws recognize the benefit of children ;

b) The activities do not interfere the least with their education , leisure and recreation in the terms established by applicable law , neither imply or risk to their health and in any case , will encourage the development of their skills and talents , and

c) The consideration received by the youth for the activities carried out will never be lower than they would receive as salary increased fourteen and under sixteen.

Article 176. For the purposes of Article 175 , in addition to arrangements Laws , regulations and standards are regarded as dangerous or unhealthy work , the following:

A. For minors from fourteen to sixteen years of age, those involving:

I. Exposure to:

1. Noise, vibration , ionizing and non-ionizing radiation or ultraviolet infrared , thermal conditions or killed or abnormal environmental pressures.

Two. Chemical contaminants in the workplace.

Three. Hazardous waste , biological agents or infectious diseases.

April. Wildlife dangerous or harmful flora.

II. work:

1. Rescue , rescue and casualty brigades.

Two. In height or confined spaces.

Three. In which operate critical equipment and processes which handle hazardous chemicals that can cause major accidents.

April. Welding and cutting.

May. In extreme weather conditions in the open, exposing them to dehydration , heat stroke , hypothermia or frostbite.

June. On roads with large volume of vehicular traffic (primary roads).

July. Agricultural , forestry, sawing , forestry , hunting and fishing.

August. Gasera productive industries , cement , mining , iron and steel, oil and nuclear.

9. Productive bricked industries , glass , ceramics and Cerera.

10. Production of the tobacco industry.

11. Related to the generation , transmission and distribution of electricity and maintenance of electrical installations.

12. In construction.

13. Have direct responsibility for the care of persons or property and securities custody.

14. With high degree of difficulty , in time pressure , high demanding responsibility , or that require sustained concentration and attention.

15. Relating to the operation, inspection , maintenance and testing of pressure vessels , cryogenic vessels and steam generators or boilers.

16. In ships.

17. Underwater and underground.

18. Street work , unless specifically authorized by the Labour Inspectorate.

III. Moderate and heavy physical exertion ; loads over seven kilograms , awkward postures , repetitive motion or prolonged periods alter their musculoskeletal system.

IV. Handling , transport, storage or shipment of hazardous chemicals.

V. Management , operation and maintenance of machinery, equipment or power tools , electrical, pneumatic or motorized , that can generate amputations , fractures or serious injury.

VI. Operation of motorized vehicles, including mechanical and electrical maintenance.

VII. Using hand tools sharps.

B. In the case of minors under eighteen years of age, those involving:

I. Industrial night work.

II. Exposure to:

a. Wildlife dangerous or harmful flora.

b. Ionizing radiation.

III. Activities as trimmers and stokers on ships.

IV. Handling , transport, storage or shipment of hazardous chemicals.

V. Work in mines.

Article 177. - The workday under sixteen years may not exceed six hours per day and must be divided into a maximum of three hours. Among the different periods of the day, enjoy an hour of rest at least.

Article 178. - You may not use the work of under sixteen in overtime and on Sundays and mandatory rest. In case of violation of this prohibition , overtime is paid with a hundred percent of the salary corresponding to the hours of the day, and the wages on Sundays and mandatory rest , in accordance with Articles 73 and 75.

Article 179. - The under sixteen will enjoy an annual period of paid vacation eighteen days , at least.

Article 180. - Employers who have to serve under sixteen are required to:

I. Demand that they exhibit the medical documentation that are fit for work ;

II. Keeping track of special inspection , showing the date of birth, type of work, hours, pay and other working conditions ;

III. Distribute work to ensure that sufficient time to fulfill their curricula ;

IV. Provide training and training in terms of this Act , and ,

V. Provide labor authorities requesting reports.

TITLE VI SPECIAL WORKS

CHAPTER I GENERAL PROVISIONS

Article 181. - Special Works are governed by the provisions of this Part and the general terms of this Act not contraríen.

CHAPTER II WORKERS CONFIDENCE

Article 182. - The working conditions of workers in confidence shall be proportionate to the nature and importance of the services rendered and shall not be inferior to those applicable to similar jobs within the company or establishment.

Article 183. - The trusted workers can not join unions as other workers, or be taken into consideration in the counts to be carried out to determine the most in the event of a strike , or be representatives of workers in the organisms that are integrated in accordance with the provisions of this Act

Article 184. - Working conditions contained in the collective agreement in force at the firm or establishment are extended to trusted employees , unless otherwise given in the same collective agreement.

Article 185. - The employer may terminate the employment relationship if there is reasonable cause loss of confidence , even if it matches the cause for dismissal referred to in Article 47.

The trusted worker may bring actions referred to Chapter IV of Title II of this Law

Article 186. - In the case referred to in the preceding article , if the employee had been promoted trusted in a position of plant it again , unless there is just cause for separation.

CHAPTER III VESSELS WORKERS

Article 187. - The provisions of this chapter apply to vessels workers , this term being understood in any sort of ship or vessel that holds Mexican flag.

Article 188. - Are subject to the provisions of this chapter , the captains and deck and engine officers , attendants and counters , radio operators , foremen , dredgers , sailors and chamber staff and kitchen, which are considered as workers by communications laws and regulations on water , and in general all persons performing any work aboard behalf of the owner, operator or charterer.

Article 189. - Workers of vessels shall have the status of Mexicans by birth do not acquire another nationality and in full enjoyment and exercise of their civil and political rights.

Article 190. - The captains , understood as those who exercise direct command of a ship , have relative to other workers as representatives of the employer.

Article 191. - It is forbidden to work in this Chapter to the age of fifteen years and under eighteen for as trimmers or stokers.

Article 192. - No employment relationship is considered the agreement to hold the captain aboard a ship with people who have been introduced to him and aimed accrued , personal services , the fare , except as provided in the next article.

Neither considered the working relationship agreement entered under the terms of the previous paragraph , with the Mexicans to be repatriated , at the request of the respective Consul.

Article 193. - People who provide their services on board only by the time the ship is in port , are subject to the provisions of this chapter as applicable.

When ships going to sea without having been able to land the persons referred to above, will be considered workers until their return to their place of origin, and shall have the rights and obligations are set out in this chapter.

Article 194. - Working conditions shall be recorded in writing. One copy shall be retained by each party, the other shall be sent to the Port Authority or the nearest Mexican Consulate , and the fourth to the Labour Inspectorate of where stipulated.

Article 195. - The letter referred to in the preceding article shall contain:

I. Place and date of signing ;

II. Name, nationality , age , sex , marital status, and address of the worker and the employer ;

III. Mention of the vessel on board of which services will be provided ;

IV. If held for a fixed or indefinite voyage or voyages ;

V. The service to be provided , specifying as accurately ;

VI. The distribution of hours of day ;

VII. The amount of wages ;

VIII. The accommodation and food to be supplied to the employee ;

IX. The annual holiday period ;

X. The rights and obligations of the worker;

XI. The percentage to be paid to workers when they try to rescue another vessel , and

XII. Other stipulations agreed to by the parties.

Article 196. - The working relationship per trip will include the term counted from the shipment of the worker until completion of discharge of the vessel or to land passengers at the port to be agreed.

If it is for a fixed or indeterminate set the port to which the employee must be reinstated , and failing this , it shall be noted that of the place where he took.

Article 197. - For the provision of Mexican workers in foreign vessels observe the provisions in Article 28.

Article 198. - When the ship is at sea and the nature of work does not allow weekly rest, the provisions in Article 73.

Article 199. - Workers are entitled to a minimum period of twelve working days of paid annual leave , which is increased by two days , up to twenty , for each subsequent year of service. Subsequently increase vacation time in two days for every five years of service.

The holidays should be enjoyed on earth and can split when required by the continuity of the work.

Article 200. - It violates the principle of equal pay provision stipulating the different wages for equal work , if you pay on ships of various categories.

Article 201. - A choice of workers , wages may be paid in the equivalent in foreign currency at the official rate of exchange prevailing on the date of the charge , when the vessel is in a foreign port.

Article 202. - The journey workers are entitled to a proportional increase in wages in the event of delay or extension thereof.

Wages can not be reduced by shortening the journey , whatever the cause.

Article 203. - The salaries and allowances of workers enjoy the preference contained in Article 113 of the vessel, its machinery, tackle , gear and cargo. To this end , the ship owner is jointly liable with the employer for wages and benefits of workers. Where there work credits from different trips , preference for the last.

Article 204. - Employers have special obligations following:

I. Providing comfortable accommodation and sanitary board ;

II. Provide healthy eating, abundant and nutritious ship workers dedicated to serving height and cabotage and dredging ;

III. Provide room and board when the ship is brought to a foreign port for repairs and conditions do not permit their stay on board. This same obligation shall continue in national port when it is not the place where you took the worker. The room and food will be provided without cost to the worker ;

IV. Pay the costs of the status of funds to the families of the workers, when the ship is abroad;

V. Grant workers time to exercise the vote in popular elections , provided that the safety of the ship and not permitted to impede his departure on the date and time set ;

VI. Allowing workers who fail to perform their duties to the state commissions or union , under the same conditions referred to in the preceding section ;

VII. Providing food and shelter, medical treatment and other therapeutic drugs in cases of disease, whatever its nature ;

VIII. Bring on board staff and healing material established by law and provisions on water communications ;

IX. Repatriate or transfer the workers agreed place , except in cases of separation for reasons not attributable to the employer , and

X. Inform the relevant Harbour Master , within twenty-four hours after being declared free pratique , of occupational accidents aboard. If the ship arrives in foreign port , the report shall be rendered to the Mexican Consul or failing that , the captain of the first national port touch.

Article 205. - Workers are especially obliged to respect and carry out the instructions and practices to prevent hazards of the sea, which will be made in the terms specified by the laws and regulations on water communications. The captains and officers will work in these cases , as representatives of the authority and not as representatives of the patterns.

Article 206. - Is prohibited on board outlets provide , without permission of the captain, alcoholic beverages to workers and introduce these vessels such effects.

It is also prohibited to workers smuggle drugs and narcotics , except as provided in Article 208 , Section III.

Article 207. - The temporary mooring of a vessel authorized by the Board of Conciliation and Arbitration , does not settle labor relations , only suspends its effects until the ship returned to service.

Repairs to ship mooring not be considered temporary.

Article 208. - These are special cases of termination of employment relationships:

I. The lack of support worker on board at the appointed time for departure or presenting , landing and not make the trip ;

II. Finding the employee intoxicated on duty while the ship is in port , leaving the ship or during navigation;

III. Use narcotics narcotics or drugs during their time on board , without a prescription.

On boarding , the employee must bring the matter to the attention of the employer and present the prescription signed by the physician ;

IV. The insubordination and disobedience to the orders of the master in his capacity of authority ;

V. The definitive cancellation or revocation of certificates of competency or sea of books required by laws and regulations;

VI. The violation of laws regarding the import or export of goods in the performance of their services , and

VII. The execution , in the performance of work by the employee , of any intentional act or omission or negligence that may endanger your safety or that of other workers , passengers or third persons , or damage, impair or jeopardize the employer's assets or third parties.

Article 209. - The termination of labor relations of workers subject to the following rules:

I. When missing ten days or less to maturity and are intended to make a new trip duration exceeds this term , workers may request the termination of labor relations , giving three days notice prior to the departure of the ship;

II. Working relationships can not be terminated when the ship is at sea or in harbor when completion is attempted within twenty-four hours before departure , unless the latter changing the final destination of the ship;

III. Nor can they be terminated employment relationships when the ship is abroad, in unpopulated areas or in port , provided that in the latter case the vessel is exposed to any risk due to bad weather or other circumstances ;

IV. When relationships are working indefinitely, the employee must give notice to the owner, operator or charterer seventy-two hours in advance ;

V. When the ship is lost by capture or sinister , it shall terminate the working relationship , being obliged the owner, operator or charterer , to repatriate workers and cover the amount of wages to its return to the port of destination or to which has been fixed by the contract and any other benefits to which they are entitled. The workers and the employer may agree to provide those work in the same category in another vessel pattern , if not reached an agreement workers will be entitled to be compensated in accordance with Article 436 ; and

VI. The change of nationality of a Mexican ship is cause for termination of employment relationships. The owner, operator or charterer is obliged to repatriate workers and cover the amount of the wages and benefits referred to in the first paragraph of the preceding section. The workers and the employer may agree to provide those work in the same category in another vessel pattern , if not reached an agreement , workers are entitled to be compensated in accordance with Article 50.

Article 210. - In cases of section V of the preceding article , if workers agree to perform work towards the recovery of the remains of the ship or cargo , shall be paid their wages for the days they work. If the salvage value exceeds the amount of wages , workers will be entitled to a bonus, in proportion to the efforts and dangers arrostrados to rescue, to be fixed by agreement of the parties or by decision the Board of Conciliation and Arbitration , which shall previously hear the opinion of the maritime authority.

Article 211. - The Rules of Work , deposited in the Board of Conciliation and Arbitration , shall be recorded in the Harbor.

The rule violations will be reported to the Labour Inspector , who , after investigation , shall notify the authority of the work , together with the opinion of the Captain of the Port.

Article 212. - Corresponds to the Labour Inspectorate to monitor compliance with the laws and other labor standards , based on the laws and regulations on water communications , when ships are in port.

Article 213. - In domestic traffic or river govern the provisions of this chapter , with the following specifications:

I. If the download takes more than a day at the point when the employment relationship ends , it shall be deemed terminated at the expiration of that period, counted from the moment the ship fondee or berth ;

II. Feeding employed patterns is mandatory, even if not contained in the contracts , if on board is provided to passengers , and in any case, in the case of vessels operating for six hours or more , or that navigating within that time , suspend navigation in unpopulated areas where it is impossible to provide food workers ;

III. The onboard enforced residence is regarded as working time , unless the rest period is four hours or more , the worker there for the impossibility of abandoning ship abandonment or lack of object because it is unpopulated ; and

IV. Weekly rest will be forced to the ground.

Article 214. - The Federal Executive shall determine how to sustain and improve the services of the House of Marino and set the input patterns.

CHAPTER IV CIVIL AVIATION WORKERS

Article 215. - The provisions of this chapter apply to the work of crews of civil aircraft bearing Mexican license plate. Their purpose , in addition to that provided for in article 2 , ensure the safety of aircraft operations , and are waived to the extent corresponding to this purpose.

Article 216. - The crew should have the status of Mexicans by birth do not acquire another nationality and in full enjoyment and exercise of their civil and political rights.

Article 217. - Working relationships referred to this chapter shall be governed by Mexican law , regardless of where the services are to be performed.

Article 218. - Should be considered aviation crew members , according to the laws and techniques for:

I. The pilot in command of the aircraft (Commander or Captain) ;

II. Officers who develop similar work ;

III. The navigator , and

IV. Attendants.

Article 219. - Will be considered representatives of the employer , by the nature of the functions performed , operations managers or flight superintendents , heads of training , chief pilots, pilot instructors or counselors , and any other officials who even if they have different job titles , carrying out similar to the above.

Holders of the above categories shall be appointed by the employer and may appear as pilot in command , without prejudice to the rights corresponding ground pilots , provided they meet the requirements of the Law of General Means of Communication and its regulations , to commit thereon.

Article 220. - The pilot in command of an aircraft is responsible for the conduct and safety of the same during the actual flight time , and is responsible for the management , care , order and safety of the crew, the passengers , baggage and cargo and mail transport it. The responsibilities and powers conferred by the Act commanders General Communications and regulations, not be reduced or modified by the exercise of the rights and obligations under the rules work.

Article 221. - For the determination of working hours will be considered the output tables and sunset, with relation to the location closest to where the aircraft is in flight.

Article 222. - For the actual flight time means the period starting from an aircraft first moves under its own power , or is towed for take -off position until it stops after the flight.

Article 223. - The total services to be provided the crew , considered the equipment used shall be fixed in the contract and shall include only the actual flight time , the path and reservation services , without may exceed one hundred eighty hours per month.

Article 224. - Effective time monthly flight crew can work contracts shall be working , taking into consideration the characteristics of the equipment used , but may not exceed ninety hours.

Article 225. - Effective time of flight of the crew shall not exceed eight hours in the day shift , seven in the evening and half past seven in the mixed , unless they are granted a rest period horizontal, before their or to fulfill those days , equal to the time flown. The excess of the stated time will be extraordinary.

Article 226. - The days of the crew shall comply with the requirements of the service and may commencement to any time of day or night.

Article 227. - When service needs or characteristics of routes require operation , the total time of service of the crew shall be divided conventionally during the corresponding day.

Article 228. - The crew may not interrupt flight service during his journey , by maturity of the working day. In case you reach the limit of their journey during flight or at an airport other than the final destination , will be required to finish it if it requires no more than three hours. If you need more time, they will be released or suspend the airport flight path nearest.

Article 229. - When using jet equipment may be reduced total time duration of services identified in this chapter.

Article 230. - When the crew service needs exceed their total time service fee for each extra hour a hundred percent corresponding wage. Over time , calculated and paid under the terms of this article shall not be subject to further payment.

Article 231. - Crews are obliged to prolong their working day on relief flights , search and rescue. The excess hours shall be paid as provided in the first paragraph of Article 67.

Article 232. - The crew serving in the furlough days will be entitled to remuneration contained in Article 75. Exceptions are cases of termination of a service that does not exceed the first hour and a half of those days , in which only receive the amount of an additional day's pay.

For the purposes of this article, the days will start at midnight and end at twenty , official time place of residence basis.

Article 233. - The crew are entitled to an annual period of thirty calendar days , not cumulative. This period can be enjoyed in proportion semiannually , and shall be increased by one day for each year of service , not to exceed sixty calendar days.

Article 234. - It violates the principle of equal pay provision stipulating the different wages for equal work , if the aircraft is provided in different category or different routes , and established seniority premiums.

Article 235. - The salary of the crew will be paid , including additional allocations corresponding fifteenth and last day of each month. Perceptions on account of night flight time and overtime , in the first half of the month after they have been made , and the amount of furlough days in the fortnight immediately to that in which they are worked.

The payments , regardless of its concept , will be made in national currency and in the place of residence of the crew , unless otherwise agreed.

Article 236. - Employers have the following specific duties:

I. Providing food, shelter and transportation to the crew for all the time to stay out of its base by reason of service. Payment will be made in accordance with the following standards:

a) In the pre-designated stations , or in those of extraordinary overnight , transportation will be by car and accommodation will be paid directly by the employer. Transportation will be provided between the airport and place of accommodation and vice versa , except in those places of residence permanent base of the crew.

b) When food can not be taken on board, the crew receive a cash allowance , which is set according to the number of meals to be made on each trip or overnight stay in extraordinary places. The amount of these allowances shall be established by mutual agreement;

II. Paying crew travel expenses , including those of the spouse and first degree relatives who are financially dependent on them, the household goods and personal effects when they are changed from their home base. The amount of these expenses are fixed by mutual agreement ;

III. Repatriate or transfer the place of recruitment to the crew whose aircraft is destroyed or unusable out of that place , paying their salaries and travel expenses , and

IV. Granting permits referred to in Article 132 sections IX and X , provided that endanger the safety of the aircraft or exit unfit for the date and time previously mentioned.

Article 237. - The crew , as they are concerned, have special obligations following:

I. Caring for aircraft that do not charge passengers or effects unrelated to the employer's interests without meeting the relevant requirements , or items prohibited by law , unless you have obtained permission from the appropriate authorities ;

II. Store in force their licenses , passports , visas and documents that are legally required for the performance of their work;

III. Appear to cover services that are assigned to the anticipation and how to establish their contract and the internal labor regulations , except for just cause ;

IV. Submit at least twice a year, regular medical examinations prescribed by law , regulations and employment contracts ;

V. Undergo trainings to establish the pattern according to the needs of the service , to maintain or increase their efficiency for promotion or use of equipment with new technical features and operate it to get the required capacity ;

VI. Plan, prepare and conduct each flight , with strict adherence to the laws , regulations and other provisions issued or approved by the Ministry of Communications and Transport and by the employer ;

VII. Make sure , before starting a trip , the aircraft meets the statutory and regulatory requirements , the security conditions , and has been properly equipped , provisioned and avituallada ;

VIII. Observe techniques in air traffic safety boletine dictate the pattern or the respective authorities at the airport base or foreign stations ;

IX. Give notice to the employer and , where appropriate, to the competent authorities , using the fastest media available to them, in case of flying any emergency situation , or when an accident occurs ;

X. Perform relief flights , Search and rescue at any time and place required;

XI. In the case of pilots in command of the aircraft , write on the log, accurately and under its responsibility , the data required by the legal provisions and do, where appropriate , the service time distribution of the other members of the crew;

XII. Submit reports , statements and representations to formulate and sign documentation for each flight required by law, and other applicable regulations , and

XIII. To inform the employer at the end of the flight , the mechanical or technical defects or presumed to warn in the aircraft.

Article 238. - When for any reason a member of the technical crew had stopped flying for 21 days or more, the crew must undergo the relevant training to the grade held at the time of the suspension and ascertain that it has the technical capability and practice and performance required for resumption of their work, in the terms established by Law General Communications and regulations.

Article 239. - The roster of aviation crews take into consideration:

I. Technical, physical and mental health of the applicant, referring to the team for the post of promotion;

II. Previous experience , determined , by specialty , by registered flight hours before the competent authority or by the instructions and practice in the case of the crew with no obligation to register these flight hours , and

III. Seniority, on equal terms.

Article 240. - The crew interested in a promotion of their specialty, will support and approve the respective training program , and license required for each specialty by the Secretariat of Communications and Transportation.

Article 241. - For computer operation having different technical characteristics which had been used , the crew member and the employer shall determine the conditions of employment.

Article 242. - It is forbidden to the crew:

I. Drinking alcoholic beverages during service delivery and within twenty-four hours prior to the initiation of their assigned flights ;

II. Use narcotics narcotics or drugs in or out of their working hours , without prescribing an aviation medicine specialist. Prior to his service , the employee must bring the matter to the attention of the employer and present the prescription signed by the physician , and

III. Run as a flight crew to decrease their physical and legal to perform flights serving his employer.

Article 243. - Is special cause for suspension of labor relations , without liability to the employer, the temporary suspension of the respective licenses , passports , visas and other documents required by national and foreign laws as is attributable to the crew.

Article 244. - These are special causes of termination or termination of labor relations:

I. The final cancellation or revocation of the documents specified in the preceding article ;

II. Meet the crew intoxicated , within twenty-four hours prior to the initiation of flight to be assigned or during the course of it ;

III. Meet the crew , at any time, under the influence of narcotics or narcotics drugs except as provided in Article 242 , Section II ;

IV. The violation of laws on the importation or exportation of goods , performance of services ;

V. The crew 's refusal , without good cause , to help run flights , search and rescue , or start or continue flight duty allotted ;

VI. The crew 's refusal to attend training programs as required to establish the pattern of service , they are necessary to maintain or increase their efficiency , for promotion or to operate equipment with new technical features ;

VII. The execution , performance of work, by the crew of any intentional act or omission or neglect that might endanger their safety or that of the members of the crew , passengers or third persons , or damage , impair or endanger the property of the employer or others , and

VIII. The breach of the obligations set forth in Article 237 and the violation of the prohibition contained in Article 242 , Section III.

Article 245. - The Federal Board of Conciliation and Arbitration , prior to the approval of the internal labor regulations , seek the views of the Secretariat of Communications and Transportation to ensure that the same will observe the provisions of the Law of General Means of Communications and regulations.

CHAPTER V RAILROAD WORKERS

Article 246. - Railroad workers must be Mexican.

Article 247. - In collective agreements may determine the staffing, taking into account the provisions of article 9.

Article 248. - In collective agreements may stipulate that trenistas workers provide services based on travel in one or two directions.

Article 249. - When an employee is nearing his retirement terms determined in collective agreements , the employment relationship may be terminated only for particularly serious cases make it impossible to continue in accordance with the provisions contained in collective agreements. In the absence of express provisions are subject to the provisions of Article 161.

Article 250. - No cause for termination of employment relationships or loss of rights , the fact that workers , force majeure , are isolated from their bosses , if they continue in their posts.

If in the same condition they abandon , to disappear again occupy the reasons for abandonment. In these cases, previously made relevant investigations , involving representatives of the union and the company , and if they find liability to the affected workers , who voluntarily checks or neglected or harmed the interests of the company , will be separated of employment. Workers who have occupied the abandoned positions have the status of agency , and being reinstated holders will continue to work in the jobs they had before or in vacated.

Article 251. - Workers who have been separated by downsizing or jobs , even when they receive the right compensation that come , shall retain the rights acquired before their separation, to return to their posts, if they return to created and also being called to service in the line of work of departure , provided they continue to belong to unions held collective agreements.

Article 252. - The days of workers shall conform to the requirements of service and may principiar at any time of day or night.

Article 253. - It violates the principle of equal pay different wage setting for equal work , if it is provided in lines or branches of varying importance.

Article 254. - It is forbidden to workers:

I. The consumption of alcoholic beverages , and traffic during the performance of his duties as an employee of the company ;

II. The consumption of narcotics or narcotics drugs unless there prescription. Before starting the service, the employee must bring the matter to the attention of the employer and present the prescription signed by the physician , and

III. Drug trafficking narcotics.

Article 255. - These are special cases of termination of employment relationships:

I. Receipt of freight or passengers out of the places mentioned by the company for these purposes , and

II. The refusal to make the trip interruption hired or without cause.

CHAPTER VI TRANSPORTATION WORKERS

Article 256. - The relationships between the drivers, drivers, operators , collectors and other workers employed on board public service motor carrier of passengers , cargo or mixed or urban outsiders , such as buses , trucks, vans or cars , and the owners or licensees of the vehicles, are relations and are subject to the provisions of this chapter.

The provision that in any way detracts from the provisions of the preceding paragraph, does not produce any legal effect or inhibit the exercise of rights arising from the services rendered.

Article 257. - They shall be fixed per day, per trip, tickets sold or circuit or kilometers and consist of a fixed amount, or a premium income or the amount exceeding a certain income , or in two or more of these modalities , but in no circumstances be less than the minimum wage.

If the wage is fixed per trip , workers are entitled to a proportionate increase in the extension or delay normal term trip causes not imputable.

Wages can not be reduced by shortening the journey , whatever the cause.

In urban transport or circuit , employees are entitled to payment of wages in the event of service interruption due to causes beyond their control.

It violates the principle of equal pay provision stipulating the different wages for equal work , if it is provided in lines or services of different categories.

Article 258. - To determine the salary of the days off will increase the remuneration they receive for the work done in the week, with a sixteen sixty six percent.

Article 259. - In determining the amount of the salary of holidays and compensation , is subject to the provisions in the second paragraph of Article 89.

Article 260. - The owner of the vehicle and the licensee or permit holder are jointly liable for the obligations arising from labor relations and law.

Article 261. - It is forbidden to workers:

I. The use of alcoholic beverages during the service and in the twelve hours before initiation;

II. Use narcotics narcotics or drugs in or out of their working hours , without a prescription. Before starting the service, the employee must bring the matter to the attention of the employer and present the prescription signed by the physician , and

III. Receive freight or passengers out of the place specified by the company for such purposes.

Article 262. - Workers have special obligations following:

I. Treat the passage with friendly and attentive and the load with caution ;

II. Undergo periodic medical examinations prescribed by law and other labor standards ;

III. Caring for the proper functioning of the vehicle and report any damage pattern to observe ;

IV. Do while traveling emergency repairs to enable their knowledge , tools and spare parts available to them. If you can not make the repairs , but the vehicle can continue to run , drive to the closest town or place designated for repair , and

V. Observe traffic regulations and technical instructions dictated by the authorities or the employer.

Article 263. - Employers have special obligations following:

I. In foreign transport pay for accommodation and meals for workers , when prolong or delay the trip for reasons not attributable to them ;

II. Make repairs to ensure the smooth operation of the vehicle and the safety of workers, consumers and the general public ;

III. Equipping vehicles and parts indispensable tool for emergency repairs , and

IV. Observe the provisions of the Traffic Regulations on operating conditions and vehicle safety.

Article 264. - These are special cases of termination of employment relationships:

I. The refusal to make the trip interruption hired or without cause. Be considered in any case cause the fact that the vehicle does not meet the security conditions necessary to safeguard the lives of workers , users and the general public , and

II. The significant decrease in volume and revenue repeated , unless there are extenuating circumstances.

CHAPTER VII PUBLIC SERVICE WORKERS IN AREAS UNDER FEDERAL JURISDICTION

Article 265. - The provisions of this chapter apply to the work of public service maneuvers cargo handling , stevedoring , stash , check, berthing, mooring , hauling , storage and transshipment of cargo and baggage , which is carried on board ship or ashore in ports , waterways, rail stations and other areas under federal jurisdiction , which is developed in boats for pilots , and complementary or related work.

Article 266. - In collective agreements maneuvers are determined subject to the same , differing from those that apply to other workers.

Article 267. - No work may be used under sixteen years.

Article 268. - Shipping companies are patterns and maneuvers , shipowners and charterers, shippers , brokers , and other persons who ordered the work.

Article 269. - The persons referred to in the previous article , which jointly ordered the work covered in this chapter , are jointly liable for the wages and allowances that apply to workers for work performed.

Article 270. - The salary may be fixed per unit time per unit of work , by weight of the package or in any other way.

If involved in a maneuver several workers , wages are distributed among them according to their categories and the proportion in which they participate.

Article 271. - The salary will be paid directly to the worker , in accordance with Article 100.

Payment made to organizations, whatever their nature, or intermediaries , to which in turn make payment to workers, not released from liability to employers.

Article 272. - Workers are entitled to daily wages be increased by sixteen sixty six percent as the rest day wages.

Also increase the daily wage in the corresponding proportion for vacation pay.

Article 273. - In determining the age of the workers , and the order in which services are to be used , the following rules shall be observed:

I. Seniority is calculated from the date it first began the worker to provide services to the employer ;

II. In collective agreements may be established seniority of each employee. The dissatisfied worker may apply to the Board of Conciliation and Arbitration to rectify their age. If no collective agreement or lack of them determination , seniority shall be determined in accordance with the provisions of Article 158 , and

III. The distribution of work shall be in accordance with the age corresponding to each worker. In collective agreements shall determine conditions deemed appropriate for work distribution.

Article 274. - Unions patterns will provide a detailed list containing the name and category of workers who must perform maneuvers in each case.

Article 275. - Workers can not be replaced in service delivery. If it breaks this prohibition , the substitute is entitled to be paid the full salary that corresponds to work performed and payment is made in accordance with the provisions of Article 100.

Article 276. - For the payment of compensation in cases of occupational hazards , the following rules shall be observed:

I. If the accident results in disability, payment will be made in accordance with Article 483 ;

II. The pattern under whose authority was given the job, be liable for accidents at work , and

III. If it's working diseases , each pattern that had used the services of the employee for 90 days , at least , in the three years preceding the date of determining the degree of incapacity for work will contribute in proportion who had used the services.

The employee may bring an action for payment of compensation against any of the standards referred to in the previous paragraph , but the defendant may bring others to trial or recourse against them.

Article 277. - In collective agreements stipulate that employers may cover a percentage of wages , so that they constitute a pension fund retirement or disability not resulting from an employment injury. In the union's constitution or special regulations approved by the assembly , we will determine the requirements for the granting of pensions.

The amounts will be given by employers to the Social Security Institute and in case it does not accept, the bank may be specified in the collective agreement. The institution will cover pensions approval of the Board of Conciliation and Arbitration.

Article 278. - In collective agreements may stipulate the establishment of a fund subject to the payment of liability for loss or damage. The amount will go to the national bank may be specified in the collective agreement , which will cover the payments under an agreement between the union and the employer, or by resolution of the Board of Conciliation and Arbitration.

Reached the amount of the fund , no new contributions , except to replenish the amounts paid.

CHAPTER VIII FARM WORKERS

Article 279. Farm workers are those who perform the tasks associated with agricultural, livestock , aquaculture , forestry or mixed , the service of an employer.

Workers in industrial forest holdings are governed by the general provisions of this law.

Farm workers may be permanent, temporary or seasonal.

Article 279 Bis. - Eventually the field worker is one that is not permanent or seasonal, plays occasional activities in rural areas , which can be determined by work and time , according to the provisions of this Act

Article 279 Ter. - Seasonal farm workers or laborers are those individuals who are hired to work on farms , livestock, forestry , aquaculture or mixed only in certain times of the year , or to conduct related activities ranging from preparation land , to the preparation of products for your first sale , whether they are produced in the open, in the greenhouse or otherwise protected , without affecting its natural state , as well as other similar agricultural, livestock , forestry , aquaculture or mixed.

It can be contracted by one or more employers for one year, for periods that in no case shall exceed twenty-seven weeks for each pattern.

It does not include seasonal farm workers , those who work in agricultural, livestock, forestry , aquaculture or mixed field acquiring products for packaging activities , re-pack , exhibition, sale or processing through a process that modify its natural state.

Article 280. - The seasonal or temporary workers who work in the field continuously for a period exceeding twenty-seven weeks for a pattern , has in its favor the presumption of being a permanent worker.

The employer shall keep a special register of the casual and seasonal workers hired each year and display it to the labor authorities when required to do so.

At the end of the season or the agricultural cycle, the employer must pay the worker corresponding proportional parts for vacations , vacation pay , bonus and any other benefits to which he is entitled, and shall deliver a certificate to each worker in the identifying all days worked and total wages earned.

Article 281. - When leases exist , the owner of the property is jointly liable with the lessee , if it does not have sufficient elements to fulfill the obligations arising from the relations with their workers.

If there are sharecropping , the landowner and the tenant shall be jointly liable.

Article 282. - Working conditions shall be made in writing, observing the provisions of article 25 and other related provisions of this Act

Article 283. - Employers have the following specific duties:

I. Paying wages precisely where the worker provide services and periods of time not exceeding one week ;

II. Provide free workers adequate and hygienic rooms , proportional to the number of family members or dependents who accompany them and, if appropriate, an individual or collective farm for animal husbandry and poultry ;

III. Keep the rooms in good condition , making repairs if necessary and expedient;

IV. Provide workers with safe water and sanitation during the working day ;

V. Keep in the workplace medicines and healing material and antidotes necessary to provide first aid to workers , their families or dependents who accompany and train staff who serve;

VI. Provide workers and their families who accompany medical care or move to the nearest place where there are medical services. They will also have the obligations referred to in Article 504 , Section II ;

VII. Provide free the worker , their families or dependents who accompany medicines and healing in cases of tropical diseases , endemic and native to the region and pay workers who become disabled , seventy -five percent of wages up to ninety days. Seasonal workers enjoy this benefit for the duration of the employment relationship.

Seasonal workers must also have life insurance for your transfers from their home to the workplace and after his return;

VIII. Allowing workers within the site:

a) Take in aquifers , the water they need for their household and their farm animals.

b) Hunting and fishing, for own use , in accordance with the provisions governing the Laws.

c) Free movement on the roads and trails established , provided it is not to the detriment of the crops and crops.

d) Hold on regional holidays usual places.

IX. Encourage the establishment of consumer cooperatives among workers ;

X. Promoting literacy among workers and their families.

The State shall ensure at all times , access to basic education for the children of seasonal farm workers or laborers. The Ministry of Education will recognize the studies in the same school year, made the children of seasonal farm workers or laborers both in their homes and in their workplaces ;

XI. Provide workers for free, safe and comfortable transportation of residential areas to places of work and back. The employer may pay their own or service for which the employee makes use of a proper public transport ;

XII. Using the services of an interpreter when workers do not speak Spanish , and

XIII. Provide childcare for the children of workers.

Article 284. - It is forbidden to employers:

I. Allow access to sellers of alcoholic beverages ;

II. Prevent entry to sellers of goods or charge a fee , and

III. Prevent workers raising farm animals in the individual or collective land for that purpose , unless it harms the crops or any other activity that takes place on site job center.

CHAPTER IX COMMERCIAL AGENTS AND THE LIKE

Article 285. - Trade agents , insurance salespeople , reps, propagandists or sales drivers and the like , are employees of the company or companies that provide their services , when their activity is permanent , unless no run work personally or only isolated part of transactions.

Article 286. - The salary commission may include a premium on the value of the goods sold or placed on the initial payment or periodic payments , or two or all three of those premiums.

Article 287. - To determine the moment of birth the right of workers to receive bonuses, the following rules shall be observed:

I. If you set a single premium at the time the transaction is perfected it as a basis , and

II. If premiums are fixed periodic payments at the time they are made.

Article 288. - The premiums that apply to workers may not be retained or deducted if subsequently revokes the operation they served basis.

Article 289. - In determining the amount of the daily wage shall be based on the average wages resulting from last year or the total earned if the employee did not meet one year of service.

Article 290. - Employees can not be removed from the area or route assigned to them , without their consent.

Article 291. - Is special cause for termination of labor relations and reiterated the significant decrease in the volume of operations , unless there are justifying circumstances.

CHAPTER X PROFESSIONAL ATHLETES

Article 292. - The provisions of this chapter apply to professional athletes such as football players , baseball , handball , boxing, fighters and the like.

Article 293. - Working relationships can be for a fixed term , indefinitely, for one or more seasons or for holding one or more events or functions. In the absence of express terms , the relationship will be indefinitely.

If after the term or completion of the season does not stipulate a new term of duration or other form , and the worker continues to provide its services, the relationship will continue indefinitely.

Article 294. - The salary may be stipulated per unit time , for one or more events or functions , or for one or more seasons.

Article 295. - Professional athletes can not be transferred to another company or club , without their consent.

Article 296. - The premium players transfer is subject to the following rules:

I. The company or club will meet professional athletes the rules or clauses which contain it;

II. The premium amount will be determined by agreement between the professional athlete and the company or club , and taking into consideration the category of events or functions , the equipment , the professional athlete and his seniority or club ; and

III. The professional athlete's participation in the premium shall be twenty-five percent , at least. If the fixed rate is less than fifty percent , will increase by five percent for each year of service , up to fifty percent , at least.

Article 297. - It violates the principle of equal pay provision stipulating the different wages for equal work , because of the category of events or functions , of equipment or players.

Article 298. - Professional athletes have special obligations following:

I. Submit to the discipline of the company or club ;

II. To attend the preparation and training practices in the place and time designated by the company or club and concentrate for events or functions ;

III. Make travel for events or functions in accordance with the provisions of the company or club. The costs of transportation, food and lodging will be borne by the company or club , and

IV. Respect local regulations , national and international governing the practice of sports.

Article 299. - It is forbidden to abuse of professional athletes all word or deed to judges or referees of events , their teammates and opponents players.

In sports that involve staff contest , the contestants must refrain from any act prohibited by the regulations.

Article 300. - These are special obligations of the patterns:

I. Organize and maintain a medical service practice periodic examinations , and

II. Giving workers a day off a week. Not applicable to professional athletes the provision in the second paragraph of Article 71.

Article 301. - It is forbidden to patterns athletes require excessive effort that would endanger their health or life.

Article 302. - The professional athletes sanctions be applied in accordance with the regulations referred to in Article 298 , Section IV.

Article 303. - These are special causes of termination and termination of labor relations ;

I. The serious misconduct or repeated offenses of indiscipline , and

II. The loss of function.

CHAPTER XI ACTORS AND MUSICIANS

Article 304. - The provisions of this chapter apply to workers and musicians actors acting in theaters , cinemas , nightclubs or variety , circus , radio and television , recording and dubbing rooms , or any other place where transmit or capture the image of the actor or musician or transmitted or becomes recorded voice or music, regardless of the procedure used.

Article 305. - Working relationships can be for a fixed or indefinite for several seasons or for holding one or more functions , representations or actions.

Not applicable the provision contained in Article 39.

Article 306. - The salary may be stipulated per unit time , for one or more seasons or for one or more functions , representations or actions.

Article 307. - It violates the principle of equal pay, the provision stipulating different wages for equal work , because of the category of functions, representations or actions , or worker actors and musicians.

Article 308. - For the provision of actors or musicians workers outside the Republic , shall be observed in addition to the rules contained in Article 28 , the following provisions:

I. It should be an advance of salary for the time contracted twenty-five percent , at least , and

II. Must be guaranteed round-trip ticket.

Article 309. - The provision of services within the Republic , rather different from the worker's residence actor or musician, will be governed by the provisions contained in the preceding article , as applicable.

Article 310. - When the nature of work required , employers are required to provide workers backstage actors and musicians comfortable , clean and safe , on the premises where the service is provided.

CHAPTER XII WORK AT HOME

Article 311. - Working from home is usually running for a pattern in the worker's home or in a place of his own choosing , without supervision or direct supervision of the provider of the work.

It will be considered that home work is done remotely using information technology and communication.

If the job is executed under conditions other than those listed in this article shall be governed by the general provisions of this Act

Article 312. - The agreement by virtue of which the employer sells raw materials or objects to a worker for the processing or Compile it in his home and later sold to the same pattern , and any such agreement or transaction constitutes homeworking.

Article 313. - Home worker is a person who works personally or with the help of family members to a pattern.

Article 314. - Are patterns that employ people at home , whether or not provide the tools or work materials and whatever form of remuneration.

Article 315. - The simultaneity of patterns does not deprive the homeworker rights under this chapter.

Article 316. - You may not use intermediaries. In the case of the company that sells the product or take home work , shall govern the provisions of Article 13.

Article 317. - Employers who employ home must register in advance with the Registrar of home work patterns which will work in the Labour Inspectorate. The register shall contain the name and address of the pattern for which to run the job and any other data that indicate the respective regulations.

Article 318. - Working conditions shall be recorded in writing. Each of the parties will keep a copy and the other will be given to the Labour Inspectorate. The notice shall contain:

I. Name, nationality , age , sex , marital status and address of the worker and the employer ;

II. Local where the job will run ;

III. Nature , quality and quantity of work;

IV. Amount of salary and date and place of payment , and

V. Other stipulations agreed to by the parties.

Article 319. - The letter referred to in the preceding article shall be delivered by the employer within a period of three working days to the Labour Inspectorate , which, within the same term , shall revise its strict liability under. If that was not set to the Act, the Labour Inspectorate , within three days , the parties will make appropriate observations, in order to make the amendments thereto. The employer must resubmit the same Labour Inspection.

Article 320. - Employers are required to keep a logbook outworkers , authorized by the Labour Inspectorate , which include the following information:

I. Name, nationality , age , sex , marital status of the employee and address or location where the job runs ;

II. Days and times for delivery and reception of the work and payment of wages ;

III. Nature , quality and quantity of work;

IV. Materials and supplies to be provided each time the worker, their value and payment for lost or damaged through the fault of the worker;

V. Form and level of wages , and

VI. The other data that indicate the regulations.

The books will be permanently available to the Labour Inspectorate.

Article 321. - The patterns delivered free to your home workers a notebook foliated and authorized by the Labour Inspectorate , to be called home work book and the recorded data is referred to in sections I , II and Article V above, and each time work is provided , those listed in section IV of this article.

The lack of book does not deprive the worker of the rights granted to you pursuant to the provisions of this Act

Article 322. - The National Commission on Minimum Wages minimum wages set different professionals work at home , and must take into consideration, among others, the following circumstances:

I. The nature and quality of work:

II. The average time for the development of products;

III. Wages and benefits received by workers of establishments and companies that develop the same or similar products , and

IV. The current market prices of the products of home work.

The books referred to in Article 320 shall be permanently available to the National Minimum Wage.

Article 323. - The wages of home workers may not be less than those paid for similar work in the company or establishment for which the work is performed.

Article 324. - Employers have the following specific duties:

I. Set wage rates in a visible place of the premises where work providing or receiving ;

II. Provide materials and working tools in the agreed dates and times ;

III. Receive timely work and pay wages in the form and dates specified ;

IV. To record in the book of each worker , at the time of work , losses or deficiencies that result , unable to take any subsequent appeal , and

V. Provide Inspectors and the National Minimum Wage reports requested.

Article 325. - The lack of timely compliance with the obligations specified in Sections II and III of the preceding article shall entitle the home worker to compensation for lost time.

Article 326. - Homeworkers have the following specific duties:

I. Put the utmost care in the custody and preservation of the materials and supplies they receive pattern ;

II. Develop products according to the agreed quality and accustomed ;

III. Receive and deliver the work in the stipulated time and date , and

IV. Compensate the employer for the loss or damage that suffer because of her materials and supplies they receive. The homeworker responsibility is governed by the provision contained in Article 110 , Section I.

Article 327. - Also have the right to the corresponding week wages are paid furlough day.

Article 328. - Homeworkers are entitled to annual leave. To determine the amount of the corresponding salary subject to the provisions in the second paragraph of Article 89.

Article 329. - The homeworker who is to stop work, have the rights under Article 48.

Article 330. - Labour Inspectors have the following specific powers and duties:

I. Check whether the people who provide home work are registered in the Registry Pattern. In case you are not, will order to register , warning them that failure to do so within a period not exceeding 10 days, subject to the sanctions stipulated by this Act ;

II. Check for worn properly and are up to date log books homeworkers and report cards home work ;

III. Ensure that the wage rate is fixed in a conspicuous place of the premises in which is received and provide work;

IV. Check if wages are paid according to the respective rate ;

V. Ensure that wages are not lower than those paid to workers in the same company ;

VI. Practice visits to the premises where the work is carried , to monitor compliance with the provisions on health and safety , and

VII. Report to the National Minimum Wage wage differences they notice in relation to those paid to workers who perform work similar.

CHAPTER XIII DOMESTIC WORKERS

Article 331. - Domestic workers are providing cleaning services , and other assistance or inherent to the home of a person or family.

Article 332. - No domestic workers and thus are subject to the general or specific provisions of this Act:

I. Persons who provide cleaning services , assistance , customer care and the like , in hotels, nursing homes , restaurants , taverns , bars , hospitals, nursing homes , schools , boarding schools and other similar establishments , and

II. The porters and watchmen of the establishments mentioned in the previous section and the apartment buildings and offices.

Article 333. Domestic workers who live in the home where they serve should enjoy a minimum daily rest of nine hours nightly plus a minimum daily rest of three hours between the morning and afternoon activities.

Article 334. - Unless otherwise expressly agreed , the domestic remuneration includes , in addition to the cash payment , food and room. For the purposes of this Act , food and housing are estimated equal to 50 % of salary to be paid in cash.

Article 335. - The National Commission on Minimum Wages minimum wages shall be paid professionals these workers.

Article 336. Domestic workers are entitled to a weekly rest day and a half uninterrupted , preferably on Saturday and Sunday.

By agreement between the parties may be agreed to build half days in periods of two weeks, but will be enjoyed a full day of rest each week.

Section 337. - Employers have special obligations following:

I. Save consideration the domestic worker , refraining from evil treatment of word or deed ;

II. Provide the employee room comfortable and hygienic , healthy and sufficient food and working conditions that ensure life and health , and

III. The employer must cooperate to provide the general education of a domestic worker , in accordance with the rules that dictate the appropriate authorities.

Article 338. - In addition to the obligations referred to in the preceding article , in cases of illness that is not working , the employer must:

I. Pay the domestic worker 's salary that corresponds up to a month ;

II. If the disease is chronic , provide care in the meantime manages to cure or worker takes care of any health care service , and

III. If the disease is chronic and the employee has served for six months at least , provide care for up to three months, or sooner if done by a healthcare worker.

Article 339. - In case of death , the employer shall pay the funeral expenses.

Article 340. - Domestic workers have special obligations following:

I. Save the employer , your family and the people who attend the home in which they serve , consideration and respect , and

II. Put the utmost care in preserving the utensils of the house.

Article 341. - Is cause for termination of employment relationships noncompliance with special obligations set forth in this chapter.

Article 342. - The domestic worker may terminate at any time the employment relationship by giving notice to the employer at least eight days in advance.

Article 343. - The employer may terminate the employment relationship without liability, within thirty days after the initiation of the service , and at any time, without having to check the cause for it, paying the appropriate compensation in accordance with articles 49 , section IV, and 50.

CHAPTER XIII A MINING WORKERS

Article 343 -A. The provisions of this chapter are applicable to all coal mines in Mexico , and all mining developments in any stage mining that is , either , prospecting, preparation , exploration and exploitation , regardless of the type of scan and operation in question , whether , underground , mines drag , open pits , inclined and vertical shots , and extraction in any of its forms, held in a traditional way, same as , for the purposes of this Act, are considered workplaces.

Article 343- B. All workplaces should have a safety management system and occupational health and with a charge of its operation, designated by the employer, in the terms established by the applicable regulations.

Article 343- C. Regardless of the obligations under this Act or other regulations imposed upon , the employer must:

I. Provide and maintain facilities under hygienic conditions so their workers can wash and eat ;

II. Counting, before and during the exploration and exploitation , with the plans , studies and analysis necessary to develop activities in safety , which should be updated whenever there is a material change in the work processes ;

III. Informing employees in a clear and understandable risks associated with its activities , the hazards they pose to their health and the prevention and protection measures applicable ;

IV. Provide the necessary personal protective equipment , to avoid the occurrence of workplace hazards and train employees in their use and operation;

V. Have adequate ventilation systems and fortification in all underground workings , which must have two exits , at least , from any work front , interconnected ;

VI. Establish a system of monitoring and control systems in each shift and work front , which will ensure that the exploitation of the mine is done safely ;

VII. Implement a system for recording and accurately know the names of all persons who are in the mine , as well as keep track of inputs and outputs of this ;

VIII. Suspend the activities and have the evacuation of workers to a safe place in case of imminent danger to the safety and health of themselves , and

IX. Do not hire or permit to hire under 18.

The operators of concessions that cover the mining claims , which are located in workplaces referred to this Chapter , shall ensure that the employer complies with its obligations. Operators of mining concessions will be secondarily liable , if an event occurs where one or more workers suffer partial or total permanent disability , or death, resulting from that event.

Article 343- D. Workers may refuse to provide services as long as the Joint Commission on Health and Safety confirm that:

I. Not have the proper training and skills to enable them to identify the risks to which they are exposed , how to avoid exposure to them and do their work in safety.

II. The employer does not give them the personal protective equipment or not trained for its use.

III. Identify imminent risk that could endanger his life , physical integrity or health or that of their coworkers.

When employees are aware of imminent risk , should be removed from the workplace exposed to that risk , making the knowledge of this fact to the employer, any member of the Health and Safety Commission or the Labour Inspectorate.

Noting the Labour Inspectorate , by any means or form, that there is an imminent risk , shall identify the existence of such risks through labor inspectors to commission for this purpose , and immediately , order measures corrective or preventive safety and hygiene in order to safeguard the life, physical integrity or health of workers. Such measures may include complete or partial suspension of the activities of the mine and even in restricting access of workers to the workplace as not to take the necessary security measures to inhibit the occurrence of an incident.

If an employer refuses to receive the labor authority , it may request the assistance of law enforcement , Federal , State or Municipal , as applicable , to enter the workplace and comply with its monitoring functions compliance with labor standards. The labor inspectorate shall notify this fact to the mining authority which would proceed to the suspension of mining works and the terms of the Law of the matter.

Article 343 -E. A controllers and direct the operation and supervision of the work and mining developments , willfully or negligently omitted to implement safety measures provided in the regulations , which have been previously identified in writing founded and reasoned opinion of the competent authority , shall apply the following penalties:

I. Fine up to 2,000 times the general minimum wage in the Federal District , when its omission there is a risk of work that generates one or more workers with permanent partial disability.

II. Fine up to 3,500 times the general minimum wage in the Federal District , when its omission there is a risk of work that generates one or more workers to permanent total incapacity.

CHAPTER XIV JOBS IN HOTELS, RESTAURANTS, BARS AND OTHER SIMILAR ESTABLISHMENTS

Article 344. - The provisions of this chapter apply to workers in hotels, nursing homes , restaurants , taverns , cafes , bars and other similar establishments.

Article 345. - The National Commission on Minimum Wages minimum wages shall be paid professionals these workers.

Article 346. - Tips are part of the wages of workers referred to this chapter in terms of Article 347.

The patterns can not be reserved or have any interest in them.

Article 347. - If it is determined , as a tip, a percentage of the drinks , the parties shall increase the salary to be made the basis for the payment of any compensation or benefit corresponding to the workers. The salary attached to this effect will be rewarding , having taken into consideration the importance of the facility where services are rendered.

Article 348. - The feed given to workers must be healthy , hearty and nutritious.

Article 349. - Workers are required to attend with care and courtesy to customers of the establishment.

Article 350. - Labour Inspectors have the following specific powers and duties:

I. Ensure that the feed given to workers is healthy , hearty and nutritious ;

II. Check that tips apply in full to workers , and

III. Ensuring respect for the rules on working time.

CHAPTER XV FAMILY INDUSTRY

Article 351. - Family Workshops are exclusively those in which both spouses work , ascendants , descendants and pupils.

Article 352. - No family workshops apply to the provisions of this Act , except the rules relating to health and safety.

Article 353. - The Labour Inspectorate will monitor compliance with the standards referred to in the preceding article.

CHAPTER XVI MEDICAL RESIDENTS

Article 353 -A. - For the purposes of this chapter , the term:

I. Medical Resident: The medical professional with Title legally issued and registered with the competent authorities , to enter a Resident Medical Receiving , to meet a residence.

II. Resident Medical Receiving: The hospital in which homes can be met , that for the purposes of the General Health Law requires the expertise of medical professionals , and

III. Residence: The set of activities required to fulfill Resident Physician training period , for post-graduate studies and practices with regard to the health discipline that seeks to engage , in a Resident Medical Receiving , over time and accordance with the requirements laid down by the respective academic provisions.

Article 353- B. - The relations between the Resident Doctors and moral or physical person to whom it reports the Resident Medical Receiving shall be governed by the provisions of this Chapter and the provisions contained in the Indenture , as no contradict them.

Section 353 - C. - Are special rights of Resident Doctors , to be entered in the contracts to be awarded to more than those stipulated in this Law , the following:

I. Enjoy the services that are necessary for the fulfillment of the residence ;

II. Exercise your residence to complete their specialty, provided they comply with the requirements of this Chapter.

Article 353- A. - These are special obligations of the Resident Physician , the following:

I. Comply stage instruction and training, according to the academic teaching program in effect at the Resident Medical Receiving ;

II. To obey the orders of those appointed to provide training or to direct the development of the work , with regard to that and him ;

III. Comply with internal Medical Receiving Residents concerned about not contrary contained in this Act ;

IV. Attend conferences theory clinical sessions , clinicopathologic , clinical, radiological , literature and other academic activities that are designated as part of specialized studies ;

V. Stay on the Resident Medical Receiving , under the terms of the next item , and

VI. Undergo and pass periodic assessment of knowledge and skills acquired , according to the provisions academic and administrative standards of the corresponding unit.

Article 353- E. - Within the time the Resident Physician must remain in the Resident Medical Receiving , according to the respective educational provisions , are included , the next working day to training in the specialty , both in relation to patients and other forms of study or practice , and to enjoy rest periods and eating food.

Article 353- F. - The working relationship will be for a specified period , not less than one year nor more than the duration of residence required to obtain the corresponding Specialization Certificate , taking into account the latter regarding termination causes identified in Article 353. G.

Under this Chapter , shall not apply the provisions of Article 39 of this law.

Article 353- G. - These are special cases of termination of the employment relationship , without liability to the employer, in addition to the provisions of Article 47, the following:

I. The breach of duty to refer the fractions I, II , III and VI of Article 353.D ;

II. The violation of the technical regulations or administrative provisions necessary to the functioning of the Resident Medical Receiving the residence is made , and

III. The commission faults own behavioral norms of the medical profession , entered in the Internal Regulations Working Resident Medical Receiving.

Article 353- H. - Are grounds for termination of the employment relationship , in addition to the provisions of Article 53 of this Law:

I. The conclusion of the Fellowship ;

II. The deletion studies academic specialty on the branch of medicine that concerns the Resident Physician.

Section 353 -I. - The provisions of this Chapter do not apply to those who only receive education or training courses as part of their professional training in health institutions.

CHAPTER XVII WORKING IN PRIVATE UNIVERSITIES AND COLLEGES

Section 353 -J. - The provisions of this Chapter apply to labor relations between workers and administrative and academic universities and colleges autonomous by law and are intended to achieve balance and social justice in the relations of work , thereby matching the autonomy , academic freedom and research and the aims of these institutions.

Article 353- K. - Academic worker is the individual that serves of teaching or research at universities or institutions referred to in this Chapter , in accordance with plans and programs established by them, administrative worker is the individual who provided nonacademic services such universities or institutions.

Article 353- L. - Is entirely up to universities or autonomous institutions regulate law academics.

For an academic worker may be considered subject to an employment relationship indefinitely, plus they perform the task of this character , it must be approved by the academic assessment carried out by the competent authority according to the requirements and procedures themselves universities or institutions established.

Article 353- M. - The academic worker may be engaged for full time or part time. Workers scholars dedicated exclusively to teaching may be hired per hour class.

Section 353 -N. - It violates the principle of equal pay different wage setting for equal work if it corresponds to different academic categories.

Article 353- Ñ. - Unions and the directives of these to be established in the universities or institutions referred to in this Chapter , shall consist only workers who provide services in each and will:

I. Academic staff ;

II. Administrative staff , or

III. Institution if it includes both types of workers.

Section 353 -O. - Unions referred to in the preceding article shall register with the Ministry of Labor and Social Security or the Board of Conciliation and Arbitration to be, as federal or local law that created the university or institution concerned.

Article 353- P. - For the purposes of collective bargaining between universities and institutions and their respective unions , will follow the rules laid down in Article 388. To this end the union of institution will be treated as union and the academic staff unions or administrative personnel will treat labor union.

Article 353- Q. - In collective agreements provisions academic workers shall not extend to administrative workers , or vice versa , except as expressly agreed.

In any case, these contracts may provide for academic staff exclusive admission or expulsion separation referred to in Article 395.

Article 353- A. - In the process of strike notice to the work stoppage must be given at least ten days prior to the date set for suspend work.

In addition to the cases provided for by Article 935, before the suspension of work , the parties or, failing the Board of Conciliation and Arbitration, those with hearing , shall determine the necessary number of workers required to continue working for that are still running work whose suspension can irreparably harm the proper conduct of an investigation or an ongoing experiment.

Article 353- S. In the Conciliation and Arbitration , Special Boards work to familiarize with labor issues in universities and autonomous colleges by law and will be integrated with the president concerned , the representative of each university or institution and academic workers representative or relevant administrative.

Article 353- T. - For purposes of the preceding article , the competent authority shall issue the respective call , establishing therein that each university or institution shall appoint its representative and conventions to be concluded paths for the election of representatives of the relevant academic workers or administrative.

Article 353 -U. - Employees of universities and institutions to which this Chapter applies enjoy social security systems in terms of their organic laws , or pursuant to agreements based on them are held. These benefits can never be less than the minimum established by the Constitution of the United Mexican States and this Act

TITLE SEVEN COLLECTIVE LABOUR RELATIONS

CHAPTER I COALITIONS

Article 354. - The law provides for freedom of association of workers and employers.

Article 355. - Temporary agreement Coalition is a group of workers or of employers for the defense of their common interests.

CHAPTER II UNIONS , FEDERATIONS AND CONFEDERATIONS

Article 356. - Union is an association of workers or employers set up to study , improve and defend their interests.

Article 357. - Workers and employers have the right to establish trade unions without prior authorization.

Any undue interference shall be punished in the manner provided for by law

Article 358. - No one can be forced to join a union or not to join him.

Any provision that establishes conventional fine in case of separation or union any way detracts from the provision in the preceding paragraph , it shall be void.

Article 359. - Unions have the right to draw up their constitutions and rules , elect their representatives, organize their administration and activities and formulate their programs.

Article 360. - Labor unions can be:

I. Union , formed by workers in the same profession , occupation or specialty ;

II. Company , formed by workers who provide services in the same company;

III. Industrial , formed by workers who provide services in two or more companies in the same industry ;

IV. National industry, made up of workers who provide services in one or more companies in the same industry , in two or more federal entities , and

V. For various occupations , formed by workers of various professions. These unions may only be formed when the city in question , the number of workers in the same occupation is less than twenty.

Article 361. - Unions of patterns can be:

I. The patterns formed by one or more branches of activity , and

II. Nationals, patterns formed by one or more branches of activity in different federal states.

Article 362. - The membership of trade unions workers aged fourteen.

Article 363. - May not join unions as other workers , workers of confidence. The union constitutions may determine the status and rights of its members, who are promoted to a position of trust.

Article 364. - Unions must be constituted with twenty employees in active service or three patterns , at least. To determine the minimum number of workers will be considered those whose employment had been rescinded or terminated within the period of thirty days prior to the date of filing of the application for registration of the union and that it is granted.

Article 364 Bis. In the registration of trade unions shall observe the principles of legality, transparency , accuracy , generosity , directness , fairness and respect for freedom , autonomy, equity and union democracy.

Article 365. - Unions must register with the Ministry of Labor and Social Security in federal competition cases and the Conciliation and Arbitration in the local competition , for which submitted in duplicate:

I. An official copy of the minutes of the constituent assembly ;

II. A list of the number , names and addresses of its members and the names and addresses of the employers , companies or establishments in which services are provided ;

III. An official copy of the bylaws , and

IV. An official copy of the minutes of the meeting at which elected the board.

The documents referred to in the preceding sections shall be authorized by the Secretary General, Organization of records and , except as provided in the bylaws.

Article 365 Bis. The authorities referred to in the preceding article shall disclose , for consultation by any person , duly updated , information from the records of the unions. They must also issue copies of the documents held in the files of records requested them , in terms of Article 8. constitutional , as provided by the Federal Law of Transparency and Access to Public Government Information and the laws governing access to information from the federal government , as appropriate.

The full text of the public versions of the statutes in the unions should be available on the websites of the Ministry of Labor and Social Welfare and Local Boards of Conciliation and Arbitration , as appropriate.

Union records shall include at least the following information:

I. address ;

II. Registration number ;

III. Name of Union ;

IV. Name of the members of the Executive Committee ;

V. Effective Date of the Executive Committee ;

VI. Number of partners and

VII. Labor union to which they belong , in your case.

The index update should be done every three months.

Article 366. - Registration may be refused only:

I. If the union is not the purpose set out in Article 356 ;

II. If not set up with the number of members specified in Article 364 , and

III. If not present the documents referred to in Article 365.

Satisfied the requirements established for the registration of trade unions, none of the authorities concerned may refuse.

If the authority to which the application was filed registration does not resolve within a period of sixty calendar days , applicants may request it to give resolution , and if it does not within three days of the filing , it shall be done registration for all legal purposes , leaving the authority must , within three days , to issue the respective certificate.

Article 367. - The Ministry of Labor and Social Security, once you have registered a union, send a copy of the resolution to the Federal Conciliation and Arbitration.

Article 368. - The registration of the union and its directive , issued by the Ministry of Labour and Social or Local Boards of Conciliation and Arbitration effects with all authorities.

Article 369. - The union's registration may be canceled only:

I. In case of dissolution , and

II. By still having the legal requirements.

The Conciliation and Arbitration Board shall decide on the cancellation of its registration.

Article 370. - The unions are not subject to dissolution , suspension or cancellation of registration, by administrative means.

Article 371. The union constitutions contain:

I. Name that distinguishes from others;

II. address ;

III. Object ;

IV. Duration. Missing this provision shall be constituted the union indefinitely ;

V. Admission of members;

VI. Obligations and rights of partners;

VII. Grounds and procedures for expulsion and disciplinary measures. In cases of expulsion following rules shall be observed:

a) The workers' assembly will meet for the sole purpose of meeting the expulsion.

b) In the case of associations composed of sections , the expulsion proceedings will be conducted before the assembly of the section , but the decision to expel shall submit to the decision of the workers in each of the sections making up the union.

c) The employee concerned shall be heard in defense , in accordance with the provisions of the statutes.

d) The assembly shall know of the evidence on which to base the procedure and offering the victim.

e) Employees can not be represented and vote by writing.

f) The expulsion must be approved by a majority of two-thirds of all union members.

g) The expulsion may be ordered only by the cases expressly set forth in the statutes, duly verified and exactly applicable to the case ;

VIII. How to call a meeting , a time of celebration of the ordinary and quorum for meetings. In the event that the policy is not timely meetings convened under the statutes , workers representing thirty -three percent of all union members or section , at least , may apply to the directive convene the assembly, and if it does not within a period of ten days , applicants may make the call, in which case , so that the assembly can meet and adopt resolutions are required to attend two-thirds of total union members or section.

The resolutions must be adopted by the fifty-one percent of union members or section , at least ;

IX. Procedure for the election of directors and membership , safeguarding the free exercise of voting modalities to be agreed by the general meeting of indirect and secret vote or direct secret ballot ;

X. Duration of the policy ;

XI. Guidelines for the management , acquisition and disposition of property , property of the union ;

XII. Payment and amount of union dues ;

XIII. Time of submission of accounts and their managers sanctions for non-compliance.

For this purpose , it shall establish internal mechanisms and procedures to ensure the resolution of disputes between members, in connection with the management of union funds.

XIV. Standards for the settlement of trade union assets , and

XV. Other rules approved by the assembly.

Article 372. - Can not be part of the leadership of trade unions:

I. Workers under the age of sixteen , and

II. Foreigners.

Article 373. The leadership of trade unions , in the terms established in their statutes , shall submit to the Assembly every six months , at least , full and detailed account of the administration of trade union assets. Accountability will include the status of union dues income and other assets , as well as your destination.

The obligation referred to in the preceding paragraph is not dispensable.

At any time any worker shall have the right to request information from the board, on the administration of the estate of the union.

If workers have not received the information about the administration of trade union assets or deem the existence of irregularities in the management of union funds , can go to the authorities and procedures specified in the respective statutes , in terms of Article 371 , section XIII of this Act

If no such procedures or if exhausted these, not provided the information or clarifications may transact with the Board of Conciliation and Arbitration applicable, compliance with these obligations.

The exercise of the shares referred to above, by no means implies the loss of union rights is not grounds for expulsion or separation dissatisfied worker.

Article 374. - Legally constituted unions are legal persons and can accommodate:

I. Acquire property;

II. Acquire property immediately and directly for the object of their institution , and

III. Defender with all authorities exercising their rights and corresponding actions.

Article 375. - Unions represent their members in defense of individual rights which they are entitled , without prejudice to the right of workers to act or intervene directly , then stopping at the request of the worker, union intervention.

Article 376. - Union representation shall be exercised by the Secretary General or the person designated by the directive, unless special provision of the statutes.

The board members who are dismissed by the employer or who resign for reasons attributable to it, shall hold office except as provided in the bylaws.

Article 377. - The obligations of unions:

I. Provide reports required by the authorities they work , where they relate exclusively to his performance as unions ;

II. Notify the authority to which they are registered , within a period of ten days , your policy changes and amendments to the statutes, accompanied by a certified copy duplicate of the respective acts , and

III. Inform the same authority every three months , at least , of the ups and downs of its members.

The obligations under this Article may be served by electronic means , in the terms specified by the authorities.

Article 378. - Unions are prohibited from:

I. Intervene in religious matters , and

II. Exercising in trade for profit.

Article 379. - The unions will dissolve:

I. By a vote of two-thirds of the members belonging to them , and

II. On expiry of the term fixed in the statutes.

Article 380. - In case of dissolution of the union, the asset shall be applied in the manner to its statutes. In the absence of specific provisions , will the federation or confederation to which it belongs and if none, the Social Security Institute.

Article 381. - Unions may form federations and confederations, will be governed by the provisions of this chapter , as applicable.

Article 382. - The members of federations or confederations may withdraw them at any time, even if there is agreement to the contrary.

Article 383. - The statutes of federations and confederations , regardless of the applicable requirements of Article 371 shall contain:

I. Name and address and those of its constituent members ;

II. Conditions of accession of new members, and

III. How their members are represented on the board and in assemblies.

Article 384. - The federations and confederations must register with the Ministry of Labor and Social Welfare.

It applies to federations and confederations as provided in the final paragraph of Article 366.

Article 385. - For purposes of the preceding article , federations and confederations submitted in duplicate:

I. An official copy of the minutes of the constituent assembly ;

II. A list with the names and addresses of its members ;

III. An official copy of the bylaws , and

IV. An official copy of the minutes of the meeting at which the board is elected.

The documentation shall be permitted in accordance with the provisions of the final paragraph of Article 365.

CHAPTER III COLLECTIVE BARGAINING AGREEMENT

Article 386. - Collective Bargaining Agreement is an agreement between one or more trade unions and one or more employers, or one or more unions of employers , in order to establish the conditions under which the work must be paid in one or more companies or establishments.

Article 387. - The employer who employs workers union members will celebrate with this obligation , when requested by a collective agreement.

If the employer refuses to sign the contract , the workers may exercise the right to strike as stated in Article 450.

Article 388. - If within the same company there are several unions, the following rules shall be observed:

I. If you attend or industrial enterprise unions or each other , the collective agreement will take place with the one with more workers within the company ;

II. If you attend craft unions , the collective agreement will take place with all major trade unions representing the professions , provided they agree. Otherwise, each union held a collective agreement for their profession , and

III. If you attend craft unions and business or industry , will hold the first collective agreement for their profession , provided that the number of its members is greater than that of workers in the same profession as part of the company union or industry.

Article 389. - The loss of the majority referred to the previous article , declared by the Board of Conciliation and Arbitration , produces the ownership of the collective bargaining agreement.

Article 390. - The collective bargaining agreement shall be in writing , under penalty of nullity. It will triplicate , giving a copy to each of the parties and deposit the same in the Conciliation and Arbitration Board or the Federal or Local Board of Conciliation , which after noting the date and time of submission of the document send it to the Federal or Local Board of Conciliation and Arbitration.

The contract shall be effective from the date and time of submission of the document, unless the parties have agreed on a different date.

Article 391. - The collective contract shall contain:

I. The names and addresses of the parties ;

II. Companies and establishments covering ;

III. Its duration or expression to be indefinite or for particular work ;

IV. The working days ;

V. On rest days and holidays;

VI. The amount of wages ;

VII. The clauses relating to the education or training of employees in the company or establishments comprising ;

VIII. Arrangements for training or initial training to be taught to those who will join the company labor or establishment;

IX. The basis for the integration and operation of the committees to be integrated in accordance with this Act and,

X. Other stipulations agreed to by the parties.

Article 391 Bis. The Conciliation and Arbitration shall publish , for consultation by any person , the information from the collective bargaining agreements that are deposited with them. They shall forward copies of such documents, in terms of the provisions of the Federal Law of Transparency and Access to Public Government Information and the laws governing access to information from the federal government , as appropriate.

Preferably, the full text of the public versions of the collective bargaining agreements should be available free on the Internet sites of the Conciliation and Arbitration.

Article 392. - In collective agreements may establish joint committees organizing to fulfill certain social and economic functions. Its decisions shall be implemented by the Conciliation and Arbitration , where the parties declare them mandatory.

Article 393. - No collective agreement shall take effect the agreement to be missing wage determination. If missing the provisions on working hours, days off and holidays, will apply the laws.

Article 394. - The collective agreement may be concluded in conditions not less favorable to employees than those contained in existing contracts in the company or establishment.

Article 395. - In the collective agreement may provide that the employer admitted solely as workers who are members of the contracting union. This clause and any others established privileges on their behalf , may not be applied to the detriment of workers who are not part of the union and already serving in the company or establishment

prior to the date on which the union requested the conclusion or revision of the collective agreement and the inclusion therein of the exclusion clause.

(Repealed the second paragraph).

Article 396. - The provisions of the collective agreement extend to all persons employed in the undertaking or establishment , whether or not members of the union who has held , with the limitation contained in Article 184.

Article 397. - The collective contract for a fixed or indefinite , or for particular work, be revised in whole or in part, in accordance with Article 399.

Article 398. - In the revision of the collective will observe the following rules:

I. If held by a single labor union or by a single employer, either party may request a review ;

II. If held by various labor unions, the review will be provided to applicants representing fifty-one percent of all union members , at least , and

III. If held by various patterns , the review will be provided that applicants have fifty-one percent of all workers affected by the contract , at least.

Article 399. - The request for review must be made at least sixty days before:

I. The expiration of the collective agreement for a specified period , if this is not more than two years ;

II. The course of two years , if the term contract is longer , and

III. The course of two years , in the case of contracts for an indefinite period or for a specific task.

For the calculation of this term are concerned, the provisions of the contract and , failing that , to the date of deposit.

Article 399 Bis. - Notwithstanding the provisions of Article 399 , collective agreements may be reviewed each year in regard to cash wages daily rate.

The request for this review shall be made at least thirty days prior to the expiration of a year since the celebration, revision or extension of the collective agreement.

Article 400. - If none of the parties requested the review under Article 399 or not exercised the right to strike, the collective agreement shall be extended by a period equal to the duration or continue indefinitely.

Article 401. - The collective bargaining agreement ends:

I. By mutual consent;

II. On completion of the work , and

III. In cases of Chapter VIII of this Title , for closing the company or establishment , provided that in the latter case , the collective agreement is applied only in the establishment.

Article 402. - If signed a collective agreement , a pattern is separated from the union that it held , the contract will govern , however , that pattern relations with the union or unions of its workers.

Article 403. - In the case of dissolution of the trade union collective contract holder or termination thereof, working conditions remain in place in the company or establishment.

CHAPTER IV CONTRACT LAW

Article 404. - Contract- law is the agreement concluded between one or more trade unions and various patterns , or one or more unions of employers , in order to establish the conditions under which the work must be paid on a particular branch of industry , and made mandatory in one or more federal entities in one or several economic areas covering one or more of such entities , or across the country.

Article 405. - Contracts - law may be held for federal jurisdiction industries or local.

Article 406. - You can apply for a contract - law unions representing two-thirds of unionized workers , at least , of a branch of the industry in one or more federal entities in one or more economic areas , covering one or more of such banks or across the country.

Article 407. The application shall be submitted to the Ministry of Labor and Social Security, if it refers to two or more federal states or federal jurisdiction industries , or the Governor of the State or Territory or the Head of Government of the Federal District , in the case of industries local jurisdiction.

Article 408. - Applicants justify that satisfy the majority requirement referred to in Article 406.

Article 409. The Ministry of Labor and Social Security, the Governor of the State or Territory or the Head of Government of the Federal District , after verifying the majority requirement , if in its judgment is appropriate and beneficial for the contract industry - law, convene a convention to labor unions and employers that may be affected.

Article 410. - The call will be published in the Official Journal of the Federation or in the official newspaper of the federal entity and in newspapers or on the media that this is appropriate and indicate the place where the convention is to be held and the date and inaugural meeting time. The date of the meeting will be appointed within a period not less than thirty days.

Article 411. The convention will be chaired by the Secretary of Labor and Social Security, or the Governor of the State or Territory or the Head of the Federal District Government , or by the representative designated for that purpose.

The convention shall establish its rules and integrate the commissions it deems appropriate.

Article 412. - The contract - law shall:

I. The names and addresses of trade unions and employers who attended the convention;

II. Entity or Entities, the area or areas it covers or govern the expression of the whole country ;

III. Its duration , which may not exceed two years ;

IV. Working conditions specified in Article 391, Sections IV , V , VI and IX ;

V. The rules under which they formulate plans and programs for the implementation of training and training in the branch of industry concerned , and ,

VI. Other stipulations agreed to by the parties.

Article 413. - In the contract - law may establish the terms referred to in Article 395. Their implementation shall be the contract administrator - union law in each company.

Article 414. - The agreement must be approved by the majority of workers referred to in Article 406 and by most employers who have at your service the same majority of workers.

Approved the agreement in the preceding paragraph , the President or the Governor of the State or Territory , as published in the Official Journal of the Federation or in the official newspaper of the State, declaring contract - law in the field of industry considered , for all companies or establishments that exist or are established in the future in the Entity or Entities, in the area or areas or covering the entire national territory.

Article 415. - If the collective agreement has been concluded by a two-thirds majority of unionized workers given branch of industry, in one or more federal entities in one or several economic areas , or across the country, may be elevated to the status of contract - law after complying with the following requirements:

I. The application must be submitted by trade unions or by employers to the Ministry of Labor and Social Security, the Governor of the State or Territory or the Head of Government of the Federal District , in accordance with Article 407;

II. Labor unions and checked patterns that satisfy the majority requirement specified in Article 406;

III. The petitioners accompany your request copy of the contract and point the authority before it is deposited ;

IV. The authority receiving the application, after verifying the majority requirement , order its publication in the Official Journal of the Federation or in the official newspaper of the State, and shall specify a period of not less than fifteen days for oppositions may be filed ;

V. If no such application is made within the period specified in the notice, the President or the Governor of the State or Territory , declare mandatory contract - law in accordance with the provisions of Article 414 , and

VI. If within the period specified in the notice such application is made , the following rules shall be observed:

a) Workers and employers have a period of fifteen days to submit written comments , accompanied by the justifying evidence.

b) The President or the Governor of the State or Territory , taking into account the data of the file , declare the obligation of contract - law.

Article 416. - The contract - law shall take effect from the date of its publication in the Official Journal of the Federation, or in the official newspaper of the State, unless the convention point to a different date.

Article 417. - The contract - law shall apply notwithstanding anything to the contrary contained in the collective agreement that the company has held , except in those areas where these provisions are more favorable to the worker.

Article 418. - In each company , contract administration - law shall the union representing inside her as many workers. The loss of most declared by the Board of Conciliation and Arbitration of the administration occurs.

Article 419. - In reviewing the contract -law applies the following rules:

I. May request a review labor unions or patterns representing the majority referred to in Article 406;

II. The application shall be submitted to the Ministry of Labor and Social Security, the Governor of the State or Territory or the Head of Government of the Federal District , ninety days before the expiration of the contract - law , at least ;

III. The authority receiving the application, after verifying the majority requirement , convene labor unions and employers affected to a convention , governed by the provisions of Article 411 , and

IV. If labor unions and employers reach an agreement , the Ministry of Labor and Social Security, the Governor of the State or Territory or the Head of Government of the Federal District , order its publication in the Official Journal of the Federation or in the newspaper Federal official entity. The reforms will take effect from the day of its publication , unless the convention indicate a different date.

Article 419 Bis. - Contracts - law may be reviewed each year in regard to cash wages daily rate.

The application of this review must be at least sixty days before the expiry of a year since the date of the celebration takes effect , revision or extension of the contract - law.

Article 420. - If neither party requested a review or not exercised the right to strike , the contract - law was extended for a period equal to that which had been fixed for its duration.

Article 421. - The contract - law will end:

I. By mutual consent of the parties representing the majority referred to in Article 406 , and

II. If at the conclusion of the review process , labor unions and employers do not reach an agreement, unless those exercising the right to strike.

CHAPTER V INTERNAL LABOR REGULATION

Article 422. - Internal labor regulation is the set of mandatory provisions for workers and employers in the development of work in a company or establishment.

No matter the rules are the rules of technical and administrative companies formulate directly to the execution of the work.

Article 423. - The rules shall include:

I. Check in and departure of employees , time spent for meals and rest periods during the day ;

II. Place and when to begin and end the working day ;

III. Days and hours set for cleaning of facilities , machinery, equipment and working tools ;

IV. Days and places of payment ;

V. Standards for the use of chairs or seats referred to Article 132, section V ;

VI. Regulations to prevent occupational hazards and instructions for administering first aid ;

VII. Unhealthy and hazardous materials not be played by children and the protection of pregnant workers should have ;

VIII. Time and manner in which workers must undergo medical examinations , previous or recurring prophylactic measures dictated by the authorities ;

IX. Permits and licenses ;

X. Disciplinary rules and procedures for implementation. The suspension at work, as a disciplinary measure shall not exceed eight days. The employee is entitled to be heard before the punishment is applied , and

XI. The other rules necessary and appropriate in accordance with the nature of the undertaking or establishment for the safety and regularity in the development work.

Article 424. - In the formation of regulation following rules shall be observed:

I. Will be developed by a joint committee of representatives of the workers and the employer ;

II. If the parties agree , either party , within eight days of its signing , will deposit with the Board of Conciliation and Arbitration ;

III. Not produce any legal effect provisions contrary to this Law , its regulations, and collective agreements and contracts - law, and

IV. Workers or the employer , at any time, the Board may request the correction of omissions of the regulation or revise its provisions contrary to this Law and other labor standards.

Article 424 Bis. The Conciliation and Arbitration shall publish , for consultation by any person , the information of the internal labor regulations that are laid before them. They shall forward copies of such documents, in terms of the provisions of the Federal Law of Transparency and Access to Public Government Information and the laws governing access to information from the federal government , as appropriate.

Preferably, the full text of the public versions of the internal labor regulations shall be available for free on the Internet sites of the Conciliation and Arbitration.

Article 425. - The regulations shall take effect from the date of your deposit. Shall be printed and distributed among workers and set at the most visible of the establishment.

CHAPTER VI COLLECTIVE MODIFICATION OF WORKING CONDITIONS

Article 426. - Labor unions or employers may request the Arbitration Conciliation and changing working conditions contained in collective agreements or contracts - law:

I. When economic circumstances justify it , and

II. When the rising cost of living rise to an imbalance between capital and labor.

The application shall comply with the provisions of sections 398 and 419 , section I , and shall be processed in accordance with the provisions for disputes of an economic nature.

CHAPTER VII SUSPENSION COLLECTIVE LABOR RELATIONS

Article 427. - It causes temporary suspension of labor relations in an enterprise or establishment:

I. Force majeure or unforeseeable circumstances not attributable to the employer, or physical or mental disability or death , which occurs as a necessary consequence , immediate and direct , the suspension of work ;

II. The lack of raw materials , not attributable to the employer;

III. Excess production in relation to their economic conditions and market circumstances ;

IV. Inability to pay , temporary in nature , and manifest notorious exploitation ;

V. The lack of funds and the impossibility of obtaining normal for further work if it is found in full by the employer, and

VI. Failure by the state ministry of quantities is required to deliver to the companies with which they had contracted labor or services , provided that those are essential , and

VII. The work stoppage, or to declare the public health authority, in cases of health emergency.

Article 428. - The suspension can affect an entire company or facility or part thereof. It will consider the ranks of workers who are suspended effect the most junior.

Article 429. - In the cases referred to in Article 427, the following rules shall be observed:

I. If this is the section I , the employer or his representative shall give notice of the suspension to the Board of Conciliation and Arbitration for it , following the procedure set out in Article 892 and following , the approval or disapproval ;

II. If it's the fractions III to V , the pattern prior to the suspension , you must obtain permission from the Board of Conciliation and Arbitration , in accordance with the provisions for disputes of an economic nature , and

III. If it's the fractions II and VI , the pattern prior to the suspension , you must obtain permission from the Board of Conciliation and Arbitration , in accordance with the provisions of section 892 et seq.

IV. If this is the section VII , the employer does not require the approval or authorization of the Board of Conciliation and Arbitration and is obliged to pay its workers compensation equivalent to a day of general minimum wage for each day of the suspension , but may not exceed one month.

Article 430. - The Board of Conciliation and Arbitration , except for the cases referred to in Section VII of Article 427, to sanction or authorize suspension , fix the compensation to be paid to workers, taking into consideration, among other circumstances , the probable time of suspension of work and the possibility of finding new jobs, but may not exceed the amount of one month's salary.

Article 431. - The union and workers every six months may request the Board of Conciliation and Arbitration to check if exist the causes of the suspension. If the board finds that not subsist , fix a term not exceeding thirty days, for the resumption of the work. If the pattern is not resumed , workers are entitled to the compensation specified in Article 50.

Article 432. - The employer must announce every opportunity the date of resumption of work. Give notice to the union , and called by the media that are appropriate in the judgment of the Board of Conciliation and Arbitration , workers who served in the company when the suspension was ordered , and is obliged to replace them in the positions they held above, wherever they occur within the time specified by the same pattern , which may not be less than thirty days from the date of the last appeal.

If the employer does not meet the obligations contained in the preceding paragraph, the workers may bring an action referred to in Article 48.

The provisions of this Article shall not apply in the case referred to Section VII of Article 427. In this course , workers will be forced to resume work as soon conclude the contingency.

CHAPTER VIII TERMINATION OF COLLECTIVE LABOR RELATIONS

Article 433. - The termination of labor relations following the closure of establishments or undertakings or permanent reduction of their work , be subject to the provisions of the following articles.

Article 434. - Are grounds for termination of labor relations:

I. Force majeure or unforeseeable circumstances not attributable to the employer, or physical or mental disability or death , which occurs as a necessary consequence , immediate and direct , the completion of the work ;

II. Inability to pay notorious and manifest exploitation ;

III. The depletion of the subject matter of an extractive industry ;

IV. Article 38 cases , and

V. The contest legally declared bankrupt or if the competent authority or the creditors resolve the decommissioning of the company or the permanent reduction of their work.

Article 435. - In the cases mentioned in the previous article, the following rules shall be observed:

I. If it's the fractions I and V , be given notice of termination to the Board of Conciliation and Arbitration for it , following the procedure set out in Article 892 and following , the approval or disapproval ;

II. If it is the fraction III , the pattern prior to the termination, you must obtain permission from the Board of Conciliation and Arbitration , in accordance with the provisions of Article 892 and following , and

III. If it is the fraction II , the pattern prior to the termination, you must obtain permission from the Board of Conciliation and Arbitration , in accordance with the provisions for disputes of an economic nature.

Article 436. - In cases of termination of the work referred to in Article 434, except the section IV , a worker is entitled to compensation of three months' salary , and receive seniority premiums referred to in Article 162.

Article 437. - In the case of reduction of work in a company or institution will take into consideration the ranks of workers , in order to be adjusted the most junior.

Article 438. - If the pattern resumed business activities or creates a similar , shall have the obligations set out in Article 154.

The provisions of the preceding paragraph applies in the case of resuming the work of the company declared in a state of insolvency or bankruptcy.

Article 439. - In the case of the introduction of machinery or new working procedures , which , leading to the downsizing, the absence of agreement , the employer must obtain the approval of the Board of Conciliation and Arbitration , in accordance with the provisions of section 892 et seq. Adjusted Workers are entitled to a compensation of four months' salary , plus twenty days for each year of service or the amount stipulated in labor contracts if more and seniority premiums referred to in Article 162.

TITLE VIII STRIKES

CHAPTER I GENERAL PROVISIONS

Article 440. - A strike is a temporary suspension of work carried out by a coalition of workers.

Article 441. - For the purposes of this Title , labor unions are permanent coalitions.

Article 442. - The strike can include a company or one or more of its establishments.

Article 443. - The strike should be limited to the mere act of suspension of work.

Article 444. - Strike is legal if it meets the requirements and pursues the objectives set out in Article 450.

Article 445. - A strike is illegal:

I. When most of the strikers engage in acts of violence against persons or property , and

II. In time of war , when workers belong to establishments or services that depend on the government.

Article 446. - Strike justified is one whose motives are attributable to the employer.

Article 447. - The strike is legal cause for suspension of the effects of labor relations for as long as it lasts.

Article 448. - The exercise of the right to strike suspended the processing of disputes of an economic nature pending before the Board of Conciliation and Arbitration , and the applications filed , unless the workers to submit the dispute to the decision of the Board.

Not applicable as provided in the preceding paragraph when the strike is aimed at the specified in Article 450 , Section VI.

Article 449. - The Board of Conciliation and Arbitration and civil authorities must uphold the right to strike , giving workers the necessary guarantees and providing them the assistance they request to suspend the work.

CHAPTER II STRIKE OBJECTIVES AND PROCEDURES

Article 450. - The strike must be intended:

I. Striking a balance between the various factors of production, harmonizing the rights of labor with those of capital ;

II. Get the employer or employers holding the collective bargaining agreement and require the revision at the end of its validity period , in accordance with the provisions of Chapter III of Title VII ;

III. Get patterns the contract - law and demand its revision at the end of its validity period , in accordance with the provisions of Chapter IV of Title VII ;

IV. Enforce the collective bargaining agreement or contract , law firms or establishments that have been violated ;

V. Enforcement of the laws on profit-sharing ;

VI. Support a strike whose purpose any of those listed in the previous sections , and

VII. Require the review of contractual wages referred to in Article 399 bis and 419 bis.

Article 451. - To suspend work requires:

I. That the strike is aimed at one or more of the above article pointing ;

II. The suspension is made by the majority of workers in the undertaking or establishment. The determination of the majority referred to this fraction as the cause may be made only to seek a declaration of non-existence of the strike , in accordance with Article 460, and in any case as a preliminary question to the suspension of work ; and

III. That previously met the requirements outlined in the following article:

Article 452. - (Repealed).

Article 453. - (Repealed).

Article 454. - (Repealed).

Article 455. - (Repealed).

Article 456. - (Repealed).

Article 457. - (Repealed).

Article 458. - (Repealed).

Article 459. - The strike is legally nonexistent if:

I. The suspension of the work is done by a number of workers than those laid down in Article 451 , Section II ;

II. There has been to one of those specified in Article 450 , and

III. Not met the requirements set out in Article 452.

Absence may not be declared a strike for reasons other than those mentioned in the previous sections.

Article 460. - (Repealed).

Article 461. - (Repealed).

Article 462. - (Repealed).

Article 463. - (Repealed).

Article 464. - (Repealed).

Article 465. - (Repealed).

Article 466. - Striking workers must continue to provide the following services:

I. Ships, aircraft , trains , buses and other vehicles that are in route , must continue to their point of destination , and

II. In hospitals , nursing homes , clinics and similar establishments continue the care of patients at the time of suspending the work until they can be transferred to another facility.

Article 467. - (Repealed).

Article 468. - (Repealed).

Article 469. - The strike will end:

I. By agreement between the striking workers and employers ;

II. If the pattern is flattened , at any time, to the requests contained in the letter of formal notice to strike and covers the salaries had not received workers;

III. For award of the person or committee that freely chosen by the parties , and

IV. For award of the Board of Conciliation and Arbitration if the striking workers submit the dispute to the decision.

Article 470. - (Repealed).

Article 471. - (Repealed).

TITLE NINE

Job Hazard

Article 472. - The provisions of this Title shall apply to all employment relationships , including special work with the limitation contained in Article 352.

Article 473. - Risks of jobs are accidents and diseases to which workers are exposed or in connection with the work.

Article 474. - Industrial accident injury is any organic or functional disturbance immediately or later , or death, suddenly produced exercise, or in connection with the work , regardless of place and time it is provided.

Are included in the above definition accidents that occur when moving the worker directly from home to the workplace and from this to that.

Article 475. Disease - work is any pathological condition resulting from the continued action of a cause whose origin or motive at work or in the environment in which the employee is obliged to provide services.

Article 475 Bis. - The employer is responsible for health and safety and risk prevention at work, under the provisions of this Act, its regulations and the Mexican official standards.

It is the obligation of workers observe preventive measures that establish safety and health regulations and official Mexican standards issued by the competent authorities , as well as patterns indicating risk prevention work.

Article 476. - Will be considered in any case working conditions which determine this Act and , where applicable, the update that made the Ministry of Labor and Social Welfare.

Article 477. - When the risks are made can produce:

I. Temporary disability ;

II. Permanent partial disability ;

III. Permanent total disability , and

IV. Death.

Article 478. - Temporary disability is the loss of faculties or aptitudes that partially or totally impossible for a person to perform the job for some time.

Article 479. - Permanent partial disability is the loss of faculty or ability of a person to work.

Article 480. - Permanent total disability is the loss of faculties or aptitudes of a person who makes it impossible to perform any work for the rest of his life.

Article 481. - The existence of previous states such as idiosyncrasies , flaws , dyscrasias , poisoning , or chronic disease , not a cause to decrease the degree of disability, or the benefits payable to the worker.

Article 482. - The subsequent consequences of workplace hazards will be considered in determining the degree of disability.

Article 483. - The compensation for occupational risks that produce disabilities , will be paid directly to the worker.

In cases of mental incapacity , tested before the Board, the compensation shall be paid to the person or persons, from those listed in Article 501, to whose care stay , in case of death of the worker , observe the provisions of Article 115.

Article 484. - To determine the compensation referred to in this Title , shall be based on the daily wage received by the worker to occur and increases the risk that apply to employment after he held , pending determination of the degree of disability , the date on which the death occurs or he perceived at the time of separation from the company.

Article 485. - The amount taken as a basis for the payment of compensation shall not be less than the minimum wage.

Article 486. - To determine the compensation referred to in this title, if the wage paid to the worker exceeds twice the minimum wage of the geographic area corresponding application to the place of supply of labor, that amount will be considered as maximum wage. If the work is provided in different geographic locations of application, the maximum salary is twice the average of the respective minimum wages.

Article 487. - Workers who suffer an occupational hazard are entitled to:

I. Medical and surgical assistance ;

II. Rehabilitation ;

III. Hospitalization, when the case requires ;

IV. Medicines and healing ;

V. The prosthetic and orthopedic appliances needed , and

VI. The compensation set out in this Title.

Article 488. - The employer is exempt from the obligations determined in the previous article , where and in the manner following:

I. If the accident occurs in the worker being found intoxicated ;

II. If the accident occurs finding the worker under the influence of a narcotic or drug, unless there is a medical prescription and that the worker had put the matter to the attention of the employer and submitted the prescription signed by the physician ;

III. If the worker intentionally causes injury alone or according to another person , and

IV. If the disability is the result of some quarrel or attempted suicide.

The pattern is in any case obliged to provide first aid and care of the transfer to the employee's home or to a medical facility.

Article 489. - Does not release the employer of liability:

I. The worker had explicitly or implicitly assumed the risks of work;

II. If the accident occurs by clumsiness or negligence of the worker , and

III. If the accident is caused by carelessness or negligence of a fellow employee or a third person.

Article 490. - In cases of negligence on the employer , compensation shall be increased by up to twenty five percent , according to the Board of Conciliation and Arbitration. There inexcusable pattern:

I. Failure to follow the laws, regulations and those contained in the official Mexican standards for safety , health and working environment ;

II. If having made previous accidents , appropriate measures are not taken to prevent recurrence ;

III. If it fails to preventive measures recommended by the commissions created by workers and employers , or labor authorities ;

IV. If workers point out the pattern of their danger and it does not take adequate measures , and

V. Circumstances similar , of the same severity as those mentioned in the previous sections.

Article 491. - If the accident results in worker temporary disability , the compensation shall consist of full salary benefits of which as long as the inability to work. This payment will be made on the first day of disability.

If after three months into a disability worker is not in a position to return to work, he or the employer may request , in view of the respective medical certificates , the reports to surrender and pertinent evidence is resolved whether to continue subject to the same medical treatment and compensation to equal or be declared permanent disability compensation to which you are entitled. These tests may be repeated every three months. The worker shall receive his salary until declared permanent disability and to determine the compensation to which you are entitled.

Article 492. - If the accident results in worker with a permanent partial disability , compensation shall be paid the percentage that sets the table disabilities valuation , calculated on the amount which would be payable if it had been total permanent disability. It will take the percentage that corresponds between the maximum and the minimum set , taking into consideration the age of the worker, the importance of the disability and the greater or lesser ability to engage in gainful activity, similar to their profession or trade. It shall also consider whether the employer is concerned about worker retraining.

Article 493. - If partial disability is the absolute loss of the powers or abilities of the worker to perform his profession, Conciliation and Arbitration Board may increase the damages up to the amount of that corresponding total permanent disability , taking into consideration the importance of the profession and the ability to play a similar category , capable of causing similar incomes.

Article 494. - The employer is not required to pay an amount greater than that corresponding to the total permanent disability if they meet more than two disabilities.

Article 495. - If the accident results in permanent disability worker total compensation shall be an amount equal to the amount of one thousand ninety days' wages.

Article 496. - The compensation to be paid to the employee in cases of partial or total permanent disability , you will be paid intact , without making deduction of wages received by him during the period of temporary disability.

Article 497. - Within two years after it had been set the degree of disability , can the worker or the employer to request a review of the extent , if an attenuation or aggravation later.

Article 498. - The employer is required to replace in their employment to workers who suffered an employment injury , if trained , provided it is presented within the year following the date on which it was determined his disability.

Not applicable as provided in the preceding paragraph if the worker received compensation for permanent total disability.

Article 499. - If a worker victim of a risk can not do your job , but someone else, the employer is obliged to provide it , in accordance with the provisions of the collective bargaining agreement.

Article 500. - When the risk , leading to the death of the worker , compensation include:

I. Two months salary for funeral expenses , and

II. The payment of the amount fixed by Article 502.

Article 501. - Will be entitled to compensation in cases of death:

I. The widow or widower who was financially dependent on the working and have an inability to fifty percent or more , and children under sixteen and over this age if they have a disability of fifty percent or more ;

II. The ancestors concur with the persons mentioned in the preceding section , unless it is proved that no worker financially dependent ;

III. In the absence of a surviving spouse , concur with the persons mentioned in the two preceding sections , the person with whom the worker lived as his spouse during the five years immediately preceding his death , or with whom he had children , provided both marriage had remained free for concubinage.

IV. In the absence of a surviving spouse , children and ancestors , people who were dependent upon the employee will compete with the person who meets the requirements outlined in the previous section , in the proportion in which each depended on him , and

V. In the absence of the persons mentioned in the previous sections, the Mexican Social Security Institute.

Article 502. - In case of death of the employee, the compensation due to persons referred to in the preceding article shall be the amount equal to five thousand days of salary , without deducting the worker compensation received during the time he was subjected to temporary disability scheme.

Article 503. - For the payment of compensation in cases of death due to employment injury , the following rules shall be observed:

I. The Labour Inspector receives notice of death, or the Board of Conciliation and Arbitration before which claims payment of compensation, practicing sent within twenty-four hours of an investigation to find out what people financially dependent on the employee and order is fixed a notice in a conspicuous place of the establishment where provided services , calling on beneficiaries to appear before the Board of Conciliation and Arbitration , within thirty days , to exercise their rights;

II. If the worker's residence in the place of his death was less than six months , it will turn urge the Board of Conciliation and Arbitration or Labour Inspector of place of last residence , so that research and practice set the notice referred to in the previous section ;

III. The Board of Conciliation and Arbitration or Labour inspector , regardless of the notice referred to in Section I, may use advertising media they deem appropriate to call the beneficiaries;

IV. The Labour Inspector , terminating the investigation , refer the case to the Board of Conciliation and Arbitration ;

V. That the requirements specified in sections preceding and verified the nature of risk , the Board of Conciliation and Arbitration , after hearing the parties , shall issue a decision , determining which persons are entitled to compensation ;

VI. The Board of Conciliation and Arbitration appreciate the relationship of husband, wife, children and ancestors , without being subject to legal evidence proving the marriage or relationship , but you can not fail to recognize it settled in the vital records , and

VII. The payment made in pursuance of the resolution of the Board of Conciliation and Arbitration frees the pattern of responsibility. People who submit to deduct their rights after the date on which payment had been verified , may deduct only its action against the beneficiaries who received it.

Article 504. - Employers have special obligations following:

I. Keep in the workplace medicines and healing material needed for first aid and train the staff to serve;

II. When you have to serve more than one hundred workers , establish a nursing endowed with healing medicines and necessary medical and surgical care. It will be staffed by competent personnel, under the direction of a surgeon. If this judgment can not be given due medical and surgical care , the employee will be transferred to the population or hospital where possible to take their healing ;

III. When you have to serve more than three hundred workers , install a hospital, medical and auxiliary personnel required;

IV. In agreement with workers , employers may contract with nursing homes or hospitals in the place that is the setting or at a distance that allows for fast and convenient transfer of workers to provide the services referred to the two previous sections ;

V. Give notice in writing or electronically to the Ministry of Labor and Social Welfare, the Labour Inspector and the Board of Conciliation and Arbitration within 72 hours of the accident occurring , providing the following information and items:

a) Name and address of the enterprise ;

b) Name and address of the worker , as well as his post or category and amount of his salary ;

c) Place and time of the accident, concise expression of facts;

d) Name and address of the persons who witnessed the accident , and ,

e) Location where the service or has provided care to the injured.

The Ministry of Labor and Social Security and the Social Security Institute shall exchange information permanently over ad of accidents presenting patterns and other statistical data necessary for the exercise of their statutory powers ; and

VI. As soon as it has knowledge of the death of a worker by workplace hazards , provide written notice to the authorities mentioned in the preceding section , providing in addition to the data and elements pointing this fraction , the name and address of the persons who may be entitled to compensation.

VII. (Repealed).

Article 505. - The Company doctors are appointed by employers. Workers may object to the appointment , stating the reasons for merge. In the event that the parties do not reach an agreement , resolve the Conciliation and Arbitration Board.

Article 506. - Doctors of the companies are required:

I. When performing the risk , to certify whether the employee is able to resume work ;

II. After the health care, certify whether the worker is able to resume work ;

III. In its opinion on the degree of disability , and

IV. In case of death , a death certificate issued.

Article 507. - The worker who refuses for cause receive medical and surgical care to provide the employer will not lose the rights granted under this Title.

Article 508. - The cause of death can be checked risk working with data that results from the autopsy , when you practice, or by any other means to determine it.

If an autopsy is performed , the intended beneficiaries may appoint a doctor to witness. They may also designate a physician who practices giving notice to the authority.

The employer may appoint a doctor to witness the autopsy.

Article 509. - In each company or facility will be organized health and safety committees as may be deemed necessary , composed of equal numbers of representatives of the workers and the employer , to investigate the causes of accidents and illnesses , propose measures to prevent and monitor compliance.

Article 510. - The fees referred to in the preceding article , shall be performed free within hours.

Article 511. - Labour Inspectors have the following specific powers and duties:

I. Monitor compliance with the laws and regulations on the prevention of occupational hazards and safety of the lives and health of workers;

II. Put on record special discover violations , and

III. Collaborate with workers and the pattern in the dissemination of health and safety standards , hygiene and sanitation.

Article 512. - The regulations of this Act and the instructions that the labor authorities issued based on them , will lay down the necessary measures to prevent occupational hazards and ensure that it is provided in a position to ensure the life and health of workers.

Article 512 -A. In order to assist in the design of national policy on safety , health and working environment , propose amendments and additions to the regulations and official Mexican standards in the field, and to study and recommend preventive measures to abate the risks in the workplace , will host the National Advisory Committee on Safety and Health at Work.

The commission shall be composed of representatives of the Ministries of Labour and Social Health , Interior , and Environment and Natural Resources , the Mexican Institute of Social Security , as well as those designated by the national organizations of workers and employers to convene the head of the Ministry of Labor and Social Welfare, who will have the capacity as Chairman of such Committee.

The Commission shall maintain ongoing communication with civil protection authorities , in order to design actions that will reduce or eliminate the loss of life , involvement of the production plant, the destruction of property , damage to the nature and disruption of essential functions of society, in the event of a natural disaster or human agents.

Section 512 -B. In each state will constitute a State Advisory Committee on Safety and Health at Work, whose purpose will be to assist in the definition of state policy on safety , health and working environment , propose amendments and additions to the regulations and Mexican official standards in the field, and to study and to propose preventive measures to abate the risks in the workplace established in their jurisdiction.

These State Advisory Committees shall be chaired by the Chief Executives of State and Government of the Federal District and its integration will include representatives of the Ministries of Labour and Social Health , Interior , and Environment and Natural Resources of

Mexican Social Security Institute , as well as those designated organizations of workers and employers to convene.

The representative of the Ministry of Labor and Social Security to the respective State Advisory Committee , shall act as Secretary thereof.

Section 512 - C. The organization of the National Advisory Committee on Safety and Health at Work and the State Advisory Committees and the Federal District Safety and Health at Work, will be identified in the regulations issued in terms of safety, health and environment working.

The inner workings of such Committees shall be fixed in each Commission Bylaws issued.

Article 512 - D. Employers must make the changes ordered by the labor authorities to adjust their premises , facilities or equipment to the provisions of this Act , its regulations or official Mexican standards on safety and health at work issuing the authorities. If the term to be granted for this purpose , there have been no changes , the Ministry of Labor and Social Welfare shall sanction the offending pattern , with higher sanction warning if the order does not meet the new deadline that be granted.

(Repealed the second paragraph).

(Repealed the third paragraph).

Article 512 - D Bis. In the case of the access restriction or limitation on the operation identified risk areas referred to in Article 541 , Section VI bis of this Law, the Ministry of Labour and Social after performing the analysis of the report that provision refers to and practice the steps it deems appropriate, decide within 72 hours whether to lift the restriction enacted or extended duration, even while correcting the irregularities that led to the suspension of activities , regardless of the imposition of the sanction appropriate for economic failure to comply with safety and health at work.

Within the period referred to in the preceding paragraph , the employer may indicate to the Secretariat as they deem appropriate and provide the evidence it deems relevant , which will be taken into account by the authority at the time to resolve.

Article 512 - D Ter. In the event that the amount determined by health authorities work stoppage during a health emergency declaration , the Ministry of Labour and Social order necessary measures to avoid affecting the health of workers, without prejudice to the imposition of appropriate sanctions and exercise of the powers of other authorities.

Section 512 -E. The Ministry of Labor and Social Welfare will establish the necessary coordination with the Ministry of Health and the Social Security Institute for the development of programs and the development of campaigns to prevent accidents and illnesses.

Article 512 -F. The authorities of the states auxiliarán to federal law enforcement in the promotion, implementation and monitoring of compliance with safety, health and working environment , in the case of companies or establishments in all other matters arising from the relations, are subject to local jurisdiction.

Such assistance shall be provided under the terms of Articles 527 -A and 529.

Article 512 -G. In the event that the workplaces are regulated by laws or regulations specialized in safety and health, the oversight applicable to other non-labor authorities , the Ministry of Labor and Social Security and the labor authorities of the entities states , according to the competence , will those assistants.

Article 513. - The Ministry of Labour and Social Welfare, prior opinion of the National Advisory Committee on Safety and Health at Work, updated tables of occupational diseases and permanent disabilities assessment of the risks arising from work , same as be published in the Official Journal of the Federation and shall be observed throughout the country.

WORK TABLE OF DISEASES

Pneumoconiosis and bronchopulmonary diseases caused by extraction of dust and fumes of animal, vegetable or mineral

1. Diseases due to the inhalation of dust from wool.

Workers in the textile industry and other handlers of this product.

Two. Diseases due to the inhalation of dust feather , horn , bone, horsehair , silk hair.

Mattress, manufacturers and haberdashery trimmings , and combing hair cutters , manufacture of brushes , brush , brush. Traces workers , butchers , meat packers.

Three. Diseases due to inhalation of wood dusts.

Carpenters , loggers, carpenters and workers in the paper industry.

April. tabacosis:

Diseases due to inhaling snuff powders.

Workers snuff industry.

May. Bagassosis: conditions due to inhalation of bagasse dust , as in the sugar industry.

Tolveros , sieves and bagaceros , workers in the paper industry and manufacture of fertilizers.

June. Suberosis: conditions due to inhalation of cork powder.

Workers cork.

July. Diseases due to the inhalation of dust grain , flour , hay , straw , jute , sisal and henequen.

Chargers , lighter , stevedores , gatherers , farmers, threshers , hat (straw hats) , packers , millers , bakers , workers hard fibers industries , furniture manufacturers , paper industry.

August. Byssinosis.

Workers yarn and cotton fabrics and other handlers of this product.

9. Canabiosis: conditions caused by inhaling dust from hemp.

Workers hemp industry.

10. Linosis: conditions caused by the inhalation of flax dust.

Workers linen industry.

11. Asthma printers (for gum arabic).

12. Anthracosis.

Mining (coal mines) , charcoal , blacksmiths , forgers , casters, stokers , soot and other workers exposed to inhalation of coal dust from coal, graphite and anthracite.

13. Siderosis.

Mining (iron mines) , smelters , polishers , welders , filers , turners and iron oxide handlers.

14. Calcinosis.

Workers handling calcium salts such as calcium sulfate and carbonate and the gypsum industry.

15. Baritosis.

Workers handling barium compounds , painters , paper industry and laboratories.

16. Estanosis.

Workers in the tin mines , furnaces and metal foundries , or rust.

17. Silicatosis.

Workers exposed to the vacuum of silicate powder (fuller's earth, clay , kaolin).

18. Diseases due to inhalation of synthetic abrasives:

Emery, carborundum , aloxite , used in the preparation of grinding , abrasive papers and polishing.

19. Silicosis.

Miners, Quarrymen , sandboxes , potters , stonemasons and rock, tunnels , roads and dams , polishing sandblasting , ceramics , cement , foundry , chemical and refractory products silica hold back.

20. Asbetosis or asbestosis.

Miners (asbestos mine) , masons , in the textile , paper , cement , insulation coating material heat and electricity.

21. Berylliosis or gluciniosis.

Diseases due to the inhalation of beryllium or beryllium dust.

Miners (beryllium mine) , and manipulate workers producing alloys for X -ray machines , electrical and aerospace industry , welding , brick oven , fluorescent and nuclear industry.

22. Conditions due to cadmium dust inhalation.

Miners , smelter workers , preparation of alloys in dentistry , photoelectric industry , telephone , coloring , glass , accumulators and welders.

23. Conditions due to dust inhalation vanadium.

Mining , oil , foundry workers, steel industry , chemical , photographic , pharmaceutical, insecticides and while cleaning mineral oil fired furnaces.

24. Diseases due to the inhalation of powders of uranium.

Miners (uranium mine) , when exposed to the action of hexa - fluoride mineral separate.

25. Conditions due to dust inhalation manganese (manganésica pneumonia).

Miners (manganese mine) , manufacturing workers -manganese steel , welding of manganese steel and other uses.

26. Diseases due to cobalt dust inhalation.

Workers exposed to the vacuum of finely divided metal powders or mixed tungsten carbide.

27. Talcosis or steatosis.

Workers in the chemical industry and cosmetic talc or soapstone handle.

28. Lung aluminosis or aluminum.

Foundry , sprays and polishes aluminum , painters and pyrotechnic in mixed form , inhalation of alumina and silica (Shaver disease) in foundry workers bauxite and abrasives.

29. Diseases due to the inhalation of powdered mica.

Manufacture of refractory glass , insulating glasses, decorative papers , neon signs, varnishes , enamels , lubricants , explosives and ceramics.

30. Diseases due to the inhalation of land, diatoms (diatomaceous earth, diatomite , tripoli , diatomite).

Workers handling products in amorphous silicas , derived from skeletons of marine animals, in plants filter candles , insulating and absorbent powders.

Respiratory diseases caused by inhalation of gases and vapors

Conditions caused by inorganic or organic chemicals that determine action simple asphyxiant or irritant of the upper respiratory tract or lung irritant.

31. Asphyxiation by azote or nitrogen.

Workers working in oxidation processes in confined spaces , cleaning and repair of wells , production of ammonia and calcium cyanamide.

32. By carbon dioxide or carbon dioxide.

Workers exposed during combustion or fermentation of carbon compounds , gasification and preparing mineral water ice, diggers and letrineros.

33. By methane , ethane, propane and butane.

Workers in the petroleum industry, coal deposits , liquid gas , coke ovens and petrochemical industry.

34. For acetylene.

Workers engaged in the production and purification , handling carbide lamps , welders chemical and petrochemical industries.

35. Irritant action of the upper airway by ammonia.

Workers in the production of this substance and its compounds, distillation of coal , oil refineries and petrochemical industries , chemical operations , ice making and refrigeration , preparation of fertilizers for agriculture, letrineros , diggers , stampers , tanneries and stables.

36. For sulfur dioxide.

Workers from the combustion of sulfur , preparation of sulfur dioxide in gaseous and liquid sulfuric acid manufacturing , dyeing , bleaching , food preservation and fumigation , refrigeration , colored paper , stampers and mining (sulfur mine).

37. For formaldehyde and formaldehyde.

Workers in manufacturing synthetic resins, food industry , photographic , fur , textiles, chemicals , rubber , shark , laboratory work , maintenance of anatomical parts and embalmer.

38. By aldehydes, acridine , acrolein, furfural, methyl acetate, methyl formate, selenium compounds , sulfur chloride, and styrene.

Workers in the chemical, petrochemical and handling of these compounds.

39. Irritant action on the lungs , by chlorine.

Workers in the preparation of chlorine and chlorinated compounds , bleaching and disinfecting , in textile and paper industry , water sterilization, and chemical manufacturing.

40. The carbonyl chloride or phosgene.

Workers in the manufacturing of dyes and other synthetic chemicals, combat gases , fire extinguishers.

41. For oxides of nitrogen or nitrous vapors.

Workers in the manufacturing and handling of nitric acid and nitrates , stampers , engravers, chemical and pharmaceutical industries , petrochemicals , explosives , synthetic dyes , welding, nitrate fertilizers and silos.

42. By sulfuric anhydride.

Workers sulfuric acid manufacture , oil refineries and chemical synthesis.

43. By ozone.

Workers using this agent in the production of peroxide and the tuning of oils, fats , flour , starch , sugar and textiles in laundering and sterilization of water in the electrical industry and in welding.

44. By bromine.

Workers handling bromine as a disinfectant , laboratory chemicals, metallurgy, chemical and pharmaceutical industry , photography and dyes.

45. By fluorine and their compounds.

Workers who handle these substances in the glass industry , engraving, silk dyeing , wood varnishing , bleaching , welding and as cement waterproofing , preparation of hydrofluoric acid , aluminum metallurgy beryllium , superphosphate and compound preparation of insecticides and rodenticides.

46. By methyl sulfate.

Workers handling this compound in various industrial operations.

47. Bronchial asthma alkaloids dichloride and diethyl ether , and poly- isocyanates of toluene diisocyanate.

Workers in the chemical, pharmaceutical , rubber , plastics and coatings.

Skin disease

Skin diseases (excluding those due to ionizing radiation) caused by mechanical factors , physical , organic or inorganic chemicals , or biological , that act as primary irritants or sensitizers , or cause chemical burns , which are generally in the forms erythematous , edematous , vesicular , eczematous or crusty

48. Dermatosis by heat.

Herreros , smelters , boilermakers , firemen , bakers , glass workers , bakers.

49. Dermatoses from exposure to low temperatures.

Workers of cold , ice manufacturing and handling and chilled products.

50. Dermatosis action of sunlight and ultraviolet rays.

Outdoor workers , salt workers , film artists , welders , glassmakers , physiotherapy cabinets , etc..

51. Dermatoses caused by hydrochloric, sulfuric, nitric, hydrofluoric , fluosilicic chlorosulfonic.

Workers manufacture of chlorine and chlorinated organics (chloracne), fatty acids, bleaching , chemical industry, handling and preparation of sulfuric acid manufacture, handling and use of hydrofluoric acid in the oil and petrochemical industries , glass etching , ceramics , laboratory equipment.

52. Dermatosis per share of caustic soda, potassium hydroxide and sodium carbonate.

Workers engaged in the production and handling of these alkalis.

53. Dermatoses , cutaneous ulceration and perforation of the nasal septum and bichromates chromate action.

Factory workers chrome dye , wallpaper , crayons , fuses , explosives , gunpowder piroxilada hunting , Swedish matches , in the textile , rubber , tanneries , dyeing , photography, photo- and electrolytic chrome.

54. Dermatosis and arsenical keratosis , nasal septum perforation.

Arsenic plant workers , dye industry , paint , colored paper , dyeing , tanning , ceramics , insecticides , rodenticides , household preparations and other handlers of arsenic.

55. Dermatosis per share of nickel and selenium oxychloride.

Smelter workers and various manipulations.

56. Dermatosis action of lime, or calcium oxide.

Workers handling lime, bleaching powder preparation , plaster, cement , chemical industry and construction workers.

57. Dermatosis action organic substances: acetic acid , oxalic acid , formic acid and derivatives phenol , cresol , dimethyl sulfate , methyl bromide , ethylene oxide , mercury fulminate , tetryl , phthalic anhydride trinitrotoluene , paraffin, tar, pitch , dinitro- benzene.

Workers of the manufacture and use of these substances (photosensitizing action of the last three).

58. Dermatosis benzol and other organic solvents.

Workers in the textile , rubber , shark , glass , chemicals , fertilizers , cement , linoleum , etc..

59. Dermatosis per share of lubricating oils , cutting (oil or elaioconiosis button) , crude oil.

Workers who use these products to work greasing, lubricating , degreasing, in the petroleum, petrochemical and derivatives.

60. Dermatosis hydrocarbon derivatives action: hexamethylene - tetramine, formaldehyde , calcium cyanamide, aniline , paraphenylene - diamine, dinitrochlorobenzene , etc. On workers using and handling these substances.

61. Calluses , fissures and cracks by mechanical action:

Chargers , lighter , stevedores , carters , spinners , combers and manipulators of fibers, hemp, wool , linen, etc.. ; Cane harvesters , vainilleros , gardeners , marble masons , blacksmiths , coopers, metal cutters , miners, masons , tailors , washerwomen , cooks, seamstresses , ironers , barbers , shoemakers , clerks , draftsmen , glaziers , carpenters , joiners , bakers , hatters , engravers , polishers , musicians, etc..

62. Dermatosis by biological agents.

Bakers , spice wheat and flour, barbers, tanners , shipyard workers parasitized grain handlers , penicillin and other drug compounds , etc..

63. Other skin. Contact dermatoses.

Handlers paintings, vegetable dyes , metal salts , cooks, dishwashers , laundry workers , miners, grocers , photographers , masons , carpenters, painters day , degreasers rag , fullers , manipulative oil and gasoline , bleach fabrics vapors through sulfur , wool spinners and collectors , doctors, nurses and laboratory.

64. Nail lesions and peringueales.

Onicodistrofias , onycholysis and paronychia exposure to solvents , moisture and trauma. Activities including the risk of exposure to these agents.

65. Other reaction type skin conditions not included in the previous groups , produced by organic chemicals (melanodermias , acromias , leucomelanodermias , lichen planus).

Activities including the risk of exposure to these agents.

Professional Eye

(Diseases of the eye caused by dust and other physical, chemical and biological)

66. Blefaroconiosis Powder (minerals, plants or animals).

Workers exposed to the action of these powders: masons , plasterers , miners , potters , grinders , grinders , polishers , cement , coal , manufacturers of aluminum and copper objects , mercury handlers , bakers , woolen , mattress makers , furriers , etc..

67. Contact Dermatitis and eczema eyelid eyelid. (Powders , gases and vapors from various origins).

Workers in the chemical- pharmaceutical , antibiotics and beauty products , petrochemical, plastics, rubber products and derivatives of para-phenylene diamine, tar , asphalt , solvents and varnishes, vanilla industry , champignon cultivation , carpenters , etc..

68. Conjunctivitis and keratoconjunctivitis (by physical agents (heat) or allergenic chemicals: ammonia, sulfur dioxide , formaldehyde , chlorine and derivatives, nitrous vapors , sulfuric acid , ozone , hydrogen sulfide, solvents and varnishes cellulose , tetrachloroethane , methyl alcohol, viscose, wool , feather , hair , pollen , cotton, wheat , peanuts , hops , snuff , mustard , vanilla , medicinal products , etc..) Blacksmiths , smelters , bakers , mills , tinsmiths , bakers , diggers , letrineros , artificial fiber workers from cellulose and other workers exposed to the action of hydrogen sulfide (hydrogen sulphide) and other agents mentioned.

69. Conjunctivitis and keratoconjunctivitis by radiation (actinic rays , infrared, short wave and X-rays). Salineros , film artists , welders , glassmakers , workers mercury incandescent lamps and exposed to ultra -violet solar workers arc lamps , mercury vapor lamps , ovens, welding, metallurgy, glassmaking , etc.. ; Radiologists and other workers in the manufacturing and handling of X -ray machines and other sources of radiant energy.

70. Pterygium. For permanent conjunctival irritation by mechanical factors (dust) physical (infra - red rays , caloric).

Herreros , smelters , bakers , mills , tinsmiths , and all workers with activities involving risk of exposure to these agents.

71. Queratoconiosis:

Embedding in the cornea of hard particles: (marble , stone , abrasive powders or metals).

All activities involving the risk of exposure to these agents.

72. Argyrosis eye. (Sales of silver).

Carvers , goldsmiths , polishers , silversmiths, glass beads manufacturers , chemical.

73. Radiation cataract. (Infra - red rays , caloric , short wavelength x-rays).

Glaziers, blacksmiths , foundry , technicians and workers Cabinet X-ray technicians and workers of atomic energy.

74. Cataract toxic. (Naphthalene and its derivatives).

All activities involving the risk of exposure to these agents.

75. Oculomotor palsy. (Carbon disulfide poisoning , lead).

All activities involving the risk of exposure to these agents.

76. Internal ophthalmoplegia. (Carbon disulfide poisoning).

All activities involving the risk of exposure these agents.

77. Retinitis , neuro - retinitis and chorio - retinitis. (Poisoning naphthalene , benzene).

All activities involving the risk of exposure to these agents.

78. Injury neuritis and trigeminal sensory branch (trichlorethylene poisoning).

All activities involving the risk of exposure to this agent.

79. Optic neuritis and amblyopia or amaurosis toxic (lead poisoning, carbon disulfide , benzene, trichlorethylene , carbon monoxide , methyl alcohol, nicotine , mercury).

All activities involving the risk of exposure to these agents.

80. Conjunctivitis pathogens.

Doctors and nurses in connection with the practice of his profession.

81. Electric ophthalmia and cataract.

Workers welding , electric furnaces or exposed to light voltaic arc during production , transport and distribution of electricity.

Poisoning

Diseases caused by absorption of dust, smoke , liquids , gases or vapors of chemical , organic or inorganic , for respiratory, digestive or skin.

82. Phosphorism and hydrogen phosphide poisoning.

Workers making phosphorus compounds or white phosphorus derivatives , catalysis in the petroleum industry, manufacturing phosphor bronze, insecticides , rodenticides , fungicidal , hydrogen phosphide , alloys and pyrotechnics.

83. Lead poisoning or lead intoxication.

Smelter workers lead, battery industry , ceramics , painters , plumbers , printers , boxes manufacturers preserves, toys , pipes, cable sheaths , welding , paints, white lead , varnish and lacquers , pigments , insecticides and other handlers lead and compounds.

84. Hydrargirism or mercurialism.

Miners (mercury mine) , handles the metal and its derivatives, manufacturers of thermometers , pressure gauges, mercury vapor lamps , felt hats , electrolysis of brine , seed conservation , fungicides , manufacture and handling of explosives and chemical-pharmaceutical industry.

85. Arsenicism and arseniado hydrogen poisoning.

Workers arsenic in plants , minerals and metals smelters , industry of dyes , paints , colored paper , dyeing , tanning , ceramics , insecticides , rodenticides , other household preparations and other handlers of Arsenic.

86. Manganesismo.

Miners (manganese mine) , crushers and metal handles , manufacturing steel alloys , copper or aluminum manufacturing dry batteries , in bleaching , dyeing and bleaching glass, welders.

87. Fever zinc smelters or tremor of welders of zinc.

Metal smelters and welders , galvanizing or tin , cast brass or galvanized metal welding.

88. Oxicarbonismo.

Workers in contact coal gas , producer gas , water gas , blast furnace , of internal combustion engines , furnaces and confined spaces , boilermakers , miners, firefighters and in all cases of incomplete combustion of coal.

89. Cyan poisoning.

Workers handling hydrocyanic acid , cyanide compounds , plants benefit from the extraction of gold and silver from their ores , smelters , photographers , producers of soda, textiles, chemical, synthetic rubber , plastics , metal heat treatment , fumigation, use of cyanogen and dyers in blue.

90. Poisoning by methyl, ethyl , propyl and butyl.

Workers using as solvents in the manufacture of paints and varnishes, in the preparation of essences and dyeing materials and chemical and petrochemical industries.

91. Hidrocarburismo by petroleum and coal tar.

Workers in the petroleum , petrochemical , coal , manufacture of perfumes and others exposed to the absorption of these substances.

92. Poisoning toluene and xylene.

Workers handling these solvents in the coatings industry , rubber , fur , gravure , manufacture of benzoic acid, benzylic aldehyde , dyes , explosives (TNT), paints and varnishes.

93. Intoxications methyl chloride and methylene chloride.

Workers using methyl chloride as a refrigerator or methylene chloride as a solvent , or in the paint industry.

94. Poisoning by chloroform, carbon tetrachloride and chloro- bromo- methane.

Workers who handle these substances as solvents , fumigants, refrigerants , fire extinguishers , etc..

95. Poisoning by methyl bromide and freon (halocarbon fluorinated derivatives).

Workers using as refrigerators , insecticides and fire extinguisher training.

96. Poisoning by the di - and tetra - chloroethylene chloroethane.

Workers who handle these substances as solvents for fats , oils , waxes , rubber , resins, lacquers dilution , degreasing wool and chemical industry.

97. Poisoning by the hexa - chloroethane.

Workers who use it to degrease aluminum and other metals.

98. Poisoning vinyl chloride or monocloretileno.

Workers in the manufacture of plastics and their use as refrigerator.

99. Poisoning the glycol mono- chlorohydrin.

Workers exposed during the manufacture of ethylene oxide and glycols , lacquer composition and handling of manure and fertilizers.

100. Poisoning by the tri - cloretileno and per - cloretileno.

Workers using these solvents in metallurgy, dry cleaners, in degreasing of metal and wool manufacturing polishes and paints.

101. Chlorinated insecticide poisoning.

Workers who manufacture or handle chlorinated aromatic derivatives as dichlorodiphenyl - trichloroethane (DDT) , aldrin , dieldrin and the like.

102. Poisoning by chlorinated naphthalenes and chlorinated biphenyls.

Workers using as electrical insulators.

103. Carbonismo sulfo.

Workers exposed during production or use of the solvent in the manufacture of rayon , cellophane, optical glass , rubber vulcanization cold as a pesticide and the extraction of fats and oils.

104. Sulfhidrismo or hydrogen sulphide poisoning.

Workers in the production of this substance , miners, aljiberos , albañaleros , oven cleaners , pipes , retorts and gas meters , gas lighting, vintners and rayon industry.

105. Poisoning diethylene dioxide (dioxane).

Workers using this solvent in the lacquer industry , lacquers , paints, inks , wax resins and plastics in histology tissue preparation.

106. Benzolismo.

Workers using benzene as a solvent in the rubber industry , waterproofing fabrics , nitrocellulose manufacturing , petrochemical , clothing , lacquer , glass , graphic arts , textiles , ceramics , paintings, gravure, footwear industry , dry cleaning, etc..

107. Poisoning by the tetra -hydro- furan.

Textile industry workers , who use it as solvent.

108. Aniline poisoning (anilismo) and compounds.

Workers in the chemical industry, dyes, inks and pharmaceuticals.

109. Poisoning by nitrobenzene , toluidine , xylidines.

Workers in the dye industry , paints, lacquers and manufacture of aniline.

110. Poison for trinitro - toluene and nitroglycerin.

Industry workers and handling of explosives.

111. Poisoning by lead tetra- acetate.

Workers in the manufacturing and handling of this antidetonante , fuel preparation , cleaning and welding of the containers containing them.

112. Poisoning by organo- phosphorus insecticides.

Workers in the production and handling of tetra -phosphate hexaetílico (TPHE) , tetraethyl pyrophosphate (HIPC) , parathion and derivatives.

113. Poisoning by dinitrophenol , dinitro - ortho-cresol , phenol and pentachlorophenol.

Workers using these compounds as fungicides and insecticides , in the manufacture of dyes , resins and preservation of wood.

114. Poisoning by benzidine , alpha- naphthylamine , beta- naphthylamine and diphenylamine.

Workers handling these substances in the rubber industry and dye manufacturing.

115. Intoxications carbamates, dithiocarbamates, clorofenoxihidroxicumarina derivatives , thallium, botanical insecticides.

Manufacture , formulation, packaging, transport and application of pesticides in general.

116. Pyridine poisoning , chlorpromazine and chemotherapy in general.

Workers engaged in the manufacture, formulation and packaging of these substances in the chemical-pharmaceutical industry.

117. Diseases caused by high-powered fuel.

(Boron hydrides , liquid oxygen , etc..).

Technicians and workers exposed in the preparation , control and management of these products.

Infections , parasitic , fungal and viral

Generalized or localized diseases caused by bacteria , parasites , fungi and viruses.

118. Anthrax.

Pastors, grooms , grooms, veterinarians, tanners , furriers , wool workers , ragpickers , handlers horsehair bristles , horns , meat and bones bovídeos , horses , sheep , goats, etc..

Workers traces and packers.

119. Glanders.

Horsemen , grooms , horse herders , veterinarians and veterinary nurses.

120. Tuberculosis.

Doctors, nurses , waiters amphitheater , housekeepers , personal biological and diagnostic laboratories , laundry staff in clinics, veterinarians, veterinary nurses , butchers and miners , when previously there silicosis.

121. Brucellosis.

Veterinarians, shepherds , butchers , farmers, milkers , dairy , laboratory technicians , plant personnel for the benefit of goat milk and cow , doctors, nurses , veterinary nurses.

122. Syphilis.

Glass Blowers (oral primary accident) physicians, nurses , waiters amphitheater (primary accident on the hands).

123. Tetanus.

Horsemen , butchers , grooms, keepers , veterinarians , agricultural industry personnel , gardeners.

124. Mycetoma and cutaneous actinomycosis.

Farm workers , bakers , millers, wheat , barley , oats and rye.

125. Hookworm.

Miners , brickmakers , potters , dumps , gardeners , sandboxes and tile manufacturers.

126. Leishmaniasis.

Chicle , rubber tappers , vainilleros , loggers in tropical regions.

127. Onchocerciasis.

Farmworkers coffee plantations.

128. Sporotrichosis.

Farmers, growers , packers soil and plants , grass and leather workers.

129. Candidiasis or moniliasis.

Fruit Bowls and workers who keep constantly wet hands or feet.

130. Histoplasmosis.

Workers guano extraction and manipulation.

131. Aspergillosis.

Animal breeders , fur cleaning and agricultural workers exposed to the fungus.

132. Coccidioidomycosis.

Workers guano extraction and manipulation , from uninfested areas or endemic , who are contracted to do work in areas infested or endemic.

133. Malaria.

Workers and peasants from uninfested areas or endemic , who are contracted to do work in areas infested or endemic.

134. Ricketsiosis. (Exanthematic typhus and similar).

Doctors , nurses, cleaning services infectious and Laboratories, provided that identify the causative agent in the patient and in the workplace.

135. Spirochaetosis. (Leptospirosis and the like).

Work performed in the sewers , mines , slaughterhouses , on Removal , laboratories and animal care.

136. Virus (hepatitis , enterovirus , rabies , psittacosis , pneumonia virus , infectious mononucleosis, polio and other).

Doctors, nurses and cleaning staff in hospitals and sanatoriums , laboratory and clinical tests , blood bank staff , provided that identify the causative agent in the patient and in the workplace.

137. Erysipeloid.

Workers in contact with animals or their carcasses , animal hair , leather and other materials, rags and other waste , laundry staff in hospitals , personnel handling soiled or contaminated.

138. Toxoplasmosis.

Slaughterhouse workers.

Diseases caused by contact with organic

139. Synthetic hormones , diseases caused by specific activity of synthetic hormones , estrogen , androgen , etc..

Staff synthesized hormone products industries.

140. Diseases caused by exposure to antibiotics.

(Penicillin , streptomycin and other large or medium similar spectrum).

Workers engaged in the manufacture, formulation and packaging of these substances in the chemical-pharmaceutical industry.

Diseases caused by mechanical factors and variations of natural elements in the working environment

141. Bursitis hygroma.

Workers in those made repeated pressures as mining (coal mines and manganese) , chargers , lighter , stevedores and others in which there is pressure on certain joints (knees , elbows , shoulders).

142. Osteoarthritis and angioneurotic disorders (dead finger).

Workers using jackhammers, drills and similar tools mechanics , drillers , riveters, stone carvers , mills , blacksmiths , boilermakers , polishers foundry workers using hammers in footwear factories , etc..

143. Retraction of the palmar fascia or tendons of the fingers.

Ropers , polishers , engravers.

144. Deformations.

Workers who adopt awkward postures , shoemakers , turners , rice pickers , porters , tailors , stone cutters , miners, seamstresses , designers , carpenters , typists , ballet dancers , etc..

145. Atrophic rhinitis , atrophic pharyngitis , laryngitis and allergies atrophic elevated temperatures.

Workers smelters , furnaces , forges , glass, boilers , rolling , etc..

146. Congeladuras.

Workers exposed as the action required to freezing temperatures , refrigerators , ice makers , etc..

147. Sudden decompression sickness , oxygen toxicity and decompression sickness traumatic. Osteoarthritis late shoulder and hip.

Workers who work breathing air to higher than atmospheric pressure: divers , underwater work and the like.

148. Evil flyers, bends , ear and sinus baro - trauma.

Aeronauts under rarefied air atmosphere during flight at high altitudes.

149. Pulmonary emphysema.

Wind instrument players , glass blowers.

150. Complex vascular cutaneous leg prolonged standing position constant or prolonged march carrying heavy loads.

Typographical , dentists , nurses, operating room , hairdressers , mail carriers , clerks, waiters, policemen and other similar activities.

Diseases caused by ionizing radiation and electromagnetic (except cancer)

151. Workers in the nuclear industry , uranium mines and other radioactive metals (arsenic , nickel , cobalt , strontium , asbestos, beryllium, radium), treatment and metallurgy, nuclear reactors use radio - elements (scintigraphy , gamma and betaterapia , isotopes) , use of radiation generators (workers and X -ray technicians), radio , sonar , lasers, masser , etc.. , who have:

a) in skin, erythema , thermal burns or necrosis ;

b) eyes , cataracts ,

c) in the blood , abnormal blood forming organs , with leukopenia , thrombocytopenia, or anemia ;

d) bone sclerosis or necrosis ;

e) sexual glands , testicular disorders with impaired sperm production and infertility , ovarian disorders and malfunctions ovular with hormonal changes ;

f) genetic effects due to mutations of chromosomes or genes ;

g) premature aging with shortening of the average duration of life.

cancer

Malignant neoplastic diseases due to the action of carcinogenic industrial physical origin , or inorganic or organic chemical or radiation- diverse location.

152. Skin Cancer: workers exposed to the action of ultraviolet rays outdoors (farmers , sailors, fishermen , laborers) to X-rays , radioactive isotopes , radium and other radioactive elements , arsenic and its compounds; pitchblende derived products distillation of coal tar, pitch, asphalt , pyrene and dibenzo (cancer of the scrotum in chimney sweeps) , creosote products of the distillation of oil shale (shale lubricating oils , paraffin oils) , petroleum products (fuel oils , greasing , paraffin , tar oil).

153. Bronchopulmonary cancer.

Miners (of uranium mines , nickel).

Workers exposed to asbestos (pleural mesothelioma), workers who handle chromate dust , arsenic , beryllium.

154. Ethmoid cancer of the nasal cavities ;

Workers employed in the refining of nickel.

155. Various cancers.

Carcinomas (and papillomatosis) of the bladder in workers aromatic amines ; leukemias and osteosarcomas by radiation exposure ; leukosis benzene.

endogenous diseases

Conditions arising from industrial fatigue.

156. Hearing loss and deafness: workers exposed to noise and vibrations , as mills , metal shredders , weavers, and trocileros coneros , blacksmiths , riveters, telegraph , radio operators , telephone operators, pilots , weapons and ammunition testers.

157. Cramps: workers exposed to repetitive movements , such as telegraph , radio - telegraph , violinists , pianists, typists , clerks , secretaries , typewriters , adding machines management , etc..

158. Chronic laryngitis with lumps on the vocal cords: teachers, singers , broadcasters, theater actors , etc..

159. Tendo - roaring wrist synovitis: laborers , masons, shovelers , fitters , turners.

160. Nystagmus of miners (coal mines).

161. Neurosis:

Pilots , telephone and other similar activities.

Article 514. - The tables referred to in the preceding article shall be reviewed whenever it is deemed necessary and convenient for the country , where there are studies and research to justify it.

In any case, the Ministry of Labor and Social Welfare and the National Advisory Committee on Safety and Health at Work should take into account the progress and advances in occupational medicine and for that purpose may be helped of technicians and medical specialists to it requires , reporting to the Legislature.

Article 515. - The Ministry of Labour and Social carry out the necessary investigations and studies , so that the President can start before the Legislature the periodic adjustment of the tables referred to in Articles 513 and 514 to progress of Occupational Medicine.

PART TWELVE

prescription

Article 516. - Shares of work prescribed in one year from the day following the date on which the obligation becomes due , except that are listed in the following articles.

Article 517. - Prescribed in a month:

I. The actions of employers to dismiss employees , to discipline their faults and to make deductions in their salaries , and

II. The actions of workers to spread the work.

In cases of section I , prescription runs from , respectively , the day after the date on which it is aware of the cause of separation or failure , from the time probing for errors or losses or damage attributable to the worker , or from the date on which the debt is due.

In cases of Section II , prescription runs from the date on which it is aware of the cause of separation.

Article 518. - Prescribe in two months the actions of workers who are dismissed from work.

Prescription runs from the day following the date of separation.

Article 519. - Prescribe in two years:

I. The actions of workers to claim the payment of compensation for employment injury ;

II. The shares of the beneficiaries in case of death from workplace hazards , and

III. Actions to seek enforcement of awards of Conciliation and Arbitration and the agreements before them.

Prescription runs , respectively, from the time they are determined by the degree of incapacity for work , from the date of the worker's death , and from the day following that on which the award had been notified of the Board or approved agreement. Where the award imposes the obligation to reinstate , the employer may request the Board to set the worker a term not exceeding thirty days to return to work, apercibiéndolo that failure to do so may the employer to terminate the employment relationship.

Article 520. - The prescription can not start or run:

I. Against the mentally incapable , but when you have discerned his tutelage under the law , and

II. Against workers who joined the military service in wartime.

Article 521. - The prescription is interrupted:

I. By the mere filing of the complaint or any promotion to the Board of Conciliation and Arbitration , regardless of the date of notification. Does not prevent the disruption that the Board is incompetent , and

II. If the person to whom the prescription runs recognizes the right of the one against whom prescribed , orally , in writing or by indubitable facts.

Article 522. - For the purposes of limitation , the months are calculated by the number of days which they belong. The first day will be full , even when it is not , but the latter must be complete and when it is a holiday , no prescription shall complete but useful first met the following.

TITLE XI LABOUR AUTHORITIES AND SOCIAL SERVICES

CHAPTER I GENERAL PROVISIONS

Article 523. - The application of labor standards falls within their respective jurisdictions:

I. The Ministry of Labor and Social Welfare;

II. In the Ministries of Finance and Public Credit and Public Education ;

III. The authorities of the Federal States , and its Directorates or Departments of Labor ;

IV. The Office for the Protection of Labor;

V. The National Employment Service ;

VI. A labor inspection ;

VII. At the National Minimum Wage ;

VIII. A National Commission for Worker Participation in Corporate Income ;

IX. Is repealed ;

X. The Federal Board of Conciliation and Arbitration ;

XI. A Local Boards of Conciliation and Arbitration , and

XII. Accountability Al Jury.

Article 524. - The Ministry of Labour and Social Welfare and Labour Departments and Divisions have the powers assigned to them by their organic laws and labor standards.

Article 525. (Repealed).

Article 525 Bis. Federal and Local Boards of Conciliation and Arbitration shall, subject to the provisions applicable budget a Professional Civil Service for hiring, promotion , retention , performance evaluation , separation and retirement of public servants.

Article 526. - Compete at the Ministry of Finance and Public Credit, the intervention that marks the Title III , Chapter VIII , and the Secretariat of Public Education, the enforcement of the obligations imposed by this Act to employers in education and act in cooperation with the Ministry of Labor and Social Welfare , training and training of workers , according to the provisions of Chapter IV of this Title.

CHAPTER II CONSTITUTIONAL COMPETENCE OF THE LABOR AUTHORITIES

Article 527. - The application of labor standards applicable to federal authorities in the case of:

I. Industrial and service branches:

1. Textiles ;

Two. electrical ;

Three. film ;

April. Hulera ;

May. sugar ;

June. mining ;

July. Metal and Steel , covering the basic mineral exploitation , profit and casting them as well as obtaining metallic iron and steel all its forms and leagues and laminates thereof;

August. Of hydrocarbons;

9. Petrochemicals ;

10. cement ;

11. Calera ;

12. Automotive, including mechanical or electrical auto parts ;

13. Chemistry, including pharmaceutical chemistry and medicine ;

14. Pulp and paper ;

15. Oils and fats ;

16. Production of food , covering only the manufacture of which they are packed, canned or packaged or intended to do so ;

17. Elaboration of beverages that are packaged or canned or intended to do so ;

18. railroad ;

19. Basic timber comprising sawmill production and manufacture of plywood or wood bonded ;

20. Glass, so it only touches the manufacture of flat glass, plain or carved or glass containers ;

21. Tabacalera , which comprises the profit or manufacture of snuff , and

22. Banking and credit services.

II. Companies:

1. Those that are directly administered or distributed by the Federal Government ;

Two. Those operating under a contract, or federal grant and industries related to them. For purposes of this provision, is acting under federal concession companies that aimed at the management and operation of public or state property regularly and continuously, to the satisfaction of the collective interest , through any administrative issued by the federal government , and

Three. Those who perform work in federal or areas that are under federal jurisdiction in the territorial waters or in those within the exclusive economic zone of the Nation.

Also correspond to the application of federal labor standards in matters concerning conflicts involving two or more federal entities , collective agreements have been made mandatory in more than one federal entity , and employer obligations in matters of training and training of their workers and health and safety at workplaces.

Article 527 -A. - In the application of labor standards concerning the training and instruction of workers and those relating to health and safety at work, the authorities of the Federation shall be aided by local establishments for firms or that in other respects derived from labor relations, are subject to the jurisdiction of the latter.

Article 528. - For the purposes of point 2 of Section II of Article 527, are companies related the permanent and directly related to the development of specific products or providing services unit.

Article 529. - In cases not covered by Articles 527 and 528, the application of labor standards for the authorities of the Federal States.

In accordance with the provisions of Article 527- A, the authorities of the Federal States shall:

I. Make available to the Federal Executive Dependencies competent to implement this Act , the information that they request them to be in a position to perform their duties ;

II. Participate in the integration and operation of the respective State Advisory Council National Employment Service ;

III. Participate in the integration and operation of the State Advisory Committee for Safety and Health at Work ;

IV. Report to the Ministry of Labor and Social Welfare violations committed by employers on health and safety and training and training and participate in the implementation of the measures taken to punish such violations and to correct irregularities in companies or establishments subject to local jurisdiction ;

V. To assist the National Committee for Productivity and Training ;

VI. Assist in the completion of formalities relating to records of job skills and,

VII. After determining general or specific request of federal authorities , take such other steps as are necessary to assist them with the aspects concerning such determination or request.

CHAPTER III ATTORNEY TO DEFEND WORK

Article 530. - The office of the Defence Force has the following functions:

I. Represent or advise workers and their unions , whenever requested , before any authority in matters that relate to the application of labor standards ;

II. Invoke the ordinary and extraordinary coming to the defense of the employee or union , and

III. Propose to stakeholders amicable solutions for the settlement of their disputes and investigate the results in minutes allowed.

Article 530 Bis. For the performance of its functions , the Office for the Protection of Labor may cite employers or unions to compromise or conciliation boards , apercibiéndolos that failing to appear at such proceedings , they shall impose the measure of constraint referred to the fraction I of Article 731 of this Act

If the service requester is who attends not compromise or conciliation board , he shall be withdrawn its request without liability to the Attorney General, stating that unless there was good cause for not appearing.

Article 531. The Federal Public Defender's Office will be integrated with an Attorney General and the Deputy Prosecutors number which is necessary for the defense of the interests of workers. They are appointed by the Secretary of Labor and Social Welfare, by the Governors of the States or by the Head of Government of the Federal District.

Article 532. - The Attorney General shall meet the following requirements:

I. Being Mexican , of age and in full exercise of their rights ;

II. Having lawfully conferred degree of Bachelor of Laws and a professional practice of not less than three years ;

III. Studies have distinguished in labor law and social security ;

IV. Not being a minister of religion , and

V. Not have been convicted of an intentional crime punishable by imprisonment.

Article 533. The Deputy Prosecutors shall meet the requirements specified in sections I, IV and V of the previous article and hold a law degree or a degree in law and obtained the patent to practice.

Article 533 Bis. The legal staff of the Office is prevented from acting as a trustee , adviser or advocate particular employer in matters relating to work , while public servants are serving it.

Article 534. - The services provided by the Office of the Defense of Labor will be free.

Article 535. - Authorities are required to provide to the Office of Labor Defense , the data and reports required for the proper performance of their duties.

Article 536. - Regulations on the function , the manner of its exercise and duties of the Office for the Protection of Labour.

CHAPTER IV NATIONAL EMPLOYMENT SERVICE

Article 537. The National Employment Service have the following objectives:

I. Study and operation promote public policies that support the creation of jobs ;

II. Design mechanisms to promote and monitor the placement of workers;

III. Organize, promote and monitor policies , strategies and programs for training and the training of workers;

IV. Register the records of job skills ;

V. Linking occupational and vocational training to the demand of the productive sector ;

VI. Design, conduct and evaluate specific programs to generate employment opportunities for young and vulnerable groups , and

VII. Coordinate with relevant authorities and standards regime labor competency certification.

Article 538. The National Employment Service will be provided by the Ministry of Labor and Social Welfare , through the administrative units of the same , to the corresponding functions that fall under the terms of its Rules of Procedure.

Article 539. - In accordance with the provisions of article above and for the purposes of 537, the Ministry of Labor and Social Security are the following:

I. In promoting jobs:

a) To pursue studies to determine the causes of unemployment and underemployment of rural labor and urban ;

b) analyze the labor market permanently through the generation and processing of information to follow up on the dynamics of employment , unemployment and underemployment in the country ;

c) Develop and regularly update the National System of Occupations , in coordination with the Ministry of Education and other competent authorities ;

d) Promote coordination among labor market actors to improve employment opportunities ;

e) To prepare reports and formulate programs to boost employment in the country and ensure its implementation;

f) Guide training to areas with higher demand for labor;

g) Propose holding employment agreements between the Federation and the Federal States , and ,

h) In general, perform all the laws and regulations entrusted to the Ministry of Labor and Social Security in this area.

II. In terms of job placement:

a) To guide job seekers to vacancies offered by employers based on their training and skills ;

b) To authorize and record , as appropriate , the operation of private agencies engaged in the placement of persons;

c) Ensure that private entities referred to in the preceding paragraph , comply with the obligations provided for under this law , regulations and administrative provisions of the labor authorities ;

d) Participate in coordination with the Ministries of Interior , Finance and Foreign Affairs, within the scope of their powers , in the recruitment of nationals going to provide services abroad ;

e) Propose the conclusion of agreements on job placement , between the Federation and the Federal States , and ,

f) In general, perform all the laws and regulations entrusted to the Ministry of Labor and Social Security in this area.

III. In terms of training or training of employees

a) (Repealed).

b) Issue Calls to form National Committees Training , Training and Productivity in industrial branches or activities it deems appropriate, and to set the foundation for the integration and operation of such committees ;

c) To consider and , if appropriate , suggest, for each branch of industry or activity , issuance of general criteria suitable for plans and training programs and training , hearing the views of the National Training Committee , Training and Productivity corresponding ;

d) To authorize and record , in terms of Article 153- C , institutions , schools or specialized agencies, and independent instructors who wish to provide training , education or training to workers , supervise its proper performance and, in appropriate, revoke the authorization and cancel the registration granted ;

e) (Repealed).

f) Review and suggest the establishment of general systems that allow, enable or train workers according to the procedure of accession conventional referred to in Article 153 -B ;

g) Rule on the penalties to be imposed for violations of the rules contained in Chapter III of Title IV Bis ;

h) To coordinate with the Ministry of Education to suggest , promote and organize training plans or programs and job training and , where appropriate, to issue certificates in accordance with the provisions of this Law, the educational arrangements and other provisions in force, and

i) In general, perform all those laws and regulations entrusted to the Ministry of Labor and Social Security in this area.

IV. On the registration of certificates of job skills:

a) Establish records related records or trained skilled workers within each of the industries or activities , and

b) In general, perform all those laws and regulations grant to the Ministry of Labor and Social Security in this area.

V. In terms of linking labor and professional training with strategic demand of the productive sector , propose and implement mechanisms to link training with the priority areas for national and regional development , as well as those showing higher rates of demand.

VI. In the field of standardization and certification of competencies , together with the Ministry of Education and other federal authorities:

a) Determine the general guidelines applicable throughout the Republic to the definition of the knowledge , skills or skills certification susceptible , as well as corresponding assessment procedures. To establish these guidelines be established

procedures to consider the needs , proposals and opinions of the various productive sectors and

b) Establish a certification scheme , applicable throughout the Republic , pursuant to which it may prove knowledge , skills or abilities, intermediate or terminal partially and cumulative , requiring an individual to carry out a productive activity , regardless of how they were acquired.

Article 539 -A. For the fulfillment of their duties in relation to companies or facilities within industrial branches or activities of federal jurisdiction , the Ministry of Labor and Social Security will be advised by an Advisory Board of the National Employment Service , composed of representatives from the public , national organizations of workers and employers national organizations , at the rate of five members each , and their alternates.

By participating Public Sector one representative each from the Ministry of Labor and Social Welfare , the Ministry of Public Education of the Ministry of Economy , the Ministry of Energy , and the Mexican Social Security Institute.

The representatives of labor organizations and employers shall be appointed according to the bases issued by the Ministry of Labor and Social Welfare.

The Secretary of Labor and Social Security may be invited to participate in the Advisory Council National Employment Service , with voice but without vote , five people whose background and experience to make contributions in the field.

The Advisory Council will be chaired by the Secretary of Labor and Social Security, will serve as the official secretary thereof as determined by the head of the Secretariat itself and its operation is governed by the regulations issued by the Board.

Article 539- B. In the case of companies or establishments subject to local jurisdiction and to perform the activities to which contract sections III and IV of Article 539, the Ministry of Labor and Social Welfare Advisory Councils will be advised by State and Federal District Service Employment National.

State Advisory Councils and Federal District National Employment Service shall consist of the Governor of the respective Federal State or Head of Government of the Federal District , who shall preside , one representative each from the Ministry of Labor and Social Security of Ministry of Education and the Mexican Social Security Institute , three representatives of local workers ' organizations and three representatives of employers' organizations of the Institution. The representative of the Ministry of Labor and Social Welfare will act as Secretary.

The Ministry of Labor and Social Welfare and the Governor of the Bank appropriate Federal or Head of Government of the Federal District issued jointly the basis under which be designated representatives of workers and employers mentioned in the Advisory Councils and formulate , in effect , invitations required.

The Secretary of Labor and Social Welfare and the Governor of the Federal State or Head of Government of the Federal District , may be invited to participate in the Advisory Councils of State and Federal District of the National Employment Service , respectively , to three persons entitled to voice but without vote , which by their background and experience to make contributions in the field.

The Advisory Councils will be subject in regard to its internal operations , the rules that purpose by each.

Article 539- C. - Auxiliarán state labor authorities to the Ministry of Labor and Social Welfare, for the performance of their duties, in accordance with the provisions of articles 527 -A and 529.

Article 539- A. - The placement service workers will invariably be free for them and will be provided, depending on the rate of application of this Law, the Ministry of Labor and Social Welfare or by the competent authorities of the Federal States , in accordance with the provisions of section II of Article 539, in both cases.

Article 539- E. - May participate in the service referred to in the preceding article , other government agencies , educational institutions , trade union or employers' organizations , charities and other civil associations which are not for profit. In these cases , it made known to the Ministry of Labor and Social Welfare for recording and monitoring purposes and that is in a position to coordinate actions in this matter.

Article 539- F. - The authorizations for the operation of employment agencies , for profit , only be granted in exceptional cases, for hiring workers required to perform special tasks.

Such approval will be granted upon request, when in the opinion of the Ministry of Labour and Social justify service provision by private and once you meet the requirements for that purpose indicate. In these cases , according to the provisions of Article 539- D , the service should be free for the workers and the rates under which are rendered must be previously set by the Ministry of Labor and Social Welfare.

CHAPTER V LABOUR INSPECTION

Article 540. - The Labour Inspectorate has the following functions:

I. Monitor compliance with labor standards ;

II. Provide technical information and advice to workers and employers about the most effective way to meet the standards of work;

III. To inform the authority deficiencies and violations of labor standards to observe in companies and establishments ;

IV. Conduct studies and collect data that have been requested by it deems appropriate and to ensure harmonious relations between workers and employers , and

V. The other powers conferred by law.

Article 541. - Labour Inspectors have the following powers and duties:

I. Monitor compliance with labor standards , especially establishing the rights and obligations of workers and employers , for regulating the work of women and children, and preventive measures that determine workplace hazards , safety and hygiene;

II. Visit the companies and establishments during working hours , day or night , after identification ;

III. Interrogate, alone or before witnesses , workers and employers, on any matter relating to the application of labor standards ;

IV. Require the production of books, records or other documents that require labor standards ;

V. Suggest violations are corrected working conditions ;

VI. Provide for the elimination of the defects in the facilities and methods of work when they are in violation of work rules or a danger to the safety or health of workers;

VI Bis. Order , after consultation with the Federal Department of Labour Inspection , the adoption of security measures for immediate implementation in the event of imminent danger to life, health or safety of people. In this case , if they are authorized , the inspectors will order the restriction of access or limit the operation identified risk areas. In this course, must give a copy of the determination to the employer for legal purposes.

Within 24 hours , labor inspectors , under the strictest responsibility , will get a detailed report in writing to the Ministry of Labor and Social Security, with a copy to the employer.

VII. Examine the substances and materials used in companies and establishments in the case of hazardous work , and

VIII. The other function conferred by law.

Labour Inspectors shall comply promptly with the instructions given by their superiors in connection with the exercise of their functions.

Article 542. - Labour Inspectors have the following obligations:

I. Sign duly authorized credential , to the workers and employers ;

II. Periodically inspect companies and establishments ;

III. Practicing extraordinary inspections when required by their superiors or when they receive any complaint regarding violations of labor standards ;

IV. Lift each inspection certificate to practice , with the intervention of the workers and the employer , stating the deficiencies and violations of labor standards , give a copy to the parties who have intervened and turnarla to the appropriate authority , and

V. Other laws impose them.

Article 543. - The facts certified by the Labour Inspectors in the record to raise in the exercise of their functions, shall be considered certain until proven otherwise.

Article 544. - It is forbidden to labor inspectors:

I. Having direct or indirect interest in the companies or establishments subject to their supervision;

II. Disclose trade secrets and manufacturing processes and exploiting them to know in the exercise of its functions , and

III. Representing or sponsor to workers or employers in labor disputes.

Article 545. - The Labour Inspectorate shall comprise a Director-General and with the number of inspectors , men and women , which is deemed necessary for the fulfillment of the functions mentioned in Article 540. They are appointed by the Ministry of Labor and Social Security and by the Governments of the Federal States.

Article 546. - To be Labour Inspector is required:

I. Being Mexican , of age , and in full exercise of their rights ;

II. Have completed high school or its equivalent ;

III. Not belonging to organizations of workers or employers;

IV. Demonstrate sufficient knowledge of labor law and social security and have the necessary expertise to carry out its functions;

V. Not being a minister of religion , and

VI. Not have been convicted of an intentional crime punishable by imprisonment.

Article 547. - These are special liability causes of Labour inspectors:

I. Not practicing the inspections referred to in Article 542, Sections II and III ;

II. Seat false facts in the record to raise ;

III. The violation of the prohibitions referred to in Article 544 ;

IV. Receive directly or indirectly any gift of workers or employers ;

V. Failing to comply with orders from his superior , and

VI. Failure to report to the Attorney General , the negotiation pattern industrial, agricultural, mining , commercial or services that skip the payment or fails to pay the minimum wage to a worker at your service.

Article 548. - The penalties that may be imposed on Labour Inspectors , regardless of what they have criminal laws are:

I. reprimand;

II. Suspension for up to three months, and

III. Dismissal.

Article 549. - In imposing sanctions following rules shall be observed:

I. The Director General will practice an investigation after hearing the person concerned;

II. The Director -General may impose the sanctions provided for in the preceding article , sections I and II , and

III. Where in the opinion of the Director General the penalty is dismissal, shall report to the Secretary of Labor and Social Security, the Governor of the State or Territory or the Head of Government of the Federal District , for its decision.

Article 550. - Regulations on the function , the manner of its exercise and duties of the Labour Inspectorate.

CHAPTER VI NATIONAL COMMITTEE ON MINIMUM WAGE

Article 551. - The National Minimum Wage Committee will work with the President, the Council of Representatives and Technical Management.

Article 552. - The Chairman of the Committee shall be appointed by the President and shall meet the following requirements:

I. Being Mexican , over thirty -five years of age and in full exercise of their rights;

II. Owning lawfully conferred degree of Bachelor of Laws or economics ;

III. Studies have distinguished labor law and economic ;

IV. Not being a minister of religion , and

V. Not have been convicted of an intentional crime punishable by imprisonment.

Article 553. - The President of the National Minimum Wage has the duties and powers:

I. Submit to the Council of Representatives on an annual work plan prepared by the Technical Department ;

II. Meet with the Director and the Technical Advisers , once a month , at least , monitor the development of the work plan and carrying out investigations it deems appropriate complementary studies ;

III. Report periodically to the Secretary of Labor and Social Commission activities ;

IV. Quote and chair meetings of the Council of Representatives ;

V. Having the organization and monitor the functioning of the Consultative Committees of the National Commission ;

VI. Chairing the work of the Consultative Committees or designate , as appropriate , who should preside ;

VII. The other powers conferred by law.

Article 554. - The Council of Representatives shall comprise:

I. With the representation of the government, composed of the President of the Commission, which will also be the Chairman of the Board and government will vote , and two advisors , informative voice , appointed by the Secretary of Labor and Social Welfare ;

II. An equal number , not less than five nor more than fifteen , and alternate representatives of unionized workers and employers , appointed every four years in accordance with the notice to that effect issued by the Ministry of Labour and Social. If workers or employers do not make the appointment of their representatives , will make the same Ministry of Labor and Social Welfare, must fall on workers or employers , and

III. The Council of Representatives shall be composed of the first July of the relevant year , at the latest.

Article 555. - Representatives advisers referred to in Section I of the preceding article , shall meet the following requirements:

I. Being Mexican , over thirty years of age and in full exercise of their rights;

II. Owning lawfully conferred degree of Bachelor of Laws or economics ;

III. Not being a minister of religion , and

IV. Not have been convicted of an intentional crime punishable by imprisonment.

Article 556. - The representatives of workers and employers must meet the following requirements:

I. Being Mexican , over twenty years and be in full exercise of their rights;

II. Not being a minister of religion , and

III. Not have been convicted of an intentional crime punishable by imprisonment.

Article 557. - The Council of Representatives has the duties and powers:

I. To determine, in the first session , how they work and the frequency of meetings;

II. Approve the annual work plan of the Technical Department ;

III. Knowing the opinion formulated by the Technical and issue resolution in which determine or modify the geographic areas in which govern minimum wages. The resolution was published in the Official Journal of the Federation;

IV. Practice and conduct research and studies directly it deems appropriate and request the TM to conduct additional research and studies ;

V. Appoint one or more committees or technical research to practice or perform special studies ;

VI. Approve the creation of advisory committees of the National Commission and determine the basis for integration and operation.

VII. Determine the opinions formulated by the advisory committees at the end of their work ;

VIII. Fix general and occupational minimum wages , and

IX. The other powers conferred by law.

Article 558. - Technical Management will be integrated:

I. With a Director appointed by the Ministry of Labor and Social Security;

II. With the number of Technical Consultants to name his Department , and

III. An equal number , as determined by the Secretary of Labor and Social Welfare Assistant Technical Advisers appointed by the representatives of workers and employers. These advisers are entitled, under the Expenditure Budget of the Federation , just compensation to be paid to those appointed by the Ministry of Labor and Social Welfare.

Article 559. - The Assistant Technical Advisor designation referred to in section III of the previous article , is revocable at any time, at the request of fifty-one percent of workers or employers that would have. The request is forwarded to the Ministry of Labor and Social Security, which after checking the majority requirement , will the corresponding declaration. The request must contain the name and address of the person to hold the office.

Article 560. - The Director , Technical Advisors and Technical Advisors Assistant , shall meet the following requirements:

I. Being Mexican , over twenty years and be in full exercise of their rights;

II. Owning lawfully conferred degree of Bachelor of Laws or economics ;

III. Not being a minister of religion , and

IV. Not have been convicted of an intentional crime punishable by imprisonment.

Article 561. - Technical Management has the following powers and duties:

I. Perform technical studies necessary and appropriate to determine the division of the Republic into geographical areas , formulate an opinion and proposal to the Board of Representatives ;

II. Propose to the Board of Representatives amendments to the Division of the Republic in geographic areas and the integration of the same , provided that circumstances exist which justify ;

III. Practice research and conduct studies necessary and appropriate for the Council of Representatives to fix minimum wages ;

IV. Suggest fixing minimum wages professionals ;

V. Post regularly occurring fluctuations in prices and its impact on the cost of living to the main towns of the country ;

VI. Resolve , upon order of the President, the queries put to them in relation to price fluctuations and their impact on the purchasing power of wages ;

VII. Technical support and research work of Consultative Committees , and

VIII. The other powers conferred by law.

Article 562. - To meet the powers referred to in section III of the preceding article , the Technical Department shall:

I. Practice and conduct research and studies necessary and appropriate to determine , at least:

a) The overall economic situation of the country.

b) The most important changes are observed in various economic activities.

c) Changes in the cost of living per family.

d) The labor market conditions and wage structures.

II. Regularly conducting investigations and studies to determine:

a) The budget required for meeting the needs of each family following , among others: those of material, such as the room , household goods , food, clothing and transportation, the social and cultural nature , such as attendance at shows, sports , training assistance to schools , libraries and other cultural centers , and those related to parenting.

b) The conditions of life and work for minimum wage workers.

III. Order all kinds of reports and studies of official institutions , federal and state and individuals dealing with economic problems , such as research institutes, social and economic , trade unions , chambers of commerce, industry and other similar institutions ;

IV. To receive and consider the studies, reports and recommendations submitted to it by workers and employers , and

V. Prepare a report of the research and studies that have conducted and presented by workers and employers and consideration of the Council of Representatives.

Article 563. - The Technical Director has the duties and powers:

I. Coordinate the work of consultants ;

II. Report periodically to the President of the Commission and the Council of Representatives , the state of the work and suggest investigations are carried out and further research ;

III. Act as Secretary to the Board of Representatives , and

IV. Having , in agreement with the President of the National Commission , the timely integration Technical Secretariats of the Advisory Committees , and

V. The other powers conferred by law.

CHAPTER VII ADVISORY COMMITTEE OF THE NATIONAL COMMITTEE OF THE MINIMUM WAGE

Article 564. - The President of the National Commission shall, in each case , the basis for the organization and functioning of Advisory Committees.

Article 565. - The Advisory Committees will be formed in accordance with the following provisions:

I. With a president ;

II. With an equal number of representatives of workers and employers , not less than three nor more than five , appointed in accordance with the provisions of Chapter II of Title Thirteen of this Act;

III. With technical advisors and specialists deemed appropriate , appointed by the President of the National Commission , and

IV. With a Technical Secretariat.

Article 566. - The representatives of workers and employers must meet the requirements set out in Article 556.

Article 567. - The Advisory Committees shall have the following powers and duties:

I. Determine in the first session and work your way up the frequency of its meetings;

II. Approve the work plan formulated by the Technical Secretariat and request , as appropriate , conducting supplementary investigations and studies ;

III. Practicing and performing research directly relevant judge for the best performance of their duties ;

IV. Order directly , when deemed appropriate , reports and studies referred to in Article 562 , Section III ;

V. Solicit feedback from workers' organizations, and the general pattern of any public or private entity ;

VI. Receive suggestions and studies submitted to it by workers , employers and generally any public or private entity ;

VII. Allege all the elements they deem necessary and appropriate to fulfill its purpose ;

VIII. Issue a report containing the opinions and recommendations it deems relevant to their areas of competence , and

IX. The other function conferred by law.

Article 568. - The Chairman of the Advisory Committee shall have the duties and powers:

I. Quote and preside over the meetings of the Commission ;

II. Subject to the Advisory Committee Work Plan formulated by the Technical Secretariat and monitor their development;

III. Report periodically to the President of the National Commission , where appropriate, the development of the work of the Advisory Committee and to inform you of such termination ;

IV. Submit to the Council of Representatives through the Chairman of the National Commission the results of the work of the Advisory Committee , and

V. The other powers conferred by law.

Article 569. - The Technical Secretariat of the Advisory Committee shall have the duties and powers:

I. Practice and conduct research studies planned in the work plan approved by the Advisory Committee and subsequently entrusted to it;

II. Order all kinds of reports and studies of departments and official institutions and public and private entities related to the subject matter of his works ;

III. To receive and consider the studies, reports and recommendations submitted to it by workers and employers ;

IV. Cleave all other items as it deems necessary or appropriate ;

V. Prepare working papers and reports required by the Commission ;

VI. Prepare a final report shall contain the results of research and studies conducted and a summary of the suggestions and studies of workers and employers and consideration of the Advisory Committee , and

VII. The other powers conferred by law.

CHAPTER VIII PROCEEDINGS BEFORE THE NATIONAL COMMISSION OF MINIMUM WAGES

Article 570. - Minimum wages are fixed each year and shall take effect the first of January next year.

Minimum wages may be reviewed at any time during its term if economic circumstances warrant:

I. On the initiative of the Secretary of Labor and Social Welfare who make the President of the National Minimum Wage written request containing statement of facts justifying it , or

II. At the request of the trade unions , federations and confederations of workers or employers subject to compliance with the following requirements:

a) The application shall be submitted to the Ministry of Labor and Social Welfare by unions , federations and confederations representing fifty-one percent of unionized workers , at least , or by employers who have to serve at least Percentage of workers said.

b) The application shall contain a statement of the grounds on which the warrant and may be accompanied by studies and accompanying documents.

c) The Secretary of Labor and Social Welfare, within five days from the date of receipt of the request and upon certification of the majority referred to in paragraph a) of this section , it shall forward to the President of the National Commission on Minimum Wages with studios and accompanying documents.

Article 571. - In the setting of minimum wages referred to in the first paragraph of Article 570 the following rules shall be observed:

I. Workers and employers have a period that expires on the last of November to present the studies they deem appropriate ;

II. The Technical Director shall submit to the consideration of the Council of Representatives , to later on the last day of November, the report referred to in section V of Article 562 of this Law;

III. The Council of Representatives , during the month of December and before the last business day of the month, will make a decision on which set minimum wages , after studying the report of the Technical Department , and opinions, studies and research presented by workers and employers. For that purpose may make such investigations and studies directly as it sees fit and apply to the Technical information;

IV. The National Commission expressed in its resolution the grounds that the warrant , and

V. Rendered the resolution, the Chairman of the Commission shall order its publication in the Official Journal of the Federation which shall be made no later than December 31.

Article 572. - (Repealed).

Article 573. - In the revision of minimum wages to which the second paragraph of Article 570 of the Act shall be observed the following:

I. The Chairman of the National Commission , within three days from the date on which it received the request from the Secretary of Labor and Social Security, or if they have submitted the organizations of workers or employers, shall convene the Council of Representatives to consider the request and decide whether the grounds that support it are sufficient to initiate the review process. If the decision is in the affirmative order to the Technical Department to prepare a report to consider the movement of prices and their impact on the purchasing power of the minimum wage as well as the most significant of the national economic situation for the Council of Representatives to have the information necessary to review the current minimum wage and set , if any , which must be established. If your resolution is negative shall inform the Secretary of Labor and Social Welfare ;

II. The Technical Director will have a term of five days from the date on which he was instructed by the President of the National Commission for the report referred to in the preceding section and send it to the Council of Representatives through the President of the Commission;

III. The Council of Representatives , within three days from the date you receive the report of the Technical Department will issue the corresponding resolution setting , where appropriate, the minimum wages to be established ;

IV. The resolution of the National Commission set the due date for the beginning of the term of the new minimum wages to be fixed , which may not be later than ten days from the date of issue of the resolution , and

V. The President of the National Minimum Wage order the publication of the decision in the Official Journal of the Federation within three days of the date on which it is issued

Article 574. - In the procedures referred to in this Chapter shall observe the following rules:

I. So you can hold meetings the Council of Representatives of the National Commission will need to happen fifty-one percent of all of its members , at least ;

II. If one or more representatives of workers or employers no longer attend any session , alternates will be called if they do not attend the session for which they were called , the Chairman of the Committee shall report to the Secretary of Labor and Social Welfare to make the appointment of the person or persons who are to serve on the Commission to replace the truants ;

III. Decisions are taken by majority vote of the members present. In case of a tie , the vote of the absent will join to the President of the Commission , and

IV. Minutes of each meeting shall be drawn up , which will sign the President and Secretary.

CHAPTER IX NATIONAL COMMISSION FOR WORKER PARTICIPATION IN COMPANY PROFITS

Article 575. - The National Committee for Worker Participation in Corporate Income and work will be integrated to determine the appropriate percentage and revising it , in accordance with the provisions of this chapter.

Article 576. - The Commission will work with the President, the Council of Representatives and Technical Management.

Article 577. - The Chairman of the Committee shall be appointed by the President and shall meet the requirements specified in Article 552.

Article 578. - The President of the Commission has the following powers and duties:

I. Submit to the Council of Representatives the work plan by the TM , which should cover all studies and investigations necessary and appropriate to evaluate the general condition of the national economy ;

II. Meet with the Director and Technical Advisors , once a month , at least , and monitor the development of the work plan ;

III. Report periodically to the Secretary of Labor and Social Commission activities ;

IV. Quote and chair meetings of the Council of Representatives , and

V. The other powers conferred by law.

Article 579. - The Council of Representatives shall comprise:

I. With the representation of the government, composed of the President of the Commission, which will also be the Chairman of the Board and government will vote , and two advisors , informative voice , appointed by the Secretary of Labor and Social Welfare , and

II. An equal number , not less than two nor more than five , and alternate representatives of unionized workers and employers , appointed in accordance with the notice to that effect issued by the Ministry of Labor and Social Welfare. If workers and employers do not make the appointment of representatives , the same Secretariat will make the corresponding appointments , which must fall on workers or employers.

Article 580. - Representatives advisers referred to in Section I of the preceding article , shall meet the requirements specified in Article 555.

The representatives of workers and employers referred to in Section II of the preceding article , shall meet the requirements specified in Article 556.

Article 581. - The Council of Representatives has the duties and powers:

I. Determine , within fifteen days of its installation , the way they work and the frequency of sessions ,

II. Approve the work plan and request the Technical Department of the same conduct investigations and complementary studies ;

III. Practice and conduct research and studies directly as it deems advisable for the better performance of their duties ;

IV. Order directly , when deemed appropriate , reports and studies referred to in Article 584 , Section II ;

V. Solicit feedback from the associations of workers and employers ;

VI. Receive suggestions and studies submitted to it by workers and employers ;

VII. Appoint one or more committees or technicians to practice and conduct special studies research ;

VIII. Cleave all other items as it deems necessary or appropriate ;

IX. Identify and review the percentage that should pertain to workers in the profits of the firms, and

X. The other powers conferred by law.

Article 582. - Technical Management will be integrated:

I. With a Director appointed by the Ministry of Labor and Social Security;

II. With the number of technical advisors to name his Department , and

III. An equal number , as determined by the Secretary of Labor and Social Security, Assistant Technical Advisor , appointed by the representatives of workers and employers. These advisers are entitled, under the Expenditure Budget of the Federation , just compensation to be paid to those appointed by the Secretariat.

Article 583. - The Director , Technical Advisors and Technical Advisors Assistant , must meet the requirements set forth in Article 560. It applies to the auxiliary Advisors Article 559.

Article 584. - Technical Management has the following powers and duties:

I. Practice and conduct research studies in the plan of work approved by the Council of Representatives and later entrusted to it;

II. Order all kinds of reports and studies of official institutions , federal and specific state dealing with economic problems , such as research institutes, social and economic , trade unions , chambers of commerce, industry and other similar institutions.

III. To receive and consider the studies, reports and recommendations submitted to it by workers and employers ;

IV. Cleave all other items as it deems necessary or appropriate ;

V. Prepare a report must contain the results of research and studies conducted and a summary of the suggestions and studies of workers and employers and consideration of the Council of Representatives , and

VI. The other powers conferred by law.

Article 585. - The Technical Director has the duties and powers:

I. Coordinate the work of consultants ;

II. Report periodically to the President of the Commission and the Council of Representatives , the state of the work and suggest investigations are carried out and further research ;

III. Act as Secretary to the Board of Representatives , and

IV. The other powers conferred by law.

Article 586. - In the operation of the Commission applies the following rules:

I. The President shall publish a notice in the Official Journal , giving workers and employers a term of three months to submit suggestions and studies, accompanied by proofs and documents ;

II. The Commission shall have the period of eight months to develop the Technical Department work plan approved by the Council of Representatives and that it satisfies the powers enumerated in Article 581, sections III to VIII ;

III. The Council of Representatives shall issue its decision within one month ;

IV. The resolution expressed the fundamentals justify. The Council of Representatives shall take into consideration the provisions of Article 118, the report of the Technical , research and studies that have made and suggestions and studies submitted by workers and employers ;

V. The resolution shall fix the percentage to be workers correspond to taxable income , without any deduction or set differences between firms , and

VI. The President shall order the publication of the decision in the Official Journal of the Federation, within five days.

Article 587. - For the review of the percentage, the Commission will meet:

I. By invitation issued by the Secretary of Labor and Social Welfare, when there studies and research to justify it , and

II. At the request of the trade unions , federations and confederations of workers or employers, subject to compliance with the following requirements:

a) The application shall be submitted to the Ministry of Labor and Social Welfare by unions , federations or confederations representing fifty-one percent of unionized workers , at least , or by employers who have to serve that percentage of workers.

b) The application shall contain a statement of the reasons and rationale to justify it , accompanied by the studies and documents.

c) The Ministry of Labor and Social Welfare, within ninety days , check the condition of the majority.

d) Verified that requirement , the same Ministry , within thirty days , convene workers and employers for the election of their representatives.

Article 588. - In the review procedure applies the following rules:

I. The Council of Representatives will consider the application and decide whether the grounds that support it are sufficient to initiate the review process. If your resolution is negative , shall notify the Secretary of Labor and Social Welfare , dissolved , and

II. The powers and duties of the President , the Council of Representatives and Technical Management and operation of the Commission, shall comply with the provisions of this chapter.

Article 589. - The unions , federations and confederations of workers or employers, may not submit a new application for review , but after ten years of the date that had been discarded or taken on the application.

Article 590. - For the procedures in this Chapter shall follow the provisions contained in Article 574.

CHAPTER X FEDERAL CONCILIATION BOARDS

Article 591. (Repealed).

Article 592. (Repealed).

Article 593. (Repealed).

Article 594. (Repealed).

Article 595. (Repealed).

Article 596. (Repealed).

Article 597. (Repealed).

Article 598. (Repealed).

Article 599. (Repealed).

Article 600. (Repealed).

CHAPTER XI LOCAL BOARDS OF CONCILIATION

Article 601. (Repealed).

Article 602. (Repealed).

Article 603. (Repealed).

CHAPTER XII FEDERAL BOARD OF CONCILIATION AND ARBITRATION

Article 604. They correspond to the Federal Conciliation and Arbitration within the scope of their competence , knowledge and resolution of labor disputes that arise between workers and employers , only between those or just between them , arising from labor relations or of facts related to them.

Article 605. - The Board shall consist of a representative of the government and representatives of workers and employers nominated by branches of industry or other activities, in accordance with the classification and call issued by the Ministry of Labour and Social.

There will be a general secretary of agreements and , if necessary , other general secretaries and assistant secretaries , as deemed appropriate, in accordance with provisions in the Internal Regulations of the Board.

The appointment and removal of the legal staff of the Board shall be conducted according to regulations approved by the plenary on professional service career and performance evaluation of the Presidents of the Special Boards.

The Chairman of the Board shall be responsible for strict compliance with this rule and the applicable provisions.

Article 605 Bis. The general secretary shall act as secretary agreements plenary. It is responsible for formulating the agenda by the Chairman and lift the minutes of the meeting , which will be approved before completion.

The Secretary General shall assist the Chairman agreements in its own powers.

The general secretaries of the Board , pursuant to its powers, are responsible for organizing , monitoring and evaluating development, resolution and timely control and efficient procedures carried out in the Special Boards and areas responsible , tending to develop in accordance with the provisions of the applicable legal and performance evaluation of public servants referred to in Section I of Article 614 of this Law

The general secretaries , monitor processing procedures your competition through the Auxiliary and Assistant Secretaries assigned to them , who, under their responsibility, shall issue in due time and form, the appropriate resolutions to ensure continuity of the process.

In the Internal Regulations of the Federal Board of Conciliation and Arbitration was established powers and responsibilities.

Article 606. The Board will work in plenary or Special Meetings , in accordance with the classification of the branches of industry and of the activities referred to in Article 605.

The Ministry of Labor and Social Security, when required by the needs of the labor and capital , may establish Special Boards , fixing the place of residence and their territorial jurisdiction.

Special Meetings established outside the capital of the Republic under the preceding paragraph , will be integrated in legal operation and the Federal Board of Conciliation and Arbitration , accounting for the consideration and resolution of labor disputes in all branches of industry and activities of federal jurisdiction , including in the territorial jurisdiction assigned to them , with the exception of disputes, _ without prejudice to the right of the worker, when it is in its interest, to attend directly to the Federal Conciliation and Arbitration.

Article 607. - The Plenary will integrate with the Chairman of the Board and all the representatives of workers and employers to the Federal District Special Meetings.

The plenary sessions and resolutions shall be governed by the provisions of Article 615 of this Act

Article 608. - When a conflict involving two or more branches of industry or activities represented at the meeting , it will integrate with the President thereof and the respective representatives of workers and employers.

Article 609. - Special Meetings will be integrated:

I. With the President of the Board, in the case of disputes, or the Chairman of the Special Board in other cases , and

II. With the respective representatives of workers and employers.

Article 610. During the trial proceedings , to formulate the draft award referred to in Articles 885 and 916 of this Act, the President of the Federal Board of Conciliation and Arbitration and the Special Meetings may be replaced by assistants , but intervene voting in person at the following resolutions:

I. Competition;

II. Personality ;

III. Nullity proceedings;

IV. Substitution pattern ;

V. In the cases of Article 772 of this Act , and

VI. In the case of collective disputes of an economic nature , which designate the expert and ordering the conduct of proceedings referred to in Article 913.

Article 611. - In plenary and Special Meetings will be the number of assistants as deemed appropriate, in order that the administration of justice is expeditious work.

Article 612. The President of the Federal Conciliation and Arbitration shall be appointed by the President and shall meet the following requirements:

I. To be Mexican by birth who does not acquire another nationality , over thirty years and be in full possession and exercise of their civil and political rights ;

II. Having legally issued title attorney or law degree and have obtained from the competent authority to exercise the patent ;

III. Have five years of practice , after the date of acquisition of title referred to in the preceding section ;

IV. Having experience in the field and have distinguished in studies of labor law and social security ;

V. Not being a minister of religion , and

VI. Enjoy good reputation and not have been convicted of an intentional crime punishable by deprivation of liberty.

Perceptions of the President of the Federal Board of Conciliation and Arbitration shall be fixed annually , subject to the applicable legal provisions.

Article 613. - The Chairman of the Board will be replaced in his temporary absences and the final , meanwhile new appointment is made by the Secretary General of greater antiquity.

Article 614. The Plenum of the Federal Conciliation and Arbitration Board has the powers and duties:

I. Issue the Rules of Procedure and the rules of professional civil service and performance evaluation of the Presidents of the Special Boards ;

II. Hear and resolve labor disputes when they affect all branches of industry and the activities represented at the meeting ;

III. Knowing the appeal lodged against the decisions of the President of the Board in the enforcement of awards made in Plenary;

IV. Standardize the criteria for resolution of the Board, when the Special Boards sustain contradictory ;

V. (Repealed).

VI. Report to the Ministry of Labor and Social Welfare of the deficiencies observed in the functioning of the Board and suggest appropriate measures to correct issue , and

VII. The other powers conferred by law.

Article 615. To standardize the criteria for resolution of Special Meetings , the following rules shall be observed:

I. The House will meet in special session , unable to deal with any other matter ;

II. So you can hold meetings in plenary , it requires the presence of a majority of the representatives of workers and employers , respectively ;

III. The Presidents of the Special Boards in Mexico , will be summoned to the session and have voice information. The representatives of workers and employers and the Chairmen of the Special Boards located outside the Federal District may attend as guests at meetings; or formulate its proposals in writing , which are included in the appropriate agenda ;

IV. Plenary Resolutions must be approved by more than half of the members present ;

V. The decisions of the Parliament that the criterion uniformen resolution shall be binding on all Special Meetings ;

VI. The same decision may be reviewed at any time at the request of fifty- one percent of the representatives of workers or employers , fifty -one percent of the Chairmen of the Special Meeting or the Chairman of the Board , and

VII. The House will publish a newsletter every three months , at least , with uniform criteria and awards of the Plenary and Special Meetings as it deems advisable.

Article 616. - Special Meetings have the powers and duties:

I. Hear and resolve labor disputes that arise in the fields of industry or the activities represented in them ;

II. (Repealed).

III. Practice research and take the decisions referred to in Article 503 ;

IV. Knowing the appeal lodged against the decisions of the President on enforcement of awards ;

V. Keeping a copy of the collective agreements and internal labor regulations.

Enacted the deposit shall transmit the file to the file of the Board , and

VI. The other powers conferred by law.

Article 617. The President of the Federal Conciliation and Arbitration Board has the powers and duties:

I. Caring for the order and discipline of the staff of the Board;

II. Chairing the plenary;

III. Special Boards preside in cases of Articles 608 and 609 , section I;

IV. Run awards made by the Plenary and Special Meetings in the cases mentioned in the previous section ;

V. Review the actions of Actuaries in the enforcement of awards that corresponds run , at the request of either party ;

VI. Fill turnarlos rogatory or the Chairmen of the Special Boards ;

VII. Submit reports on injunctions brought against the awards and resolutions issued by the Plenary and Special Boards presiding ;

VIII. Hear and resolve of the precautionary measures to be promoted in industrial disputes ;

IX. Submit to Parliament regulations service career and performance evaluation of the Presidents of the Special Boards , and

X. The other powers conferred by the Laws.

Article 618. - The Presidents of the Special Boards have the following duties and powers:

I. Caring for the order and discipline of the Special Board staff ;

II. Sort the execution of the awards made by the Special Board ;

III. Hear and resolve precautionary measures ;

IV. Review the actions of Actuaries in the enforcement of awards and the precautionary measures at the request of either party ;

V. Complete the exhortations that are referred by the President of the Board;

VI. Submit reports to the protections that are filed against the rulings and decisions taken by the Special Board ;

VII. Report to the President of the Board of the deficiencies observed in performance and suggest appropriate measures to correct issue , and

VIII. Meet and successfully pass the performance evaluation procedures established in accordance with the respective regulations , and

IX. The other function conferred on the Laws.

Article 619. - The General Secretaries of the Board have the powers and duties:

I. Coordinate the integration and management of the Board to file their own responsibility;

II. Attest to the actions of the Board in the area of competence , and

III. Other than this Act conferring

Article 620. - For operation of the Plenary and Special Boards following rules shall be observed:

I. In the House requires the presence of the Chairman of the Board and a majority of the representatives of workers and employers , respectively. In case of a tie , the Chairman shall have a casting vote ;

II. In the Special Boards following rules shall be observed:

a) During the processing of individual disputes and collective legal nature , simply the presence of the Chairman or the Assistant , who will conduct the hearing, to completion.

If present one or more of the representatives , decisions are taken by majority vote.

If not present any of the representatives , the President or the Assistant shall make the orders to proceed , except in the case of which relate to personality , competence , acceptance testing , dismissal of the action referred to in Article 773 and replacing pattern. The President himself agreed to summon the representatives at a hearing for the resolution of such issues, if any concurs , issue the appropriate decision.

b) The hearing to discuss and vote on the award shall be governed by the provisions of the following fraction.

c) In the case of collective disputes of an economic nature , besides the President requires the presence of a representative , at least.

d) In cases of a tie, the vote of the absent or representatives will be added to the President or to the Auxiliary ;

III. For discussion and voting audience award will require the presence of the President or the President special and fifty percent of the representatives of workers and employers , at least. If you go less than fifty percent , the President may new day and

time for the hearing is held , if neither a majority, alternates will be cited , with the exception of business knowledge truants. If no alternates attend , the Chairman of the Board or the Special Board shall report to the Secretary of Labor and Social Security to designate the persons replacing. In case of a tie , the Chairman shall have a casting vote.

CHAPTER XIII LOCAL BOARDS OF CONCILIATION AND ARBITRATION

Article 621. - Local Boards of Conciliation and Arbitration work in each of the federal states. It is up the knowledge and resolution of labor disputes are not within the jurisdiction of the Federal Board of Conciliation and Arbitration.

Article 622. The Governor of the State or Head of Government of the Federal District , as required by the needs of labor and capital, may establish one or more Boards of Conciliation and Arbitration fixing the place of residence and their territorial jurisdiction.

Article 623. The plenary will integrate with the Chairman of the Board and representatives of workers and employers.

Integration and operation of Local Boards of Conciliation and Arbitration shall be governed by the provisions contained in the previous chapter. The powers of the President and the Secretary of Labor and Social Welfare shall be exercised by the Governors of the States and in the case of Mexico , by the President of the Republic and the Head of Government of the Federal District , respectively.

Article 624. Perceptions of the Chairmen of the Boards of Conciliation and Arbitration of the states and the Federal District shall be fixed annually , subject to the applicable legal provisions.

TITLE XII LEGAL STAFF OF THE CONCILIATION AND ARBITRATION

Article 625. The staff of the Conciliation and Arbitration shall be composed of actuaries , secretaries , officials conciliators , auxiliary , assistant secretaries , general secretaries and presidents of Special Board.

The Ministry of Labor and Social Welfare, the Governors of the Federal Government and the Head of the Federal District, determine the number of people that each Board should consist.

Article 626. - The Actuaries must meet the following requirements:

I. Being Mexican , seniors and be in full exercise of their rights;

II. Having legally issued title attorney or law degree and have obtained from the competent authority to exercise the patent ;

III. Studies have distinguished in labor law ;

IV. Not being a minister of religion , and

V. Enjoy good reputation and not have been convicted of an intentional crime punishable by imprisonment.

Article 627. - The Secretaries shall meet the following requirements:

I. Being Mexican , seniors and be in full exercise of their rights;

II. Having legally issued title attorney or law degree and have obtained from the competent authority to exercise the patent ;

III. Studies have distinguished in labor law ;

IV. Not being a minister of religion , and

V. Enjoy good reputation and not have been convicted of an intentional crime punishable by imprisonment.

Article 627 -A. The public service of reconciliation is provided through specialized public servants in the conciliation , officials called conciliatory , the members of the Boards or their legal staff.

Article 627- B. Officials conciliators must meet the following requirements:

I. Being Mexican , over thirty years old , and in full exercise of their rights ;

II. Having legally issued title attorney or law degree and have obtained from the competent authority to exercise the patent ;

III. Having two years of professional practice in the workplace, after obtaining a bachelor's degree in law, having distinguished himself in studies of labor law and have been trained on conciliation ;

IV. Not being a minister of religion , and

V. Not have been convicted of an intentional crime punishable by deprivation of liberty.

Article 627- C. Throughout the procedure and before the pronouncement of the awards , the Boards will be required to encourage the parties to resolve the disputes through conciliation. Agreements to arrive , if , once ratified and approved by them, produce legal effects inherent to execution against awards.

Article 628. - The Auxiliary shall meet the following requirements:

I. Being Mexican , over twenty years and be in full exercise of their rights;

II. Having legally issued title attorney or law degree and have obtained from the competent authority to exercise the patent ;

III. Having three years of professional practice in the workplace, after obtaining a law degree or law degree , and have excelled in labor law studies ;

IV. Not being a minister of religion , and

V. Enjoy good reputation and not have been convicted of an intentional crime punishable by imprisonment.

Article 629. The General Secretaries shall meet the requirements specified in sections I, II , IV and V of the preceding article , have five years of professional practice in the workplace, after obtaining a law degree or law degree , studies have distinguished labor law and minimum of one year experience as a public servant in the field of labor.

Article 630. The Special Board presidents and assistant secretaries shall meet the requirements outlined in the previous article.

Article 631. Perceptions of the Presidents of the Federal Special Boards of Conciliation and Arbitration shall be fixed annually , subject to the provisions applicable budget.

Article 632. The legal staff of the Boards shall not act as agent, adviser or advocate employer in labor matters.

Article 633. The Presidents of the Special Boards are appointed every six years by the Secretary of Labor and Social Welfare, by the Governor of State or Head of Government of the Federal District.

Article 634. The appointments of the Secretaries-General and Assistant Secretaries shall be deemed to be appointed, in regard to the functions and needs of the position.

Article 635. - The Presidents of the Special Boards will be replaced in his temporary absences and the final , meanwhile new appointment is made by the Assistant business that is considering.

Article 636. - The breach of the obligations of the legal staff of the Boards , which is not a ground for dismissal , is punishable by reprimand or suspension from office for up to three months.

Article 637. - In the imposition of penalties referred to in the preceding article applies the following rules:

I. The Chairman of the Board perform a research with the interested audience and impose the corresponding penalty to the actuaries , secretaries , assistants and officials conciliators , and

II. In the case of the general secretaries , assistant secretaries and chairmen of the Special Meeting , the Chairman of the Board shall report to the Secretary of Labor and Social Welfare, the State Governor or Head of Government of the Federal District , who , after hearing to interested dictate the corresponding resolution.

Article 638. - To impose sanctions shall consider the circumstances and background of the official.

Article 639. - The imposition of a sanction has the effect of inhibiting the official business knowledge that may have been at fault.

Article 640. - These are special faults of Actuaries:

I. No notifications pursuant to the provisions of this Act;

II. Not timely notify the parties, except for just cause ;

III. No timely practice proceedings , except for just cause ;

IV. To state false facts in the record to raise in the exercise of their functions;

V. No records returned immediately after practicing the steps , and

VI. Other established laws.

Article 641. - Special faults are the Secretaries:

I. Delaying the processing of a business without cause;

II. No account promptly to the Board of promotions ;

III. Do not give immediate notice to the President of the deposits made by the parties;

IV. Not authorize proceedings that do not intervene or certifications that are appropriate;

V. False facts attest ;

VI. Submit a file to the representatives of workers or employers , without demanding a receipt ;

VII. Require timely No representatives to sign the resolutions ;

VIII. Not timely inform the President of the events referred to in the preceding section ;

IX. No record the minutes of the proceedings which involve or settle in them false facts ;

X. No awards swell within the period specified in this Act;

XI. Thicken awards in terms other than those contained in the vote , and

XII. Other established laws.

Article 641 -A. Special faults are conciliators officials:

I. Know of a business they are disqualified under the provisions of this Act ;

II. Not be present at the conciliation hearings or assigned to them at any stage of the trial, when the Board or any of its members deem necessary conciliatory function , except for just cause ;

III. Not address the parties promptly and with due consideration ;

IV. Delaying the reconciliation of a business justification ;

V. Not informing the Conciliation and Arbitration that are attached on the results achieved in conciliation hearings entrusted to them , at intervals determined by them ;

VI. Not accountable to the Conciliation and Arbitration of his secondment to the conventions parts have arrived for purposes of approval where appropriate , and

VII. Other established laws.

Article 642. - Special vacancy in Auxiliaries:

I. Know of a business they are disqualified under the provisions of this Act ;

II. Delaying the processing of a business;

III. Vote resolution manifestly illegal or unjust ;

IV. Allow to thicken awards within the period specified in this Act;

V. Thicken awards in terms other than those stated in the vote ;

VI. Stop dictating the respective agreements within the terms stated in this Act;

VII. Refrain from timely inform the Chairman of the Special Board about criminal misconduct or any of the representatives of workers or employers , and

VIII. Other established laws.

Article 643. - These are special fouls the Presidents of the Special Boards:

I. The cases mentioned in sections I , II , III and VI of the preceding article ,

II. Failure to provide timely execution of awards ;

III. Not timely inform the President of the Board of the criminal misconduct or any of the representatives of workers or employers before the Special Board to preside ;

IV. Failure to report to the Attorney General to a negotiation pattern industrial, agricultural, mining , commercial or services that have been convicted of final award to pay the minimum wage or the differences that have stopped covering one or more of its employees ;

V. Not to comply with the processes , methods and performance evaluation mechanisms and of the obligations under the regulations issued by the Plenary of the Board , and

VI. Other established laws.

Article 644. They are general causes for dismissal of actuaries , secretaries , officials conciliators , auxiliaries, general secretaries , assistant secretaries and Presidents of the Special Boards:

I. Violating the prohibition of Article 632 of this Law;

II. Failure to attend more than three consecutive days to their jobs without just cause ; absent frequently during working hours , and repeated failure to comply with the obligations of the position;

III. Receive directly or indirectly any gift of the parties and

IV. Committing five fouls , at least , other than the special causes for dismissal , according to the authority which made the appointment.

Article 645. - These are special reasons for dismissal:

I. Of Actuaries: to state false facts in the record to raise in the exercise of their functions;

II. Conciliators officials:

a) No account for Conciliation and Arbitration of his assignment on the conventions have arrived the parties for purposes of approval where appropriate.

b) Know of a business they are disqualified under the provisions of this Act ;

III. From the secretaries: false facts attest or maliciously and substantially alter the facts in writing authorizing proceedings ;

IV. Of the auxiliary

a) Know of any business they are disqualified.

b) To vote a decision or express an opinion manifestly illegal or unjust.

c) Hold or unduly delay the processing of a case , and

V. General Secretaries , Assistant Secretaries and Chairmen of the Special Boards:

a) The cases mentioned in paragraphs a) and c) of the preceding section.

b) Voting resolution manifestly illegal or unjust.

c) Failing to provide promptly to the enforcement of awards.

d) The cases referred to in Article 643 , Section V of this Act

Article 646. The removal from office of the legal staff of the Special Meetings shall be ordered by the authority which made the appointment.

Article 647. - The sanctions referred to in this Title shall be without prejudice to the criminal liability.

TITLE XIII REPRESENTATIVES OF WORKERS AND EMPLOYERS

CHAPTER I REPRESENTATIVES OF WORKERS AND EMPLOYERS IN FEDERAL AND LOCAL BOARDS OF CONCILIATION AND ARBITRATION

Article 648. The representatives of workers and employers on the Boards shall be elected at conventions, which are organized and operated every six years in accordance with the provisions of this Chapter.

Article 649. - It held as many conventions as Special Meetings must operate on the Board of Conciliation and Arbitration.

Article 650. The first day of October of the year for appropriate , the Secretary of Labor and Social Security, the Governor of the State or Head of Government of the Federal District , published in the Official Journal of the Federation or in the official newspaper of the federal entity and one of the major newspapers , the call for the election of representatives.

Article 651. - The notice shall contain:

I. The distribution of the branches of industry and of the activities that should be represented on the Board;

II. The authority to which it should be presented lists and credentials ;

III. The place and the date of filing of the documents referred to in the preceding section , and

IV. The place , location, date and time of event of the convention , in accordance with Article 659.

Article 652. - The employee representatives shall be elected at conventions by delegates who previously designated in accordance with the following standards:

I. They are entitled to appoint delegates to conventions:

a) Labor unions duly registered.

b) The free workers who had provided services to an employer for a period not less than six months during the year prior to the date of the call, when no registered unions ;

II. Be considered members of trade unions registered workers in them, when:

a) they are providing services to an employer.

b) They would have provided services to an employer for a period of six months during the year prior to the date of the announcement ;

III. Free Workers referred to in Section I , paragraph b) , designate a delegate to every enterprise or establishment , and

IV. The credentials of delegates shall be issued by the leadership of trade unions or by designating free workers.

Article 653. - The representatives of the employers shall be appointed by the same conventions patterns or their delegates , in accordance with the following standards:

I. They are entitled to participate in the election:

a) The duly registered employers' unions , whose members have workers in their service.

b) independent patterns have workers in their service ;

II. Patterns unions appoint a delegate ;

III. Independent patterns may attend the convention in person or be represented by proxy signed by two witnesses and certified by the Labour Inspector , and

IV. The credentials of delegates shall be issued by the leadership of trade unions.

Article 654. - For purposes of the preceding articles, workers and employers form the following standards:

I. Labor unions will form the register of members that meet the requirements of Article 652 , Section I , paragraph a) ;

II. Free workers form the pattern of workers involved in the appointment of the delegate ;

III. Patterns unions form the patterns of workers in the service of its members, and

IV. Independent patterns form the standards of its workers.

Article 655. - The registers contain the following information:

I. Names and addresses of trade unions and employers ;

II. Name , nationality, age , gender, and firm or establishment in which they are employed , and

III. Names the employer or employers , address and branch of industry or activity they are engaged.

Article 656. The standards shall be submitted to the Ministry of Labor and Social Security, the Governor of the State or Head of Government of the Federal District , the 20th of October in the year of the Call at the latest.

Article 657. - Labour Inspectors verify and certify the accuracy of the rolls.

Article 658. - The credentials must register with the Ministry of Labor and Social Security or to the Directorates or Departments of Labor Federal Entities , on November 15 of the year of the election, at the latest.

The registering authority shall certify, in view of the data of the labor inspector , the number of votes of each credential.

Article 659. - The convention will be held on December 5 in even years that correspond , in the capitals of the Republic , the States , or on the place of residence of the Board.

Article 660. - In running conventions following rules shall be observed:

I. For each Special Board held a convention of workers and other patterns ;

II. Delegates and independent patterns will be presented at conventions, provided their credentials ;

III. The conventions work with the number of delegates and independent patterns concur ;

IV. Delegates and independent patterns , the conventions have a number of votes equal to workers certified display their credentials ;

V. The convention will be installed by the Secretary of Labor and Social Welfare, by the Governor of the State or Head of Government of the Federal District or the person designated by them ;

VI. Installed the convention, shall register credentials and choice of the board , which shall consist of a President , two secretaries and two Members. Will take part in the election, with the number of their voting , delegates and independent patterns whose credentials had been recorded. The computation is done by two of the participants, specially designated ;

VII. Installed the board , it shall review the credentials , giving them read aloud. The conventions may only discard those that do not meet the requirements set out in Article 652 and 653, or if it is found that voters do not belong to the branch of industry or activities represented at the convention ;

VIII. Approved credentials will proceed to the election of representatives , by a majority vote. For each owner will choose an alternate , and

IX. After the election, shall be drawn up , a copy shall be deposited in the archives of the Board , another was sent to the Ministry of Labor and Social Security, the Governor of the State or Territory or the Head of Government of the Federal District , and two delivered to the elected representatives or alternate , to serve them credential.

Article 661. If no officer or independent pattern attends the convention or it does not make the election of representatives on December 5 , it is understood that stakeholders delegate authority to the Secretary of Labor and Social Welfare in the State Governor or the Chief Federal District Government.

Article 662. - Elected representatives , provided with their credentials , will be presented at once to the Ministry of Labor and Social Security, or the Department of Labor or Department of State, for review of the same and for personal identification.

Article 663. The first working day of the following January , the Secretary of Labor and Social Welfare, The Governor of the State or Head of Government of the Federal District , elected representatives take the legal protest and after exhorting to administer prompt justice and expeditiously constituted declare federal or local Board of Conciliation and Arbitration and the Permanent Settlement.

Article 664. In the appointment of representatives of workers and employers in the Special Boards established outside the capital of the Republic , shall follow the provisions of this Chapter , with the following specifications:

I. The notice shall indicate the territorial jurisdiction of the Board;

II. The convention will be held at the residence of the Board , and

III. Shall be entitled to attend the election of representatives , union workers or the free and the patterns that should be represented on the Board.

Article 665. - The representatives of workers and employers must meet the following requirements:

I. Being Mexican , over twenty years and be in full exercise of their rights;

II. Completion of compulsory education ;

III. No ecclesiastical office , and

IV. Not have been convicted of an intentional crime punishable by imprisonment.

Article 666. - Representatives receive the remuneration to them by the federal and local budgets.

Article 667. - The representatives of workers and employers shall hold office for six years.

Article 668. The Secretary of Labor and Social Welfare, the Governors of States and Head of Government of the Federal District , known for the resignations of the representatives , accepting or discarding them , after having obtained the cause.

Article 669. - The office of attorney is revoked in accordance with the following standards:

I. May request revocation of two-thirds of the workers in the branches of industry or activities represented in the Special Board or patterns at their service that most workers ;

II. The application shall be submitted to the Secretary of Labor and Social Welfare, the Governor of the State or Head of Government of the Federal District ;

III. The authority receiving the application, after verifying the majority requirement , make the relevant declaration and call the alternate, in order to render legal protest , and

IV. A lack of alternate or revocation of the appointment when it is concerned, to be the revocation request , they shall be the names of the substitutes.

Article 670. The temporary or permanent absence of the representatives shall be filled by the alternates. In the absence of these or if called by the Chairman of the Board is not present within ten days of the request, the Secretary of Labor and Social Security, the Governor of the State or

Head of Government of the Federal District , shall make the appointment of substitute , which should be conducted by an employee or employer.

Article 671. - Causes for accountability of representatives of workers and employers:

I. Know of a business for which you are disqualified pursuant to this Act;

II. Litigating in some other special board except in his own behalf, his parents , spouse or children ;

III. Missing without cause at the conclusion of the hearings;

IV. Refusing to cast their vote in any resolution;

V. Refuse to sign any resolution;

VI. Subtract a record office , without giving receipt to the Secretary ;

VII. Subtract from some record any record or modify the contents of the minutes after signed by the parties, test them , or destroy in whole or in part the folios of a file;

VIII. Retain a record or improperly refusing to return when required by the Secretary;

IX. Vote resolution manifestly illegal or unjust ;

X. Receive directly or indirectly any gift of the conflicting parties , and

XI. Litigating an alternate representative to the Board that the owner is in office or litigate this being in the alternate functions.

Article 672. - The sanctions against representatives of workers and employers are:

I. reprimand;

II. Suspension for up to three months, and

III. Dismissal.

Article 673. - Are grounds for dismissal:

I. Those indicated in Article 671, Sections I , II , VI , VII , IX , X and XI;

II. The non-attendance to five plenary sessions a year without just cause , and

III. The refusal to vote three resolutions or committing five fouls other than the grounds for dismissal , within a period of one year , without just cause.

Article 674. - The sanctions representatives of workers and employers will be imposed by the Jury of Responsibilities of Representatives, which will be integrated:

I. With a representative of the Secretary of Labor and Social Security, the Governor of the State or Head of Government of the Federal District , and

II. With one representative of workers and other patterns , and their alternates , elected every six years by the conventions referred to this chapter.

Article 675. - In proceedings before the jury applies the following rules:

I. The Chairman of the Board and the Chairmen of the Special Boards must report to the Jury the faults of which they are aware ;

II. People who are interested in business may also expose the faults of which they are aware ;

III. They put the allegations to the attention of the defendant and defense will be heard by himself, by someone you trust , or both ;

IV. The Jury shall have the broadest powers to investigate the facts , must summon the accused to practice proceedings ;

V. The defendant may offer evidence it deems appropriate , and

VI. After the reception of the evidence, the jury hear arguments and issue resolution , communicating , if damning , the Authority to enact appropriate dismissal.

CHAPTER II REPRESENTATIVES OF WORKERS AND EMPLOYERS IN THE NATIONAL COMMISSION OF MINIMUM WAGES AND ADVISORY COMMITTEES

Article 676. - Are applicable to the election of representatives of workers and employers in the National Minimum Wage , the provisions contained in the previous chapter , in the manner of the following articles.

Article 677. - On May 15 the corresponding odd-numbered year , the Secretary of Labor and Social summon workers and employers for the election of their representatives. Notices will be published in the Official Journal of the Federation and in major newspapers as deemed appropriate.

Article 678. - The notice shall contain:

I. Determining the number of representatives to be chosen for establishing the National Commission , in accordance with the provisions of Article 554 Fraction II ;

II. The distribution of the number of representatives it has been determined between the different economic activities by importance ;

III. Authorities to be submitted to the the lists and credentials ;

IV. The place and the date of filing of the documents referred to in the preceding section , and

V. The place and time conventions to be concluded.

Article 679. - The Convention will be held on the 25th of June of odd-numbered year , which corresponds in the Capital of the Republic.

Article 680. - For the election of representatives to the National Commission held a convention of workers and other patterns for each of the groups to which they had distributed the branches of economic activity.

Article 681. - Are entitled to participate in the election workers ' unions and employers and independent patterns. Representatives to the National Commission shall be elected by all union workers and patterns of voting Republic.

Article 682. - The Secretary of Labor and Social Security may delegate the authorities of the Federal States , in whole or in part, the powers are in the certification of standards and credentials and the functioning of the conventions.

Article 682 -A. - The advisory committee shall be established by resolution of the Council of Representatives of the National Commission , to be published in the Official Journal of the Federation and shall contain:

I. The subject matter of the Advisory Committee ;

II. The duration of their work ;

III. The number of representatives of workers and employers to the Advisory Committee to be appointed by the representatives of workers and employers before the National Commission ;

IV. The term for the appointment of representatives , the requirements to be met in each case and place to be determined for the notification of the appointment , and

V. The place and date on which will formally start the work of the Advisory Committee.

CHAPTER III REPRESENTATIVES OF WORKERS AND EMPLOYERS IN THE NATIONAL COMMISSION FOR WORKER PARTICIPATION IN COMPANY PROFITS

Article 683. - In the election of representatives of workers and employers in the National Commission for the Participation of Workers in Corporate Income , shall follow the provisions of the two previous chapters , with the following article mode.

Article 684. - The call for the determination or revision of the percentage of profits, contain:

I. Determining the number of representatives to be chosen to serve on the Commission , in accordance with Article 579 , Section II , as well as the distribution of branches of industry and activities , according to their importance , the number of representatives had been determined ;

II. The place and date of presentation of the lists and credentials , and

III. The place , date and time conventions to be concluded.

TITLE XIV LABOUR LITIGATION

CHAPTER I PROCEDURAL PRINCIPLES

Article 685. The process of labor law will be public, free , instant , predominantly oral and conciliatory and start parte. Boards will be required to take the necessary measures to achieve greater economy, and simplicity of the process concentration.

When worker demand is incomplete , in that it does not understand all the benefits under this Act arising from the attempted action or appropriate, in accordance with the facts presented by the employee , the Board, at the time of admitting the claim , will remedy this. This notwithstanding that when demand is obscure or vague proceed under the terms provided in Article 873 of this Act

Article 686. - The process of labor law and procedures paraprocesales , shall be heard and decided in the terms indicated in this Law

Boards ordered to correct any irregularity or omission notaren the conduct of the proceedings , for the purpose of regulating the procedure , without implying that they can revoke their own resolutions , as provided in Article 848 of this Law

Article 687. - At the hearings, written , promotions or allegations , no particular form is required , but the parties shall state the petitioner's arguments.

Article 688. The administrative and judicial authorities are bound in the scope of their respective competences, to assist the Boards of Conciliation and Arbitration , if it should refuse to be liable under the terms of the laws applicable to the case. The Boards shall assist each other in the exercise of their functions.

CHAPTER II CAPACITY , PERSONALITY AND LEGITIMACY

Article 689. The parties to the process of labor, individuals or companies who can prove their legal interest in the process and bringing actions or oppose exceptions.

Article 690. - People who may be affected by the decision to rule in a dispute may intervene in it , checking its legal interest in it, or be called to judgment by the Board.

Interested parties may appear at trial or be called to it even before the conclusion of the hearing of offering and admission of evidence , to show what they deem appropriate. The Board , with a stay of proceedings and citation of the parties, shall issue a resolution noting the date and time for the holding of the relevant hearing which shall be held within ten working days following the date of the hearing or appeal of the third, notifying personally reported the same agreement with five days in advance.

Article 691. Child workers have the capacity to stand trial without authorization , but should not be assessed in view, the Board sought from the Office of the Defense of Labor for the purpose. For minors 16 years , the Office of Labor Defense will designate a representative when not they have.

The provisions of the preceding paragraph shall also apply in the case of alleged beneficiaries of a deceased worker.

Article 692. - The parties may appear in court directly or through legally authorized agent.

In the case of proxy , personality is credited according to the following rules:

I. When acting as a proxy respondent individual, may do so by proxy or power of attorney signed by the grantor and two witnesses , without having to be ratified before the Board;

II. The attorneys counsel employers or of the parties , whether or not agents of these, should prove to be lawyers or law graduates with professional certificate or persons who have current intern letter issued by the competent authority for such a profession. May only be allowed to others for notifications and receive documents, but they may not appear at the hearing or make any promotion ;

III. When acting as a proxy respondent corporation, may prove his testimony by attorney or proxy signed before two witnesses , after verifying that empowers who is legally authorized to do so , and

IV. The union representatives credited with certification personality they extend the relevant registration authority , having been registered union leadership. They may also appear through legal representative , who in all cases shall be an attorney , law graduate or intern.

Article 693. Boards may have the personality accredited representatives of workers or unions , federations and confederations without being subject to the rules of the preceding article , provided that exhibited documents come to the conclusion that , indeed, represents the interested party.

Article 694. - Workers , employers and unions may empower by simple appearance , after identification , to the Boards of the place of residence , to represent the work before any authority , the personality will be credited with the copy certified is issued thereof.

Article 695. - The representatives or agents may prove their personality according to the above guidelines , in each of the trials in their appearance , exhibiting simple copy photocopy for comparison with the original document or certified by authority , which will be returned to immediately , leaving in cars duly certified copy.

Article 696. - The power to grant the worker to be represented in court, to sue conferred shall mean all principal and accessory benefits that apply , although not expressed in it.

Article 697. - Whenever two or more persons exercising the same act or oppose the same exception in the same judgment must litigate together and with a common representation , unless the litigant interests opposed.

If it is the parties actors , the appointment of the common representative shall be made in the application, or in the settlement hearing , and exceptions demand offering and admission of evidence, whether it is the defendants , the appointment shall be made in the defense or the audience that has been mentioned. If they did the appointment stakeholders within the terms indicated , the Conciliation and Arbitration Board will selecting from among the people themselves.

The Common Representative shall have the rights , duties and responsibilities inherent in a judicial representative.

CHAPTER III ATTRIBUTIONS

Article 698. - It shall be the Local Boards and Conciliation Conciliation and Arbitration of the Federal , hear disputes arising within their jurisdiction , which are not within the jurisdiction of the Federal Boards.

The Federal Board of Conciliation and Arbitration cognizance of labor disputes in the case of industrial branches , businesses or matters contained in Articles 123, section A, paragraph XXXI , of the Constitution and 527 of this Act

Article 699. - When in disputes referred to the first paragraph of the preceding article , are exercised in the same demand action obligations related to training and training or health and safety , knowledge of these matters will be of the jurisdiction of the Federal Special Board of Conciliation and Arbitration , according to its jurisdiction.

In the case referred to in the preceding paragraph, the Local Board , recognizing the demand , order will make a copy of it and documents submitted by the plaintiff, which shall immediately forward to the Federal Board for the conduct and resolution , exclusively , of training and training issues , health and safety and , under the terms stated in this Act

Article 700. - Competition by territory is governed by the following rules:

I. (Repealed).

II. In individual disputes , the actor can choose between:

a) The Board of the place of the contract.

b) The Board of the defendant's domicile.

c) The Board of the place of supply of services, if they were provided in several places, shall be the Board of the last one.

III. In the federal jurisdiction disputes , the Federal Board of Conciliation and Arbitration , under the terms of Article 606 of this Law , in the local jurisdiction disputes , with the place where the enterprise is located or establishment;

IV. In the case of cancellation of the registration of a trade union , the Board of where it was ;

V. In conflicts between employers and workers each , the Board where the defendant , and

VI. When the defendant is a union , the Board of domicile of the same.

Article 701. The Conciliation and Arbitration of office shall be declared incompetent in any state of the process , even before hearing the evidence presentation , they exist in the

record data to justify it. If the Board is declared incompetent, with citation of the parties, shall immediately forward the case to the Board or the court considers competent , if this or that , upon receiving the record, is declared incompetent in turn , shall immediately transmit the record authority to decide the competition , in terms of Article 705 of this Act

Article 702. - No plea consider the defense in the refusal of the employment relationship.

Article 703. - Competition issues , on labor , can be made only by demurrer.

The demurrer should oppose your period demand and the respective hearing exceptions , accompanying elements relied upon , at which time the Board after hearing the parties and receive evidence as it deems appropriate , which must relate solely to the question of incompetence , issue resolution instantly.

Article 704. - When a Special Board considers that the dispute before it, is the responsibility of another of the same board , with citation of the parties, shall be declared incompetent and sent the case to the Special Board considers competent. If this upon receiving the record is declared incompetent in turn , forward it to the authority should decide the question of jurisdiction , for it determines what the Special Board should continue to hear the dispute.

Article 705. - The competitions are made:

I. By the President of the Federal Board of Conciliation and Arbitration , in the case of the Special Boards of it, with each other;

II. By the President of the Local Board of Conciliation and Arbitration , in the case of Special Meetings of the same federal entity and

III. For the corresponding instances of the Judiciary of the Federation, when arising between:

a) Local Boards or Federal Conciliation and Arbitration and the Federal Court of Conciliation and Arbitration.

b) Local and Federal Boards Boards of Conciliation and Arbitration.

c) Local Boards of Conciliation and Arbitration of various federal entities.

d) Local Boards or Federal Conciliation and Arbitration and other court.

Article 706. - Void everything done before the Board incompetent , unless the act of admission of the claim and the provisions of Articles 704 and 928 fraction V of this Act or , if applicable , when it has concluded an agreement to end the business , in the conciliation period.

CHAPTER IV IMPEDIMENTS AND EXCUSES

Article 707. - Government representatives , workers or employers before boards and auxiliaries , are prevented to hear lawsuits involving when:

I. Are related by consanguinity within the fourth degree or affinity within the second , with either party ;

II. Have the same relationship within the second degree , with the legal representative , attorney or solicitor of any party ;

III. Have direct or indirect personal interest in the trial ;

IV. Some of the litigants or lawyers was complainant , complainant or accuser of the official in question , his spouse or incorporated in part on a criminal , taken against any of them , provided you have exercised appropriate criminal action ;

V. Be attorney or advocate any party or expert or witness in the same trial , or having expressed an opinion on it ;

VI. Be a partner , tenant, employee or employer or financially dependent on either party or their representatives ;

VII. Be guardian or conservator, or been under the guardianship or conservatorship of the parties or their representatives , and

VIII. Be debtor , creditor, heir or beneficiary of any of the parties or their representatives.

Article 708. - Government representatives , workers or employers before the Boards , and auxiliaries are not objectionable , but should disqualify himself from hearing the judgments involved , when they are included in any of the cases referred to in the previous article. Failure to do so will incur the liability referred to in this Act

Article 709. - The excuses will be graded flat, and in processing the following rules shall be observed:

I. The instruct and decide:

a) The Chairman of the Board , in the case of the Chairman of a Special Board or Conciliation or Assistant Representative of Workers or Employers.

b) The Secretary of Labor and Social Welfare , being the President of the Federal Board and Governor of the State or Head of Government of the Federal District , in the case of the President of the Local Board.

II. The excuse should promote writing and under oath , before the authorities specified in the preceding section, within 48 hours after they are aware of the impediment. Upon request shall accompany the supporting evidence ;

III. The authority to decide on the excuse , its receipt , rule outright with the items you have for it or may indicate day and time to appear before it the person, so that after hearing and receive evidence immediately proceed to judgment ; and

IV. If the excuse is declared inadmissible , the competent authority may sanction , which is excused with warning or suspension from office for up to eight days and in case of recurrence in the same case , it will be removed.

Article 710. - When a party knows that the representative of the Government , employers or workers before the Board or the Assistant are prevented for some judgment and refrain from doing so , may appear before the authorities specified in Section I of the previous article written by the complaint , which must accompany the evidence to establish the disability and shall be processed in accordance with the procedure outlined in section III of that provision.

If the obstacle is found to replace it as follows:

a) The Chairman of the Board by the Secretary General of greater antiquity ;

b) The Chairman of the Special Board for the Auxiliary Board itself , and this by the Secretary;

c) The Chairman of the Permanent Conciliation Board by the Secretary thereof , and

d) The representatives of workers and employers by their respective alternates.

Regardless of the substitution, the official will be punished prevented , under the terms provided in Section IV of Article 709 of this Act

Article 711. The procedure is not suspended while the complaint is processed impediment.

CHAPTER V BOARDS PERFORMANCE

Article 712. - When the worker ignore the pattern name or corporate name of where you work or worked , must specify at least in its initial written demand for the company 's home , hotel, office or where he worked or paid work and dedicated activity pattern.

The mere filing of the complaint in the preceding paragraph interrupts the limitation on who happens to be the employer of the worker.

Article 713. - In any hearing will require the physical presence of the parties or their representatives or agents , except as otherwise provided by the Act

Article 714. - The actions of the Boards should be practiced in days and hours, under penalty of nullity , provided that this Act does not provide otherwise.

Article 715. - They are days every year with the exception of Saturdays and Sundays , the mandatory rest , the holidays to bring the official calendar and those that the Board suspend its work.

Article 716. - Working hours are those between seven and nineteen hours , except the strike procedure , in which all are working days and hours.

Article 717. - The Chairmen of the Boards , those of the Special Boards and Auxiliaries, may enable legal holiday for you diligence practice , when there is justifiable cause , stating clearly what is concrete and this , together with the steps that have to be practiced.

Article 718. - The hearing or proceeding is initiated business days and time may be continued to completion, without suspend without express authorization. In case of suspension should be continued the next business day , the Board shall include in the record the reason for the suspension.

Article 719. - When the specified date is not carried out the practice of some diligence , the Board shall include in the record the reason for which was not practiced and point in the same agreement, the date and time for that to occur same.

Article 720. - The hearings shall be public. The Board may , ex officio or upon request , to be closed , when required by the best law business, morals or good customs.

Article 721. - All court proceedings are authorized by the Secretary , except proceedings entrusted to other officers , the proceedings at the hearing shall be recorded in the minutes , which shall be signed by the persons therein intervened , want and know it. When any member of the Board omits sign the minutes of the proceedings in which he was present shall mean that you are happy with them. From the minutes of the hearings autograph copies thereof to each of the parties appearing.

Article 722. - The statements that yield the parties, their agents or anyone else before the Meetings , the made under oath and under pain of the penalties incurred if falsely claim to authority.

The statements of experts in law, be filed under oath , without requiring any warning.

Article 723. - The Board, in accordance with the provisions of this Act, must issue to the applicant , a certified copy of any document or record that contained in the file. You must also certify that exhibit photocopy portions of any document or record that appears in the record, prior alignment is done with the original.

Article 724. The Plenum of the Federal Conciliation and Arbitration or the Local Boards of Conciliation and Arbitration , decide the creation , dissemination and use of technological tools which include systems for consultation and performance of the parties in the procedures set out in Chapter Fourteen of this Act

You can also agree that the records be concluded definitively discharged upon certification thereof microfilming or conservation through any other scientific technical procedure to permit consultation.

Article 725. - In case of loss or disappearance of the record or any record , the Secretary, the report of the archivist, shall certify that the lack anterior and posterior of the case or proceeding. The Board , on its own initiative or upon request , it will inform the parties , a claim for the investigation of the case and immediately arrange replacement cars, incidentally.

Article 726. - In the previous article , the Board shall indicate , within seventy -two hours , day and time to have a hearing in which the parties must provide all items, records and copies held by their power. The Board may order to practice those actions and steps necessary to replace the car , taking into account, where appropriate, the provisions of Article 724 of this Act

Article 727. The Board , on its own , make the appropriate report to the prosecutor responsible for the disappearance of the case or proceeding , enclosing a copy of the minutes and other steps taken in that connection.

Article 728. - The Chairmen of the Boards and Auxiliaries, may impose disciplinary measures , to maintain good order in the conduct of hearings or proceedings , and demand that they keep the respect and consideration due.

Article 729. The disciplinary measures that may be imposed are:

I. reprimand;

II. Fine, do not exceed 100 times the general minimum wage in the Federal District at the time the violation is committed. In the case of workers , the fine shall not exceed the amount of his wages or salary in a day. For the purposes of this article, is not considered proxies workers , and

III. Expulsion of the premises of the Board , the person who resists enforce the order , will be evicted from the premises with the help of the police.

Article 730. - When the facts giving rise to the imposition of a disciplinary penalty may constitute the commission of a crime , the Board shall issue a detailed affidavit and turn it over to the Public Prosecutor for leading effects.

Article 731. - The Chairman of the Board, the Special Boards and Auxiliaries may use jointly and severally , any coercive measures necessary for people to attend the hearings in which their presence is indispensable or to ensure compliance with its resolutions.

Pressure means that can be employed are:

I. Fine, do not exceed 100 times the general minimum wage in the Federal District at the time of committing the contempt. In the case of workers , the fine shall not exceed the amount of his wages or salary of a day. For the purposes of this article, shall not be considered proxies workers ;

II. Presentation of the person with the help of the police , and

III. Arrest for up to thirty -six hours.

Article 732. - The disciplinary and coercive measures be imposed outright, without any proceedings , and must be grounded and motivated. May be challenged under the terms stated in this Act

CHAPTER VI PROCEDURAL RULES

Article 733. - The terms begin to run the day following the effective date of the notice and be counted on them the day of maturity.

Article 734. In terms not count the days when the Board ceases to act according to the work schedule approved by the House, and when by accident or force majeure actions can take place. The work stoppage notices published in the newsletter or on the podium work in your case.

Article 735. - When performing any act or practice of procedural or exercise of a right, have not set a term, this will be the three days.

Article 736. - In computing terms , the months are calculated by the thirty calendar days , and those days were considered twenty-four hours , counted twenty-four to twenty-four hours , unless otherwise provided in this Act

Article 737. When the address of the defendant is outside the place of residence of the Board, the Board extended the term in question , depending on the distance , at the rate of one day for every 200 miles , 3 to 12 days , taking into account transportation and the general means of communication.

Article 738. - Within the terms set by the parties, shall be forfeited its right to due exercise , indict without rebellion.

CHAPTER VII NOTIFICATIONS

Article 739. - The parties , in their first appearance or writing, must state address within the residence of the Board to be notified , if they do , personal notifications shall be by newsletter or by courts , as appropriate, in as provided in this Act

They should also note the defendant's address for notifications , or the last place where the employee provided services. The notification is personal and shall be served as provided in Article 743.

The person appearing as a third party in a lawsuit , you should note address within the residence of the Board to be notified , if not, is subject to the provisions at the end of the first paragraph of this article.

In case the parties may bring interested parties should indicate in their initial promotion their domicile to receive notifications.

Article 740. When demand is not expressed on behalf of the employer or the company in which the employee works or worked , personal notice thereof shall be subject to the procedure laid down in Article 743 of this Law as pertains, must ensure the actuary the place where the notifying is precisely indicated by the applicant, and shall be deemed notice to the employer, but by making it ignore the name.

Article 741. - Personal notifications will be made at the address specified in the file, even while not designated or local new home for it, and carried out in these conditions , shall take full effect.

Article 742. - Will personally be following notifications:

I. The site to trial and if it is the first handed down provided therein;

II. The order of filing of judgment than dictate Conciliation and Arbitration in the records referred to them by other Boards ;

III. The resolution in which the Board has no jurisdiction ;

IV. The car that falls to be sentenced for defense ;

V. The decision ordering the resumption of proceedings , which proceedings were interrupted or suspended for any legal cause ;

VI. The order summoning to interrogatories ;

VII. The resolutions to be strangers to know the third trial;

VIII. The award ;

IX. The order granting or point end date for which the employee is reinstated ;

X. An order that orders the reinstatement of proceedings;

XI. In the cases referred to in Articles 772 and 774 of this Act , and

XII. In urgent cases or special circumstances in the opinion of the Board.

Article 743. - The first personal notification shall be in accordance with the following standards:

I. The actuary should be satisfied that the person to be served , live, work or have their domicile in the house or premises , the Court pointed to the notice;

II. If present the applicant or his representative , the clerk shall notify the resolution, delivering a copy of it , whether it is moral person , the clerk shall ensure that the person understands the diligence is representative or legal representative of the former;

III. If not present the applicant or his representative , will be left for you to wait subpoena the next day, at a specific time ;

IV. If however the summons is not present the applicant or his representative , notification will be made to any adult person who is in the house or premises , and if they be these closed , fix a copy of the resolution at the door input ;

V. If the house or premises designated for notification refuses the applicant , his representative or the person requesting the inquiry , to receive notice , it will be instructive to be fixed by the door of the same , enclosing a copy of the resolution , and

VI. In the case of Article 712 of this Act , the clerk shall ensure that the designated location in cars, is that they are rendered or services were provided.

In all the cases mentioned in this article , the actuary settle right in cars, clearly indicating the items of evidence on which it rests.

Article 744. - Subsequent personal notifications will be the registrant or authorized person , the same day that the decision is taken whether it satisfies the premises of the Board or at home having designated and if it is found to be present , you leave a copy of the resolution approved by the actuary , if the house or building is closed , fix the copy in the front door or in the workplace.

The actuary settle right in cars.

Article 745. - The House of the Federal and Local Boards of Conciliation and Arbitration , may agree to publish a bulletin containing the list of notifications that are not personal.

Article 746. - They shall take effects the notifications made to the parties to the Labour Bulletin , unless they are personal. When not post bulletin board , such notification shall be in the bar of the Board.

The Secretary shall include in the record the date of the respective publication and daily instead set local visible the Board, a copy of the Labour Bulletin or , where appropriate, lists podiums notifications , collecting some and others, to solve any questions arising about the omission of a publication.

The notification lists must be authorized and sealed in its date by the Secretary. The publication of notices shall contain the date , the case number and the names of the parties to the proceedings in question.

Article 747. - The notification shall have effect as follows:

I. The personal: the day and time that are practiced , counting from moment to moment , whatever the time of the notification has been made , unless otherwise provided in the Act , and

II. The other , the day following its publication in the Gazette or in the bar of the Board.

Article 748. - The notifications must be made during business hours with a twenty-four hours in advance , at least , the day and time that diligence be effected , unless otherwise provided by the Act

Article 749. - The notifications made to the attorney or persons legally authorized expressly by the parties, accredited by the Board, shall have the same effect as if they had been made to them.

Article 750. - The notices , summonses or subpoenas must be made within five days of its date , unless expressly by resolution or by law otherwise exist.

Article 751. - The letter of notification shall contain at least:

I. Place, date and time the notification is practiced ;

II. The file number;

III. The name of the parties;

IV. The name and address of the person or persons entitled to notice , and

V. A certified copy of the resolution to be appended to the certificate.

Article 752. - Are null notifications which are not engaged in accordance with the provisions of this Chapter.

CHAPTER VIII EXHORTATIONS AND OFFICES

Article 753. The proceedings that can not be practiced in the place of residence of the Board hearing the trial shall be performed by urge the President of the Board of Conciliation and Arbitration or the Special domiciled in to be practiced , and, not having in that place , to the nearest authority to appropriate place in Mexico.

Article 754. - The steps are practiced abroad, shall be allowed only when it is demonstrated that they are essential to prove the basic facts of the claim or its defense.

In the case referred to in the preceding paragraph, the office will be fought for , taking into account the provisions of international treaties or conventions.

Article 755. - In the absence of treaties or agreements shall be been to the following rules:

I. Shipments will be sent through the diplomatic channel , to the place of residence of the appropriate authority, the signatures must be legalized by the authorities that issue , and

II. Legalization is not required signatures, if the laws or practices of the country where the office is open , do not establish that requirement.

Article 756. - In the exhortations that must be completed, within Mexico, legalization is not required signature of the issuing authority.

Article 757. - The Board shall issue letters rogatory and offices , the day after that on which the resolution took effect that order.

Article 758. - The exhortations and offices that receive the authorities referred to in Article 753, shall be provided within seventy -two hours of receipt and must fill within five days , except in cases where by the nature of what is to be practiced , necessarily requires more time , in this case , the requested authority shall determine which believes appropriate without fixed term may not exceed fifteen days.

Article 759. - When delay compliance with a warrant will be recalled its own motion or on application, the requested authority , despite a reminder if the delay continues , the authority issuing the letters will inform the immediate superior of the petitioner.

Article 760. - The Board at the request of a party, to deliver the warrant and its attachments to the previous bidder be expected to leave the Court, who under the strictest responsibility to deliver the requested authority for filling out.

The bidder shall return the warrant filled out under the strictest responsibility for issuing the letters.

CHAPTER IX INCIDENTS

Article 761. - The incidents are handled within the main file which promotes , except as provided in this Act

Article 762. - Incidents are handled as special preliminary ruling the following questions.

I. Nullity ;

II. Competition;

III. Personality ;

IV. Accumulation , and

V. Excuses.

Article 763. When in a hearing or proceeding incident is promoted lack of personality , managed immediately hearing the parties and resolved , continuing the procedure.

In other cases referred to the previous article, we set a day and time for the celebration of incidental hearing to be held within twenty-four hours , in which the parties may present evidence and documentary and instrumental to immediately resolve the incident , continuing the procedure.

Incidents that have not designated a special procedure in this Act shall be settled up listening to the parties.

Article 764. - If the Court indicate that a person manifests knowledgeable of a resolution, the wrong done or omitted notification shall take effect as if made under the Act in this case, the motion for dismissal to be promoted will be disposed of plane.

Article 765. (Repealed).

CHAPTER X ACCUMULATION

Article 766. - In the work processes that are pending before the Conciliation and Arbitration , it must build its own motion or on application, in the following cases:

I. In the case of actions brought by the same actor against the same defendant , in which claim the same benefits ;

II. When they are the same parts , but the services are different , but derived from the same relationship;

III. In the case of actions brought by various actors against the same defendant , whether the dispute arose from the same act derived from the employment relationship, and

IV. In all cases , which by their very nature the benefits claimed or facts that motivated , can cause rulings.

Article 767. - If declared from the accumulation , the most recent judgment or judgments shall accumulate to oldest.

Article 768. - Lawsuits regarding employer obligations for training and worker training and health and safety in the workplace , not

be combined with any other action. If any of these actions is exercised jointly with others derived from the same employment relationship shall be governed by the provisions of Article 699.

Article 769. - The accumulation declared admissible the following effects:

I. In the case of Section I of Article 766, it shall have no effect acted in judgment or judgments accumulated and only take effect the oldest trial proceedings , and

II. In the cases covered by sections II, III and IV of Article 766, the conflicts will be resolved by the Board itself in a single resolution.

Article 770. - For the processing and resolution of accumulation , shall follow the rules contained in Articles 761 to 765.

Jurisdiction will build the Board of Conciliation and Arbitration to formal proceedings , observed in the leading, the provisions of Chapter III of this Title.

CHAPTER XI IN THE CONTINUATION OF THE PROCESS AND THE EXPIRATION

Article 771. - The Presidents of the Auxiliary Boards and take care , under the strictest responsibility , that trials before they are processed are not inactive , providing what is appropriate under the Act to make an award , unless otherwise specified.

Failure to comply with the above, will be subject to the penalties established by the Laws of administrative responsibilities of public servants.

Article 772. When , to continue the process of judgment in the terms of the preceding article , is necessary and this promotion of worker not completed within a period of forty- five calendar days , the President of the Board shall order that he personally required for this , apercibiéndolo that , otherwise , will operate the revocation as provided in the following article.

If the worker is sponsored by a Labor Attorney , the Board shall notify the agreement concerned the worker and the Office of Labor Defense , for appropriate action. If it was sponsored by the Office , you will be told to this agreement , to the effect that intervene with the worker and clarify the legal consequences of the lack of promotion , and to give you legal advice in case the worker requests it.

Article 773. The Board , at the request of a party, shall be withdrawn from the action brought by any person who does not do any promotion at the end of four months , provided that such promotion is necessary for proceeding and that comply with the provisions of Article above. No such term shall be deemed to operate if the evidence has the actor or is due to be issued a resolution on promotion of the parties mentioned in this article, or the practice of an errand , or remember is pending the return of a Warrant or receiving reports or copies as ordered to different authority within the procedure.

For purposes of the preceding paragraph, the Board shall summon the parties to a hearing , in which after hear and receive evidence offered , which must relate solely to the propriety or impropriety of withdrawal , issue resolution.

Article 774. - In case of death of the worker , meanwhile beneficiaries appear for trial , the Board will make the request to the Attorney for the Defense of Labor, under the terms and for the purposes referred to in Article 772 of this Act

Article 774 Bis. At any stage of the proceedings , the parties may , by conciliation , to conclude an agreement to end the trial, also , the defendant may accept in whole or in part as claimed. In the first case , it will terminate the trial , the second , will continue the proceeding pending.

Article 775. - Assistant Attorney shall have the powers and responsibilities of a trustee , shall provide necessary promotions proceeding until its final completion.

Gathered the requirements referred to in previous articles , cease assistant attorney representation at trial that intervened.

CHAPTER XII TEST

Section One General Rules

Article 776. - Are eligible for admission, all the evidence they are not contrary to morality and the law , and in particular the following:

I. confessional ;

II. Documentary ;

III. testimonial ;

IV. expert ;

V. Inspection ;

VI. presumptive ;

VII. Instrumental performances , and

VIII. Photography , cinema film , fingerprint records , audio and video, or other information technology and communication, such as computer systems, optical electronic media , fax , email, digital document , electronic signature or password, in overall, the means provided by the discoveries of science.

Article 777. - The evidence must relate to the disputed facts they have not been admitted by the parties.

Article 778. - The evidence must be offered at the hearing , unless they refer to subsequent events or having finally prove the faults that may be invoked against witnesses.

Article 779. - The Board discard those tests which are unrelated to the suit in question or are useless or irrelevant , stating the reason for it.

Article 780. - The tests will be offered include all the elements necessary for its relief.

Article 781. - The parties may freely interrogate the persons involved in the presentation of evidence on disputed facts , hold each other the questions they deem appropriate , and to examine the documents and objects exhibited.

Article 782. - The Board may order with citation of the parties , examination of documents , objects and places , its recognition by actuaries or experts and , in general, take such measures as it deems appropriate to clarify the truth and will require the parts for exhibiting the documents and objects concerned.

Article 783. Any authority or person outside the trial that have documents in their possession that may help clarify the truth should contribute them to the audience by offering and admission of evidence or , even before the proceedings closed when you are required by the Board of Conciliation and Arbitration.

Article 784. - The Board relieved of the burden of proof on the worker , when other means are in a position to come to the knowledge of the facts , and for that purpose require the master to exhibit documents , according to the laws , has the legal obligation to retain in the company, under penalty that no reporting is presumed that the facts alleged by the worker. In any case , the employer shall prove that when there is controversy over:

I. Date worker's income ;

II. Age of the worker;

III. Worker's absences ;

IV. Cause of termination of employment;

V. Termination of contract of employment or to work or given time , in the terms of articles 37 , paragraph I , and 53 , section III of this Act;

VI. Evidence of having given written notice to the employee or the Board of Conciliation and Arbitration of the date and cause of his dismissal ;

VII. The employment contract ;

VIII. Working day ordinary and extraordinary , when it does not exceed nine hours per week ;

IX. Payments and mandatory days off , as well as the bonus ;

X. Enjoy and vacation pay ;

XI. Sunday premium payments , vacation and seniority ;

XII. Amount and payment of wages ;

XIII. Payment of employee participation in company profits , and

XIV. Incorporation and contributions to the Social Security Institute , the National Housing Fund and the Savings System for Retirement.

The loss or destruction of the documents mentioned in this article, by accident or force majeure, does not relieve the employer to prove his statement by other means.

Article 785. If any person is prevented by illness or other cause to go to the local board to answer interrogatories ; recognize the content or signing a document or give evidence , and justifies the view of the same , by a medical certificate or other reliable evidence that exhibit under oath , indicate new date for the sufficiency of the evidence and , to survive the impediment , may order the secretary , accompanied by members of the Board who wish, moves into the place where it is unable to the sufficiency of the evidence. Failure to meet the person , shall be declared or recognized confessed documents referred diligence either, deserted the test, as appropriate.

Medical certificates shall contain the name and professional license number of whom issued , the date and the pathological condition that prevents the appearance of the accused. Medical certificates issued by public social security institutions do not require ratification.

Section Two

The Confessional

Article 786. Either party may request a quote your counterpart to attend to answer interrogatories.

If a corporation , the confessional can vent through its legal representative or agent with authority to answer interrogatories.

Unions or organizations of workers or employers absolve positions through its general secretary or member of the statutorily authorized representative or by proxy with express powers.

Article 787. - The parties may also request that you cite to interrogatories personally principals, administrators, managers and, in general , people who exercise functions of leadership and management in the enterprise or establishment , as well as members policy unions , when the facts giving rise to the conflict belong to them and they have been attributed to the claim or defense , or that by reason of their duties they ought to be known.

Article 788. - The Board ordered the ITM is acknowledged personally or through their agents , apercibiéndolos concur that without the date and time indicated , they shall be confessed to the positions they articulate.

Article 789. - If the person summoned to answer interrogatories , is not met by the date and time indicated , shall act on the warning referred to in the preceding article shall be declared and confessed to the positions that would have been articulated and qualified legal.

Article 790. - In the outpouring of confessional evidence following rules shall be observed:

I. The positions may be made orally or in writing , that displays the interested party at the time of the hearing;

II. The positions will be made freely but be specified with the facts , not to be insidious or useless. They are insidious positions that tend to obscure the intelligence of which it must respond to obtain a confession against the truth , are those that deal with useless facts that have been previously confessed or that are not in contradiction with any credible evidence or fact that recorded in cars or on which there is no dispute;

III. The pardoning should be identified with any official document under oath , answer for himself without assistance. Not invoke draft answers, but will be allowed to consult any notes if the Board , after meeting resolves that are needed to aid his memory ;

IV. When positions are formulated orally , shall be recorded verbatim in the respective minutes , they are made in writing , it will add to the file sent and shall be signed by articulating and absolving ;

V. Positions will be classified previously as not meeting the requirements specified in section II , the Board will dispose cars settling in the foundation and concrete reason that supports your resolution;

VI. The answer absolving agreeing or disagreeing positions ; may add explanations it deems appropriate or the Board requests it , the answers also be recorded verbatim in the respective minutes , and

VII. If absolving refuses to answer or answers are elusive , the Board of its own motion or on application, give him a warning in the act of having it for confessed if it persists.

Article 791. - If the person to answer interrogatories is resident outside of where you are to the Board, the Board shall deliver Warrant , accompanying , in a closed and sealed, the specifications previously approved positions , of which a copy must be removed to stored in the secret of the Board.

The Board will receive the confessional exhorted the terms under which prompted the Board issuing the letters.

Article 792. - Will be taken by states and spontaneous confession , the statements contained in the position to formulate the articulating.

Article 793. When the person to whom interrogatories stated for facts labore own and not for the company or establishment, after fact checking , test the bidder will be required to provide the address where you need to be cited. In case the bidder ignore the address , it will inform the Board prior to the date set for the celebration of the presentation of evidence hearing , and the Board may ask the employer to provide the last address you have registered that person. In the event that the person referred to in this Article has ceased to provide services to the company for a period longer than three months , the test will change the nature of a testimonial.

If the person summoned does not attend the date and time indicated , the Board will submit by using the security forces.

Article 794. - Will be taken by states and spontaneous confession of the parties, without being offered as evidence , the statements contained in the records and proceedings of the trial.

Section Three

From Documentaries

Article 795. - Public documents are those whose development is mandated by the Act to an officer invested with public trust, as well as those issued in the exercise of their functions.

Public documents issued by the authorities of the Federation , States , Federal District and municipalities, will faith in the judgment without legalization.

Article 796. - Are private documents that do not meet the conditions laid down in the preceding article.

Article 797. - The original private documents submitted by the party bidder who is in his power, if they are object in terms of content and signature will be left in cars until its completion should not be challenged, the bidder may request a refund of the original, certified copy previous cars.

Article 798. - If the private document is single or photostatic copy may be requested , should be objected , the certifying or comparison with the original , to this effect , the bidder shall specify the place where the original document is located.

Article 799. - If the original document to be performed on the alignment or certifying is held by a third party, shall be obliged to display it

Article 800. - When a document comes from third party unrelated to the trial , it is contested , it must be ratified in its content and signed by the subscriber , to which should be mentioned in the terms of Section VII of Article 742 of this Act

The opposing party may ask any questions in relation to the facts contained in the document.

Article 801. - The concerned shall submit the original of private documents , they are part of a book, record or file , copy to be exhibited Part compulse that point , indicating the place where they are located.

Article 802. - Is reputed author of a paper that subscribes private.

Subscribing means of a written placement footnote or outside it to the handwritten signature of the author or his fingerprint, as an expression of the will to make it yours.

The subscription does full faith of the formulation of the document on behalf of the subscriber when ratified in content and signature or fingerprint , except in cases where the content is not repute from the author , a fact which should be supported by appropriate evidence and stated in Article 33 of this Law

Article 803. - Each part display documents or objects offered as proof for documents in the car. If it reports , or copies , which should be issued by any authority , the Board shall order them directly.

Article 804. - The employer has an obligation to preserve and exhibit at trial the following documents are required:

I. Individual employment contracts are held , where no collective agreement or applicable law ;

II. Lists scratched or payroll , when carried in the workplace , or wage payment receipts ;

III. Controls for assistance, when carried in the workplace ;

IV. Proof of payment of profit sharing , vacation and Christmas bonuses and premiums referred to this Act, and payments , contributions and social security contributions , and

V. Other than by the law.

The documents set forth in paragraph I shall be kept for the duration of the employment relationship and one year later, those listed in Sections II , III and IV , in the last year and a year after the employment relationship is terminated , and the aforementioned in fraction V , as it specified in laws that govern it.

Article 805. - The breach of the provisions of the preceding article shall be presumed that the facts that the actor expresses in its application, in relation to such documents, unless the contrary is proved.

Article 806. - Whenever one of the litigants or testimony requested copy of a document or record that piece work in public offices, the opposing party shall be entitled to , at its expense , will add to the conducive creating the same document , part or file.

Article 807. - Existing documents in place which promotes the trial, which are held by the counterparty, authorities or third parties will be subject to alignment or certifying , at the request of the bidder , through the clerk.

Existing documents rather than the residence of the Board, who are in any of the cases mentioned in the preceding paragraph, shall be checked or certified there at the request of the bidder, by warrant directed to the appropriate authority.

For the certifying or matching appropriate , must be displayed in the offer of proof hearing , a copy of that by this means should be perfected.

Article 808. To make faith in the Republic , documents from abroad must be duly legalized by the diplomatic or consular authorities , in the terms established by the laws or international treaties concerning.

Article 809. - The documents submitted in a foreign language must be accompanied by a translation , the Board shall immediately appoint ex officio official translator , who will submit and affirm, under oath , the translation done within the period of five days , which may be extended by the Board, if in its opinion is justified.

Article 810. - Copies presume the existence of the original , according to the rules from , but if in doubt its accuracy , must be ordered with original collation that took as long as this has been offered.

Article 811. - If you object to the authenticity of any document in content , signature or fingerprint , the parties may offer evidence regarding the objections , which will , if they are coming , in the audience of presenting evidence to referred to in Article 884 of this Act

Article 812. - When public documents contain statements or representations made by individuals, only prove that they were made before the authority that issued the document.

The declarations or statements in question tested against those who attended the event did or they were made , and expressed their agreement with them.

Section Four

From Testimonial

Article 813. - The party offering testimony must meet the following requirements:

I. The witnesses must be provided in connection with the disputed facts that are intended to prove to his testimony, to a maximum of five witnesses to each event , with the understanding that its relief is subject to the provisions in Section X of Article 815 of this Act ;

II. Contain the names of the witnesses , when impediment to present directly to the Board may request the quote, noting the cause or valid reasons that hinder them, in which case you should provide their addresses and if found them incorrect , will bidder by the presentation;

III. If the witness resides outside the place of residence of the Board, the bidder must provide proof to , accompanying interrogatories , the tenor of which shall be considered the witness , to do so , will be declared void. Also display copies of the interrogation , which are made available to other parties , so that within a period of three days to submit its list of cross-examination in a sealed envelope , and

IV. When the witness is a public servant of higher command , in the opinion of the Board, may make a statement through trade, observing the provisions of this article that apply.

Article 814. The Board , in the case of Section II of the preceding article , shall order summoning the witness to submit its statement at the time and day to be stipulated , with the warning to be submitted by the police.

Article 815. - In the outpouring of testimony following rules shall be observed:

I. The bidder submitted directly test their witnesses , except as provided in Article 813, and the Board shall receive their testimony;

II. The witness must be identified before the Board under the terms of the provisions of Section IV of Article 884 of this Law;

III. Witnesses shall be examined separately , in the order in which they were offered. The interrogation shall be made orally , except as provided in sections III and IV of Article 813 of this Law;

IV. After taking the witness conduct protest with truth and warn of the penalties incurred by false witnesses , shall contain the name , age, marital status, address , occupation and where they are working and then proceed to take his statement ;

V. The parties will formulate the questions orally and directly. The Board will support those that are directly related to the matter in question and that have not been done before at the same witness or implied with the answer ;

VI. First ask the bidder for the test and then to the other parties. The Board , when it deems appropriate, directly examine the witness ;

VII. The questions and answers will be recorded in the file being written literally one and the other ;

VIII. The witnesses are required to give the reason for this , and the Board shall apply with respect to the answers not bearing in itself ;

IX. The witness heard his statement , signed in the margins of the leaves containing it and this should be noted by the secretary , if you do not know or can not read or sign the statement will be read by the secretary and print their fingerprints and once ratified , it may be changed in the substance or in writing ;

X. Only hear the evidence of three witnesses for each event that is intended to prove , in the case to be presented more than three witnesses , the offeror shall designate test including who the desahogarán , and

XI. The sufficiency of this test is indivisible , unless one of the witnesses filed out of the place of residence of the Board and that the test has to vent by urge , in which case the Board shall take appropriate measures so that the other witnesses not aware vented ' previous statements.

Article 816. - If the witness does not speak Spanish , render his statement through an interpreter , to be appointed by the Board, to protest their faithful performance. When the witness so requests, in addition to settle your statement in Spanish , shall be written in their own language , by him or by the interpreter.

Article 817. - The Board , turning the urge to vent the testimony , interrogations accompanied with cross-examination questions and rated , under which the test should vent , but the parties can expand , and shall notify the requested authority the names of persons who have the authority to intervene in the proceedings.

Article 818. - The objections and strikeouts witnesses shall be made orally at the conclusion of the sufficiency of the evidence for later appreciation by the Board.

When false objected to a witness , the Board will receive evidence at the hearing of presentation of evidence referred to in Article 884 of this Act

Article 819. - The witness who fails to attend the hearing, despite being subpoenaed , he will act on the warning decreed , and the Board shall adopt the measures necessary to appear to give his statement , the date and time indicated.

Article 820. - A single witness may be conviction , if in the same circumstances exist that are guaranteed to do so unsuspected veracity of distorting the facts on which states , if:

I. It was the only one who noticed the facts ;

II. The statement is not in conflict with other evidence available in the record , and

III. Concurrence witness circumstances that are a guarantee of truth.

Section Five

From the Expert

Article 821. - Expert evidence will focus on issues related to some science , art , or art.

Article 822. - The expert must have knowledge in science , art or art on which should cover its opinion , if the profession or art estuvieren legally regulated , experts should prove to be authorized under the Act

Article 823. - Expert evidence should be provided indicating the matter on which it must relate , displaying the respective questionnaire , with a copy to each of the parties. The omission of the questionnaire will result in the Board not support the test.

Article 824. - The Board shall appoint experts as working men , when requested.

Article 825. - In the sufficiency of expert evidence will observe the following provisions:

I. Each party shall submit its expert personally the day of the hearing, except as provided in the preceding article ;

II. Experts protest to hold office under the Act and immediately surrender its opinion , unless you ask for cause you draw new date for surrender his opinion;

III. The day appointed for the hearing having respective verificative the or expert who attend the same yield their opinion. If anyone does not run parallel to the audience , without justification in the opinion of the Board, shall specify the new date for surrender, the Board dictating measures to appear ;

IV. The parties and members of the Board may ask the experts the questions they deem appropriate , and

V. In case of any discrepancy in the opinions , the Board shall appoint a third expert.

Article 826. - The expert umpire appointed by the Board must be excused within forty- eight hours of notification of the appointment , provided that either of the cases referred to in Chapter Four of this Title.

The Board flatly qualify excuse , declared admissible expert be appointed again.

Article 826 Bis. - When the opinion rendered by an expert is notoriously false, biased or inaccurate , the Board shall give the Prosecutor's Office to determine if there is a crime.

Section Six

Inspection

Article 827. - The party offering the inspection shall specify the subject matter of the same , the place to be practiced ; covering periods and objects and documents that must be examined. By offering the test, must be in the affirmative , setting the facts or issues that are to be credited with the same.

Article 828. - Admitted proof of inspection by the Board, shall specify the day , time and place for relief , if the documents and items held by either party , the Board appraised of that , if not display them , presumably be taken by certain facts that try to prove , provided that such documents referred to in Article 804 of this Act if the documents and

objects are in the hands of outsiders to the dispute, shall apply coercive measures as appropriate.

Article 829. - In testing the sufficiency of inspection following rules shall be observed:

I. The actuary , to the relief of the test will stick strictly to the orders of the Board ;

II. The actuary is required to put it documents and items to be inspected ;

III. The parties and their attorneys may attend the inspection procedure and make objections or observations they deem pertinent , and

IV. From the coach will rise affidavit to be signed by those who take part in it and which is added to the file , right before the Court.

Section Seven

The presumptive

Article 830. - Presumption is the consequence that the Act or the Board deducted from a known fact to ascertain the truth of another unknown.

Article 831. - There is a legal presumption when the Act expressly provides , no presumption of a human when done properly tested one that follows is the result of that.

Article 832. - The one that has in its favor a legal presumption, is only required to prove the fact that the sheath.

Article 833. - The legal and human presumptions , rebuttable.

Article 834. - The parties to provide presumptive evidence , indicate what it is and what it is credited with.

Section Eight

Of Instrumental

Article 835. - The instrumental is the set of actions contained in the record , formed out of the trial.

Article 836. - The Board is obliged to take into account the actions contained in the record of the trial.

Section Nine

From the Elements Contributed by Advancement of Science.

Article 836 -A. In the event that the parties offer evidence, those listed in Section VIII of Article 776, the offeror shall provide the Board with the tools , equipment or items needed for you to assess the content of the records and reproduce the sounds and images , by the time required for relief.

In case the bidder duly justified his disability to provide those items , the Board will provide it.

Article 836 -B. To the relief or valuation of the evidence referred to in this Section , shall apply:

a) Certificate Authority: to agencies and entities of the Federal Public Administration and certification service providers that, according to the legal provisions , have recognized this quality and have the technological infrastructure for the issuance , registration and administration of digital certificates and to provide services related thereto ;

b) Password: the unique set of alphanumeric characters that a user uses to access a service , program or system and can be associated with a physical medium, magnetic or biometric ;

c) Certificate Digital: the digital record issued by a Certification Authority which guarantees the authenticity of the identity data of the certificate holder ;

d) Password: the unique set of secret characters to validate the identification of the person who was assigned an Access Key to access a service, program or system ;

e) Private Key: the character set that generates the digital certificate holder exclusive and secret way to create advanced electronic signature ;

f) Public key data in a digital certificate enabling the identification of the signatory and the verification of the authenticity of your electronic signature ;

g) To: the person appointed by the issuer to receive the data message ;

h) Digital Document: The information can only be generated , accessed , modified and processed electronically, and sent through a data message ;

i) Issuer: the person who sends a digital document or data message;

j) Electronic signature: data set in electronic form are linked or associated with a data message for any technology and are used to identify the signatory in relation to the data message to indicate that approval of the information contained in the message data ;

k) Advanced Electronic Signature: the character set that allows the identification of the signatory in electronic documents or data messages as a result of using your digital certificate and private key and produces the same legal effect as handwritten signatures ;

l) Signer: a person who uses an electronic signature or advanced electronic signature to sign digital documents and , where appropriate, data messages ;

m) Electronic Media: a technological devices to perform the transmission and reception of data messages and digital documents ;

n) Electronic Media: a technological devices for processing, printing , display , storage , reproduction , retrieval, extraction and storage of information;

ñ) Message Data: the exchange of information between a sender and a receiver through electronic media ;

o) Personal Identification Number (PIN): the password used in services, systems or programs to access or identity , and

p) Information system: a set of technological elements to create , send, receive , store or process information.

Article 836 - C. The party offering a digital document or any electronic means, shall comply with the following:

I. Submit a print or digital copy of , and

II. Fostering minimum data for digital document location in the electronic medium in which it is located.

Article 836 - D. In testing the sufficiency of the electronic media , the following rules shall be observed:

I. The Board shall appoint the experts that will be needed to determine whether the information contained in the digital document is complete and unaltered , as was generated from the first moment , placing it in time and space between the sender and recipient.

The Board may commission the clerk to associate or expert appointed attesting place, date and time that is available to them in the middle which contains the digital document.

II. If the digital or electronic document , is held by the bidder , it must make available to the nominated surveyors or the means needed to render an opinion , do not apperceived that the test will be declared void.

III. If the digital or electronic document is held by the counterparty , it must also be made available from or expert appointed , with the warning that if not done, will establish the presumption being that the facts that the bidder expressed in relation to the digital document.

IV. If the digital or electronic document is in the possession of another person, that is required to make it available to the Board under the warnings set out in Article 731 of this Act

For purposes of this Article, subject to the provisions in Section Five of this chapter on expert evidence.

V. The parties and members of the Board may do or experts designated the questions they deem appropriate.

To the relief of the test referred to in this Article , the Board at any time may assist one human and technological elements necessary to best provide.

CHAPTER XIII LABOR DECISIONS

Article 837. - The decisions of the labor courts are:

I. Agreements: If measurements refer to simple procedural or when deciding any matter within the business ;

II. Cars incidental or interlocutory decisions: when resolved in or out of court an incident , and

III. Awards: when deciding on the merits of the dispute.

Article 838. - The Board shall render its decisions in the event that respective end of the proceedings or within forty -eight hours in which those written for promotions , unless otherwise provided in this Act

Article 839. The resolutions of the Boards shall be signed by the members of them and the secretary on the day the vote , in the terms of Article 620 of this Act

Article 840. - The award:

I. Place, date and Board to pronounce it ;

II. Names and addresses of the parties and their representatives ;

III. Extract the application and answer , reply and rejoinder and , where appropriate, of the counterclaim and reply to it, which shall contain clearly and concisely the requests of the parties and the facts in issue ;

IV. Enumeration of the evidence admitted and vented ' awareness and appreciation , noting the facts to be regarded as established ;

V. Extract the allegations ;

VI. The legal reasons or equity , jurisprudence and doctrine might support them , and

VII. The paragraphs.

Article 841. The awards will be issued in truth known and in good faith , and appreciating the facts of consciousness , without rules or formalities subject to overestimation of the tests, but the Conciliation and Arbitration are required to study in detail the rendered , making the evaluating them. Also, stating the reasons and legal grounds on which they rest.

Article 842. - The awards must be clear, precise and consistent with the claim, defense , _y other claims made in a timely trial.

Article 843. - At the awards , in the case of economic benefits, the salary will be determined as a basis for conviction; quantifying the amount of the benefit will be brought under the measures which must be complied with the resolution. Only by exception, may be ordered to open settlement incident.

Article 844. - When the sentence is liquid quantity shall be specified in the award itself , without incident, according to the foundation which must be completed.

Article 845. - If any or all of the representatives of workers or employers to the Board , which attend the hearing or proceeding to refuse to vote , will be required in the act by the Secretary who will tell the responsibilities incurred if they do not. If refusal persists , the Secretary shall affidavit to that effect is submitted to the appropriate authority to

determined that the liability incurred under Articles 671 to 675 of this Act

In these cases, the following rules shall be observed:

I. If it shall be taken by the president or assistant and representatives that vote. In case of a tie, the vote of the absent representatives will join the President or auxiliary ;

II. If it's award:

a) If after the injunction insist refusal , are excluded from the business knowledge and the Chairman of the Board or Special Board will call substitutes.

b) If the alternates are not presented to the Board within which they point , which may not be longer than three days, or refuse to vote on the award, the Chairman of the Board or Special Board shall report to the Secretary Labour and Social Security, the Governor of the State or Head of Government of the Federal District , to designate the persons who substituyan , in case of a tie, it is understood that the absent add your vote to the President.

Article 846. - If voted resolution one or more representatives to the Board , refuse to sign , will be required in the act by the Secretary and , if he persists in his refusal upon certification of the same Secretary , the resolution shall take effect law, without prejudice to any liability incurred by the neglectful.

Article 847. - Once notified of the award, either party , within a period of three days , the Board may request clarification of the resolution, to correct errors or clarify a point. The Board resolved within the same period , but may be varied by no sense of resolution.

The filing of enlightenment, does not interrupt the term for challenging the award.

Article 848. - The decisions of the boards do not support any resource. Boards can not revoke their resolutions.

The parties may enforce the liability incurred by Board members.

CHAPTER XIV A REVIEW OF THE IMPLEMENTING ACTS

Article 849. - Against acts of presidents , clerks or officers legally authorized in enforcement of awards , agreements , resolutions that put an end to the third party with and the dictates on precautionary measures appropriate to the review.

Article 850. From the review know:

I. The Special Board of Conciliation and Arbitration corresponding integrated with representatives of employers and workers and the auxiliary hearing the case , pursuant to Article 635 of this Act, in the case of acts of the Presidents of the thereof;

II. The Chairman of the Board or the relevant Special Board , in the case of acts of actuaries or legally authorized officials , and

III. The Board of Conciliation and Arbitration with the participation of the Secretary General of Agreements , in the case of acts of the President of this or in the case of a conflict that affects two or more branches of industry.

Article 851. - The review must be submitted in writing to the competent authority within three days after they are aware of the act which is contested.

Article 852. - In the review process the following rules shall be observed:

I. By promoting the review is provide respective evidence ;

II. Brief review will view the other parties for three days , to manifest what serves his interests and provide the evidence they deem relevant , and

III. Was summoned to a hearing of evidence and arguments , within ten days of the presentation of the review , which will be accepted and evidence from desahogarán and issue a decision.

Declared from the review , revised the act that originated in the appropriate manner and apply disciplinary sanctions to those responsible , as I indicated in Articles 637 to 647 of this Act

Article 853. Should the claim against the coercive measures that impose the Chairmen of the Special Boards and Conciliation and Arbitration , as well as the help of these.

Article 854. - In the processing of the claim will observe the following rules:

I. Within three days after it becomes aware of the extent , promote the claim in writing , providing supporting evidence ;

II. When admitted the claim request the official who issued the challenged measure , render its written report regarding funded and motivated act was challenged and attaching relevant evidence , and

III. The Board will schedule a hearing , which must take place during the ten days following the date on which the claim is admitted , to receive and accept evidence and issue resolution.

Article 855. - From result from the complaint, which was amended to the extent necessary urgency and apply to officer the penalty provided in Article 672 of this Act

Article 856. The Chairmen of the Boards may require the party seeking review or gross impropriety grievance in a fine of up to 100 times the general minimum wage in force in the Federal District at the time of submission.

It is well understood that the opinion inadmissible when its Chairman , as the case appears to be promoted in order to delay or impede the administration of justice.

CHAPTER XV PRECAUTIONARY MEASURES

Article 857. - The Chairmen of the Boards of Conciliation and Arbitration , or the Special thereof, at the request of a party, may decree the following precautionary measures:

I. Attachment, fear that when absent or hide the person against whom it is filed or a complaint has been filed , and

II. Embargo precautionary necessity for ensuring the assets of a person, company or establishment.

Article 858. - The precautionary measures may be requested to file the lawsuit , or later , whether it be in writing or in appearance. In the first case , previously the site will be processed and the second , in a separate. In any case , the application will notify the person against whom the ruling is requested.

Article 859. - The roots shall be ordered plane and its effect will be to prevent the defendant not to be absent from his place of residence , while legitimate representative , sufficient instructions and funds.

Article 860. - The person who breaks the hold decreed , will be responsible for the crime of disobedience to a command authority. To this effect , the President of the Board shall make the complaint in question to the prosecutor concerned.

Article 861. To declare a provisional seizure , the following rules shall be observed:

I. The applicant shall determine the amount claimed and render it deems appropriate tests to prove the necessity of the measure ;

II. The Chairman of the Board , taking into consideration the circumstances of the case and the evidence submitted , within twenty-four hours after one in which the prompt, may order the provisional seizure if , in its opinion , is necessary providence ;

III. The judgment ordering the seizure will determine the amount by which it should be practiced , and

IV. The Chairman of the Board shall adopt measures must abide by the embargo , in order not to stop or hinder the development of the activities of the company or establishment.

Article 862. - In the case of Section II of the previous article , providence is considered necessary when the applicant finds that the defendant has different judgments or claims before judicial or administrative authorities set up by others against him, and that the amount , at the discretion of the President , there is a risk of insolvency.

Article 863. Providence will be held even if not present the person against whom it is rendered. The owner of the seized property shall be the depositary of them , without having to accept the charge or protest perform it , with the responsibilities and privileges of the same , observing the provisions of this Act as applicable. In case of corporate entity , the depositary will be the manager or general manager or who have legal representation of it.

In the case of real estate, on request , the Board shall request the registration of provisional seizure in the Public Registry of Property.

Article 864. - If the defendant is given sufficient security deposit or will not take out the injunction be lifted or has been decreed.

CHAPTER XVI PROCEEDINGS BEFORE CONCILIATION BOARDS

Article 865. (Repealed).
Article 866. (Repealed).
Article 867. (Repealed).
Article 868. (Repealed).
Article 869. (Repealed).

CHAPTER XVII STANDARD PROCEDURE BEFORE THE BOARDS OF CONCILIATION AND ARBITRATION

Article 870. - The provisions of this Chapter governing the processing and settlement of individual and collective disputes of a legal nature with no special handling of this Act

Article 871. - The procedure will begin with the presentation of the application, before the officers of Parties or the Receiver Unit competent Board , which will turn it to the House or the Special Board , as appropriate, on the day before completion the work of the Board.

Article 872. - The demand shall be in writing , accompanied by as many copies of the same , as defendants have. The actor in his initial written application shall indicate the facts in favor of its requests and can accompany you consider relevant evidence to prove his claims.

Article 873. The Board , within twenty-four hours , counted from the time of receipt of the application, shall issue a resolution , which set a day and time for the celebration of the settlement hearing , demand and exceptions , which must occur within the fifteen days following the date on which you received the statement of claim. This agreement will be personally notified the parties ten days in advance of the hearing at least giving the defendant a collated copy of the lawsuit and the settlement admisorio , warning them of the provisions of section 879 of this Act

When the actor is an employee or their beneficiaries , the Board, in case notare any irregularity in the writ of summons or contradictory actions which he is exercising or has not clarified the basic salary of the action , the agreement will point out defects or omissions incurred prevent and to remedy them within a period of three days. Such approval shall be served personally to the actor.

Article 874. - The lack of reporting of some or all of the defendants , requires the Board to officially note new date and time for the holding of the hearing, unless the parties attend the same or if the actor abandons actions filed against defendants who have not been notified.

The parties comparecieren the audience , will be notified of the new date for the meeting , which were notified and did not attend , will be notified by newsletter or bar of the Board , and those who were not notified they will personally.

Article 875. The hearing referred to in Article 873 in two stages:

a) In conciliation ;

b) demand and exceptions ;

c) (Repealed).

The hearing will begin with the appearance of the parties to attend the same , those who are absent may intervene when they are submitted , provided that the Board did not take the agreement of the requests in the corresponding stage.

Article 876. - The conciliation stage will be held as follows:

I. The parties appear in person to the Board and will be assisted by their lawyers employers , consultants or agents. If it comes to corporations , the representative or agent shall have the authority to take a compromise that forces his client ;

II. The Board , through the conciliation officer or his legal staff will intervene to hold talks between the parties and the urge to try and reach a settlement. We propose options for fair and equitable solution that , in his opinion , be appropriate to terminate the dispute;

III. If the parties reach an agreement , it will terminate the conflict. The corresponding agreement approved by the Board , will produce all the legal effects inherent to an award ;

IV. (Repealed).

V. The Board , through the conciliation officer or his legal staff , shall, without hindering the process and being in personal contact with the parties and even before the closure of the instruction , they reach a settlement , always insisting on options fair and equitable solution for both , if the parties do not reach an agreement they will by protesters , from the stage of demand and exceptions, and

VI. Had it not crowded parties to the settlement , they shall be dissatisfied with any arrangement and shall be delivered to the stage of demand and exceptions.

Article 877. (Repealed).

Article 878. - The stage of demand and exceptions , be conducted according to the following rules:

I. The President or other officer conciliatory and legal staff of the Board again urge the parties to resolve the dispute through a settlement and , if they persist in their attitude , give the floor to the actor for exposing their demand ;

II. If the claimant is the employee or his beneficiaries and does not meet the requirements omitted or not remedy the deficiencies which have been indicated in the approach of the additions to the application, the Board will prevent you to do it then.

The actor will present his claim, ratifying it , rinsing or modifying , detailing the petitioner's arguments. In case of modification , clarification or straightening demand , when the actor is an employee or their beneficiaries , may do so only once at this stage. Case for clarification or modification of the application , the Board, at the request of the defendant, indicate new date within the

within ten days , for the continuation of the hearing to enable it to answer the complaint in its entirety , in case of straightening, the Board shall proceed in the same way , but ex officio ;

III. Exposed demand by the plaintiff, the defendant shall where appropriate, to give answer to the complaint orally or in writing. In the latter case shall deliver to the actor a simple copy of your answer , if not, the Board shall be issued at the expense of the defendant;

IV. In its defense the defendant oppose exceptions and defenses , and must refer to each and every one of the facts alleged in the complaint, affirming them or denying them , and expressing to ignore when they are not themselves , can add the explanations it deems fit. The silence and evasive will make you have as admitted those on which no controversy arises , and there shall be no evidence to the contrary. The outright denial of right confession matter of fact. The admission of these do not imply the acceptance of the right ;

V. A plea does not relieve the defendant answer the complaint at the hearing and , if it does not and the Board has jurisdiction , it shall be answered in the affirmative the demand ;

VI. The parties may by once, replicate and contrarreplicar briefly settling on record their claims if requested ;

VII. If the defendant upbraids the actor , will proceed to answer immediately, or, at the request of the same , the Board agreed to suspend the hearing , then pointing to a date within ten days , and

VIII. At the end of the demand period and exceptions will be summoned to the hearing of offering and admission of evidence , that will take place within ten days. If the parties agree on the facts and the dispute is reduced to a point of law, shall be declared closed cars taking turns instruction to resolution.

Article 879. The settlement hearing , demand and exceptions will be held , even if the parties do not concur.

If the actor does not appear to demand and exceptions period , it shall be reproduced on demand via their appearance or initial brief.

If the defendant does not attend , the demand shall be answered in the affirmative , notwithstanding that at the stage of offering and admission of evidence showing that the actor was no worker or employer, that there was no dismissal or that are not true the facts stated in the application.

Article 880. The hearing of offering and admission of evidence will be developed in accordance with the last paragraph of Article 875 of this Act and in accordance with the following standards:

I. The actor will offer its evidence regarding disputed facts. Immediately after the defendant offered its evidence and may object to its counterpart and that in turn may object to the defendant;

II. The parties may submit new evidence , provided that relate to those offered by the counterparty as well as tending to justify their objections to the amendments , pending the hearing is closed , and for once ;

III. The parties shall provide their tests , observing the provisions of Chapter XII of this Title , and

IV. Once the offer, the Board shall immediately terminate upon the evidence that supports and discard. Otherwise, the Board may reserve to meet within five days.

Article 881. - After the stage of offering and admission of evidence will be admitted only those relating to subsequent events or strikeouts.

Article 882. (Repealed).

Article 883. The Board , in the same agreement that supports testing, set a day and time for the celebration of the presentation of evidence hearing , which must occur within ten working days , and shall in the case , which turn the trades and exhortations necessary to collect the information or issuing copies to be any authority or person outside the trial show that the offeror has applied with the warnings specified in this Act , and shall adopt the necessary measures so that the day of the audience can vent all the evidence that has been admitted.

When , by the nature of the evidence admitted , the Board considers that it is possible to let go of them in a single hearing , in such resolution shall specify the days and times you must vent, but do not keep the order in which they were offered , trying to be receive first the actor and then those of the defendant. This period shall not exceed thirty days.

Article 884. - The presentation of evidence hearing will be conducted according to the following rules:

I. Open the hearing , it shall vent all tests are properly prepared , trying to be the actor's first and immediately the defendant or, in his case, which have been identified to vent on your date ;

II. If any of the evidence admitted is not in properly prepared , will be brought new day and time for relief within ten days , making use of coercive measures ;

III. If the vent tests are only copies or documents to be officials or others forward , the Board will require them in the following terms:

a) In the case of authorities , the Board shall be required to submit such documents or copies, if not fulfilled , at the request of a party, the Board shall notify the immediate superior to to enforce the sanctions , and

b) In the case of others, the Board shall issue the appropriate enforcement measures , until there is submission of copies or relevant documents ;

IV. The Board shall require the person appearing to vent the corresponding test to identify with any official document , and , if not done at the time of the hearing, shall be given three days to do so, apercibiéndola that , if otherwise , it will not effect the corresponding statement , and

V. At the conclusion of the presentation of the evidence , the Board granted the parties a period of two days to submit their arguments in writing.

Article 885. At the conclusion of the presentation of evidence , the allegations made by the parties and upon certification by the secretary of that there are no tests for venting , you will view the parties for the term of three days to express their approval for such certification under the pain of

if after the period specified not do so and any vent tests , had pursued in them shall be the same for all legal purposes and shall proceed as provided in paragraph below. In the event that the parties to the hearing scheduled venting , proving that one or some evidence offered is not vented , the Board, with citation of the same , indicate within eight days following date and time for their relief. The evidence has been pending , the parties shall make allegations within twenty-four hours.

Having done this , the auxiliary , ex officio , declared closed the investigation and , within ten days thereafter, make written the draft award , which shall contain the elements listed in Article 840 of this Act

I. An extract of the demand and response, reply and rejoinder , and where appropriate, of the counterclaim and answered it ;

II. The marking of the disputed facts ;

III. An account of the evidence admitted and vented ' , and appreciation in conscience , pointing out the facts to be regarded as established ;

IV. The grounded and motivated considerations arising , if any , of the alleged and proven , and

V. The paragraphs.

Article 886. - The draft award copies thereof to each of the members of the Board.

Within five working days following the day on which it has received a copy of the project, any member of the Board may request that the proceedings be practiced as it considers appropriate to clarify the truth.

The Board , with citation of the parties indicate , where appropriate, date and time for the relief , within a period of eight days , the tests were not carried out or practice of the procedures requested.

Article 887. - Once the term referred to the previous article , awarded to members of the Board, or if applicable , vented ' proceedings in this term as ordered , the President of the Board shall summon members same , for discussion and vote , which must occur within ten days after they have completed the term fixed or sufficiency of the respective proceedings.

Article 888. - The discussion and vote on the draft award will take place at a meeting of the Board, the secretary certifying the presence of the participants who attend the vote , in accordance with the following standards:

I. It will read the draft resolution and the allegations and the comments made by the parties ;

II. The President will make the business discussion with the result of the action taken , and

III. After the discussion, we shall vote , and the President shall declare the result.

Article 889. - If the draft judgment is passed , no additions or modifications , will rise to the level of award and immediately signed by the members of the Board.

If the project is make changes or additions shall order the clerk to immediately write the award, in accordance with the approved. In this case , the result will be recorded.

Article 890. - Thickened the award , the Secretary shall, in his case , the signatures of the Board members who voted in the business and , once obtained, to submit the case to the clerk , to immediately notify the award personally to parts.

Article 891. - If the Board considers that a party acted with malice or bad faith , it may impose a fine on the award , pursuant to the provisions of Section II of Article 729 of this Act

CHAPTER XVIII SPECIAL PROCEDURES

Article 892. - The provisions of this Chapter governing the handling of disputes arising in connection with the application of articles 5. fraction III , 28, section III , 151 , 153 , section X , 158 , 162 , 204 , Section IX , 209 , fraction V , 210 , 236 , sections II and III , 389 , 418 , 425 , section IV , 427 fractions I , II and VI, 434, fractions I, III and V , 439 , 503 and 505 of this Act conflicts aimed at the collection of benefits that do not exceed the amount of three months' salary.

Article 893. - The procedure will begin with the presentation of the statement of claim , in which the plaintiff may offer evidence to the Board its authority, which ten days notice , summon a conciliation hearing , demand and exceptions , testing and resolution , which shall take place within fifteen working days from the date the claim was filed or at the conclusion of the investigations referred to in Article 503 of this Act

Article 894. - The Board , citing the demanding , give him a warning that failure to attend the hearing referred to in the following article will by accepted requests from the plaintiff , unless they are contrary to the provisions of the Act

Article 895. - The conciliation hearing , demand and exceptions , testing and resolution , will be held in accordance with the following standards:

I. The Board shall endeavor to reconcile the parties , in accordance with Sections I and II of Article 876 of this Law;

II. Not possible above, each of the parties will present what he considers appropriate , make your requests and offer and render the evidence that has been admitted ;

III. If offered the count of workers , shall follow the provisions contained in Article 931 of this Act , and

IV. After the reception of the evidence, the Board shall hear the allegations and issue resolution.

Article 896. - If the plaintiff or petitioner attends the hearing , it shall be reproduced his written or initial appearance , and in your case, offered evidence which had accompanied. If it comes to the application of Article 503 of this Act, the Board shall issue its decision taking into account the arguments and evidence submitted by the persons who exercised rights under the performance that generated the deceased worker.

When controvert the right of the intended beneficiaries , suspended the hearing and marked its resumption within fifteen days , so that the parties can offer and provide evidence related to the points at issue.

If you do not attend other parties, will act on the warning referred to in Article 894 of this Act

Article 897. - For the processing and resolution of conflicts referred to in this Chapter , the Board shall consist of the Assistant , except in cases of Articles 389 , 418 , 424 , section IV , 427, fractions II , III and VI , 434, fractions I, III and V , and 439 of this Act shall intervene where the President of the Board or the Special Board.

Article 898. - The Board , for the purposes of Article 503 of this Law, request the employer to provide the names and addresses of registered beneficiaries before him and government institutions , may also order the practice of any proceedings , or use the media deems appropriate, to summon all persons financially dependent on the deceased worker to exercise their rights before the Board.

Article 899. - In special procedures shall follow the provisions of Chapters XII and XVII of this title , as applicable.

Section One

Social Security Individual Disputes

Article 899 -A. Individual conflicts social security are aimed at claiming the granting of benefits in cash or in kind , from the various insurance that make up the compulsory Social Security , organized and administered by the Social Security Institute , and those under the Social Security Act and the Law Institute of the National Housing Fund for Workers to fill the Institute of National Housing Fund for Workers and Administrators Retirement Funds , as well as those are applicable under collective bargaining agreements or contracts -Law containing benefits social security.

The jurisdiction of these conflicts , because of land be vested in the Federal Special Conciliation and Arbitration of the place in which the clinic is the Mexican Social Security Institute to which they are assigned the insured or their beneficiaries.

In case of demand -related benefits only the return of funds for retirement and housing , competition correspond to Special Federal Board of Conciliation and Arbitration of the Federation where you are the last person entitled workplace.

Article 899- B. Individual conflicts social security , may be raised by:

I. The workers, policyholders, pensioners or their beneficiaries , who are holders of rights under insurance comprising the compulsory Social Security ;

II. Workers who are holders of rights under the National Housing Fund for Workers or their beneficiaries ;

III. The individual account holders Savings System for Retirement of employees subject to this Act or the beneficiaries , and

IV. Workers who are applicable collective bargaining agreements or contracts -Law containing benefits social security.

Article 899- C. The demands on conflict referred to this section shall contain:

I. Name , address and date of birth of the petitioner and the documents proving his personality ;

II. Factual and causes that give rise to the claim ;

III. The claims of the petitioner , clearly stating what is asked ;

IV. Name and address of companies or establishments in which he has worked , positions held ; activities ; antiquity generated and contributions to the social security ;

V. Social security number or identification reference as insured, annuitant or beneficiary , clinic or family practice unit assigned ;

VI. In your case , the last state of the individual account retirement savings , certificate issued by the Mexican Institute of Social Security pension granting or denial of , or evidence of credit granting or denial of housing ;

VII. Documents issued by employers , the Mexican Social Security Institute , the Institute of the National Housing Fund for Workers and Administrator for Retirement Fund or , where appropriate, acknowledgment of their request and, in general , the information necessary to ensure the conduct of proceedings in accordance with due immediacy ;

VIII. The other evidence it deems appropriate to prove their claims , and

IX. Necessary copies of the application and its attachments , to run served notice.

Article 899- D. Social security agencies , as provided by Article 784 must show the documents , according to the Laws, have a legal obligation to issue and maintain , under penalty that no reporting is presumed the facts alleged by the petitioner. In any case , it is for social security organizations , prove that when there is controversy over:

I. Join date social security scheme ;

II. Number of weeks of contributions in the fields of insurance;

III. Average salary of the petitioners quote ;

IV. State housing account and retirement contributions of the insured ;

V. Provisions of the insured or withdrawals on accounts resources ;

VI. Granting pensions or annuities ;

VII. Duration of rights, and

VIII. Partial payments granted to policyholders.

Article 899- E. In the case of benefits due to workplace hazards or general diseases , the procedure is subject to the following rules:

The parties shall designate their medical experts in the application and in the reply to the same , which shall have the register referred to in Article 899- F.

Should the actor skip the appointment of medical expert or ask the Board to appoint one in terms of the provisions of Article 824 of this Act, this will prevent you to remedy the omission within a period of three days , apercibiéndolo that in case of failure to do so will reject the statement of claim.

Expert evidence will be integrated with the expert opinions rendered by the experts of the parties, and which render the expert appointed by the Special Board of knowledge.

The Board, appoint such experts , ensure that the same institution depend differently than those designated by the parties, unless the body of medical experts referred to in Article 899- G of the Act , do not count on any that satisfies these circumstances.

Advice should contain:

I. Data identification and accreditation of the medical profession of each of the experts ;

II. Actor identification data , specifying the document that proved his identity ;

III. Diagnosis of the conditions claimed;

IV. Case of risk rating and valuation work , the arguments to determine the causal relationship between the specific activity undertaken by the worker and disability status score or valuation which is determined ;

V. The conviction means which are based the conclusions of expertise , including reference to medical studies which have subjected the worker , and

VI. In his case, the percentage of valuation, functional organic decline , or the determination of disability status.

The parties have a period of ten working days from the conclusion of the initial hearing , that his experts agree and protest and express charge conferred to the Board as justified , the requirements for the issuance of the expert and , as appropriate , to the determination of causation, work injury case.

The Board shall be responsible for notification of the experts so designated and shall adopt the measures it deems appropriate to expedite the issuance of the expert opinions and require the worker to be present at the completion of medical studies or procedures requiring experts.

Within thirty days of the conclusion of the initial hearing , the Board shall set a day and time for the hearing to receive the expert with citation of the parties, with the understanding that failure to appear , they will forfeit their right to cross-examine or observations.

If the plaintiff does not attend the proceedings ordered by the Board referred to in paragraph c) of this section , or if you leave medical studies or procedures ordered , will attest to the lack of

interest , to the effect that the dropout is decreed test , except for justifiable reasons referred to in Article 785 of this Act

The Board shall apply to the experts enforcement measures established by this Act , to ensure the timely issuance of the opinion.

The parties to the hearing on sufficiency of the medical expert , by itself or through a professional in medicine, may submit any comments or questions they deem appropriate in relation to the considerations and conclusions of the medical expert evidence.

Board members may question the expert or experts who appear to diligence.

The Board credited determine whether the causal link between the specific activity undertaken by the worker and the work environment reported in the statement of claim and the risk occupational work, to qualify as such.

The Board may require the authorities , public institutions and decentralized bodies , the information in their possession and to contribute to the clarification of the facts may also request medical studies in public health institutions or private practice all kinds of inquiries and inspections in undertakings or establishments in which the employee has worked and , if necessary , be assisted by expert opinion on other matters.

In the enforcement of the award the parties may agree on the modalities of its implementation.

Article 899- F. Medical experts involved in conflicts involving the risk rating and valuation work and general diseases , must be registered in the register of the Federal Board of Conciliation and Arbitration.

To this end, the medical expert must satisfy the following requirements:

I. Be legally authorized and qualified to practice as a doctor ;

II. Be in good standing;

III. Having three years of professional experience related to occupational health ;

IV. Not have been convicted of an intentional crime punishable by imprisonment , and

V. Observe the provisions of Article 707 of this Act and the provisions of the Federal Law of Administrative Responsibilities of Public Servants in relation to the causes of disability and excuse.

If during the period of six months medical experts fail on more than three occasions , with the timely submission of medical reports that are required , without justified cause , according to the President of the Federal Conciliation and Arbitration shall be given from the register of medical experts and may not return but after two years, counted from the date of withdrawal.

Article 899- G. The Federal Board of Conciliation and Arbitration integrate a body of medical experts specializing in occupational medicine, for which public institutions that provide health services , shall appoint medical experts may be requested by the Board , pursuant to Regulation corresponding.

CHAPTER XIX PROCEDURES FOR COLLECTIVE DISPUTES OF AN ECONOMIC NATURE

Article 900. - Collective disputes of an economic nature , are those whose approach aims at the modification or implementation of new working conditions , or suspension or termination of collective labor relations , unless this Act unless another procedure.

Article 901. - In the handling of conflicts referred to in this Chapter , the Boards should ensure , first, that the parties reach an agreement. To this end, they may attempt conciliation at any stage of the proceedings has not been given the decision to end the conflict.

Article 902. - The exercise of the right to strike suspended the processing of disputes of an economic nature , pending before the Board of Conciliation and Arbitration and the applications filed , unless the workers state in writing , agree to submit the dispute to the decision of the Board.

Not applicable as provided in the preceding paragraph, when the strike is intended as stated in Article 450 , Section VI.

Article 903. - Collective disputes of an economic nature may be raised by labor unions holding collective labor contracts , for the majority of workers in a company or establishment , provided that affect professional interest , or the pattern or employers , by application in writing , which shall include:

I. Name and address of that promotes and documents supporting his personality ;

II. Factual and causes that led to the conflict , and

III. The claims of the petitioner , clearly stating what is asked.

Article 904. - The petitioner , as appropriate, must accompany the application as follows:

I. Public or private documents that tend to check the economic situation of the company or establishment and the need for the measures requested ;

II. The ratio of workers who provide services to the company or establishment, stating their names, jobs they perform, they receive salary and seniority ;

III. An opinion expressed by the expert on the economic situation of the company or establishment;

IV. It deems appropriate tests to prove their claims , and

V. Necessary copies of the application and its attachments , to run served notice.

Article 905. - The Board , immediately after receiving the demand , summon the parties to a hearing shall be held within five days.

Article 906. - The hearing was held in accordance with the following standards:

I. If the petitioner does not attend the hearing , he shall be withdrawn its application;

II. If the other party does not attend , he shall be dissatisfied with any arrangement. The petitioner made a statement of the facts and the causes that led to the conflict and ratify their request ;

III. If both parties concur , the Board, after hearing their arguments, the urge to seek a settlement. Members of the same may make the suggestions they deem appropriate for the settlement of the conflict;

IV. If the parties reach an agreement , it will terminate the conflict. The agreement, approved by the Board , will produce all the legal effects inherent to an award ;

V. If no agreement is reached , the parties will make a statement of the facts and reasons that led to the conflict and formulate their requests and which by their nature can not vent , they set a day and time for this;

VI. Finished the exhibits of the parties and made their requests , it shall be offered and where appropriate, to unburden the evidence admitted ;

VII. The Board , in the same hearing, appoint three experts , at least , to investigate the facts and causes that led to the conflict , giving them a term not to exceed thirty days , to issue its opinion as to how that, in his opinion , the conflict can be resolved without prejudice to each party may designate an expert to be associated with those appointed by the Board or render separate opinion , and

VIII. Workers and employers may appoint two commissions made to the number of persons determined by the Board, to accompany the expert on research and they indicate the observations and suggestions they consider appropriate.

Article 907. - The experts appointed by the Board shall meet the following requirements:

I. Being Mexican and in full exercise of their rights ;

II. Be legally authorized and qualified to practice the art , science or art about to be the expert , except where authorization is not required , but should have the knowledge of the subject in question , and

III. Not have been convicted of an intentional crime.

Article 908. - The parties , within the first ten days of the term referred to Section VII of Article 906, may submit to the experts, or through the Board or by the Commission , observations , reports, studies and other elements that can contribute to the determination of the causes that led to the conflict , to be considered by the experts, in their opinions.

Article 909. - The experts appointed by the Board , conduct investigations and studies they consider appropriate , and may act as widely , having, in addition to those inherent in their performance, the following powers:

I. Order all kinds of reports and studies of the authorities and official institutions , federal and specific state dealing with economic problems , such as

research institutes of social and economic , trade unions , chambers of commerce, industry and other similar institutions ;

II. Practice all types of inspections in the undertaking or establishment and review their books and documents , and

III. Browse to the parties and persons connected with the workers or the company as it deems appropriate.

Article 910. - The opinion of the experts shall contain at least:

I. The events and causes that led to the conflict ;

II. The relationship between the cost of family life and the wages received by the workers ;

III. Average wages are paid in company or establishments of the same branch of industry and general working conditions that govern them ;

IV. Economic conditions in the undertaking or establishment or establishments ;

V. The general condition of the industry which includes the company or establishment;

VI. The general market conditions ;

VII. The statistical indices that tend to define the national economy and

VIII. The way in which , in his view , the conflict can be resolved.

Article 911. - The opinion of the experts will be added to the file and give a copy to each of the parties.

The Secretary settle right in cars of the day and time you handed over the copies to the parties, or the refusal to receive them.

Article 912. - The parties , within seventy-two hours of receiving a copy of the opinion of experts, can make the observations they deem appropriate in connection with the facts, considerations and conclusions of the same opinion.

The Board , if objections to the opinion, summoned to a hearing at which experts will attend to answer questions put to them by the parties and in respect of surveys that paid , is able to offer tests aimed to check the falsity of the facts and considerations contained in the opinion.

Article 913. - The Board has the broadest powers to take such measures as it deems appropriate , in order to complete , clarify or define the issues discussed by the experts , and to request new reports to the authorities , institutions and individuals to be referred to in Article 909 , Section I of this Chapter , examine the experts or ask any further opinion or appoint committees to practice or conduct research or studies.

Article 914. - The authorities , institutions and individuals referred to the previous articles are required to provide reports , answering questionnaires and render the statements apply to them.

Article 915. - The evidence has , the Board granted the parties a period of seventy- two hours to formulate their arguments in writing apercibidas that failure to do so , they will forfeit their right.

Article 916. - After the term for the submission of briefs , the auxiliary instruction and declared closed within fifteen days prepare a report which shall contain:

I. A summary of the presentations and requests of the parties;

II. An excerpt from the opinion of the experts and the observations they had made the parties;

III. An enumeration and assessment of the evidence and of the action taken by the Board;

IV. An extract of the allegations , and

V. Submit the reasons and rationale that can serve to resolve the conflict.

Article 917. - The opinion shall be added to the file and give a copy to each of the representatives of workers and employers , to the Board. The Secretary settle right in cars of the day and time you were handed copies or refusal to receive them.

Article 918. - The Chairman of the Board cited for discussion and voting hearing , which must occur within ten days after they are delivered to representatives copies of the opinion, and will be held according to the rules established in the Article 888 of this Act

Article 919. - The Board , in order to achieve balance and social justice in the relations between workers and employers , by resolution may increase or decrease the staff, the day , the week of work, wages and overall , change the working conditions of the company or establishment , but in no case can reduce the minimum rights set forth in the law.

CHAPTER XX PROCEDURE FOR A STRIKE

Article 920. - The strike procedure will begin by presenting a list of demands , which must meet the following requirements:

I. Will write to the employer and he formulated the requests , announce the purpose of going on strike if they are not satisfied , specifically expressed object and point the same day and time that work be suspended , or the term pre-strike ;

II. Be submitted in duplicate to the Board of Conciliation and Arbitration. If the company or establishment are located in different place of residence the Board, the writing may be submitted to the nearest labor authority or senior political authority of the place of location of the company or establishment. The authority making the site will forward the file , within twenty-four hours , to the Board of Conciliation and Arbitration , and telegraph or telephone notify the Chairman of the Board.

III. The notice for the suspension of the work will occur, at least six days prior to the date for cessation of work and ten days in advance in the case of public services , observing the provisions of this Act period shall be reckoned from the date and time notified remaining pattern.

Article 921. - The President of the Board of Conciliation and Arbitration or authorities referred to in Section II of the preceding article , under its strict liability the employer will get a copy of the letter of formal notice within forty-eight hours of of receipt.

The notification shall have the effect of making the employer , throughout the term of the notice , a repository of company or establishment affected by the strike, with the powers and responsibilities of the office.

Article 922. - The pattern , within forty-eight hours of notification, shall file its written response to the Board of Conciliation and Arbitration.

Article 923. - Will not be processed to the notice of a strike when it is not made in accordance with the requirements of Article 920 or is filed by a union other than the owner of the collective bargaining agreement or the contract manager law or when it seeks to require the signing of a collective agreement , however there is already one placed in the Conciliation and Arbitration Board jurisdiction. The Chairman of the Board , before starting the processing of any notice of strike , should ensure the above , order the appropriate certification and written notice of the decision to the petitioner.

Article 924. - A notification from the list of demands with a strike , shall cease enforcement of any judgment , nor be practiced , however, assurance , action or eviction, against the company or establishment , or sequester assets the premises in which they are installed , unless before the strike broke the case of:

I. Ensuring the rights of workers , especially benefits, wages , pensions and other benefits payable , up to the amount of two years' wages of the worker;

II. Credits arising from non-payment of contributions to the Social Security Institute ;

III. Ensure the collection of contributions that the employer has an obligation to make the Institute of National Housing Fund for Workers , and

IV. Other tax credits.

Always be preferential rights of workers, on the credits to which they relate fractions II , III and IV of this rule , and in any case the proceedings relating to the exceptions mentioned in the previous sections, will be practiced without affecting the strike procedure.

Article 925. - For the purposes of this Chapter , the term public services the communications and transport, light and electricity , the clean, the utilization and distribution of water for the service of the people , the gas , toilets , those in hospitals, cemeteries and power , when referring to basic necessities , provided that in the latter case affecting a full service branch.

Article 926. - The Conciliation and Arbitration Board shall summon the parties to a conciliation hearing , which avenirlas endeavor , without prejudice statement on the existence or non-existence , justification or lack of justification for the strike. This hearing may be postponed only upon request of workers and only once.

Article 927. - The settlement hearing shall conform to the following standards:

I. If the employer opposed the objection of lack of personality to answer the petitions, the Board previously resolved this situation and, if it is declared unfounded , will continue the hearing

where you will observe the standards set by the conciliation proceedings before the Conciliation and Arbitration Board as applicable;

II. If workers do not attend the settlement hearing , shall not the term for suspension of work ;

III. The Chairman of the Board may employ coercive measures to force the employer to attend the settlement hearing , and

IV. The effects of the notice referred to in Article 920 paragraph II of this Act , shall not be suspended by the settlement hearing or pattern of wayward to attend it.

Article 928. - In the procedures referred to in this chapter applies the following rules:

I. For operation of the Plenary and Special Boards observe the provisions in Article 620, but the president personally intervene in the following resolutions:

a) Lack of personality.

b) Lack of jurisdiction.

c) Cases of Articles 469, 923 and 935.

d) Declaration of absence or illegality of a strike.

II. No general rules shall apply in respect of terms to notices and subpoenas. Notices shall become effective from the date and time that are made ;

III. All days and hours will be working. The Board shall have permanent guards for this purpose;

IV. Not be reportable under the terms of Article 710 of this Act, the members of the Board, nor accept any incidents that the lack of personality that may be raised , by the employer, in the response to the site, and the workers , within forty-eight hours after they are made aware of the first class of the pattern. The Board , within twenty-four hours of the promotion, after hearing the parties , issue resolution , and

V. You can not issue any competition promoted. If the Board made the site once the pattern , notes that the matter is not your competence , will make the corresponding declaration.

Workers have a period of twenty four hours to designate the Board to consider competent , so that _le inspect the files. The performances remain valid , but the term for suspension of work shall run from the date the Board notifies the employer designated competent receiving the record , what will inform the parties in the resolution of incompetence.

Article 929. - Workers and employers of the company or establishment , or third parties , may request the Board of Conciliation and Arbitration , within seventy-two hours following the suspension of work , declare the nonexistence of the strike for the reasons specified in Article 459 or for not meeting the requirements of Article 920 of this Act

If no request for the declaration of absence , will be considered a strike exists for all legal purposes.

Article 930. - In the process of declaration of absence of the strike , the following rules shall be observed:

I. The request to declare the nonexistence of the strike , shall be in writing , accompanied by a copy for each of the deployed patterns and coalition of workers unions or emplazantes. The request shall state the reasons and legal basis for it. It may be argued then causes other than lack ;

II. The Board will notify the application and hear the parties at a hearing, which will also be offering and taking of evidence , to be held within a period not exceeding five days ;

III. The evidence must relate to the causes of absence in the application mentioned in section I , and when the application has been submitted by third parties, which also tend to check their interest. The Board will accept only those that meet the above requirements ;

IV. The tests will surrender at the hearing, except as provided in the following article. Only in exceptional cases the Board may defer the receipt of which by their nature can not vent at the hearing;

V. After the reception of the evidence , the Board, within twenty-four hours , decide on the existence or nonexistence of the legal status of the strike , and

VI. For the resolution of absence , will be referred to the representatives of workers and employers to serve on the Board. The judgment shall be rendered by those who attend , and in case of a tie, the President will be added to the _votos of the absent.

Article 931. - If offered as evidence the count of workers, the following rules shall be observed:

I. The Board shall indicate the place, date and time to be effected ;

II. Only entitled to vote the company workers who apply to the count ;

III. Be considered an employee of the company who had been dismissed from work after the date of submission of the site;

IV. Not count the votes of confidence workers or those workers who entered the work after the date of filing of the notice of a strike , and

V. Objections to workers who apply to the count , must be in the very act of diligence, in which case the Board will schedule a hearing to offer and test-taking.

Article 932. - If the Board declares the state's legal nonexistence strike:

I. Workers shall set a term of twenty four hours to return to their job ;

II. Above must notify through union representation , workers admonishing that the mere failure to comply with the resolution, will be completed labor relations , except for just cause ;

III. Declare that the pattern has not incurred no liability and workers come to work within the period specified , shall be free to recruit others, and

IV. Dictate the measures considered for the job can be resumed.

Article 933. - In the classification procedure illegality of the strike , shall follow the rules contained in Article 930 of this Act

Article 934. - If the Board of Conciliation and Arbitration states that the strike is illegal , it shall terminate the working relationship of the strikers.

Article 935. - Before the suspension of work , the Board of Conciliation and Arbitration , after hearing the parties , determine the necessary number of workers who must continue to work to continue running the work , whose suspension seriously harm the security and preservation premises, machinery and raw materials or the resumption of work. For this purpose, the Board may order the adoption of the measures it deems appropriate.

Article 936. - If the strikers refuse to provide the services referred to in Articles 466 and 935 of this Act, the employer may use other workers. The Board , if necessary , request the assistance of the police , so that they can provide such services.

Article 937. - If the conflict because of the strike by workers subjected to the decision of the Board, the regular procedure or the procedure for disputes of an economic nature , as appropriate.

If the Board stated in the award that the reasons for the strike are attributable to the employer , condemn him to the satisfaction of the demands of the workers as they are from , and the payment of wages for the days that the strike had lasted. In no event will the pattern sentenced to pay the wages of workers who had declared a strike in terms of section 450 , section VI of this Act

Article 938. - If the strike is to the conclusion or revision of contract law , shall follow the provisions of this Chapter , with the following specifications:

I. The notice of a strike by unions allied presented with a copy for each of the patterns deployed , or by individual company or establishment , to the Board of Conciliation and Arbitration , or to the authorities referred to in Article 920 Section II of this Act;

II. In the letter of formal notice shall specify the day and time the work is suspended , it shall be thirty or more days after the date of its submission to the Board of Conciliation and Arbitration.

III. If the notice is filed with the Board of Conciliation and Arbitration , the President , under its strict liability , employers will get a copy of the letter of formal notice directly within twenty-four hours of its receipt, or rotate within the necessary exhortos same term , which must vent the requested authority , under its strict liability , within twenty four hours of receipt. Desahogados rogatory should be returned within the same twenty-four hours, and

IV. If the notice is filed with the other authorities referred to in section I , these under the strictest responsibility , will go directly to patterns written copy of the site , within twenty-four hours after its receipt. Once the site , send the file to the Board of Conciliation and Arbitration within the same twenty-four hours.

TITLE XV IMPLEMENTATION PROCEDURES

CHAPTER I SECTION ONE

General Provisions

Article 939. The provisions of this Title governing enforcement of awards made by the Boards of Conciliation and Arbitration. They also apply to arbitral awards to judgments given in collective disputes of an economic nature and the agreements to the Boards.

Article 940. The enforcement of awards referred to in the preceding article corresponds to the Chairmen of the Boards of Conciliation and Arbitration and the Special Meetings , for which purpose will dictate the measures necessary for the prompt and expeditious implementation.

Article 941. - When the award is to be executed by the Chairman of other Board will direct you to the proper insertions encourage and empower you to make use of coercive measures , in case of opposition to the diligence of execution.

Article 942. - The President urged may not know of the exceptions opposing parties.

Article 943. - If when completing a warrant , opposes any party that had not been heard by the President issuing the letters , suspended the completion of the warrant , upon granting bail to secure the amount of the amount for which execution was dispatched and damages that may be caused. Granted bail, will return the warrant to the President issuing the letters.

Article 944. - The expenses incurred in the enforcement of awards , shall be borne by the party who does not comply.

Article 945. The awards must be completed within fifteen days following the day on which the notice takes effect.

The parties may agree on the modalities of its implementation.

Article 946. - The execution must be shipped to the fulfillment of a duty or the payment of cash amounts , specifically named in the award , understood it , the quantified in it.

Article 947. - If the employer refuses to submit their differences to arbitration or to accept the award rendered , the Board:

I. Shall terminate the employment relationship;

II. Condemn compensate the employee with the amount of three months' salary ;

III. Proceed to establish the liability resulting to the pattern of the conflict, in accordance with Article 50 , sections I and II , and

IV. In addition , condemn the payment of overdue wages and interest , if any , as provided in Article 48 , and the payment of the premium -old , under the terms of Article 162.

The provisions of this Article shall not apply in cases of actions contained in Article 123 , Section XXII , paragraph A of the Constitution.

Article 948. - If the refusal to accept the award rendered by the Board regardless of workers will terminate the employment relationship in accordance with the provisions of Article 519 paragraph III , last paragraph of this Act

Article 949. Whenever running an award be delivered a sum of money or the performance of a right to work , the President shall ensure that personally granted. Should the defendant filed outside the place of residence of the Board, will turn urge the President of the Board of Conciliation and Arbitration or the judge nearest to your home to fill that enforcement of the award.

Section Two

Of Procedure of the Embargo

Article 950. - After the period specified in Article 945, the President , at the request of the party who obtained , shall issue an order of injunction and seizure.

Article 951. - During execution of the payment order and yet following rules shall be observed:

I. Was made in the place where the services provided or rendered in the new home of the debtor or in the room , office, establishment or place designated by the clerk in the minutes of notification in accordance with Article 740 of this Law;

II. If you are not the debtor , diligence be practiced with any person present ;

III. The Clerk will require payment to the person requesting the inquiry and if not made the same be seized ;

IV. The Clerk may, if necessary, without prior authorization, request the assistance of the police and break the locks of the premises in which they must practice diligently ;

V. If no one is present , the actuary shall perform the embargo and authorized copy of the diligence in the door of the room in which the arrest was made , and

VI. The Clerk , under his responsibility , lien only goods necessary to ensure the amount of the sentence , their interests and implementation costs.

Article 952. - There are only exempt from seizure:

I. Goods that are the heritage of family ;

II. Those who belong to the household , provided they are of essential use ;

III. Machinery, instruments, tools and animals of an enterprise or establishment , as are necessary for the development of their activities.

May be seized the company or establishment , in accordance with Article 966 of this Law;

IV. The crops before they are harvested , but not planting rights ;

V. The weapons and horses of active duty military , essential for employment in accordance with the laws ;

VI. The right of usufruct, but not the fruits thereof;

VII. Use rights and housing , and

VIII. Easements , unless the estate is garnish , to whom are constituted.

Article 953. - The attachment proceedings can not be suspended. The actuary resolve issues that may arise.

Article 954. - The Clerk , taking into consideration setting out the parties, determine the assets to be covered by the ban, preferring those that are more easily performed.

Article 955. - When the embargo should fall in assets located outside of where expertise is rendered , the Clerk will move to the place where the party obtaining manifest found and after identification of the goods, perform the embargo.

Article 956. - If the goods seized money or credits were realized in the act , the Clerk will lock however and made available to the Chairman of the Board , who shall decide immediately whether to pay the actor.

Article 957. - If the goods seized are furniture in storage will of the person, that under his responsibility designated by the party obtaining. The depositary shall inform the President executor of where the property seized shall custody. The party obtaining may request a change of custodian.

Article 958. - If the goods seized are credits , fruits or products , shall be notified to the debtor or tenant, that the payment amount is to the President executing apperceived double payment in case of disobedience.

Article 959. - The Actuary required to suing so that you display documents and related agreements , so that the record stating and attesting to the conditions specified therein.

Article 960. If you come to make a claim , will designate a custodian store it at guard , who is obliged to do everything necessary to not alter or impair the right of the title and try to represent all actions and resources that Law gives credit to cash and are subject also to the obligations imposed by the laws of the holders.

Article 961. - If the claim was disputed , but will be reported to the authority before which the proceedings concerned , and the name of a depositary, to enable it to discharge its obligations under the end of the previous article.

Article 962. If the goods seized they be buildings, the President executor , under its responsibility , order , within 24 hours , registration at the Public Registry of Property.

Article 963. - If the embargo rests urban farm and its products or on these only , the repository administrator will have the character with the powers and duties:

I. May hold leases, under these conditions: volunteer time for both parties , the amount of income can not be less than that fixed in the final contract require the lessee guarantees necessary for compliance, and gather in all cases the authorization of the President Executor ;

II. Charging time the income on their deadlines, proceeding against delinquent tenants under the Act ;

III. Make payments without prior approval of taxes and any fees for property , and cover the recurrent costs of conservation and toilet ;

IV. Submit to the appropriate office , demonstrations and statements that the Act prevents matter ;

V. Submit for approval to the President Executor , budgets for the cost of repair or construction ;

VI. Check the permission of the President Executor , levies farm reporting , and

VII. Monthly accountable management and deliver the balance on a deposit ticket , which will provide the President Executor.

The depositary that fails to fulfill the obligations outlined in this article, shall be entitled to the penalties provided in the respective laws.

Article 964. - If the embargo lies with a company or establishment , the following rules shall be observed:

I. The depositary will charge controller to the box , being obliged to:

a) Monitor the accounting:

b) Managing the negotiation and management of enterprise and the practice therein , in order to produce the best possible performance , and other acts inherent in his position.

II. If the depositary considers that the administration is not conveniently or likely to impair the rights of the garnishee , the President shall inform the Executor , for it , hearing the parties and the auditor at a hearing , resolve it deems appropriate , and

III. Whenever a third party depositary , granted bail to the President Executor , for the sum to be determined and will be accountable for its actions in the terms and manner prescribed therein.

Article 965. - Actor may request the extension of the embargo:

I. When the goods seized are not sufficient to cover the amounts for which execution dispatched after the appraisal given them , and

II. When you promote a third party and has been issued order accepting.

The President may order enforcer enlargement if , in his opinion , the circumstances referred to in the preceding sections , without the knowledge of the defendant.

Article 966. - When you practice several liens on the same property , the following rules shall be observed:

I. If done in execution of work credits are payable in successive order embargoes except for duty preference ;

II. The embargo practiced in executing a work credit , even if it later is preferred over those charged by authorities other than the Board of Conciliation and Arbitration provided that the embargo will remain fincado practice before the auction.

When President Executor is aware of the existence of a lien , shall inform the authority which he practiced , that the seized goods are subject to the payment of credit preferential continue working and implementing procedures to make payment. The resulting net balance after making the payment , will be made available to the authority which the arrest was effected.

Preference issues that arise , be heard and determined by the Board who knows the business, to the exclusion of any other authority , and

III. That there rearrested can continue execution of the award or agreement , but topped the assets are paid to the first distrainor the amount of your credit , except for duty preference.

Section Three

Auctions

Article 967. - Concluded the attachment proceedings , proceed to the auction of the property, in accordance with the rules contained in this Chapter.

Before the auction or plead fincarse the award , the defendant may release the seized property , paying cash immediately and the amount of the amounts established in the award and implementation costs.

Article 968. - In embargoes following rules shall be observed:

A. If the goods seized are furniture:

I. It will make its assessment by the person appointed by the President executioner where the executor President realizes that the valuation of assets is significantly lower or higher than its value , order the practice of another , stating the reasons for which considers that the appraisal does not match the value of the property ;

II. Serve as a basis for the amount of the valuation auction , and

III. The auction will be announced in the newsletter or on the podium work of the Board , as appropriate and in the town hall or government office designated by the President executor.

B. If the goods seized are properties:

I. Appraisal is taken as that of a legally authorized appraiser who shall be appointed by the Chairman of the Board and, if applicable , shall be in accordance with the provisions of Section I , paragraph A of this section;

II. The exhibit arrestor liens certificate issued by the Public Registry of Property, 10 years before the date you ordered the auction. If the Court shall do and other certificate will be asked to register only on the period or periods not cover it , and

III. The order provided that the auction will be published only once , in the labor bulletin or the bar of the Board , if any and shall, for once, in the Treasury of each state and the newspaper largest circulation of where assets are located , summoning bidders.

Be summoned personally to creditors in the certificate of encumbrances , in order to assert their rights.

Article 969. - If the goods seized are a company or establishment will observe the following procedure:

I. An appraisal is made by an expert to be requested by the President of the Board of Nacional Financiera , SNC , or any other official institution ;

II. Serve as a basis for the auction the amount of valuation ;

III. It applies the provisions of section III , paragraph A previous article regarding furniture, and

IV. If the company or establishment is integrated with real property, liens collect the certificate referred to in Section II paragraph B above article.

Article 970. Legal position is covering two-thirds of the appraisal. The person to attend as a bidder shall submit in writing its position and display on a deposit ticket Nacional Financiera , SNC , the amount of 10 percent of your bid.

Article 971. - The auction is conducted in accordance with the following standards:

I. The date and time indicated will be held on the premises of the Board ;

II. It will be conducted by the Chairman of the Board , who shall be opened ;

III. The President shall wait a term which shall not be more than half an hour, for posture ;

IV. The president judge of the positions , and allow a minute between bid and auction ;

V. The actor will attend the auction as a bidder , by submitting a written bid , without satisfying the requirement referred to in Article 974 of this Act , and

VI. The President declared fincado the auction for the highest bidder.

Article 972. - Stagecoach tack will not be suspended. The Chairman of the Board immediately resolve the issues raised by stakeholders.

Article 973. - If there are no bidders, the actor may be awarded order goods for the price of their position , or request the holding of new auction houses net of twenty percent in each. The subsequent almonedas be held within thirty days of the date of the last.

Article 974. - The winner will exhibit within the next three days, the total amount of its position , failed to appreciate that failure to do so will be the displayed amount for the actor , and the President shall announce new date for the conclusion of the auction.

Article 975. - Shown the total price of the award , the President shall declare fincado the auction and the following shall apply:

I. Immediately cover the plaintiff and other creditors in their order , and if there are remaining , will be delivered to the defendant ;

II. If it comes to real estate, will be observed ;

a) The former owner shall submit to the Chairman of the Board , all documents related to the property that was auctioned.

b) If it wins the worker must be free of all liens , taxes and fiscal duties.

c) The writing must be signed by the previous owner , within five days of the notice to him by the respective public notary. If not, the President will make in their rebellion , and

III. Signed writing, the purchaser will be in possession of the property.

CHAPTER II PROCEDURE OF THE THIRD PARTY WITH CREDIT AND PREFERENCES

Section One From Third parties

Article 976. - Third party domain may be exclusive or preferential. The first aim to achieve the lifting of the embargo practiced in property owned by third parties , the latter preferably being paid to obtain a loan with the proceeds of property seized.

Article 977. Third parties are heard and determined by the House or by the Special Board hearing the main trial , sustanciándose incidentally , according to the following rules:

I. The third party shall be filed in writing, enclosing the title for the decision and relevant evidence;

II. The Board ordered the mediation is handled in a separate and summon the parties to a hearing within ten days , in which you hear and after the evidence has , issue resolution;

III. As for the offer, acceptance and presentation of the evidence , observe the provisions of Chapter XII , XVII and XVIII of Title Fourteen of this Act;

IV. Third parties do not suspend the proceedings. The third party domain exclusionary act suspends only the auction , the preferred loan repayment , and

V. If declared from the third party , the Board shall order the lifting of the embargo and , if necessary , order it to pay the stated preferred credit.

Article 978. - The intervenor may file an application with the requested authority who practiced but must designate domicile in the place of residence of the Board issuing the letters , to make it personal notifications , if the designation does not , all notices will be by newsletter or by courts.

The requested authority , to return the warrant , forward the demand for third party.

Section Two

Preference of Credits

Article 979. Where a conflict exists individually or collectively , workers may apply to the Board for the purposes of Article 113, which prevents the court or administrative authority to be processed before the trials in which they seek to enforce claims against the employer to , before conducting the auction or the awarding of the property seized , are notified to ensure that the law preemption granted by that provision.

If the goods seized are insufficient to cover the claims of all workers , be made pro rata leaving intact their rights.

Article 980. - The preference shall be dealt with according to the following rules:

I. The preference shall be requested by the employee before the Board at which examines the conflict into by indicating specifically what the authorities to substantiate those trials in which to adjudicate or off employer's assets , accompanying your request sufficient copies to run to the parties contesting in legal proceedings ;

II. If the trial is pending before the judicial authority , prevent the Board informing him that the seized goods are subject to the payment of wage claims preferred and therefore , before finishing or award the property of the employer, shall notify the worker in order that appear to derive their rights , and

III. In the case of tax credits, installments due to the Mexican Social Security Institute , or contribution to the Institute of National Housing Fund for Workers , the Board simply referred automatically to the appropriate authority , indicating the existence of labor claims whose benefits have yet to be covered , so that before awarding or off the employer's assets are appropriate under the preceding article.

Article 981. - When in trials before the Board award has been issued for cash amounts or for final settlement , the Board shall advise the court or administrative authority has been prevented in the previous article , remitting certified copy of the award, in order to be taken into account when applying the same product auctioned or foreclosed property.

If the pattern before the auction had made payment to rid their property, it should be covered with the amount of the claims in that it had acted prevention.

CHAPTER III PROCEDURES PARAPROCESALES OR VOLUNTEERS

Article 982. - Is determined under the provisions of this Chapter , all matters , as mandated by the Act , by its nature or at the request of a party, require the intervention of the Board, without being promoted jurisdictional conflict between parties determined.

Article 983. - In the procedures referred to in this Chapter , the worker , union or employer concerned may attend the relevant Board , orally or in writing requesting the intervention of the same and expressly stating the person whose statement is required , the thing that is to be displayed , or the care that is required to be carried out.

The Board agreed within twenty four hours of the request and , if necessary , set a day and time to conduct due diligence and order , if necessary , the citation of the persons whose statements are sought.

Article 984. - When provision of the Act or of any authority or by agreement of the parties, will have to give deposit or bond , the interested party or parties may appear before the Chairperson of the Board or the Special Meeting , which the receive and , where appropriate, notify the interested party.

The cancellation of the bond or deposit back , also can be processed before the President of the Board or Special Board who immediately agreed to subpoena the beneficiary and after verifying that fulfilled the obligations secured by the bond or deposit , authorize cancellation or return.

Article 985. When the Ministry of Finance and Public Credit, without objection mediated worker , modify the overall taxable income declared by the deceased , and this has challenged that decision , may request the Board of Conciliation and Arbitration within 3 days that in submitting the corresponding challenge the suspension of additional distributions of profits to workers, to which attached:

I. The guarantee granted in favor of the workers who will be by:

a) The additional amount to be distributed to the workers.

b) The legal interest computed for one year.

II. A copy of the decision of the Ministry of Finance and Public Credit , and

III. The name and address of the representatives of unionized workers , non-union and trust.

Article 986. - The Board to receive the employer's written review that meets the requirements outlined in the previous article, in which case immediately be conveyed to the representatives of the workers, so that within three days express what they deem appropriate; I remember after the period leading.

If the application does not meet the standard of legal requirements , the Board will reject.

Article 987. When workers and employers reach an agreement or settlement of a worker , out of court , may appear before the Conciliation and Arbitration and Special request for approval and ratification , in the terms referred to in the second paragraph of Article 33 of this Act, for which purpose will be identified to the satisfaction of the former.

In the agreement under which terminates the employment relationship should be broken the amount provided to the worker by way of salary, accrued benefits and profit sharing. In the event that the Joint Committee for Equity in Earnings in the company or establishment has not yet determined the individual participation of workers shall be left to save their rights, until such time as the project is formulated individual deal.

Any agreements on the terms of this Article shall be approved by the Board of Conciliation and Arbitration competent , do not affect the rights of workers , and have definite effects , so it will rise to the level of binding award.

Article 988. - Workers over fourteen but under sixteen , who have not completed their compulsory education, may appear before the Board of Conciliation and Arbitration competent requesting authorization to work , and accompanied by the documents they deem appropriate , to establish the compatibility between studies and work.

The Board of Conciliation and Arbitration , immediately after receiving the request , agree the appropriate course.

Article 989. - Employees may request , through the Board of Conciliation and Arbitration for which the employer will issue a written record containing the number of days worked and wages earned , in the terms established by Article 132 Section VII of this Act

Article 990. - The employee or their beneficiaries to receive any money under agreement or settlement , may attend the Meeting in person accordingly.

Article 991. In cases of termination under Article 47 , the employer may appeal to the Board of Conciliation and Arbitration competent to request notifies the worker notice that the above provision is concerned, by the means indicated in it. The Board , within five days of receipt of the promotion , it shall notification.

(Repealed the second paragraph).

TITLE XVI RESPONSIBILITIES AND SANCTIONS

Article 992. The violations of labor standards committed by employers or workers shall be punished in accordance with the provisions of this title , regardless of responsibility to them for breach of its obligations , without prejudice to the penalties provided in other jurisdictions legal and the legal consequences that come in goods and services concession .

The quantification of financial penalties in this Title are set , there will be calculation based on the daily quota of general minimum wage in the Federal District , at the time of commission of the violation .

For the imposition of sanctions, be taken into account:

I. The intentional or not the act or omission constituting the offense;

II. The seriousness of the offense;

III. The damage which has occurred or may occur ;

IV . The financial capacity of the offender , and

V. The offender recidivism .

In all cases of recidivism will double the fine imposed for the previous offense .

Recidivism is defined for the purposes of this Law and other provisions derived therefrom , each of the subsequent violations at the same precept , committed within two years from the date of the act in which the offense was stated above, where this had been disproved .

When a single act or omission was affecting several workers , penalty shall be imposed for each of the affected workers. If a single act or omission incurred various offenses , the penalties that apply to each of them independently .

When the fine is applied to a worker , it can not exceed the amount specified in Article 21 of the Constitution .

Article 993. The pattern that does not meet the rules determining the percentage or the exclusive use of Mexican workers in enterprises or establishments shall be fined the equivalent of 250-2500 times the general minimum wage.

Article 994 . Fine will be imposed , for the equivalent of :

I. From 50 to 250 times the minimum wage , the employer who does not comply with the provisions contained in Articles 61 , 69, 76 and 77;

II. From 250 to 5000 times the minimum wage , the employer who fails to fulfill the obligations under Chapter VIII of Title III on Workers Participation in corporate profits ;

III. From 50 to 1500 times the minimum wage to the employer who fails to comply with the obligations under Article 132, Sections IV , VII , VIII , IX , X , XII , XIV and XXII ;

IV . From 250 to 5000 times the minimum wage , the employer who does not comply with the provisions of Section XV of Article 132;

V. From 250 to 5000 times the minimum wage , the employer who fails to comply with the installation of their establishments the health and safety rules or laws set measures to prevent occupational hazards ;

VI. From 250 to 5000 times the minimum wage , the employer who commits any act or discriminatory behavior in the workplace , to perform acts of sexual harassment or tolerate or allow acts of sexual harassment against their workers , and

VII . From 250 to 2500 times the minimum wage , the employer who violates the prohibitions contained in Article 133, Sections II , IV , V , VI and VII , and 357 second paragraph.

Article 995. The employer who violates the prohibitions contained in Article XIV and XV 133 fractions , and the rules governing the work of women and children, be punished by a fine of from 50 to 2500 times the minimum wage .

Article 995 Bis . The employer who violates the provisions of Article 22 bis , first paragraph of this Act , be punished with imprisonment of 1-4 years and a fine from 250 to 5,000 times the minimum wage .

Article 996. The owner, operator or charterer , shall be liable to a fine equivalent to:

I. From 50 to 500 times the minimum wage , does not meet the provisions contained in Article 204 , Section II , and 213 , Section II , and

II. From 50 to 2500 times the minimum wage , which does not comply with the obligation under Article 204 , Section IX.

Article 997. The employer who violates the protective rules of field work and from work to home, you will be fined the equivalent of 250-2500 times the general minimum wage.

Article 998. The employer who does not provide a domestic worker to lack of education, primary school attendance , shall be imposed a fine equivalent to 50-250 times the minimum wage .

Article 999. The employer who violates the protective rules of work in hotels , restaurants , bars and other similar establishments shall be liable to a fine equivalent to 50-2500 times the minimum wage .

Article 1000 . The breach of the rules on remuneration of work, working hours and breaks, Law contained in a contract or in a collective bargaining agreement , is punishable by a fine equivalent to 250-5000 times the general minimum wage .

Article 1001. The employer who violates the rules contained in the Internal Labor Regulations shall be liable to a fine equivalent to 50-500 times the minimum wage .

Article 1002. For violations of labor standards is not sanctioned by this chapter or any other provision of this Act, the offender shall be imposed a fine equivalent to 50 to 5000 times the minimum wage .

Article 1003 . - Workers , employers and trade unions , federations and confederations of each other , they can complain to the Labour authorities violations of labor standards.

The Presidents of the Special Boards and labor inspectors , have the obligation to report to the Attorney General to a negotiation pattern industrial, agricultural, mining , commercial or services you have stopped paying their workers or pay less than that indicated as minimum wage .

Article 1004. - The employer of any bargaining industrial, agricultural, mining , commercial or service that delivers one or more of its employees in amounts below the minimum wage set general or has delivered payment vouchers that cover higher sums of those actually delivered , shall be punished by the following penalties:

I. With imprisonment from six months to three years and a fine that amounts to 800 times the minimum wage , as established by Article 992, when the amount of the omission does not exceed the amount of one month's minimum wage of the geographic area of corresponding application ;

II. With imprisonment from six months to three years and a fine that amounts to 1600 times the minimum wage , as established by Article 992, when the amount of default is greater than the amount of one month but not exceeding three months general minimum wage of the geographic area corresponding application , and

III. With imprisonment from six months to four years and a fine that is equal to 3200 times the minimum wage , as established by Article 992, if the omission exceed three months minimum wage of the geographic area of application.

(Repealed the last paragraph) .

Article 1004 -A. The pattern does not allow inspection and supervision authorities practice work in his establishment, he shall pay a fine of 250-5000 times the general minimum wage.

Article 1004- B . The breach of the obligations referred to in Article 15-B of the Act, shall be punishable with fine equivalent of 250-2500 times the general minimum wage.

Article 1004- C . Who use subcontracted personnel in a malicious way , in terms of Article 15-D of this Act shall be liable to a fine equivalent 250-5000 times the general minimum wage.

Article 1005 . The Attorney for the Defense of Labor or the agent or representative of the employee, will be imposed penalty of six months to three years in prison and a fine of 125-1250 times the general minimum wage in the Federal District in the following cases :

I. When no valid reason to refrain from attending two or more hearings , and

II. When no valid reason to refrain from promoting in the trial over the span of three months.

Article 1006. Anyone who present false documents or witnesses will be imposed a penalty of six months to four years and a fine of 125-1900 times the general minimum wage in the Federal District . In the case of workers , the fine will be the salary paid to the employee in a week.

Article 1007 . - The penalties set forth in the preceding article shall be without prejudice to any liability for damages that would not prove the proxy.

Article 1008. The administrative penalties referred to in this Chapter shall be imposed , where appropriate, by the Secretary of Labor and Social Welfare, by the Governors of the States or by the Head of Government of the Federal District , who may delegate the exercise of these powers to the subordinate officials deem appropriate , by agreement is published in the official newspaper concerned.

Article 1009 . - The authority , after hearing the person concerned , impose the sanction.

Article 1010 . - The penalties will be paid by the authorities designated by law.

TRANSIENT

Article 1. - This Act shall enter into force on the 1st day . May 1970 , with the exception of Articles 71 and 87 will come into force on the 1st day . July 1970 , and Article 80 shall enter into force on the 1st day . September 1970 .

Article 2. - It repeals the Federal Labor Law of August 18, 1931 , in the manner referred to in the preceding article .

Article 3. - The individual employment contracts or collective establishing rights , benefits or entitlements in favor of workers, lower than those granted this law will not produce hereinafter legal effect , meaning replaced the respective clauses by establishing this Act

Individual employment contracts or collective agreements or establishing rights , benefits or entitlements in favor of workers in excess of that granted this Act shall continue to have effect .

Article 4. - In the application of Article 159, in relation to the 132, section XV , collective agreements containing educational and training systems already in operation on the date of publication of this Act , and the laying down conditions for practice exam or fitness test and possession of the right knowledge so that workers can move up in cases of vacancies or newly created positions in accordance with the age they are concerned, will continue to apply .

Article 5. - To pay seniority premiums referred to in Article 162 workers already providing services to a company on the date of entry into force of this Act, the following rules shall be observed :

I. The workers with less than ten years old , who are separated from employment voluntarily within one year after the date of entry into force of this Act, shall be entitled to pay them twelve days of salary ;

II. Those who are older than ten and less than twenty years , who voluntarily separate from employment within two years following the date referred to in the preceding section, shall be entitled to pay them salary twenty-four days ;

III. Those who are older than their twenties who voluntarily separate from employment within three years of the date referred to in the preceding sections , shall be entitled to pay them thirty-six days of salary ;

IV . After the terms referred to in the preceding sections are subject to the provisions in Article 162 , and

V. Workers who are dismissed from their jobs or who resign for cause within one year following the date of the coming into effect of this Act is entitled to get paid twelve days salary. After one year , regardless of the date of separation, shall be entitled to the premium attached to them for the years that have elapsed from the date of entry into force of this Act

Article 6. - The installed daycare companies or establishments continue to operate until the Mexican Social Security Institute to take care of them .

Article 7. - This shall not apply to the review of the resolution of December 13, 1963 issued by the National Commission for Worker Participation in corporate profits , but until you meet ten years from the date cited.

Article 8. - In the case of companies registered with the Mexican Social Security Institute , the obligations contained in Article 504 will be in charge of companies, to the extent that the Institute is not obliged to lend them in accordance with law

Article 9. - The Ministry of Labour and Social Welfare, the Governors of the States and Territories and the Head of the Federal District , reorganizing Conciliation Permanent and Conciliation and Arbitration , in accordance with the provisions of this Act , within a period of three months , counted from the date thereof .

Article 10 . - The same authorities referred to the previous article authorities reorganized the remaining work in accordance with the provisions of this Act, within the period of three months.

Article 11. - Do not require the requirements specified in Articles 626 , part II , 627 , Section II , 628 , sections II and III , and 629 of Title Twelve , legal staff stated in Article 625 , which has the status of basis and at the time of entry into force of this Act, serving on the Boards of Concilliation and Arbitration and Conciliation .

Article 12. - The lawsuits pending before the Conciliation and Arbitration _Juntas continue to be processed in accordance with the provisions of the Federal Labour Act of August 18, 1931 , in the meantime making the reorganization referred to article 9 . Transient . Performed the reorganization , trials are executed in accordance with the provisions of this Act, the Board shall inform the parties that the processing time will be subject to the procedures established in this Act

In proceedings pending before the Conciliation , evidence will be received which offer the parties and forwarded the case to the Permanent Conciliation or Arbitration Conciliation and appropriate .

The Conciliation and Arbitration shall continue to business referred to in Article 600 , Section IV , you already know .

Article 13. - It empowers the Regional Commissions and the National Minimum Wage to establish the minimum wage increases general and current professional field .

To make the minimum wage leveling referred to in the preceding paragraph , observe the following procedure :

I. Within three days of the entry into force of this decree , the regional commissions dictate Minimum Wage resolution setting the minimum wage increases .

II. The presidents of the regional commissions under its responsibility, communicate to the National Minimum Wage relevant resolutions within 24 hours of the date of promulgation .

III. The President of the National Minimum Wage convene the Council of Representatives and submit the same to the relevant opinion within three days of receipt of the communications referred to in the preceding section, dictate resolution confirming or revising those who have given the regional commissions , having set the increment to be applied to the current minimum wage , to be modified as required taking into account the provisions of the resolution issued by the Ministry of Labor and Social Welfare dated March 19 1982.

IV . The President of the National Minimum Wage sent to the Official Journal of the Federation, for publication , the resolution of the Council of Representatives containing the minimum wages established corresponding to the increase .

Mexico , D. F. , December 2, 1969 . Luis L. Leon Uranga , S. P. - Joaquín Gamboa Pascoe , D. Q. - Arturo Esposito Mogel , S. S. - Briseno Alberto Ruiz , D. S. - Headings .

In compliance with the provisions of Section I of Article 89 of the Political Constitution of the Mexican United States , for its due publication and observance , I issue this Decree at the residence of the Federal Executive in Mexico City , Federal District , twenty-third day of December 1969 . - Gustavo Diaz Ordaz . - Category . - the Secretary of Labor and Social Welfare, Salomon Gonzalez Blanco. - Category . - the Secretary of the Interior, Office Manager , Mario Moya Palencia. - Category . - the Secretary of Foreign Affairs, Antonio Carrillo Flores. -

Category . - the Secretary of Defense , Marcelino García Barragán . - Category . - the Secretary of the Navy , Antonio Vázquez del Mercado. - Category . - the Secretary of Finance and Public Credit, Antonio Ortiz Mena . - Category . - the National Heritage Secretary , Manuel Franco Lopez. - Category . - the Secretary of Industry and Commerce, Octavian Campos Salas . - Category . - the Secretary of Agriculture and livestock, Juan Gil Preciado . - Heading . - The Secretary of Communications and Transport , José Antonio Padilla Segura. - Category . - The Secretary of Public Works, Gilberto Valenzuela . - Category . - The Secretary of Water Resources , José Hernández Terán . - Category . - The Secretary of Education, Agustin Yañez . - Category . - The Secretary of Health and Welfare, Salvador Aceves Parra. - Category . - The Secretary of the Presidency , Emilio Martinez Manautou . - Category . - The Head of the Department of Land Affairs and Colonization , Norberto Aguirre Palancares . - Category . - the Head of the Department of Tourism, Agustin Salvat . - Category . - the Head of the Federal District , Alfonso Corona del Rosal . - Category .

TRANSITIONAL ARTICLES OF DECREE OF REFORM

DECREE various legal regulations are reformed .

Published in the Official Journal of the Federation on January 23, 1998

SINGLE ARTICLE . - Are amended Articles 20 and 32 , Section I , and Section I is added to Article 47 BIS of the Mexican Foreign Service Act , are amended Articles 4 , Section I , 117 , 161, first paragraph , and 173, second paragraph , and Article 148 BIS added to the chapter called "From Recruitment " and a subsection F) to section II of Article 170 of the Organic Law of the Mexican Army and Air Force ; Article 57 is amended and a subsection E) section I of Article 105 of the Organic Law of the Navy of Mexico , is amended by Article 4 , Section I , of the Code of Military Justice , Article 5 is added BIS to the Military Service Law ; Amends Sections 106 and 108 of the Organic Law of the Judicial Power of the Federation; 4, first paragraph , of the Organic Law of the Federal Tax Court , 9 , section I of the Act on the Treatment for Young Offenders Federal District on Ordinary Matters and for the Republic in Federal Matters , 20 , paragraph a) , 22 and 23 , in their respective sections I, of the Organic Law of the Attorney General of the Republic, 19, 34 and 35 , in their respective fractions I, of the Organic Law of the Attorney General of the Federal District , 76 , 91, 103 , 114 and 120 , in their respective subsections a) of the Federal Code of Electoral Institutions and Procedures , 22 and 50 , in their respective first paragraphs , of the Navigation Act ; 7, first paragraph and you will be a second paragraph , Amends Sections 38 and 40 , first paragraph , of the Civil Aviation Act , 189 , 216 and 612, section I of Federal Labor Law , 267 of the Social Security Act ; 156 , section I , and 166 , second paragraph , of the Law Institute of Security and Social Services for State Workers, 28 , first paragraph , 50 , section IV , and repealing section III of article 51 of the Law on Social Security Institute for the Mexican Armed Forces ; Amends Sections 21 , section I of the Federal Act on Public Entities , 51 of the Law Regulating Article 27 Nuclear Constitutional , 9 , section I of the Law of National Human Rights Commission , 8 , section I of the Federal Public Brokerage , 6 , second paragraph , of the Organic Law of the National Institute of Anthropology and History , 32 , sections I to III , the Foreign Investment Law , 14 , Section I of the Act that establishes the basis for the Coordination of National Public Security System , the 5th . , Section I of the Regulatory Commission Act Energy , 10 , fraction I and 14 , Section I of the Systems Act Retirement Savings , 12 , paragraph I , of the Organic Law of Agrarian Tribunals ; 39 , Section I of the Law of the Bank of Mexico , 26 , paragraph I , of the Federal Law of Economic Competition ; 121, Section I of the Federal Act on State Employees , Regulatory Section " B " of Article 123 of the Constitution , and 15 , Section I and last paragraph of the Law of the National Banking and Securities , to read as follows:

....

TRANSIENT

ONLY . - This Decree shall enter into force on March 20, 1998 .

Mexico , DF , on December 12, 1997 . - Sen . Heladio Ramirez Lopez , President. - Dip . Luis Meneses Murillo , President . - Sen . Jose Antonio Valdivia , Secretary . - Dip . Jaime Castro López , Secretary . - Rubrics . "

In compliance with the provisions of Section I of Article 89 of the Constitution of the United Mexican States, and for its due publication and observance , I issue this Decree at the residence of the Federal Executive in Mexico City , Federal District , on the thirtieth day of December 1997 . - Ernesto Zedillo Ponce de Leon. - Category . - the Secretary of the Interior , Emilio Chuayffet Chemor . - Category .

DECREE amending article 74 of the Federal Labor Law .

Published in the Official Journal of the Federation on January 17, 2006

SINGLE ARTICLE . - It amends Article 74 of the Federal Labor Law , to read as follows :

....

TRANSIENT

ARTICLE ONE . - This Decree shall enter into force on the day following its publication in the Official Journal of the Federation.

ARTICLE TWO . - For the commemoration in 2006 of the birth of Benito Juarez , Hero of the Americas , the fraction III , will take effect in 2007.

Mexico , DF , on December 15, 2005 . - Dip . Heliodorus Escárraga Diaz , President . - Sen . Enrique Jackson Ramírez , President . - Dip . Garduño Patricia Morales , Secretary. - Sen . Michelle Aguilar Gonzalez , Secretary. - Rubrics . "

In compliance with the provisions of Section I of Article 89 of the Constitution of the United Mexican States, and for its due publication and observance , I issue this Decree at the residence of the Federal Executive in Mexico City , Federal District , on the sixteenth day of January, two thousand and six. - Vicente Fox Quesada. - Category . - the Secretary of the Interior, Carlos María Abascal Carranza. - Category .

DECREE amending several federal laws , in order to update all those articles that refer to the Secretaries of State whose name was modified and the Government of the Federal District in the leading , as well as remove the mention of administrative departments are no longer valid .

Published in the Official Journal of the Federation on April 9, 2012

ARTICLE FORTY- EIGHT. Amends Sections 126 , section VI , 407 , 409 , 411, first paragraph , 415, section I; 419, Sections II and IV , 512 -E , 531 , 539 -A, second paragraph , 549 , section III , 622 ; 623 and 625 , second paragraph , 633 , 637 , section II ; 650 , 656, 660 , Sections V and IX , 661 , 663 , 668 , 669 , Section II , 670 , 674 , section I , 709 , Section I , paragraph b) 845 , Section II , paragraph b) , and 1008 , of the Federal Labor Law , to read as follows :

....

TRANSIENT

First . This Decree shall enter into force on the day following its publication in the Official Journal of the Federation.

Second . From the date of entry into force of this Decree shall supersede the provisions that contravene or are opposed to it.

Mexico , DF , on February 21, 2012 . - Dip . Guadalupe Acosta Naranjo , President . - Sen . Jose Gonzalez Morfin , President . - Dip . Arizmendi Laura Campos , Secretary. - Sen . Renan Cleominio Zoreda Novelo, Secretary . - Rubrics . "

In compliance with the provisions of Section I of Article 89 of the Constitution of the United Mexican States, and for its due publication and observance , I issue this Decree at the residence of the Federal Executive in Mexico City , Federal District , to March 30 , two thousand twelve . - Felipe de Jesus Calderon Hinojosa . - Category . - The Interior Secretary Alejandro Poire Romero Alfonso . - Category .

DECREE amending, supplementing and repealing various provisions of the Federal Labor Law .

Published in the Official Journal of the Federation on November 30, 2012

Article One. - It AMEND the articles 2 , the 3rd , the 4th , section I , paragraph a) ; grades 5, section VII , 25 , sections I , II and IV , 28 , 35, 43 , first paragraph , and fraction II , 47 , Sections II , VIII , and second , third and fourth paragraphs , 48, 50 paragraph III, 51, section II , 56 , 97 , section IV , 103 Bis , 110 , Sections V and VII, 121 , Section II , 132 , fractions XVI , XVII , XVIII and XXVI , 133, first paragraph and sections I and V , 134 , Section II , the title of Chapter III of Title IV Bis , to read as " from Productivity , Education and Training of Workers" ; 153 -A , 153- B , 153- C , 153- D , 153- E , 153- F , 153 -G , 153- H , 153 -I , 153- J , 153- K , 153- L , 153- N , 153- Q , 153- S , 153 -U , 153- V , first paragraph , 154 , first paragraph , 157 , 159 , 168 , 170 , sections II and IV , 173 , 174 , 175 , 176 , 279, first paragraph , 280 , 282 , 283 , current fractions II and IV , V , VI and VII, 284 , section III , 285 , 311 , current second paragraph , 333 , 336 , 337 , section II , 353 -A , Section II , 353 - S , 366 , section III, the last paragraph , 371, sections IX and XIII , 373 , 427 , section VI , 429, sections I and III , 430 , 435 , sections I and II , 439 , 476 , 490 , section I , 502 , 503 , sections I , II , III and IV, 504, fraction V , 512 -A , 512 -B , first and second , 512 - C , first paragraph , 512 - D , first paragraph , 512 -F , first paragraph , 513, first paragraph , 514 , 515 , 521 , section I , 523, fraction V ; 527, sections I and II , No. 2 , 529, fractions II , III and V ; 532 , section IV , 533 , the title of Chapter Once Title IV , to read as " the National Employment Service " , 537 , 538 , 539 , sections I , paragraphs b), c) , d), e) , f) and h) , II , paragraphs a), d) and f) , III , paragraphs b), c) , d) and h) , 539 -A, first and third paragraphs , 539 -B , 541 , section VI , 546, fractions II and V ; 552 , section IV , 555, fraction III , 556 , Section II , 560 , section III , 604 , 605, second paragraph , 606, first paragraph , 607 , 610, first paragraph and Sections IV and V present ; 612 , 614, first paragraph and section I , 615, first paragraph and sections II, III , IV , VI and VII, 617, first paragraph and section VII , 618 , Section II , 619 , sections I and II , 620 , sections I , II , paragraph a) , third subparagraph, and III , 624 , 625, first paragraph , 626, current fractions II , III and IV, 627, current fractions II , III and IV, 628, fractions II , III , IV and V , 629 , 630 , 631 , 632 , 634 , 637 , sections I and II , 642, current fraction IV; 643, Sections I , III and IV, 644, first paragraph and sections I and II , 645, current fraction IV; 646 , 648 , 664, first paragraph , 685, first paragraph , 688 , the title of Chapter II of Title Fourteen , to read as " from Capacity, Personality and Legitimacy " , 689 , 691 , 692, fractions II and IV , 693 , 698 , second paragraph , 700 , Section II , paragraphs a) , b) and c) ,

701 , 705 , sections I , II and III , 711 , 724 , 727 , 729, first paragraph and fraction II , 731 , Section I , 734 , 737 , 739, second paragraph , 740 , 742, Section XI , 743, fractions II and IV , 753 , 763 , 772 , 773 , 776 , Section VIII , 783 , 784, fractions V , VI , VIII , IX and XIV, 785 , 786 , 790 , section III , 793 , 802 , second paragraph , 804 , section IV and last paragraph , 808 , 813 , sections I , II , and IV , 814 , 815, fractions II , IV , VI and VII, 816 , 817 , 823 , 824 , 825, fractions III and IV , 828 , 839 , 840, sections III , IV and VI, 841 , 850 , 853 , 856, first paragraph , 857 , Section II , 861, first paragraph and sections II, III and IV, 863 , 873 , 875, first and second paragraphs , 876 , sections I , II and V , 878 , sections I , II , V , VII and VIII , 879, first paragraph , 880, first paragraph and fractions II and IV , 883 , 884 , sections I , II , current III and IV , 885, the first paragraph , 886 , 888, first paragraph and section I , 891 , 939 , 940 , 945, first paragraph , 947 , section IV , 949 , 960 , 962 , 965, fraction II and last paragraph , 966 , Section II , 968 , section A, Sections I and III, paragraph B, sections I, II and III , 969 , sections I and III , 970 , 977, first paragraph , 979 , first paragraph , 985, first paragraph , 987 , 991, first paragraph , 992 , 993 , 994 , 995 , 996 , 997 , 998 , 999 , 1000, 1001 , 1002 , 1003, second paragraph , 1004 , sections I , II and III , 1005, first paragraph , 1006 , was ADDED in articles 3 . Bis , 15-A , 15-B , 15 -C , 15-D , 22 Bis , 28 -A, 28 -B , 39-A , 39 -B , 39 -C , 39 -D , 39 -E , 39 -F , 42 , with a fraction VIII , 42 Bis , 43 , with a fraction V , 47 , with a fraction XIV Bis and penultimate paragraph , 51 , with a fraction IX , from the current section IX to be fraction X ; 56 Bis , 83 , with a second paragraph , from the former second paragraph to be third , 101 , with a second paragraph , 121, with a second paragraph to section IV , 127 , with a paragraph IV Bis , 132 , with fractions XVI Bis ; nineteenth Bis, Bis XXIII , XXVI and XXVII Bis Bis , 133, with fractions XII , XIII , XIV and XV , 135, with a fraction XI -F 153 Bis , 170, with a fraction II Bis , Bis 175 ; 279, with a final paragraph , 279 Bis , 279 Ter , 283 , with fractions IV , IX , X , XI , XII and XIII , 311 , with a second paragraph , from the former second paragraph to be third , a Chapter XIII Bis called "From the Works in Minas " to Part Six, comprising Articles 343- A, 343- B , 343- C , 343- D and 343 -E , 357, with a second paragraph , 364 bis , 365 bis , 377, with a final paragraph , 391

Bis , 424 bis , 427, with a fraction VII , 429, with a fraction IV , 432, with a third paragraph , 475 bis , 504, with a final paragraph to section V , 512 Bis - D , 512 - D Ter ; 512 -G , 525 Bis , 527 , Section I , with a numeral 22 , 530 bis , 533 bis , 539 , with fractions V and VI , 539 -A, with a paragraph fourth , passing the previous quarter to be fifth paragraph ; 541, with a fraction VI Bis , 605, with a third and fourth paragraphs , 605 Bis , 610, with a fraction II , subsequent recorriéndose ; 617, with fractions VIII and IX , from the current fraction VIII to be X ; 618 , with a fraction VIII , from the current fraction VIII to be IX , 623, with a first paragraph , first paragraph above going to be second, 626, with a fraction II , subsequent recorriéndose , 627, with a fraction III , recorriéndose subsequent , 627 -A , 627- B , 627- C , 641 -A , 642, with sections IV , V and VI , the current passing sections IV and V to be VII and VIII , 643, with a fraction V , current passing fraction V to be VI , 645, with a fraction II , subsequent recorriéndose , and a subsection d) of the current fraction IV; 690, with a second paragraph , 739, with a third and fourth paragraphs , 771, with a second paragraph , 774 Bis , 784, with a final paragraph , 815, with sections X and XI , 826 Bis , a Section Nine , entitled " of the Elements Contributed by Progress of Science" , Chapter XII of Title fourteen , comprising Articles 836- a, 836- B , 836- C and 836 - D , 884, with a fraction IV , passing the current IV to be V , 885, with a second paragraph , a Section One , Chapter Fourteen Title XVIII , called " Social Security Individual Disputes " , which contains Articles 899 -A to 899 - G , 985, with a paragraph III, 995 Bis , 1004 -A , 1004- B and 1004 - C , and REPEAL Sections 153 -O , 153- P , 153- R , 153- V , fourth paragraph , 395 , second paragraph , 512 - D , second and third paragraphs ; 523 , Section IX , 525 , 539 , section III , paragraphs a) e) Chapters X and XI of Title Eleven , comprising articles 591 to 603 , 614, fraction V , 616 , Section II , 700 , Section I , 765 ; Title XVI Chapter Fourteen , comprising 865 articles at 869 , 876 , section IV , 875, first paragraph , subparagraph c) 877 , 882 , 991, second paragraph , 1004, last paragraph of the Federal Labor Law , to read as follows :

Transients

First . This Decree shall enter into force on the day following its publication in the Official Journal of the Federation.

Second . Employers will have thirty-six months from the entry into force of this Decree , to make the adjustments to the premises of the workplace in order to facilitate access and development of activities for people with disabilities.

Also , employers will have twelve months from the entry into force of this Decree , to proceed with the formalities leading to affiliate the workplace to National Fund for Workers Consumption .

Third . The Federal Executive , the Governors of the States and Head of Government of the Federal District , in the scope of their respective powers, have a term of six months to adapt the regulatory arrangements that apply to the provisions contained in this Decree.

Fourth . The Ministry of Labor and Social Welfare shall issue tables diseases valuation work and permanent disability resulting from occupational hazards , within a period of six months from the entry into force of this Decree , as it will applying the tables referred to in articles 513 and 514 are amended .

Fifth . The Federal States , within their respective jurisdictions , shall have a term of up to three years to transform the Boards of Conciliation and Arbitration Conciliation Local , for which purpose shall include within their budgets , sufficient financial resources to ensure implementation , functioning and operation . These budgets must be reviewed and approved , where applicable, by the appropriate Legislature .

Sixth . Federal and Local Boards of Conciliation and Arbitration shall take the professional career service referred to Article 525- bis of the Law, according to their legal status from the first day of January 2014.

Seventh . The Presidents of the Federal and Local Boards of Conciliation and Arbitration established guidelines for the training system , training and staff legal update its respective Board within six months of coming into force these reforms .

Eighth . The Public Service of Reconciliation should be integrated at the latest for the budget year following that of the entry into force of the present reforms .

Ninth . The Defence Deputy Prosecutors Labour do not have the title and the professional card referred to in Article 533 shall have a term of five years to get it , as from the entry into force of the present reforms .

Labour Inspectors have no secondary education certificate or its equivalent referred to in Article 546 , Section II , will have a term of three years to obtain , from the entry into force these reforms .

The legal staff of the Conciliation and Arbitration does not have the professional title and the certificate referred to in Articles 626 , part II , 627 , Section II , 627- B , Section II , 628, and 629 count fraction II with a term of five years to get it , as from the entry into force of the present reforms .

Tenth . The remuneration referred to in Article 631 shall come into force from next Expenditure Budget of the Federation and the states.

Eleven . The trials started with the preceding provisions of this Act must be concluded in accordance with them.

Twelfth . The abolition of the Permanent Conciliation shall take effect ninety calendar days after that in the entry into force of this Decree.

The competent authority shall make the necessary actions for matters which are in process , are addressed by the Conciliation and Arbitration appropriate.

The competent authority shall take appropriate administrative measures for staff in the permanent Conciliation extinct.

Thirteen . The Federal Board of Conciliation and Arbitration shall establish the registration of medical experts in the field of occupational medicine referred to in Article 899- G of this Decree , within thirty days after the entry into force.

Medical experts in the field of occupational medicine will have a period of six months from the Federal Conciliation and Arbitration set the record referred to in the preceding paragraph , to obtain the corresponding register after the deadline indicated, the Board does not receive the expert experts emitting lacking registration.

Fourteen. Expenses that are generated as a result of the entry into force of this Decree , shall be made under the approved expenditure budget , so no additional resources will be needed in the current fiscal year , and will increase the budget regularized .

Mexico , DF , on November 13, 2012 . - Dip . Jesus Murillo Karam, President. - Sen . Ernesto Javier Cordero Arroyo , President . - Dip . Javier Orozco Gomez , Secretary . - Sen . Lilia Guadalupe Merodio Reza , Secretary. - Rubrics . "

In compliance with the provisions of Section I of Article 89 of the Constitution of the United Mexican States, and for its due publication and observance , I issue this Decree at the residence of the Federal Executive in Mexico City , Federal District , to November 29th , two thousand twelve . - Felipe de Jesus Calderon Hinojosa . - Category . - The Interior Secretary Alejandro Poire Romero Alfonso . - Category .

SUPPLEMENTS

SELECTED GOVERNMENT AND BUSINESS CONTACTS

MEXICAN GOVERNMENT AGENCIES

Secretaria de Comercio y Fomento Industrial (SECOFI)
(Secretariat of Commerce and Industrial Development)
Lic. Jaime Zabludosky
Under Secretary of Foreign Trade and Investment
Alfonso Reyes No. 30, Piso 9
Colonia Hipodromo-Condesa
06140 Mexico, D.F.
Tel: (011-52-5) 729-9101/ 9102
Fax: (011-52-5) 729-9307

Secretaria de Comercio y Fomento Industrial (SECOFI)
(Secretariat of Commerce and Industrial Development)
Lic. Carmen Quintanilla Madero
Director General of Standards
Puente de Tecamachalco No. 6
Lomas de Tecamachalco
53950 Naucalpan, Edo. de Mexico
Tel: (011-52-5) 729-9475/ 9476/ 9478
Fax: (011-52-5) 729-94-84

Instituto Mexicano de la Propiedad Industrial
(Mexican Institute of Industrial Property and Technological Development)
Lic. Jorge Amigo Castañeda
Director General
Periferico Sur No. 3106
Colonia Jardines del Pedregal
01900 Mexico, D.F.
Tel: (011-52-5) 624-0401/ 0402
Fax: (011-52-5) 624-0406

Secretaria de Educacion Publica (SEP)
(Secretariat of Public Education)
Lic. Fernando Serrano Migallon
Director General of Copyrights
Mariano Escobedo No. 438, 7o Piso
Colonia Nueva Anzures
11590 Mexico, D.F.
Tel: (011-52-5) 230-7630
Fax: (011-52-5) 250-0380

Secretaria de Comercio y Fomento Industrial (SECOFI)
(Secretariat of Commerce and Industrial Development)
Ing. Luis Raul Escudero
Mines General Coordinator
Morena No. 811, piso 2
Colonia Narvarte
03020 Mexico, D.F.
Tel: (011-52-5) 639-3575/4575
Fax: (011-52-5) 639-0814

Secretaria de Energia (SE)
(Secretariat of Energy)
Ing. Jorge Eduardo Navarrete Lopez
Under Secretary of Policy and Energy Development
Avenida Insurgentes No. 890, Piso 15
Colonia Roma Sur
03100 Mexico, D.F.
Tel: (011-52-5) 448-6070/ 6071/ 6072
Fax: (011-52-5) 448-6325

Secretaria de Medio Ambiente, Recursos Naturales y Pesca
(SEMARNAP)
Dra. Julia Carabias Lillo
(Secretariat of the Environment, Natural Resources, and Fisheries)
Lateral Anillo Periferico Sur 4209 - Piso 6
Fracc. Jardines de la Montana
14210 Mexico, D.F.
Tel: 628-0602/ thru 0605
Fax: 628-0644

Secretaria de Comunicaciones y Transporte (SCT)
(Secretariat of Communications and Transport)
Dr. Aaron Dychter Poltolarek
Under Secretary of Transportation

Edificio "C" - Piso 1 - Ala Oriente
Xola y Avenida Universidad
Colonia Narvarte
03028 Mexico, D.F.
Tel: (011-52-5) 519-4468/ 530-7390
Fax: (011-52-5) 519-48-71

MEXICAN TRADE ASSOCIATIONS/CHAMBERS OF COMMERCE

American Chamber of Commerce of Mexico, A.C.
Mr. John Bruton
Executive Vice President
Lucerna No. 78
Colonia Juarez
06600 Mexico, D.F.
Tel: (011-52-5) 724-3800
Fax: (011-52-5) 703-2911

United States Hispanic Chamber of Commerce
CONCANACO-SERVYTUR
Lic. Flavia Farinetti
Director of International Affairs
Balderas No. 144, Piso 3
Colonia Centro
06079 Mexico, D.F.
Tel: (011-52-5) 709-2281
Fax: (011-52-5) 709-1177

Camara Nacional de Comercio de la Ciudad de Mexico - (CANACO)
(National Chamber of Commerce of Mexico City)
Lic. Roman Vidal Tamayo
Director of Trade Development
Paseo de la Reforma No. 42 - Piso 3

Colonia Centro
06048 Mexico, D.F.
Tel: (011-52-5) 592-0371
Fax: (011-52-5) 703-2958

Confederacion de Camaras Nacionales de Comercio, Servicios y Turismo - (CONCANACO-SERVITUR)
(Confederation of National Chambers of Commerce)
Ing. Alejandro Aguilera Gomez
Director General

Balderas No. 144, Piso 3
Colonia Centro
06079 Mexico, D.F.
Tel: (011-52-5) 709-5910/ 1117
Fax: (011-52-5) 709-1177

Camara Nacional de la Industria de la Transformacion
(National Manufacturing Industry Chamber)
Lic. Luis Miguel Pando Leyva
Director General
Avenida San Antonio No. 256
Colonia Ampliacion Napoles
03849 Mexico, D.F.
Tel: (011-52-5) 563-61-12
Fax: (011-52-5) 598-58-88

Confederacion de Camaras Industriales de los Estados Unidos Mexicanos (CONCAMIN)
(Confederation of Industrial Chambers of Mexico)
Lic. Rene Espinoza
Director General
Manuel Ma. Contreras No. 133, Piso 2
Colonia Cuauhtémoc
06500 Mexico, D.F.
Tel: (011-52-5) 535-6589
Fax: (011-52-5) 535-6871

Asociacion Nacional de Import adores y Exportadores de la Republica Mexicana, A.C. (ANIERM)
Association of Importers and Exporters of Mexico
Ing. Luis Rebollar Corona
President
Monterrey No. 130
Colonia Roma 06700
Tel: (011-52-5) 584-9522
Fax: (011-52-5) 584-5317

Asociacion de Instituciones Financiara
Morgan Guaranty Trust Company of New York
Torre Optima
Sr. Eduardo Cepeda
Director General

Paseo de las Palmas 405 - Piso 16
Lomas de Chapultepec
11000 Mexico, D.F.
Tel: 540-9333
Fax: 540-9548

It should be noted that there are hundreds of specialized and regional associations and chambers in Mexico, which could not be included here.

MEXICAN COMMERCIAL BANKS

Banca Serfin, S.A.
Prol. Paseo de la Reforma No. 500
Col. Lomas de Santa Fé
01219 Mexico, D.F.
Tel: 257-8000
Fax: 257-8000 ext. 47195

Lic. Adolfo Lagos Espinoza
Director General

Banco del Atlantico, S.A.
Hidalgo 128, Coyoacan
04030 Mexico, D.F.
Tel: 6261778
Fax: 6589062
Lic. Fernando Ramos Gonzalez de Castilla
Director General

Impulsora Bursatil, S.A. de C.V. (Inbursa)
Paseo Las Palmas #736, Planta Baja
Col. Lomas de Chapultepec
11000 Mexico D. F.
Tel: 2021122
Fax: 5205326
Lic. Jose Ponce
Director, Area Internacional

Banco Internacional, S.A.
P. de la Reforma 156, Piso 3
Col. Juárez
06600 Mexico, D.F.
Tel: 7212983
Fax: 7212993
C.P. Antonio del Valle Ruiz
Director General

Banco Mercantil del Norte, S.A.
Institucion de Banca Multiple Grupo
Financiero
(Banorte)
Madero 22, Mezzanine
Col. Centro
06000 Mexico, D.F.
Tel: 5127440
Fax: 5124114
Lic. Francisco Gonzalez Martinez
Director General

Banco Santander Mexicano, S.A.
P. de la Reforma 211, Piso 16
06500 Mexico, D.F.
Tel: 629-3222/592-5472
629-3000 SWB
Fax: 629-3337
Lic. Enrique Castillo Sanchez-Mejorada
Director General

Banco Nacional de Mexico, S.A. (Banamex)
Isabel la Catolica 44, Piso 1
06089 Mexico, D.F.
Tel: 2255178
Fax: 7099446
C.P. Alfredo Harp Helu
Presidente del Comite de Direccion

Bancomer, S.A.
Ave. Universidad #1200, Piso 2
Col. Xoco
03339 Mexico, D.F.
Tel: 6213301
6213434 SWB
Fax: 6213988
Ing. Ricardo Guajardo Touche
Director General

Bank of America Mexico
P. de la Reforma 116, Piso 12
Col. Juarez
06600 Mexico, D.F.
Tel: 591-0011/546-15-25
Fax: 546-8026/2404
Mr. James F. McCabe
Director General

Bankers Trust S. A. de C. V.
Casa de Bolsa
Bosque de Alisos 45 "A", Piso 3
Col. Bosques de las Lomas

05120 Mexico, D.F.
Tel: 257-6651
257-6600 SWB
Fax: 557-6660
Ing. Adalberto Palma Gomez
Representante de Bankers Trust Co.

Bancrecer, S.A.
P. de la Reforma 116
Mexico, D.F. 06600
Tel: 566-0217
Fax: 329-6164
Mr. Manuel Somoza
Director General

Citibank S.A.
Reforma 390, Piso 18
Col. Juarez
06695 Mexico, D.F.
Tel: 2113030
Fax: 2075457

Lic. Julio A. de Quesada
Director General

Multibanco Inverlat, S.A.
Blvd. M. Avila Camacho #1, Piso 18
11560 Mexico, D.F.
Tel: 2292000
2292929 SWB
Fax: 2292157
Mr. William P. Sutton (ext. 2531)
Director General

Banco Bilbao Viscaya Probursa
Montes Urales 620, Piso 3
Lomas de Chapultepec
11000 Mexico, D. F.
Tel: 3258888/325-8000/06/25
325-8999 SWB
Fax: 3258054/8009
Lic. Jose Madariaga Lomelin
Presidente Ejecutivo

MEXICAN DEVELOPMENT BANKS

Banco Nacional de Comercio Exterior (Bancomext)
Camino a Sta. Teresa 1679, Piso 12, Ala Sur
Col. Jardines del Pedregal
01900 Mexico, D.F.
Tel: 227-9000 SWB
Fax: 6529408
Actuario Enrique Vilatela Riba
Director General

Banco Nacional de Crédito Rural, SNC (Banrural)
Agrarismo #227, Col. Escandon
11800 Mexico, D.F.
Tel: 2731465/273-1945
2715566 SWB
Fax: 271-5519/8132/723-1300
Lic. Oscar Terroba Garza
Director General

Banco Nacional de Obras y Servicios Publicos, S.N.C. (Banobras)
Calle Tecoyotitla #100
Col. Florida
01030 Mexico, D.F.
Tel: 7236202/6205/6192
Fax: 7236108
Lic. Jaime Corredor Esnaola
Director General

Banco Nacional del Ejercito, Fuerza Area y Armada, S.N.C. (Banjercito)
Ave. Industria Militar #1055
Lomas de Sotelo
11200 Mexico, D.F.
Tel: 5578661/395-2704/626-0549
5579188 SWB
Fax: 5576249
Gral de Brigada Int. Rafael Paz del Campo
Director General

Nacional Financiera, SNC
Insurgentes Sur 1971, Torre III y IV, Piso 8
Col. Guadalupe Inn
01020 Mexico, D.F.
Tel: 3257050/51
3256000
Fax: 3257249
Lic. Roberto Casillas Contreras Medellin
Director Internacional

REPRESENTATIVE OFFICES OF U.S. BANKS IN MEXICO

American Express Bank, (Mexico)S.A.
Av. Patriotismo 635, Piso 3
Col. Ciudad de los Deportes
03710 Mexico, D.F.
Tel: 326-2907
Fax: 326-2908
Ing. Jose Falomir
Director General

Bank One, Milwaukee, National Association
Rio Sena 54, Planta Baja
Col. Cuauhtemoc
06500 Mexico D.F.
Tel: 546-7178/566-2997
Fax: 546-7178/566-2997
Mr. Carlos Damaso Galguera
Representative

California Commerce Bank
Emilio Castelar 75 - PH
Col. Chapultepec Polanco
II560 Mexico, D.F.
Tel: 725-8760
Fax: 725-8676
Ing. Rene M. Popovits
Representative

CoBank National Bank for Cooperatives
Insurgentes Sur 1802, Piso 3
Col. Florida San Angel
01030 Mexico, D.F.
Tel: 661-2776, 661-9408, 661-9785
Fax: 661-9408
David A. Barraza
Representative

Continental Bank, National Association
Blvd. Manuel Avila Camacho 1, Piso 1,
Despacho 101
Col. Los Morales Polanco
Mexico, D.F. 11510
Tel: 395-3887
Fax: 395-4588
Federico Gonzalez Gomez
Representative

First Chicago Bank Mexico, S.A.
Institucion de Banca Multiple
Ruben Dario No. 281, Piso 10
Col. Bosque de Chapultepec
11580 Mexico, D.F.
Tel: 283-3300
Fax: 283-3320
Gregory G. Tallas
Director General

Morgan Guaranty Trust Company of New
York
Banco J.P. Morgan
Torre Optima
Paseo de las Palmas 405 - Piso 16
Lomas de Chapultepec
11000 Mexico, D.F.
Tel: 540-9333
Fax: 540-9548
Sr. Eduardo Cepeda
Director General

NationsBank of Texas, National Association
Edificio Torre Optima
P. de las Palmas 405 piso 10
Lomas de Chapultepec
11000 Mexico, D.F.
Tel: 540-8900
Fax: 540-8989
Lic. Roberto Sanchez Procissi
Representative

Republic National Bank of New York,
Mexico, S.A.
Campos Eliseos No. 1 - A
Col. Chapultepec Polanco
11560 Mexico, D.F.
Tel: 254-6059
Fax: 327-5114
Daniel Becker Feldman
Representative

The Chase Manhattan Bank, N.A.
Chemical Bank
Prol. P. De la Rforma 600, PB
Col. Santa Fe Peña Blanca
01210 Mexico, D.F.
Tel: 540-9703
540-9700 SWB
Fax: 540-9866
John Donnely
Representative

The First National Bank of Boston
Bosque De Alisos No. 47-B-3 Piso
Col. Bosque Lomas
Mexico, D.F. 05120
Tel: 257-7900
Fax: 257-7979
Stephen Thomas Griesemer
Representative

U.S. EMBASSY TRADE PERSONNEL

U.S. Embassy, Mexico City
Mr. Kevin C. Brennan
Minister-Counselor for Commercial Affairs
Mr. John Harris
Commercial Counselor
Paseo de la Reforma No. 305
Colonia Cuauhtemoc
06500 Mexico, D.F.
Tel: (011-52-5) 211-00-42, Ext. 3730
Fax: (011-52-5) 207-89-38
Mail: P.O. Box No. 3087
Laredo, TX 78044-3087

U.S. Trade Center, Mexico City
Mr. Robert W. Miller
Director
Liverpool No. 31
Colonia Juarez
06600 Mexico, D.F.
Tel: (011-52-5) 591-01-55
Fax: (011-52-5) 566-11-15
Mail: P.O. Box No. 3087
Laredo, TX 78044-3087

U.S. Agricultural Trade Office
Mr. Marvin Lehrer
Director
Edificio Virreyes, PH-2
Monte Pelvoux No. 220
Lomas de Chapultepec
11000 Mexico, D.F.
Tel: (011-52-5) 202-04-34
Fax: (011-52-5) 202-05-28
Mail: P.O. Box No. 3087
Laredo, TX 78044-3087

U.S. Consulate General, Monterrey
Mr. Robert Jones
Commercial Officer
Avenida Constitution No. 411 Pte.
64000 Monterrey, NL
Tel: (011-52-8) 45-21-20
Fax: (011-52-8) 42-51-72
Mail: P.O. Box No. 3098
Laredo, TX 78044-3098

U.S. Consulate General, Guadalajara
Ms. Virginia Krivis
Commercial Officer
Progreso No. 175
44100 Guadalajara, Jalisco
Tel: (011-52-3) 625-29-98
Fax: (011-52-3) 625-35-76
Mail: P.O. Box No. 3088
Laredo, TX 78044-3088

U.S. Consulate General, Tijuana
Ms. Wanda Barquin
Commercial Officer
Tapachula 96
22420 Tijuana, Baja California Norte
Tel: (011-52-6) 681-7400
Fax: (011-52-6) 686-5211
Mail: P.O. Box 439039
San Diego, Ca. 92143-9039

WASHINGTON-BASED U.S. GOVERNMENT COUNTRY CONTACTS

U.S. Department of Commerce
International Trade Administration
Office of NAFTA
Ms. Juliet Bender
Director
14th Street & Constitution Avenue, N.W.
Room No. 3022
Washington, D.C. 20230
Tel: (202) 482-0507
Fax: (202) 482-5865
Flash Fax: (202) 482-4464
(Flash Fax is a system through which firms can receive a wide variety of documents on doing business in Mexico automatically via fax)

U.S. Company Advisement/Advocacy at the IDB
Commerce Department Liaison Unit
Office of U.S. Executive Director L. Ronald Scheman
Inter-American Development Bank
1300 New York Avenue, N.W. Mail Stop E0209
Washington, D.C. 20577
Tel: (202) 623-3822
Fax: (202) 623-2039

Export-Import Bank of the United States
Ms. Paula Swain Priestley
Loan Officer for Mexico

International Business Development
811 Vermont Avenue, N.W.
Washington, D.C. 20571
Tel: (202) 565-39-21
Fax: (202) 565-33-80

U.S. Trade and Development Agency
Mr. Albert W. Angulo
Program Director
Latin American and the Caribbean
1621 N. Kent Street, Rm. 309
Rosslyn, VA 22209
Tel: (703) 875-4357
Fax: (703) 875-4009

U.S. Department of State
Bureau of Inter-American Affairs
Office of Mexican Affairs
Mr. Amb. John Leonard
Director
21st and C Streets, N.W., Rm. 4258
Washington, D.C. 20520
Tel: (202) 647-9894
Fax: (202) 647-5752

Office of the United States Trade Representative
Mr. John Melle
Director of Mexican Affairs
600 17th Street, N.W.
Washington, D.C.
Tel: (202) 395-3412
Fax: (202) 395-3911

U.S.-BASED PARTNERS FOR MEXICO

United States Chamber of Commerce
Mr. Andrew Howell
Assistant Director, Latin American Affairs
1615 H Street, N.W.
Washington, D.C. 20062-2000
Tel: (202) 463-5490
Fax: (202) 463-3126

United States-Mexico Chamber of Commerce
Mr. Martin Rojas
Communications Director
1730 M. Street N.W. Suite 112
Washington, D.C. 20056
Tel: (202) 296-5198
Fax: (202) 728-0768

United States Hispanic Chamber of Commerce
Mr. Jose F. Niño
President
1030 15th Street, N.W., Suite 206
Washington, D.C. 20005
Tel: (202) 842-1212
Fax: (202) 842-3221

InterAmerican Development Bank
Public Information Center
1300 New York Avenue, N.W.
Washington, D.C. 20577
Tel: 202/6232096; Fax: 202/6231928

U.S. STATE TRADE OFFICES IN MEXICO

STATE OF ARIZONA TRADE, TOURISM AND INVESTMENT OFFICE PH. (011-525) 566-9850
Sr. Manuel Diaz, Director General 566-9847
P. de la Reforma 10 - 7th. floor FAX 566-9642
Col. Tabacalera
06030 Mexico D. F.
E-mail dbarreir@infocel.net.mex

ARKANSAS STATE OFFICE
Sr. John Leonard
Durango 341-4
Col. Roma PH. (011-525) 211-6308
06700 Mexico D. F. FAX 211-5776
E-mail: 74174.504@compuserv.com

CALIFORNIA STATE OFFICE
Sr. Reinhold C. Schrader, Director Gral.PH. (011-525)747-8260
P. de la Reforma No. 265 - 14 floor
Col. Cuauhtemoc
06500 Mexico D. F. FAX 747-8229
E-mail: ref@californiaagency com.mex

CONNECTICUT STATE OFFICE
Noe Dela Flor, Director

Havre 67-107 PH. (011-525)514-1769
Col. Juarez 525-6807
06600 Mexico, D.F. FAX 514-8449

FLORIDA TRADE OFFICE
Sra. Guadalupe M. Martinez, Directora
PH.(011-525) 546-1518
Rio Marne 17 - 301 546-3438
Col. Cuauhtemoc 546-1919
06500 Mexico D.F, FAX 535-2475
E-mail: martinezflmx@iserve.net.mx

GEORGIA TRADE OFFICE
Lic. Steven Rosenberg - Representante PH. (011-525) 207-8011
Planeacion Avanzada, S. A. de C. V. 207-9836
P. de la Reforma 382 - 302 FAX 208-2179
Col. Juarez
06600 Mexico D. F.
Internet: Gdittmexico@serve.net.mx

HISPANIC CHAMBER OF COMMERCE
Sr. Juan Pablo de la Calle, Representante
Av. Insurgentes Sur No. 1700 Piso 4
PH.(011-525) 663-3535
Col. Florida 661-7744
01050 Mexico D. F. FAX 661-6486

IDAHO STATE OFFICE
Ing. Armando M. Orellana Villers, Representante
Av. Ninos Heroes No. 2905-6 PH. (011-53) 121-2158
44520 Guadalajara, Jal. FAX 121-1778
Internet: 74173.667@compuserv.com

ILLINOIS STATE OFFICE
Sr. Raymundo Flores - Director General PH. (011-525) 533-6666
P. de la Reforma 265 Piso 14
Edif. Torre Reforma FAX 533-5163
Col. Cuauhtemoc
06600 Mexico D. F.
Internet: Ilray@ibm.net

IOWA STATE OFFICE
Lic. Antoinette Allegretti, President
Trade, Management Services, Inc.
Kansas No. 63-1B
Col. Napoles PH. (011-525) 682-2458
03810 Mexico D. F. FAX 536-0561
Interntet:tallegretti@attmail.com

INDIANA TRADE OFFICE
Lic. Ana L. Carreón, Director PH. (011-525) 550-1014
Av. Revolucion 1909 616-2486
Col. San Angel 616-2984
01000 Mexico D. F. FAX 550-1014
Internet:indiana@intmex.com

LOUISIANA TRADE OFFICE
Sra. Nancy Alicia Paez, Director General
Chalchihui 137 PH. (O11-525) 520-9369
Col. Lomas de Chapultepec
11000 Mexico D. F. FAX 520-9369
E-mail: epax@genemp.com.mx

MARYLAND TRADE OFFICE
Mr. Noe de la Flor, Director
Havre 67, Dep. 107 PH. (011-525) 514-1769
Col. Juarez
06600 Mexico, D.F.
E-mail: indelaflor@serve.net.mx

MICHIGAN TRADE OFFICE
Sr. Manuel Otalora - Director General PH. (011-525) 611-8958
Acordada No. 18-201
Col. San Jose Insurgentes FAX 563-8150
03900 Mexico D. F.
E-mail: fhanhausen@aol.com

MINNESOTA TRADE OFFICE
Sr. William G. Allen - Representante
3 M de Mexico S. A. de C. V. PH. (011-525) 626-0400
Av. San Juan de Aragon 516
Col. Carrera Lardizabal
07070 Mexico D. F. FAX 728-2238
KENTUKY
Dr. Francisco Lugo
Av. De La Paz 1900 (temporary address)

MISSOURI AGRICULTURAL & TRADE OFFICE
Sr. Francisco Cortes, Director PH. (011-536) 16-6250
Mexicaltzingo No. 2189 16-6251
44150 Guadalajara, Jal. FAX 16-6554

NEW MEXICO STATE OFFICE
Mr. Rahul Kapur, Director General PH. (011-

525) 208-1515
Florencia 57, piso 3 FAX 207-7512
Col. Juarez
06600 Mexico D. F.
Internet: Nmexico@intmex.com

NORTH CAROLINA TRADE OFFICE
Sr. Kennedy C. Lonan
Av. Magnocentro No. 11, Piso 5
Col. Centro Urbano Huixquilucan PH. (011-525) 245-9041
52760 Mexico D. F. FAX 245-9049
Internet:70454.1031@Compuserve.com

OHIO TRADE OFFICE
Sr. Robert Steen
P. de la Reforma 390 Piso 17
Edificio Citibank
Col. Juarez PH. (011-525) 525-3132
06600 Mexico D. F.
OKLAHOMA TRADE OFFICE
Sr. Guillermo Mondlak Haussman
Representative
Horacio 1751-601 PH. (011-525) 589-9502
Col. Polanco FAX 589-9402
11510 Mexico, D.F.

OREGON REPRESENTATION OFFICE
C.P. Joaquin Frias Maures
PROCORFI Consultores
Jose Maria Velasco No. 67 PH. (011-525)660-1104/0979
San Jose Insurgentes /0665
03900 Mexico D. F. FAX 593-5982

GOVERNMENT OF PUERTO RICO OFFICE
Lic. Roberto Pedroza Diaz
Director General
Andres Bello 10 Piso 19 PH. (011-525)282-9175/76
Polanco FAX 282-9187
11510 Mexico D. F.

PENNSYLVANIA STATE OFFICE
Mr. Joaquin Frias, Director
Jose Ma. Velasco No. 67 PH. (011-525)660-1104
Col. San Jose Insurgentes FAX 593-5982
03900 Mexico, D.F.
Internet: Pennpro@internet.com.mex

RHODE ISLAND STATE OFFICE
Sr. Michael G. Taylor, Representative
Blvd. A. Lopez Mateos No. 2601
Col. Progreso San Angel PH. (011-525) 683-1277
01080 Mexico D. F.

SAN ANTONIO CITY OFFICE
(CASA DE LA CIUDAD DE SAN ANTONIO)
Mr. Daniel G. Rodriguez, Representative
Rio Nilo 80 - 502 PH. (011-525) 525-3131
Col. Cuauhtemoc FAX 207-7598
06500 Mexico, D.F.
E-mail: casame@rag.acnet.net

TEXAS STATE OFFICE
Sr. Phillip Hendrix - Director PH. (011-525) 546-8173
Hotel Ma. Isabel Sheraton
Paseo de la Reforma 325-PB
Col. Cuauhtemoc FAX 546-4830
06500 Mexico, D.F.
Internet: Texasmexico@iserve.net.mx

UTAH STATE OFFICE
Division of Economic Development
Mrs. Guadalupe M. de Escalante, Director
Florencia No. 39 piso 3 PH. (011-525) 525-5606
Col. Juarez
06600 Mexico D. F. FAX 525-5786
Internet:escalante@serve.net.mx

WASHINGTON TRADE OFFICE
Sr. Noe de la Flor, Director
Havre 67 - 107 PH. (011-525) 525-6807
Col. Juarez 514-1769
06600 Mexico D. F. FAX 514-8449

WISCONSIN STATE OFFICE
Mr. Vince Lencioni, Director
Rio Danubio No. 80 piso 2 PH: (11-525) 533-4745
Col. Cuauhtemoc
06500 Mexico D.F. FAX 207-6879
E-mail:wtom@data.net.mx

MARKET RESEARCH FIRMS IN MEXICO

A.C. Nielsen Company
Sr. Roberto O. Pedraza P.
Commercial Manager
Blvd. Manuel Avila Camacho No. 191, pisos 7 y 8
Colonia Chapultepec Morales
11570 Mexico, D.F.
Tel: (011-52-5) 395-03-99
Fax: (011-52-5) 580-1957

Acus Consultores, S.C.
Ing. Alberto Calvo Mercado
General Director
Parque Lira No. 79, Despacho 408
Col. San Miguel Chapultepec
11850 Mexico, D.F.
Tel.: (525) 272-40-32
Fax: (525) 272-4969

Arthur D. Little de Mexico, S.A.
Lic. Andrew Wigard
Director
Sinaloa No. 149, Piso 10
Colonia Roma Norte
06700 Mexico, D.F.
Tel: (011-52-5) 208-75-64
Fax: (011-52-5) 207-75-92

Bimsa, S.A. de C.V.
Lic. Cesar Ortega de la Roquette
Vice President and Director General
Ingenieros Militares No. 91
Colonia Lomas de Sotelo
11200 Mexico, D.F.
Tel: (011-52-5) 395-34-88
Fax: (011-52-5) 395-86-48

The Boston Consulting Group
Monterrey Office
Calzada del Valle 40906, Piso 4
Garza Garcia, Nuevo Leon, CP 66220
Tel: (011-52-8) 356-6400
Fax: (011-52-8) 356-6699

Dun & Bradstreet, S.A. de C.V.
Mr. Carlos T. Blanco
General Director
Durango No. 263, piso 5
Col. Roma
06700 Mexico, D.F.
Tel: (011-52-5) 229-6900, 511-3766
Fax: (011-52-5) 514-96-40, 511-00-65

Infotec
Dr. Alberto Sanchez Osio
Deputy Director
Avenida San Fernando No. 37
Colonia Toriello Guerra-Tlalpan
14050 Mexico, D.F.
Tel: (011-52-5) 606-00-11 Exts. 1021/1025
Fax: (011-52-5) 606-13-07

Newell, Arano y Asociados, S.A. de C.V.
Sr. Polux Arano Diaz de la Serna
Director General
Avenida Cuernavaca No. 43
Colonia Condesa
06140 Mexico, D.F.
Tel: (011-52-5) 211-82-95
Fax: (011-52-5) 211-82-62

Norris & Elliott, S.A. de C.V.
Ing. Agustin Pesquiera Rebeil
President
Leibnitz No. 11, 4o Piso
Colonia Anzures
11590 Mexico, D.F.
Tel: (011-52-5) 254-64-02
Fax: (011-52-5) 254-47-67

Technomic de Mexico, S.A.
Sr. Antonio Iñiguez
General Manager
Rio Guadalquivir No. 50, Piso 3
Colonia Cuauhtemoc
06500 Mexico, D.F.
Tel: (011-52-5) 208-13-25
Fax: (011-52-5) 207-47-28

Wilsa, S.A.
Sr. Wilbert Sierra
Director General
Cozumel No. 60
Colonia Condesa
06140 Mexico, D.F.
Tel: (011-52-5) 286-15-31
Fax: (011-52-5) 286-94-57

In Mexico there are only two companies having infrastructure to perform consumption trend surveys nationwide:

A.C. NIELSEN COMPANY
Boulevard Manuel Avila Camacho No. 191, pisos 7 y 8
Col. Chapultepec Morales
11570 Mexico, D.F.

Tel: (011-52-5) 395-03-99
Fax: (011-52-5) 580-1957
Contact: Roberto O. Pedraza, Commercial Manager

BIMSA ECONOMETRICS, S.A. DE C.V.
Sofocles No. 118
Col. Chapultepec Polanco
11560 Mexico, D.F.
Tel & fax: (011-52-5) 580-0288 (11 lines)
Contact: Lic. Daniel Chiquiar Cikurel, Director
Internet: www.bimsa.com.mx

Other two companies doing market research that could perform surveys through contractors nationwide:

SELECT
Av. Nuevo Leon No. 54
Col. Hipodromo Condesa
Mexico, D.F.
Tel: (011-52-5) 256-0981, 256-1098, 256-1426, 553-4952
Fax: (011-52-5) 553-4641
Contact: Dr. Ricardo Zermeno

MACROASESORIA ECONOMICA
Insurgentes Sur No. 2065, 1er. Piso, Torre B
Col. San Angel
01000 Mexico, D.F.
Tel: (011-52-5) 726-9200 ext. 19209
Fax: (011-52-5) 726-9300
Contact: Lic. Jaime Herrera

MAJOR NEWSPAPERS AND BUSINESS JOURNALS:

Alto Nivel
Hda. Del Rosario No. 195
Col. Prados del Rosario
02410 México, D.F.
Tel: (011-52-5) 382-7376
Fax: (011-52-5) 382-7387
Circulation: 25,100
Printing Data: Size: 9.6 x 7.6"; three 2.2" colummns
Contact: Ms. Patricia Arrieta, Advertising

America Economía
Published by: Dow Jones & Co., Inc.
Isaac Newton No. 286, Piso 9
Col. Chapultepec Morales
11560 México, D.F.
Tel: (011-52-5) 254-2400, 254-2415, 254-1352
Fax: (011-52-5) 254-7510
Circulation: 13,500
Printing Data: Size; 10.8 x 8.1"; three 2.2 colummns
Contact: Mrs. Norma T. N. De Alcázar, Advertisement Director

Business Mexico (Monthly)
Published by: The American Chamber of Commerce of Mexico
Lucerna 78
Col. Juárez
06600 México, D.F.
Tel: (011-52-5) 724-3800 ext. 3335
Fax: (011-52-5) 703-2911 or 703-3908
Circulation: 10,000
Printing Data: Size: 9.8 x 7.5"; three 2.2" colummns
Contact: Ms. Diane Hemelberg de Hernández, Editor
Cristina Bustos, Advertising

El Nuevo Inversionista
Published by: Videovisa Publicaciones, S.A. de C.V.
Acoxpa No. 444, Piso 5
Tel: (011-52-5) 229-3100 ext. 3210, 3107 and 1464
Fax: (011-52-5) 229-3100 ext. 1421
Circulation: 17,000
Printing Data: Size: 9.3 x 7.3"; three 2.2 colummns
Contact: Ms. Guadalupe Pardo Aguirre, Commercial Director

Entrepreneur
Published by: Impresiones Aéreas, S.A. de C.V.
Arquímedes No. 5
Col. Polanco
11560 México, D.F.
Tel: (011-52-5) 769-8935
Fax: (011-52-5) 726-8968
Circulation: 20,000
Printing Data: Size: 9.4 x 7.1"; three 2.2" colummns

Contact: Ms. Tata Sandoval, Marketing Director

Expansión
Published by Grupo Editorial Expansión, S.A. de C.V.
Sinaloa No. 149, 9th. Floor
Col. Roma Sur
06700 Mexico, D.F.
Tel: (011-52-5) 207-2176
Fax: (011-52-5) 511-6351
Circulation: 24,000
Printing Data: Size: 9.8 x 7.1"; three 2.2" colummns
Contact: Adriana Mondragón, Angelina Gamboa, Advertising

Mundo Ejecutivo
Edited by: Grupo Internacional Editorial, S.A. de C.V.
Río Nazas No. 34
Col. Cuauhtémoc
06500 México, D.F.
Tel: (011-52-5) 566-4144, 566-0543, 209-9930
Fax: (011-52-5) 566-0564
E-mail: mundoeje@inetcorp.net.mx
Internet: http://www.mundoeje.com.mx
Circulation: 22,000
Contact: Mr. Emilio Flores, Commercial Manager

MAJOR NEWSPAPERS

EL ECONOMISTA
Av. Coyoacán No. 515
Col. Del Valle
03100 México, D.F.
Tel: (011-52-5) 237-0791
Fax: (011-52-5) 682-9369
internet: http://www.economista.com.mx
Circulation: 35,000
Printing Data: Offset; 170 Agata lines, four colummns
Contact: Mr. Alejandro Ortíz, Advertising Executive

EL FINANCIERO
Lago Bolsena No. 176
Col. Anáhuac
11320 México, D.F.
Tel: (011-52-5) 227-7600, ext. 7647
Fax: (011-52-5) 227-7687
Internet: http://www.elfinanciero.com.mx
Circulation: 135,000
Printing Data: Offset; 180 Agata lines, four colummns
Contact: Lic. Francisco Javier Badiola Contreras, Deputy Commercial Director

El Financiero Weekly International Edition
2300 S. Broadway
Los Angeles, CA 90007
Tel: (213) 747-7547, (800) 433-4872
Fax: (213) 747-2489

EL UNIVERSAL
Published by: El Universal Compañía Periodística Nacional
Bucareli No. 8
Col. Centro
06040 México, D.F.
Tel: (011-52-5) 521-0010, 709-1313, ext. 1030, 1031, 1032
Fax: (011-52-5) 521-8080
http:\\www.el-universal.com.mx
Circulation: 170,000
Printing Data: 300 Agata lines, eight colummns
Contact: Lic. José Luis Grosvenor Ibarra, Sales Manager

EXCELSIOR
Published by: Excelsior, Compañía Editorial, S.C. de R.L.
Av. Paseo de la Reforma No. 18
Col. Centro
06600 México, D.F.
Tel: (011-52-5) 705-4444
Fax: (011-52-5) 546-0787
Internet address:
http://www.excelsior.com.mx
http/worldnews.net/excelsior/excelsior.hmtl
Circulation: 200,000
Printing Data: 280 lines, eight colummns
Contact: Mr. Gabriel Manzanilla Aragón, Advertising Chief

REFORMA
Published by: Consorcio Interamericano de Comunicación, S.A. de C.V.
Av. México Coyoacán No. 40
Col. Santa Cruz Atoyac
03310 México, D.F.
Tel: (011-52-5) 628-7878
Fax: (011-52-5) 628-7466
Internet: http://www.infosel.com.mx/

Circulation: 94,000
Printing Data: Offset; 21¼", eight colummns

Contact: Lic. Jesús Vazquez, Advertising Director

BASIC TITLES ON MEXICO

IMPORTANT!
All publications are updated annually!
Please contact IBP, Inc. at ibpusa3@gmail.com for the latest ISBNs and additional information

TITLE
Mexico Export-Import and Business Directory
Mexico A "Spy" Guide - Strategic Information and Developments
Mexico A Spy" Guide"
Mexico Air Force Handbook
Mexico Air Force Handbook
Mexico Banking & Financial Market Handbook
Mexico Banking & Financial Market Handbook
Mexico Business and Investment Opportunities Yearbook
Mexico Business and Investment Opportunities Yearbook
Mexico Business and Investment Opportunities Yearbook Volume 1 Strategic Information and Opportunities
Mexico Business Intelligence Report - Practical Information, Opportunities, Contacts
Mexico Business Intelligence Report - Practical Information, Opportunities, Contacts
Mexico Business Law Handbook - Strategic Information and Basic Laws
Mexico Business Law Handbook - Strategic Information and Basic Laws
Mexico Business Law Handbook - Strategic Information and Basic Laws
Mexico Business Law Handbook - Strategic Information and Basic Laws
Mexico Business Law Handbook Volume 2 Investment and Trade Laws Volume 2 Investment and Trade Laws
Mexico Business Success Guide - Basic Practical Information and Contacts
Mexico Clothing & Textile Industry Handbook
Mexico Clothing & Textile Industry Handbook
Mexico Clothing & Textile Industry Handbook
Mexico Company Laws and Regulations Handbook
Mexico Company Laws and Regulations Handbook - Strategic Information and Basic Laws
Mexico Constitution and Citizenship Laws Handbook - Strategic Information and Basic Laws
Mexico Country Study Guide - Strategic Information and Developments
Mexico Country Study Guide - Strategic Information and Developments Volume 1 Strategic Information and Developments
Mexico Criminal Laws, Regulations and Procedures Handbook - Strategic Information, Regulations, Procedures
Mexico Customs, Trade Regulations and Procedures Handbook
Mexico Customs, Trade Regulations and Procedures Handbook
Mexico Diplomatic Handbook - Strategic Information and Developments
Mexico Diplomatic Handbook - Strategic Information and Developments
Mexico Ecology & Nature Protection Handbook
Mexico Ecology & Nature Protection Handbook
Mexico Ecology & Nature Protection Laws and Regulation Handbook
Mexico Economic & Development Strategy Handbook
Mexico Economic & Development Strategy Handbook
Mexico Education System and Policy Handbook

TITLE
Mexico Electoral, Political Parties Laws and Regulations Handbook - Strategic Information, Regulations, Procedures
Mexico Energy Policy, Laws and Regulation Handbook
Mexico Energy Policy, Laws and Regulations Handbook
Mexico Energy Policy, Laws and Regulations Handbook
Mexico Export-Import and Business Directory
Mexico Export-Import and Business Directory
Mexico Export-Import and Business Directory
Mexico Export-Import Trade and Business Directory
Mexico Export-Import Trade and Business Directory
Mexico Fishing and Aquaculture Industry Handbook - Strategic Information, Regulations, Opportunities
Mexico Foreign Policy and Government Guide
Mexico Foreign Policy and Government Guide
Mexico Government and Business Contacts Handbook
Mexico Government and Business Contacts Handbook
Mexico Immigration Laws and Regulations Handbook - Strategic Information and Basic Laws
Mexico Industrial and Business Directory
Mexico Industrial and Business Directory
Mexico Insolvency (Bankruptcy) Laws and Regulations Handbook - Strategic Information and Basic Laws
Mexico Internet and E-Commerce Investment and Business Guide - Strategic and Practical Information: Regulations and Opportunities
Mexico Internet and E-Commerce Investment and Business Guide - Strategic and Practical Information: Regulations and Opportunities
Mexico Investment and Business Guide - Strategic and Practical Information
Mexico Investment and Business Guide - Strategic and Practical Information
Mexico Investment and Business Guide - Strategic and Practical Information
Mexico Investment and Business Guide - Strategic and Practical Information
Mexico Investment and Business Guide Volume 2 Business, Investment Opportunities and Incentives
Mexico Investment and Business Profile - Basic Information and Contacts for Succesful investment and Business Activity
Mexico Investment and Trade Laws and Regulations Handbook
Mexico Investment, Trade Strategy and Agreements Handbook - Strategic Information and Basic Agreements
Mexico Justice System and National Police Handbook
Mexico Justice System and National Police Handbook
Mexico Labor Laws and Regulations Handbook - Strategic Information and Basic Laws
Mexico Land Ownership and Agriculture Laws Handbook
Mexico Medical & Pharmaceutical Industry Handbook
Mexico Medical & Pharmaceutical Industry Handbook
Mexico Mineral & Mining Sector Investment and Business Guide - Strategic and Practical Information
Mexico Mineral & Mining Sector Investment and Business Guide - Strategic and Practical Information
Mexico Mining Laws and Regulations Handbook
Mexico Oil & Gas Sector Business & Investment Opportunities Yearbook
Mexico Oil & Gas Sector Business & Investment Opportunities Yearbook
Mexico Oil and Gas Exploration Laws and Regulation Handbook
Mexico Privatization Programs and Regulations Handbook
Mexico Privatization Programs and Regulations Handbook
Mexico Recent Economic and Political Developments Yearbook
Mexico Recent Economic and Political Developments Yearbook
Mexico Recent Economic and Political Developments Yearbook

TITLE
Mexico Research & Development Policy Handbook
Mexico Research & Development Policy Handbook
Mexico Research & Development Policy Handbook
Mexico Starting Business (Incorporating) in....Guide
Mexico Tax Guide
Mexico Tax Guide
Mexico Tax Guide Volume 1 Strategic Information and Basic Regulations
Mexico Taxation Laws and Regulations Handbook
Mexico Telecom Laws and Regulations Handbook
Mexico Telecommunication Industry Business Opportunities Handbook
Mexico Telecommunication Industry Business Opportunities Handbook
Mexico Transportation Policy and Regulations Handbook
Mexico: How to Invest, Start and Run Profitable Business in Mexico Guide - Practical Information, Opportunities, Contacts

BASIC LAWS AND REGULATIONS AFFECTING BUSINESS[1]

COUTRY	LAW TITLE
Mexico	1917 Constitution of Mexico
Mexico	1994 Electoral Code (with amendments of 2002)
Mexico	Act and Banking Commission Securities
Mexico	Act Civil Liability for Nuclear Damage
Mexico	Act Credit Union
Mexico	Act Expropriation
Mexico	Act Federal Animal Health
Mexico	Act Federal Transparency and Access to Public Government Information
Mexico	Act General Business Corporation
Mexico	Act Industrial Property
Mexico	Act Liability Nuclear Damage
Mexico	Act of the National Institutes of Health
Mexico	Act Public Service Electric Energy
Mexico	ACT Public Service Electric Power.
Mexico	Act Regulations National Water
Mexico	Act Regulations Navigation
Mexico	Act Snuff Control
Mexico	Act, the National Hydrocarbons Commission
Mexico	Administrative Proceedings Code of the State of Campeche Drawings
Mexico	Agricultural Law
Mexico	Airport Law
Mexico	Assemblea Legislation Legislative District of the Federal
Mexico	Assistance Act and Family Violence Prevention.
Mexico	Attorney Colima State Code
Mexico	Bank Act Mexico
Mexico	Bankruptcy Law
Mexico	Bylaws of the Federal Commission on Competition
Mexico	Cadastral and Registration Law of the State of Sonora

[1] For ordering texts of specific laws in English, French or other languages, please contact Global Investment Center USA at ibpusa3@gmail.com

Mexico	Campeche State Law
Mexico	Chiapas State Laws
Mexico	Chihuahua State Law
Mexico	Civic Justice Act for the Federal District
Mexico	Civil Aviation Law
Mexico	Civil Code Hidalgo
Mexico	Civil Code of the Federal District
Mexico	Civil Code of the Republic of Mexico
Mexico	Civil Code of the State of Aguascalientes
Mexico	Civil Code of the State of Baja California
Mexico	Civil Code of the State of Campeche
Mexico	Civil Code of the State of Chiapas
Mexico	Civil Code of the State of Chihuahua
Mexico	Civil Code of the State of Coahuila
Mexico	Civil Code of the State of Colima
Mexico	Civil Code of the State of Durango.
Mexico	Civil Code of the State of Guanajuato
Mexico	Civil Code of the State of Guerrero Number 358
Mexico	Civil Code of the State of Jalisco
Mexico	Civil Code of the State of Nayarit
Mexico	Civil Code of the State of Nuevo Leon
Mexico	Civil Code of the State of Oaxaca
Mexico	Civil Code of the State of Queretaro
Mexico	Civil Code of the State of Quintana Roo
Mexico	Civil Code of the State of San Luis Potosi
Mexico	Civil Code of the State of Sinaloa
Mexico	Civil Code of the State of Sonora
Mexico	Civil Code of the State of Tabasco
Mexico	Civil Code of the State of Tamaulipas
Mexico	Civil Code of the State of Tlaxcala
Mexico	Civil Code of the State of Veracruz
Mexico	Civil Code of the State of Yucatan
Mexico	Civil Code of the State of Zacatecas
Mexico	Civil Code Tamaulipas
Mexico	Civil Procedural Code of the State of Coahuila de Zaragoza
Mexico	Civil Procedure Code of the Free and Sovereign State of Guerrero No. 364
Mexico	Coahuila State Law
Mexico	Code Fiscal State of Quintana Roo
Mexico	Code for the Protection and Defense of Children Chihuahua State
Mexico	Code Municipal Fiscal State Quintana Roo
Mexico	Code of Administrative Justice for the State of Durango.
Mexico	Code of Administrative Justice of the State of Michoacan de Ocampo
Mexico	Code of Administrative Procedures for the State of Veracruz Contentious
Mexico	Code of Civil Procedure for the Federal District
Mexico	Code of Civil Procedure for the Free and Sovereign State of Quintana Roo
Mexico	Code of Civil Procedure for the Sonora
Mexico	Code of Civil Procedure for the State of Baja California
Mexico	Code of Civil Procedure for the State of Colima
Mexico	Code of Civil Procedure for the State of Durango.
Mexico	Code of Civil Procedure for the State of Nayarit

Mexico	Code of Civil Procedure for the State of Oaxaca
Mexico	Code of Civil Procedure for the State of San Luis Potosi
Mexico	Code of Civil Procedure for the State of Sinaloa
Mexico	Code of Civil Procedure for the State of Tabasco
Mexico	Code of Civil Procedure for the State of Veracruz
Mexico	Code of Civil Procedure for the State of Zacatecas
Mexico	Code of Civil Procedure for the State of Zacetacas
Mexico	Code of Civil Procedure Jalisco State
Mexico	Code of Civil Procedure of the State of Aguascalientes
Mexico	Code of Civil Procedure of the State of Campeche
Mexico	Code of Civil Procedure of the State of Chiapas
Mexico	Code of Civil Procedure of the State of Mexico
Mexico	Code of Civil Procedure of the State of Michoacán
Mexico	Code of Civil Procedure of the State of Querétaro
Mexico	Code of Civil Procedure of the State of Tamaulipas
Mexico	Code of Civil Procedure of the State of Tlaxcala
Mexico	Code of Electoral Institutions and Procedures for the State of Campeche
Mexico	Code of Electoral Institutions and Procedures the State of Quintana Roo
Mexico	Code of Federal institutions and procedures electoral
Mexico	Code of Judicial Organization of the State of Chiapas
Mexico	Code of Justice for young offenders in the State of Durango
Mexico	Code of Military Justice
Mexico	Code of Procedure and Administrative Justice for the State of Guanajuato
Mexico	Code of Regulations to the Federal Law on Economic Competition
Mexico	Colima State Law
Mexico	Commercial Code
Mexico	Companies Act Interest Public Limited Liability
Mexico	Companies Act Social Solidarity
Mexico	Constitution for the State of Guanajuato
Mexico	Constitution of Querétaro
Mexico	Constitution of the State of Aguascalientes
Mexico	Constitution of the State of Baja California Sur
Mexico	Constitution of the State of Durango.
Mexico	Constitution of the State of Guerrero
Mexico	Constitution of the State of Hidalgo
Mexico	Constitution of the State of Morelos
Mexico	Constitution of the State of Nuevo Leon
Mexico	Constitution of the State of Oaxaca
Mexico	Constitution of the State of Puebla
Mexico	Constitution of the State of Quintana Roo
Mexico	Constitution of the State of Sonora
Mexico	Constitution of the State of Tabasco
Mexico	Constitution of the State of Tamaulipas
Mexico	Constitution of the State of Veracruz
Mexico	Constitution State of Michoacan de Ocampo
Mexico	Constitution Tamaulipas State
Mexico	Contract Law Insurance
Mexico	Corporations Act Corporations
Mexico	Credit Institutions Act 2008
Mexico	Criminal Code of the Federal District

Mexico	Customs Law
Mexico	Elections Code of the State of Colima
Mexico	Electoral Code of the State of Durango
Mexico	Electoral Code of the State of Sonora
Mexico	Electoral Code of the State of Veracruz
Mexico	Electoral Law of the State of Hidalgo
Mexico	Environmental Law of the Federal District.
Mexico	Expropriation Act
Mexico	Family Code of the State of Zacatecas
Mexico	Federal Code of Civil Procedure
Mexico	Federal Code of Electoral Institutions and Procedures
Mexico	Federal Consumer Protection
Mexico	Federal Copyright Law.
Mexico	Federal Gambling Law And Law Of Acquisitions, Leases and public sector services
Mexico	Federal Labor Law
Mexico	Federal Law In Cinematography
Mexico	Federal Law of Administrative Responsibilities Public Servants Of Federal Law To prevent and eliminate discrimination
Mexico	Federal Law of Economic Competition
Mexico	Federal Law of Education
Mexico	Federal Law of Games and Draws
Mexico	Federal Law of Public Advocacy
Mexico	Federal Law of the Sea
Mexico	Federal Law of the Sea
Mexico	Federal Law of Transparency and Access to Public Government Information
Mexico	Federal Law on Metrology and Standardization
Mexico	Federal Law on Monuments and Archaeological Areas, Artistic and Historic Monuments
Mexico	Federal Law on Plant Varieties
Mexico	Federal Law on Plant Varieties
Mexico	Federal Law Protection Consumer
Mexico	Federal Plant Variety Law
Mexico	Federal Radio and Television Law
Mexico	Federal Tax Code
Mexico	Federal Tax Law Car
Mexico	Federal Tax Law on Auto miles
Mexico	Federal Telecommunications Act
Mexico	Federal Telecommunications Law
Mexico	Financial Code of the Federal District 2005
Mexico	Fiscal Code of the Federation
Mexico	Fisheries Act
Mexico	Foreign Investment Law
Mexico	Foreign Trade Law of
Mexico	Forest Law
Mexico	General law of Commercial Companies
Mexico	General Law of Ecological Equilibrium and Environmental Protection
Mexico	General Law of National Assets
Mexico	General Law of Organizations and Auxiliary Credit Activities
Mexico	Guerrero State Law
Mexico	Health Law
Mexico	Hidalgo State Law

Mexico	Investment Companies Act
Mexico	Jalisco State Law
Mexico	Land Law
Mexico	Law Business Flat Tax
Mexico	Law Energy Regulatory Commission
Mexico	Law Federal Telecommunications
Mexico	Law for Equality between Women and Men
Mexico	Law for the Protection of the Rights of Children and Adolescents.
Mexico	Law for the Sustainable Use of Energy
Mexico	Law for Transparency and Ordering of Financial Services
Mexico	Law General Cooperative Societies
Mexico	Law General Goods National
Mexico	Law Libraries General
Mexico	Law of Civil Protection
Mexico	Law of Commercial Companies
Mexico	Law of Federal Plant Protection
Mexico	Law of Fiscal Coordination
Mexico	Law of Fisheries and Aquaculture Sustainable
Mexico	Law of Industrial Property
Mexico	Law of Limited Liability Companies Public Interest
Mexico	Law of Persons with Disabilities
Mexico	Law of Ports
Mexico	Law of roads, bridges and federal motor carrier
Mexico	Law of the Bank of Mexico
Mexico	Law of the National Human Rights Commission
Mexico	Law of the State of Sonora Water
Mexico	Law on Access to Public Information of the State of Sonora,
Mexico	Law on Biosafety of Genetically Modified Organisms
Mexico	Law on Military Courts
Mexico	Law on Special Tax on Production and Services
Mexico	Law on the Promotion and Development of Bioenergy
Mexico	Law on Value Added Tax
Mexico	Law Transportation and Highways of the Federal District.
Mexico	Laws Nayarit
Mexico	Laws of the State of Aguascalientes
Mexico	Laws of the State of Chiapas
Mexico	Laws of the State of Durango
Mexico	Laws of the State of Veracruz-Llave
Mexico	Laws Sonora
Mexico	Laws State of Yucatan
Mexico	Mar Federal Law
Mexico	Mediation and Conciliation Law of the State of Aguascalientes
Mexico	Mercantile Corporations Act
Mexico	Mexican Civil Code of the Republic
Mexico	Mexican Postal Service Law
Mexico	Mexico Bank Act
Mexico	Mexico Bank Act
Mexico	Mexico State Law
Mexico	Mining Act
Mexico	Mining Act Regulations

Mexico	Monetary Law of the United States of Mexico
Mexico	Morelos State Laws
Mexico	Mortgage Corporation Law on Federal
Mexico	Municipal Tax Code for the State of Zacatecas
Mexico	National Security Act
Mexico	Navigation Act
Mexico	Oaxaca State Law
Mexico	Organic Law of Agrarian Courts
Mexico	Organic Law of National Financial
Mexico	Organic Law of Petróleos Mexicanos and Subsidiary Entities
Mexico	Organic Law of the Attorney General of the Republic
Mexico	Organic Law of the Federal Court of Fiscal and Administrative
Mexico	Organic Law of the Federal Court of Fiscal and Administrative Justice
Mexico	Organic Law of the Judicial Power of the Federation.
Mexico	Organic Law of the National Bank of the Army, Air Force and Navy
Mexico	Organic Law of the National Savings Bank and Financial Services
Mexico	PEMEX Law
Mexico	Penal Code Chihuahua
Mexico	Penal Code of the Federal District (Mexico)
Mexico	Penal Code of the State of Baja California
Mexico	Penal Code of the State of Campeche
Mexico	Penal Code of the State of Chiapas
Mexico	Penal Code of the State of Coahuila
Mexico	Penal Code of the State of Colima
Mexico	Penal Code of the State of Durango.
Mexico	Penal Code of the State of Guanajuato
Mexico	Penal Code of the State of Guerrero
Mexico	Penal Code of the State of Hidalgo
Mexico	Penal Code of the State of Mexico
Mexico	Penal Code of the State of Michoacán
Mexico	Penal Code of the State of Nayarit
Mexico	Penal Code of the State of Nuevo Leon
Mexico	Penal Code of the State of Oaxaca
Mexico	Penal Code of the State of Queretaro
Mexico	Penal Code of the State of Quintana Roo
Mexico	Penal Code of the State of Sinaloa
Mexico	Penal Code of the State of Tabasco
Mexico	Penal Code of the State of Tamaulipas
Mexico	Penal Code of the State of Tamaulipas
Mexico	Penal Code of the State of Tlaxcala
Mexico	Planning Act
Mexico	Political Constitution of the State of Chiapas
Mexico	Political Constitution of the State of Coahuila
Mexico	Political Constitution of the State of Jalisco
Mexico	Political Constitution of the State of Tlaxcala
Mexico	Political Constitution of the State of Yucatan
Mexico	Political Constitution of the State of Zacatecas
Mexico	Private Security Act for the Federal District.
Mexico	Procedure Election Law for the Federal District
Mexico	Prosecutor Sonora State Code

Mexico	Prosecutor Tamaulipas State Code
Mexico	Public Service Law Electricity
Mexico	Puebla State Law
Mexico	Regulation Civil Aviation Law
Mexico	Regulation of Environmental Law Federal District
Mexico	Regulation of the Federal Law of Tourism
Mexico	Regulations of the National Bank for Foreign Trade
Mexico	Regulations to the Mining Act
Mexico	Revenue Code of Aguascalientes State
Mexico	Revenue Code of Zacatecas
Mexico	Rules Of The Federal Plant Variety
Mexico	Rules Of The Law Industrial Property
Mexico	Rules Of The Law Of National Water
Mexico	Securities Exchange Act
Mexico	Service Act Tax Administration
Mexico	Social Insurance Law
Mexico	State Civil Code of Mexico
Mexico	State Civil Code Puebla
Mexico	State Constitution Baja California
Mexico	State Constitution Campeche
Mexico	State Constitution Chihuahua
Mexico	State Constitution Colima
Mexico	State Constitution Nayarit
Mexico	State Constitution of San Luis Potosi
Mexico	State Law California
Mexico	State Law Federal District
Mexico	State Law Guanajuato
Mexico	State Law Michoacán
Mexico	State Law Nuevo Leon
Mexico	State Law Querétaro
Mexico	State Law Sinaloa
Mexico	State Law Zacatecas
Mexico	State Laws of Quintana Roo
Mexico	State Laws San Luis Potosi
Mexico	State of Aguascalientes Electoral Code
Mexico	State Penal Code Jalisco
Mexico	State Penal Code San Luis Potosi
Mexico	State Tax Code San Luis Potosi
Mexico	Statute of Government of the Federal District
Mexico	Superior Court Organic Law of the Federal District.
Mexico	Tabasco State Law
Mexico	Tamaulipas State Law
Mexico	Tax Act Cash Deposit
Mexico	Tax Act Income
Mexico	Tax Code of the State and Municipalities of Baja California Sur
Mexico	Tax Code of the State of Colima Municipal
Mexico	Tax Code of the State of Durango Municipal
Mexico	Tax Code of the State of Durango.
Mexico	Tax Code of the State of Nayarit
Mexico	Tax Code of the State of Querétaro

Mexico	Tax Code of the State of Zacatecas
Mexico	Tax Code Sinaloa State
Mexico	Tax Code Tabasco State
Mexico	Tax Law General Import and Export
Mexico	Telecommunications Act Federal
Mexico	Tlaxcala State Law
Mexico	Urban Code for the State of Aguascalientes
Mexico	Urban Code for the State of Zacatecas
Mexico	Urban State Code Zacetacas
Mexico	Vehicle Registration Act Public
Mexico	Water Law
Mexico	Wildlife Act
Mexico	Zacatecas State Law

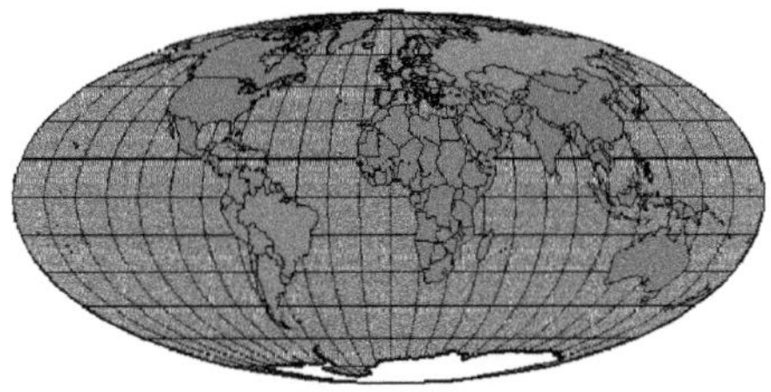

GLOBAL LABOR LAWS AND REGULATIONS HANDBOOK - STRATEGIC INFORMATION AND BASIC LAWS LIBRARY

Price: $149.95 Each

1. Albania Labor Laws and Regulations Handbook - Strategic Information and Basic Laws
2. Algeria Labor Laws and Regulations Handbook - Strategic Information and Basic Laws
3. Andorra Labor Laws and Regulations Handbook - Strategic Information and Basic Laws
4. Angola Labor Laws and Regulations Handbook - Strategic Information and Basic Laws
5. Antigua & Barbuda Labor Laws and Regulations Handbook - Strategic Information and Basic Laws
6. Antilles (Netherlands) Labor Laws and Regulations Handbook - Strategic Information and Basic Laws
7. Argentina Labor Laws and Regulations Handbook - Strategic Information and Basic Laws
8. Armenia Labor Laws and Regulations Handbook - Strategic Information and Basic Laws
9. Australia Labor Laws and Regulations Handbook - Strategic Information and Basic Laws
10. Austria Labor Laws and Regulations Handbook - Strategic Information and Basic Laws
11. Azerbaijan Labor Laws and Regulations Handbook - Strategic Information and Basic Laws
12. Bahamas Labor Laws and Regulations Handbook - Strategic Information and Basic Laws
13. Bangladesh Labor Laws and Regulations Handbook - Strategic Information and Basic Laws
14. Barbados Labor Laws and Regulations Handbook - Strategic Information and Basic Laws
15. Belarus Labor Laws and Regulations Handbook - Strategic Information and Basic Laws
16. Belgium Labor Laws and Regulations Handbook - Strategic Information and Basic Laws
17. Belize Labor Laws and Regulations Handbook - Strategic Information and Basic Laws
18. Bermuda Labor Laws and Regulations Handbook - Strategic Information and Basic Laws
19. Bolivia Labor Laws and Regulations Handbook - Strategic Information and Basic Laws
20. Bosnia and Herzegovina Labor Laws and Regulations Handbook - Strategic Information and Basic Laws
21. Botswana Labor Laws and Regulations Handbook - Strategic Information and Basic Laws
22. Brazil Labor Laws and Regulations Handbook - Strategic Information and Basic Laws
23. Brunei Labor Laws and Regulations Handbook - Strategic Information and Basic Laws
24. Bulgaria Labor Laws and Regulations Handbook - Strategic Information and Basic Laws
25. Cambodia Labor Laws and Regulations Handbook - Strategic Information and Basic Laws
26. Cameroon Labor Laws and Regulations Handbook - Strategic Information and Basic Laws
27. Canada Labor Laws and Regulations Handbook - Strategic Information and Basic Laws
28. Cayman Islands Labor Laws and Regulations Handbook - Strategic Information and Basic Laws
29. Chile Labor Laws and Regulations Handbook - Strategic Information and Basic Laws
30. China Labor Laws and Regulations Handbook - Strategic Information and Basic Laws
31. Colombia Labor Laws and Regulations Handbook - Strategic Information and Basic Laws
32. Comoros Labor Laws and Regulations Handbook - Strategic Information and Basic Laws
33. Cook Islands Labor Laws and Regulations Handbook - Strategic Information and Basic Laws
34. Costa Rica Labor Laws and Regulations Handbook - Strategic Information and Basic Laws

35.	Croatia Labor Laws and Regulations Handbook - Strategic Information and Basic Laws
36.	Cuba Labor Laws and Regulations Handbook - Strategic Information and Basic Laws
37.	Cyprus Labor Laws and Regulations Handbook - Strategic Information and Basic Laws
38.	Czech Republic Labor Laws and Regulations Handbook - Strategic Information and Basic Laws
39.	Denmark Labor Laws and Regulations Handbook - Strategic Information and Basic Laws
40.	Dominica Labor Laws and Regulations Handbook - Strategic Information and Basic Laws
41.	Dominican Republic Labor Laws and Regulations Handbook - Strategic Information and Basic Laws
42.	Dubai Labor Laws and Regulations Handbook - Strategic Information and Basic Laws
43.	Ecuador Labor Laws and Regulations Handbook - Strategic Information and Basic Laws
44.	Egypt Labor Laws and Regulations Handbook - Strategic Information and Basic Laws
45.	El Salvador Labor Laws and Regulations Handbook - Strategic Information and Basic Laws
46.	Equatorial Guinea Labor Laws and Regulations Handbook - Strategic Information and Basic Laws
47.	Estonia Labor Laws and Regulations Handbook - Strategic Information and Basic Laws
48.	Falkland Islands Labor Laws and Regulations Handbook - Strategic Information and Basic Laws
49.	Fiji Labor Laws and Regulations Handbook - Strategic Information and Basic Laws
50.	Finland Labor Laws and Regulations Handbook - Strategic Information and Basic Laws
51.	France Labor Laws and Regulations Handbook - Strategic Information and Basic Laws
52.	Georgia Labor Laws and Regulations Handbook - Strategic Information and Basic Laws
53.	Germany Labor Laws and Regulations Handbook - Strategic Information and Basic Laws
54.	Gibraltar Labor Laws and Regulations Handbook - Strategic Information and Basic Laws
55.	Greece Labor Laws and Regulations Handbook - Strategic Information and Basic Laws
56.	Grenada Labor Laws and Regulations Handbook - Strategic Information and Basic Laws
57.	Guam Investment & Business Guide
58.	Guatemala Labor Laws and Regulations Handbook - Strategic Information and Basic Laws
59.	Guernsey Labor Laws and Regulations Handbook - Strategic Information and Basic Laws
60.	Guyana Labor Laws and Regulations Handbook - Strategic Information and Basic Laws
61.	Haiti Labor Laws and Regulations Handbook - Strategic Information and Basic Laws
62.	Honduras Labor Laws and Regulations Handbook - Strategic Information and Basic Laws
63.	Hungary Labor Laws and Regulations Handbook - Strategic Information and Basic Laws
64.	Iceland Labor Laws and Regulations Handbook - Strategic Information and Basic Laws
65.	India Labor Laws and Regulations Handbook - Strategic Information and Basic Laws
66.	Indonesia Labor Laws and Regulations Handbook - Strategic Information and Basic Laws
67.	Iran Labor Laws and Regulations Handbook - Strategic Information and Basic Laws
68.	Iraq Labor Laws and Regulations Handbook - Strategic Information and Basic Laws
69.	Ireland Labor Laws and Regulations Handbook - Strategic Information and Basic Laws
70.	Israel Labor Laws and Regulations Handbook - Strategic Information and Basic Laws
71.	Italy Labor Laws and Regulations Handbook - Strategic Information and Basic Laws
72.	Jamaica Labor Laws and Regulations Handbook - Strategic Information and Basic Laws
73.	Japan Labor Laws and Regulations Handbook - Strategic Information and Basic Laws
74.	Jersey Labor Laws and Regulations Handbook - Strategic Information and Basic Laws
75.	Jordan Labor Laws and Regulations Handbook - Strategic Information and Basic Laws
76.	Kazakhstan Labor Laws and Regulations Handbook - Strategic Information and Basic Laws
77.	Kenya Labor Laws and Regulations Handbook - Strategic Information and Basic Laws

78. Kiribati Labor Laws and Regulations Handbook - Strategic Information and Basic Laws
79. Korea, North Labor Laws and Regulations Handbook - Strategic Information and Basic Laws
80. Korea, South Labor Laws and Regulations Handbook - Strategic Information and Basic Laws
81. Kuwait Labor Laws and Regulations Handbook - Strategic Information and Basic Laws
82. Kyrgyzstan Labor Laws and Regulations Handbook - Strategic Information and Basic Laws
83. Laos Labor Laws and Regulations Handbook - Strategic Information and Basic Laws
84. Latvia Labor Laws and Regulations Handbook - Strategic Information and Basic Laws
85. Lebanon Labor Laws and Regulations Handbook - Strategic Information and Basic Laws
86. Libya Labor Laws and Regulations Handbook - Strategic Information and Basic Laws
87. Liechtenstein Labor Laws and Regulations Handbook - Strategic Information and Basic Laws
88. Lithuania Labor Laws and Regulations Handbook - Strategic Information and Basic Laws
89. Luxemburg Labor Laws and Regulations Handbook - Strategic Information and Basic Laws
90. Macao Labor Laws and Regulations Handbook - Strategic Information and Basic Laws
91. Macedonia, Republic Labor Laws and Regulations Handbook - Strategic Information and Basic Laws
92. Madagascar Labor Laws and Regulations Handbook - Strategic Information and Basic Laws
93. Malaysia Labor Laws and Regulations Handbook - Strategic Information and Basic Laws
94. Malta Labor Laws and Regulations Handbook - Strategic Information and Basic Laws
95. Man Labor Laws and Regulations Handbook - Strategic Information and Basic Laws
96. Mauritius Labor Laws and Regulations Handbook - Strategic Information and Basic Laws
97. Mauritius Labor Laws and Regulations Handbook - Strategic Information and Basic Laws
98. Mexico Labor Laws and Regulations Handbook - Strategic Information and Basic Laws
99. Micronesia Labor Laws and Regulations Handbook - Strategic Information and Basic Laws
100. Moldova Labor Laws and Regulations Handbook - Strategic Information and Basic Laws
101. Monaco Labor Laws and Regulations Handbook - Strategic Information and Basic Laws
102. Mongolia Labor Laws and Regulations Handbook - Strategic Information and Basic Laws
103. Morocco Labor Laws and Regulations Handbook - Strategic Information and Basic Laws
104. Myanmar Labor Laws and Regulations Handbook - Strategic Information and Basic Laws
105. Namibia Labor Laws and Regulations Handbook - Strategic Information and Basic Laws
106. Netherlands Labor Laws and Regulations Handbook - Strategic Information and Basic Laws
107. New Caledonia Labor Laws and Regulations Handbook - Strategic Information and Basic Laws
108. New Zealand Labor Laws and Regulations Handbook - Strategic Information and Basic Laws
109. Nicaragua Labor Laws and Regulations Handbook - Strategic Information and Basic Laws
110. Nigeria Labor Laws and Regulations Handbook - Strategic Information and Basic Laws
111. Northern Mariana Islands Labor Laws and Regulations Handbook - Strategic Information and Basic Laws
112. Norway Labor Laws and Regulations Handbook - Strategic Information and Basic Laws
113. Pakistan Labor Laws and Regulations Handbook - Strategic Information and Basic Laws
114. Panama Labor Laws and Regulations Handbook - Strategic Information and Basic Laws
115. Peru Labor Laws and Regulations Handbook - Strategic Information and Basic Laws
116. Philippines Labor Laws and Regulations Handbook - Strategic Information and Basic Laws
117. Poland Labor Laws and Regulations Handbook - Strategic Information and Basic Laws
118. Portugal Labor Laws and Regulations Handbook - Strategic Information and Basic Laws
119. Romania Labor Laws and Regulations Handbook - Strategic Information and Basic Laws
120. Russia Labor Laws and Regulations Handbook - Strategic Information and Basic Laws

121. Samoa (American) Investment & Business Guide
122. Samoa (Western) Labor Laws and Regulations Handbook - Strategic Information and Basic Laws
123. Saudi Arabia Labor Laws and Regulations Handbook - Strategic Information and Basic Laws
124. Scotland Labor Laws and Regulations Handbook - Strategic Information and Basic Laws
125. Serbia Labor Laws and Regulations Handbook - Strategic Information and Basic Laws
126. Singapore Labor Laws and Regulations Handbook - Strategic Information and Basic Laws
127. Slovakia Labor Laws and Regulations Handbook - Strategic Information and Basic Laws
128. Slovenia Labor Laws and Regulations Handbook - Strategic Information and Basic Laws
129. South Africa Labor Laws and Regulations Handbook - Strategic Information and Basic Laws
130. Spain Labor Laws and Regulations Handbook - Strategic Information and Basic Laws
131. Sri Lanka Labor Laws and Regulations Handbook - Strategic Information and Basic Laws
132. St. Helena Labor Laws and Regulations Handbook - Strategic Information and Basic Laws
133. Sudan Labor Laws and Regulations Handbook - Strategic Information and Basic Laws
134. Suriname Labor Laws and Regulations Handbook - Strategic Information and Basic Laws
135. Sweden Labor Laws and Regulations Handbook - Strategic Information and Basic Laws
136. Switzerland Labor Laws and Regulations Handbook - Strategic Information and Basic Laws
137. Syria Export Import & Business Directory
138. Taiwan Labor Laws and Regulations Handbook - Strategic Information and Basic Laws
139. Tajikistan Labor Laws and Regulations Handbook - Strategic Information and Basic Laws
140. Thailand Labor Laws and Regulations Handbook - Strategic Information and Basic Laws
141. Tunisia Labor Laws and Regulations Handbook - Strategic Information and Basic Laws
142. Turkey Labor Laws and Regulations Handbook - Strategic Information and Basic Laws
143. Turkmenistan Labor Laws and Regulations Handbook - Strategic Information and Basic Laws
144. Uganda Labor Laws and Regulations Handbook - Strategic Information and Basic Laws
145. Ukraine Labor Laws and Regulations Handbook - Strategic Information and Basic Laws
146. United Arab Emirates Labor Laws and Regulations Handbook - Strategic Information and Basic Laws
147. United Kingdom Labor Laws and Regulations Handbook - Strategic Information and Basic Laws
148. United States Labor Laws and Regulations Handbook - Strategic Information and Basic Laws
149. Uruguay Labor Laws and Regulations Handbook - Strategic Information and Basic Laws
150. US Labor Laws and Regulations Handbook - Strategic Information and Basic Laws
151. Uzbekistan Labor Laws and Regulations Handbook - Strategic Information and Basic Laws
152. Venezuela Labor Laws and Regulations Handbook - Strategic Information and Basic Laws
153. Vietnam Labor Laws and Regulations Handbook - Strategic Information and Basic Laws

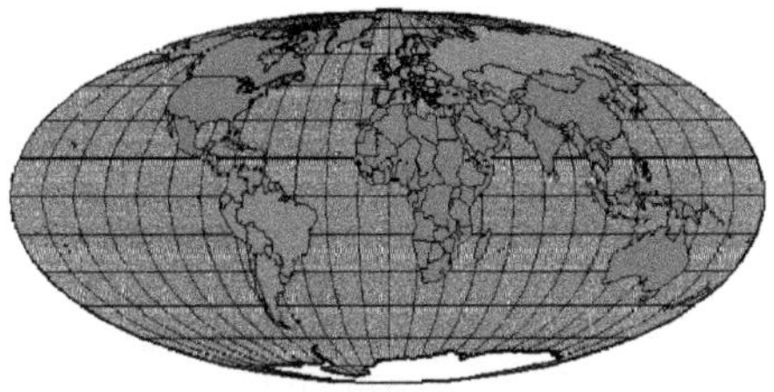

GLOBAL

SOCIAL SECURITY SYSTEM, POLICIES LAWS AND REGULATIONS HANDBOOK - STRATEGIC INFORMATION AND BASIC LAWS LIBRARY

Price: $9995 Each

1.	Albania Social Security System, Policies, Laws and Regulations Handbook
2.	Algeria Social Security System, Policies, Laws and Regulations Handbook
3.	Andorra Social Security System, Policies, Laws and Regulations Handbook
4.	Angola Social Security System, Policies, Laws and Regulations Handbook
5.	Antigua and Barbuda Social Security System, Policies, Laws and Regulations Handbook
6.	Argentina Social Security System, Policies, Laws and Regulations Handbook
7.	Armenia Social Security System, Policies, Laws and Regulations Handbook
8.	Australia Social Security System, Policies, Laws and Regulations Handbook
9.	Austria Social Security System, Policies, Laws and Regulations Handbook
10.	Azerbaijan Social Security System, Policies, Laws and Regulations Handbook
11.	Bahamas Social Security System, Policies, Laws and Regulations Handbook
12.	Bahrain Social Security System, Policies, Laws and Regulations Handbook
13.	Bangladesh Social Security System, Policies, Laws and Regulations Handbook
14.	Barbados Social Security System, Policies, Laws and Regulations Handbook
15.	Belarus Social Security System, Policies, Laws and Regulations Handbook
16.	Belgium Social Security System, Policies, Laws and Regulations Handbook
17.	Belize Social Security System, Policies, Laws and Regulations Handbook
18.	Benin Social Security System, Policies, Laws and Regulations Handbook
19.	Bermuda Social Security System, Policies, Laws and Regulations Handbook
20.	Bhutan Social Security System, Policies, Laws and Regulations Handbook
21.	Bolivia Social Security System, Policies, Laws and Regulations Handbook
22.	Botswana Social Security System, Policies, Laws and Regulations Handbook
23.	Brazil Social Security System, Policies, Laws and Regulations Handbook
24.	British Virgin Islands Social Security System, Policies, Laws and Regulations Handbook
25.	Brunei Social Security System, Policies, Laws and Regulations Handbook
26.	Bulgaria Social Security System, Policies, Laws and Regulations Handbook
27.	Burkina Faso Social Security System, Policies, Laws and Regulations Handbook
28.	Burma (Myanmar)
29.	Burundi Social Security System, Policies, Laws and Regulations Handbook
30.	Cameroon Social Security System, Policies, Laws and Regulations Handbook
31.	Canada Social Security System, Policies, Laws and Regulations Handbook
32.	Cape Verde Social Security System, Policies, Laws and Regulations Handbook
33.	Central African Republic Social Security System, Policies, Laws and Regulations Handbook
34.	Chad Social Security System, Policies, Laws and Regulations Handbook
35.	Chile Social Security System, Policies, Laws and Regulations Handbook
36.	China Social Security System, Policies, Laws and Regulations Handbook
37.	Colombia Social Security System, Policies, Laws and Regulations Handbook
38.	Congo (Brazzaville) Social Security System, Policies, Laws and Regulations Handbook
39.	Congo (Kinshasa) Social Security System, Policies, Laws and Regulations Handbook
40.	Costa Rica Social Security System, Policies, Laws and Regulations Handbook
41.	Cote d'Ivoire Social Security System, Policies, Laws and Regulations Handbook
42.	Croatia Social Security System, Policies, Laws and Regulations Handbook

43.	Cuba Social Security System, Policies, Laws and Regulations Handbook
44.	Cyprus Social Security System, Policies, Laws and Regulations Handbook
45.	Czech Republic Social Security System, Policies, Laws and Regulations Handbook
46.	Denmark Social Security System, Policies, Laws and Regulations Handbook
47.	Djibouti Social Security System, Policies, Laws and Regulations Handbook
48.	Dominica Social Security System, Policies, Laws and Regulations Handbook
49.	Dominican Republic Social Security System, Policies, Laws and Regulations Handbook
50.	Ecuador Social Security System, Policies, Laws and Regulations Handbook
51.	Egypt Social Security System, Policies, Laws and Regulations Handbook
52.	El Salvador Social Security System, Policies, Laws and Regulations Handbook
53.	Equatorial Guinea Social Security System, Policies, Laws and Regulations Handbook
54.	Estonia Social Security System, Policies, Laws and Regulations Handbook Estonia
55.	Ethiopia Social Security System, Policies, Laws and Regulations Handbook
56.	Fiji Social Security System, Policies, Laws and Regulations Handbook
57.	Finland Social Security System, Policies, Laws and Regulations Handbook
58.	France Social Security System, Policies, Laws and Regulations Handbook
59.	Gabon Social Security System, Policies, Laws and Regulations Handbook
60.	Gambia Social Security System, Policies, Laws and Regulations Handbook
61.	Georgia Social Security System, Policies, Laws and Regulations Handbook
62.	Germany Social Security System, Policies, Laws and Regulations Handbook
63.	Ghana Social Security System, Policies, Laws and Regulations Handbook
64.	Greece Social Security System, Policies, Laws and Regulations Handbook
65.	Grenada Social Security System, Policies, Laws and Regulations Handbook
66.	Guatemala Social Security System, Policies, Laws and Regulations Handbook
67.	Guinea Social Security System, Policies, Laws and Regulations Handbook
68.	Guyana Social Security System, Policies, Laws and Regulations Handbook
69.	Haiti Social Security System, Policies, Laws and Regulations Handbook
70.	Honduras Social Security System, Policies, Laws and Regulations Handbook
71.	Hong Kong Social Security System, Policies, Laws and Regulations Handbook
72.	Hungary Social Security System, Policies, Laws and Regulations Handbook
73.	Iceland Social Security System, Policies, Laws and Regulations Handbook
74.	India Social Security System, Policies, Laws and Regulations Handbook
75.	Indonesia Social Security System, Policies, Laws and Regulations Handbook
76.	Iran Social Security System, Policies, Laws and Regulations Handbook
77.	Iraq Social Security System, Policies, Laws and Regulations Handbook
78.	Ireland Social Security System, Policies, Laws and Regulations Handbook
79.	Isle of Man Social Security System, Policies, Laws and Regulations Handbook
80.	Israel Social Security System, Policies, Laws and Regulations Handbook
81.	Italy Social Security System, Policies, Laws and Regulations Handbook
82.	Jamaica Social Security System, Policies, Laws and Regulations Handbook
83.	Japan Social Security System, Policies, Laws and Regulations Handbook
84.	Jordan Social Security System, Policies, Laws and Regulations Handbook
85.	Kazakhstan Social Security System, Policies, Laws and Regulations Handbook
86.	Kenya Social Security System, Policies, Laws and Regulations Handbook
87.	Kuwait Social Security System, Policies, Laws and Regulations Handbook
88.	Kyrgyzstan Social Security System, Policies, Laws and Regulations Handbook
89.	Laos Social Security System, Policies, Laws and Regulations Handbook
90.	Latvia Social Security System, Policies, Laws and Regulations Handbook
91.	Lebanon Social Security System, Policies, Laws and Regulations Handbook
92.	Lesotho Social Security System, Policies, Laws and Regulations Handbook
93.	Liberia Social Security System, Policies, Laws and Regulations Handbook
94.	Libya Social Security System, Policies, Laws and Regulations Handbook
95.	Liechtenstein Social Security System, Policies, Laws and Regulations Handbook
96.	Lithuania Social Security System, Policies, Laws and Regulations Handbook
97.	Luxembourg Social Security System, Policies, Laws and Regulations Handbook
98.	Madagascar Social Security System, Policies, Laws and Regulations Handbook

99. Malawi Social Security System, Policies, Laws and Regulations Handbook
100. Malaysia Social Security System, Policies, Laws and Regulations Handbook Malaysia
101. Mali Social Security System, Policies, Laws and Regulations Handbook Mali
102. Malta Social Security System, Policies, Laws and Regulations Handbook Malta
103. Marshall Islands Social Security System, Policies, Laws and Regulations Handbook
104. Mauritania Social Security System, Policies, Laws and Regulations Handbook
105. Mauritius Social Security System, Policies, Laws and Regulations Handbook
106. Mexico Social Security System, Policies, Laws and Regulations Handbook
107. Micronesia Social Security System, Policies, Laws and Regulations Handbook
108. Moldova Social Security System, Policies, Laws and Regulations Handbook
109. Monaco Social Security System, Policies, Laws and Regulations Handbook
110. Morocco Social Security System, Policies, Laws and Regulations Handbook
111. Namibia Social Security System, Policies, Laws and Regulations Handbook Namibia
112. Nepal Social Security System, Policies, Laws and Regulations Handbook Nepal
113. Netherlands Social Security System, Policies, Laws and Regulations Handbook Netherlands
114. New Zealand Social Security System, Policies, Laws and Regulations Handbook New Zealand
115. Nicaragua Social Security System, Policies, Laws and Regulations Handbook Nicaragua
116. Niger Social Security System, Policies, Laws and Regulations Handbook Niger
117. Nigeria Social Security System, Policies, Laws and Regulations Handbook Nigeria
118. Norway Social Security System, Policies, Laws and Regulations Handbook Norway
119. Oman Social Security System, Policies, Laws and Regulations Handbook Oman
120. Pakistan Social Security System, Policies, Laws and Regulations Handbook Pakistan
121. Panama Social Security System, Policies, Laws and Regulations Handbook Panama
122. Papua New Guinea Social Security System, Policies, Laws and Regulations Handbook Papau New Guinea
123. Paraguay Social Security System, Policies, Laws and Regulations Handbook Paraguay
124. Peru Social Security System, Policies, Laws and Regulations Handbook Peru
125. Philippines Social Security System, Policies, Laws and Regulations Handbook Philippines
126. Poland Social Security System, Policies, Laws and Regulations Handbook Poland
127. Portugal Social Security System, Policies, Laws and Regulations Handbook Portugal
128. Qatar Social Security System, Policies, Laws and Regulations Handbook Qatar
129. Romania Social Security System, Policies, Laws and Regulations Handbook Romania
130. Russia Social Security System, Policies, Laws and Regulations Handbook Russia
131. Rwanda Social Security System, Policies, Laws and Regulations Handbook Rwanda
132. Samoa Social Security System, Policies, Laws and Regulations Handbook
133. San Marino Social Security System, Policies, Laws and Regulations Handbook
134. Sao Tome and Principe Social Security System, Policies, Laws and Regulations Handbook
135. Saudi Arabia Social Security System, Policies, Laws and Regulations Handbook
136. Senegal Social Security System, Policies, Laws and Regulations Handbook
137. Serbia Social Security System, Policies, Laws and Regulations Handbook
138. Seychelles Social Security System, Policies, Laws and Regulations Handbook
139. Sierra Leone Social Security System, Policies, Laws and Regulations Handbook
140. Singapore Social Security System, Policies, Laws and Regulations Handbook
141. Slovak Republic Social Security System, Policies, Laws and Regulations Handbook
142. Slovenia Social Security System, Policies, Laws and Regulations Handbook S
143. Solomon Islands Social Security System, Policies, Laws and Regulations Handbook
144. South Africa Social Security System, Policies, Laws and Regulations Handbook
145. South Korea Social Security System, Policies, Laws and Regulations Handbook
146. Spain Social Security System, Policies, Laws and Regulations Handbook
147. Sri Lanka Social Security System, Policies, Laws and Regulations Handbook
148. Sudan Social Security System, Policies, Laws and Regulations Handbook
149. Swaziland Social Security System, Policies, Laws and Regulations Handbook
150. Sweden Social Security System, Policies, Laws and Regulations Handbook
151. Switzerland Social Security System, Policies, Laws and Regulations Handbook
152. Syria Social Security System, Policies, Laws and Regulations Handbook
153. Taiwan Social Security System, Policies, Laws and Regulations Handbook

154. Tajikistan Social Security System, Policies, Laws and Regulations Handbook
155. Tanzania Social Security System, Policies, Laws and Regulations Handbook Tanzania
156. Thailand Social Security System, Policies, Laws and Regulations Handbook
157. Togo Social Security System, Policies, Laws and Regulations Handbook
158. Trinidad and Tobago Social Security System, Policies, Laws and Regulations Handbook
159. Tunisia Social Security System, Policies, Laws and Regulations Handbook
160. Turkey Social Security System, Policies, Laws and Regulations Handbook
161. Turkmenistan Social Security System, Policies, Laws and Regulations Handbook
162. Uganda Social Security System, Policies, Laws and Regulations Handbook
163. Ukraine Social Security System, Policies, Laws and Regulations Handbook
164. United Kingdom Social Security System, Policies, Laws and Regulations Handbook
165. United States Social Security System, Policies, Laws and Regulations Handbook
166. Uruguay Social Security System, Policies, Laws and Regulations Handbook
167. Uzbekistan Social Security System, Policies, Laws and Regulations Handbook
168. Vietnam Social Security System, Policies, Laws and Regulations Handbook
169. Yemen Social Security System, Policies, Laws and Regulations Handbook
170. Zambia Social Security System, Policies, Laws and Regulations Handbook
171. Zimbabwe Social Security System, Policies, Laws and Regulations Handbook

www.ingramcontent.com/pod-product-compliance
Ingram Content Group UK Ltd.
Pitfield, Milton Keynes, MK11 3LW, UK
UKHW051457290926
15471UKWH00008B/1263

9 781438 781273